UNCIVIL MOVEMENTS

Leigh A. Payne

UNCIVIL MOVEMENTS

The Armed Right Wing and Democracy in Latin America

The Johns Hopkins University Press
Baltimore and London

© 2000 The Johns Hopkins University Press
All rights reserved. Published 2000
Printed in the United States of America on acid-free paper
9 8 7 6 5 4 3 2 1

The Johns Hopkins University Press
2715 North Charles Street
Baltimore, Maryland 21218-4363
www.press.jhu.edu

Library of Congress Cataloging-in-Publication Data will be found
at the end of this book

A catalog record for this book is available from the British Library.

ISBN 0-8018-6242-6

To Adrah and Don Payne

Contents

Figures and Tables

Acknowledgments

As I think over my many *thank you*'s, I am humbled. I have a tale to tell of an embarrassment of riches. Some of my debts are matters of professional accounting, the funds and the release time from teaching that made long periods of travel to Argentina, Brazil, and Nicaragua possible, not to mention the time to write up the research collected on those travels. Thanks are owed to the Fulbright Commission, the Social Science Research Council, and the University of Wisconsin–Madison.

I also have an endless number of colleagues to thank. There were those who graciously read individual chapters and the whole manuscript, providing me with insights and perspectives I could never have gained on a solo journey. In particular, I must mention my colleagues at the University of Wisconsin's Political Science Department who commented extensively on early drafts: Michael Barnett, Edward Friedman, Michael Schatzberg, and Crawford Young. I must also thank the anonymous reader at the Johns Hopkins University Press who helped me think through some of the painful and awkward parts of the book. Then there are my colleagues in Spanish and Portuguese who patiently and graciously helped me with various translations and interpretations of text: Severino Albuquerque, Ksenija Bilbija, and Catherine Jagoe.

My undergraduate and graduate students over the years have participated in various parts of this project, often unwittingly. But sometimes they got paid for their work. This project benefits from the perseverance, care, and diligence of Andy Baker, Lynne Baum, Anne Carelli, Mara Connor, Jennifer Cyr, Alison Dieterichs, Elizabeth Garden, Darren Hawkins, John Malley, Marisol Pagés, and Heidi Smith.

And then there were those who helped with the mechanics of putting this whole thing together. In particular, I thank Laura Gerke and also Diane

Morauske for their friendly assistance at various stages. To the editors at Johns Hopkins University Press, once again, it has been a pleasure to work with you. This is aimed especially at Henry Tom, who took an interest in this project at an early stage, and Mary Yates for her painstaking copy-editing.

To my friends in Madison—Brad, Carol, Catherine, David, Ksenija, Marci, Ned, Richard, and Toma—thank you for taking care of me during this process.

To my husband, Steve Meili, who survived another book project, I cannot thank you enough for your editing, your patience, your fathering, your care. Abbe and Zack, my children, kept a tight hold over me, never allowing me to completely give way to the impulse to cloister myself off from the world in order to write the book, thereby helping me to keep some balance in my life.

I have dedicated this book to my parents, Adrah and Don Payne. This book is about people who couldn't be more different from you, you who believe in the inherent goodness of human beings.

Abbreviations

AAA	Argentine Anticommunist Alliance (Alianza Anticomunista Argentina)
ANC	National Constituent Assembly (Assembléia Nacional Constituinte)
ARDE	Democratic Revolutionary Alliance (Alianza Revolucionaria Democrática)
ARENA (Brazil)	National Alliance for Renewal (Aliança de Renovação Nacional)
ARENA (El Salvador)	Nationalist Republican Alliance (Alianza Republicana Nacionalista)
AWB	Afrikaner Resistance Movement (Afrikaner Weerstandsbeweging)
CELS	Center for Legal and Social Studies (Centro de Estudios Legales y Sociales)
CONADEP	Argentine Commission on the Disappeared (Comisión Nacional sobre la Desaparición de Personas)
CONTAG	Confederation of Agricultural Workers (Confederação Nacional de Trabalhadores de Agricultura)
CNA	National Confederation of Agriculture (Confederação Nacional de Agricultura)
CPT	Pastoral Land Commission (Comissão Pastoral de Terra)
EPS	Sandinista People's Army (Ejército Popular Sandinista)
ESG	Superior War College (Escola Superior de Guerra)
FAMUS	Relatives and Friends of those Killed by Subversion (Familiares y Amigos de los Muertos en la Subversión)
FDN	Nicaraguan Democratic Front (Frente Democrática Nicaragüense)

FMLN	Farabundo Martí National Liberation Front (Frente Farabundo Martí para la Liberación Nacional)
FPA	Parliamentary Block for Agriculture (Frente Parlamentar de Agricultura)
FRAPH	Revolutionary Front for the Advancement and Progress of Haiti (Front Révolutionnaire pour l'Avancement et le Progrés d'Haïti)
FREPASO	National Solidarity Front (Frente del País Solidario)
FSLN	Sandinista National Liberation Front (Frente Sandinista por la Liberación Nacional)
INCRA	Institute for Colonization and Agrarian Reform (Instituto Nacional de Colonização e Reforma Agrária)
INDA	National Agricultural Development Institute (Instituto Nacional de Desenvolvimento Agrário)
INRA	Nicaraguan Agrarian Reform Institute (Instituto Nicaragüense de Reforma Agraria)
MBR-200	Bolívar Revolutionary Movement (Movimiento Bolivariano Revolucionario)
MDB	Brazilian Democratic Movement (Movimento Democrático Brasileiro)
MILPAS	People's Anti-Sandinista Militias (Milicias Populares Anti-Sandinista)
MINeII	Movement for National Independence and Ibero-American Integration (Movimiento por Independencia Nacional e Integración Ibero-Americana)
MIRAD	Ministry of Reform and Agrarian Development (Ministério da Reforma e do Desenvolvimento Agrário)
MODIN	Movement for Dignity and Independence (Movimiento por la Dignidad y la Independencia)
MRS	Sandinista Renewal Movement (Movimiento de Renovación Sandinista)
MST	Landless Peasant Movement (Movimento Sem Terra)
PJ	Peronist Party (Partido Justicialista)
PLC	Liberal Constitution Party (Partido Liberal Constitucionalista)
PMDB	Party of the Brazilian Democratic Movement (Partido do Movimento Democrático Brasileiro)
PNRA	National Plan for Agrarian Reform (Plano Nacional de Reforma Agrária)

PRN (Nicaragua)	Party of Nicaraguan Resistance (Partido de Resistencia Nicaragüense)
PRN (Argentina)	Process of National Reconstruction (Proceso de Reconstrucción Nacional)
PRONAL	National Project Party (Proyecto Nacional)
PT	Workers' Party (Partido dos Trabalhadores)
SNI	National Intelligence Service (Serviço Nacional de Informações)
SRB	Brazilian Rural Society (Sociedade Rural Brasileira)
TFP	Tradition, Family, and Property (Tradição, Familia, e Propriedade)
UCD	Union of the Democratic Center (Unión del Centro Democrático)
UCR	Radical Party (Unión Cívica Radical)
UDN-FARN	Nicaraguan Democratic Union–Armed Revolutionary Forces (Unión Democrática Nicaragüense–Fuerza Armada Revolucionaria Nicaragüense)
UDR	Rural Democratic Union (União Democrática Ruralista)
UNO	National Opposition Union (Unión Nacional Opositora)

Introduction

On 6 December 1998, Venezuelans elected Hugo Chavez to the presidency. Chavez represented for his electorate a political alternative, a protest against a two-party system that had grown distant from, and unresponsive to, its popular base. Mobilizing against *"los corruptos,"* Chavez broke into the closed political system, swept to victory by votes from Venezuela's poor.

Viewed in this way, Chavez becomes a symbol of democracy's triumph. But such an interpretation ignores Chavez's past. He could run for the presidency only because of a presidential pardon in 1994. From 1992 to 1994 he was in jail, serving time for a coup attempt. Rather than being a healthy sign for Latin American democracy, in other words, Chavez represents a disturbing phenomenon that has emerged in other Latin American countries: the rise of antidemocratic groups that compete and gain power within the democratic system.

Unlike Venezuela, whose authoritarian period ended in the 1940s, the countries examined in this book are still undergoing a transition from authoritarian rule. Just when the political opening allowed new social movements and political institutions to press for greater democracy, extreme right-wing movements surfaced to check that process. These movements consisted of the same actors who had previously threatened Latin American democracy: the military, landholders, and paramilitary forces. This book examines three of these cases: putschist military officers in Argentina, murderous landlords in Brazil, and violent paramilitary squads in Nicaragua.

In Argentina a band of military leaders staged four coup attempts between 1987 and 1990. Called the Carapintada (painted faces) owing to their use of war paint, they took up arms, seized military installations, and threatened the democratic government with violence if it did not alter its policies.

The main motivation behind the Carapintada's uprisings were the civilian government's trials of military officers for the murder and disappearance of an estimated thirty thousand individuals during the military regime's Dirty War against subversion. The Carapintada won their demands. The democratic government ended the trials, exonerated military officers both for their human rights abuses and for their later involvement in coup attempts, and eventually pardoned the leaders of the military regime for ordering the disappearances. The Carapintada transformed themselves into a political party, MODIN (Movement for Dignity and Independence), which at one point became the nation's third most powerful political party.

Brazilian landowners formed an association in 1985 to check the rising power of the landless peasant and ecology movements. Members of the UDR (Rural Democratic Union) were involved in the murder of hundreds of leaders of those rural social movements. These landlords operated with impunity. Almost without exception, they avoided investigation, prosecution, trial, and prison. Indeed, at the peak of Brazil's rural violence, the UDR became a powerful lobby within the democratic government, successfully overturning even a very moderate agrarian reform law.

The 1979 Nicaraguan Revolution ended forty-two years of dictatorship by the Somoza family backed by its repressive National Guard, but it did not end the country's violence. On the contrary, the National Guard, supported by the U.S. government, took up arms against the revolutionary government of the FSLN (Sandinista National Liberation Front). Together with sectors of the peasantry, indigenous communities, and disgruntled revolutionaries, the National Guard formed the Contras (shorthand for *Contrarevolucionarios,* or counterrevolutionaries) who fought for ten years in a civil war against the leftist FSLN government and its policies and practices. The war ended in 1990, when a candidate favorable to U.S. and Contra interests defeated the Sandinista candidate for president. The Contras formed a new political party, the PRN (Party of Nicaraguan Resistance), which competed in democratic elections at the local and national level. At the same time, the Contras reorganized into armed bands of Recontras, who continued to use violence against the Sandinistas and also against the Chamorro government.

These episodes might suggest that the region is facing another round of authoritarian conspiracies against democracy. But this book advances a different view. It contends that these groups are neither new, necessarily oriented toward toppling new or weak democracies, nor uniquely Latin American. Instead, such *uncivil movements* are a common feature of democracy. While they may eventually become part of an authoritarian conspiracy under certain conditions, they are not necessarily or endemically oriented toward supplanting democracies. Instead, their violence, along with their use of democratic institutions, discourse, and practices, enhances their capacity to shape democracies. Indeed, when they prove capable of securing their demands within the democratic system, they have little need to overthrow it. Therefore, uncivil movements emerge in countries like Venezuela whose authoritarian period is buried in the past, in countries without an authoritarian legacy, and in countries that have recently experienced authoritarian rule.

While uncivil movements do not actively dismantle democracies, they can nevertheless threaten them. Uncivil movements pose an insidious threat to democracy. They expose certain pathologies of democracy and civil society: they show that the same institutional processes designed to channel demands from civil society also give political expression and power to uncivil groups. Uncivil movements also employ the same mobilizational strategies used by social movements within civil society: like social movements, they claim to identify and empower a new political constituency, conscious of its identity while struggling to overcome its marginal status in the political system.

This book analyzes uncivil movements and their impact on democracy. It begins, in chapter 1, with a definition of uncivil movements. It explains how they both resemble and differ from other types of political movements. The chapter develops the concept of uncivil movements as pathologies of democracy and civil society by showing how they appropriate institutional and social movement strategies to their own uncivil ends. Chapter 2 sets forth an explanatory model of uncivil movements. It analyzes the mobilizational strategies adopted by uncivil movements to enhance their power, specifically political framing, cultural cues, and movement myths. The chapter also examines the limitations on uncivil movements' political power, suggesting ways in which willing governments can check their impact. Chapters 3, 4, and 5 apply the uncivil movements analytical framework to the Argentine Carapintada, the Brazilian UDR, and the Nicaraguan Contras, respectively. Each chapter narrates its particular case, emphasizing the political, cultural, and movement factors. The chapters are organized to facilitate comparisons across cases, with the conclusion of each chapter developing the building blocks of greater comparative insights. Chapter 6 summarizes the book's findings about the relationship of uncivil movements to democratic change. It does so by drawing not only on the Latin American and "transitional" cases but also on comparative cases outside the region and in so-called consolidated democracies. The chapter illustrates that neither re-democratization alone nor an authoritarian past determines the rise and success of these movements; rather, these factors interact, following similar patterns, in each context. The chapter also uses these comparative cases to suggest policy options for democracies facing uncivil movements. It examines how different types of governments have been able to suppress certain movements without provoking a direct assault on democracy. Based on these findings, the chapter offers insights on the prospects of democratic stability in light of uncivil movements.

As for methodology, I explain uncivil movements' threat to democracy through structured, focused comparison and process tracing as elaborated by Alexander George and others.[1] I follow the evolution of three different movements using a variety of different sources for tracing those movements, for example, published accounts, newspaper clippings, participant observation, and open-ended interviews. The research for this book took place over three years, in three different countries, on three different movements, and in three different languages. This labor-intensive comparative case study method allowed me to overcome some of the limitations of a single case. The temptation to make generalizable claims based on a single case was checked by careful analysis of how events played out in the other cases. I rejected various preliminary building blocks each time I introduced a new case study into the analysis. Processes that seemed to hold the key for one case simply did not have equal importance in other cases. Looking at uncivil movements outside Latin America and the democratic-transitions context further allowed me to explore the dynamic relationship between factors in a way that would have been impossible if I had focused on only one of the Latin American cases.

Case selection was critical. The three Latin American cases were chosen to represent the range of authoritarian movements in Latin America's recent past. The Argentine Carapintada epitomized a military-style authoritarian movement. The UDR represented a landholding elite authoritarian movement. The Contras exemplified paramilitary-style movements with strong backing from the United States. I had also originally selected these movements because they appeared to represent three explanations for mobilization by authoritarian movements. Borrowing Crawford Young's typology, I saw the Carapintada as a primordial group, the UDR as an instrumental group, and the Contras as a group "constructed" by external forces.[2] What

I found instead was a set of movements that shared primordial, instrumental, and "socially constructed" attributes.

The Carapintada, for example, possesses some primordial features. Officer training involves a process of socialization, customs, rites, and language not unlike those Clifford Geertz describes in his seminal analysis of cultural identity.[3] Thus, when the democratic governments threatened that identity by prosecuting officers who had carried out their military duty fighting the War against Subversion, military officers rebelled. That threat triggered primordial identities and mobilization around them. It also caused the Carapintada not only to identify a threat but also to recognize a shared identity, and the power to mobilize that identity to conquer the threat.

But primordial identity in the Carapintada case turned out to be a weak indicator of mobilization. Only a minority of officers responded to the Carapintada's call to arm themselves against perceived threats to the identity and dignity of the armed forces. In other words, even those who share a deep attachment to an identity may not concur with the tactics used by a particular movement at a particular time. Moreover, the movement drew support from civilians who shared neither training nor identity with the Carapintada officers.

The primordial traits in both the UDR and the Contras also raised questions about the category's utility in explaining the Carapintada. In Brazil, even landholders not engaged in farming nevertheless identified themselves as landholders and felt threatened by the democratic government's agrarian reform policies. Landholding is more than a way of life; it is a cultural background, an identity. Indeed, because of this emotional tie to land, the government—even if it had been willing and able to do so—could not easily buy off the UDR with material compensation for land expropriated for agrarian reform. The intensity of landholding identity led to radical action rather than negotiated settlement. But while most landholders shared the deep emotional attachment to the land, few joined the UDR. The UDR case thus further challenged the view that deep-seated emotions and identity necessarily lead to radical mobilizations.

One group within the Contras—the Miskito Indians—most resembled Geertz's primordial group. While many Miskito leaders had fought with the Sandinistas and celebrated the triumph over Somoza, they felt betrayed by the Sandinista government. They perceived that government as reneging on the promise of autonomy for the indigenous Atlantic Coast region. Some Miskito leaders even felt that the Sandinista government had imposed greater state control over them than the Somoza government had done. The Sandinistas eventually granted regional autonomy, but only after many of the Miskito leaders had already joined the Contras. Rather than return to their newly autonomous region, the Miskitos remained in the armed struggle to defeat the Sandinistas. In that struggle they joined forces not only with groups who failed to share their cultural identity and cultural goals but also with their former enemies: Somoza's National Guard.

A primordial explanation, in short, describes why certain threatening events may trigger deep emotions within a particular group. And yet it ignores the question of why only some of the individuals who share that primordial identity mobilize and why primordial groups would unite with one enemy against another. Cultural anthropology and constructivist approaches suggest that primordial identities may compete with other identities, undermining their mobilizing potential.[4] In the model presented here, mobilization depends on the threat generated by the political context but also on the historical and cultural context that contributes to developing a collective identity. For successful mobilization to occur, movements must take advantage of cultural and political contexts to build support for uncivil action behind old as well as new identities. In sum, the kind of identity (and threat) that primordialism points to is present in all of the cases of uncivil movement mobilization studied here. But how and when movements can use that identity to mobilize has yet to be explained. The uncivil movement approach outlined in this book does so.

Employing an instrumental approach to analyze the UDR proved as limiting as the primordial analysis. I originally viewed the UDR as a movement seeking to protect the material well-being of Brazilian landholders. When the democratic governments and rural social movements began to expropriate or invade private land, landowners reacted by mobilizing against that threat to their economic and political interests. But as I mentioned before, many of the UDR's landholders no longer depended on the land for income. Moreover, most of them were not directly affected by expropriation or invasion. Something more than their material interests compelled them to join the movement. I found that interest and identity issues converged in explaining the UDR's mobilization and evolution.

Moreover, I found traces of instrumentalism within the Carapintada and the Contras. One of the Carapintada rebellions, for example, explicitly demanded higher salaries for military officers. Two of the Carapintada's top leaders faced prosecution for human rights violations and mobilized the movement to protect themselves from jail sentences. The prospects of food, wages, medical care, and clothing lured Nicaraguan peasants into the Contras. This compensation for military service helped them to overcome rural poverty exacerbated by the civil war. While pervasive, instrumentalism proves relatively weak as a prime motivator for uncivil movements. Instead, it plays a contributing role. Instrumentalism becomes part of the process of framing a catalyst threat around which uncivil movements mobilize.

I had originally perceived the Contras as a movement largely invented by the U.S. government to serve its foreign policy needs. This view is not totally without merit. While insurgency surely would have existed—in fact *did* exist—without the United States' support, the strength of the counterrevolutionary forces and their capacity to prolong the war has to be attributed to the United States. Even the Contras, while criticizing the United States for backing down before the insurgency could militarily defeat the Sandinistas, admit that they could not have sustained the war without the United States. But just as the Reagan administration drew on U.S. historical images by referring to the Contras as "freedom fighters" and the "moral equivalent of our founding fathers" to drum up political support in the United States for the Contra war, the Contras engaged in their own construction of Nicaraguan meaning behind the movement: they were the true peasant sons of the revolutionary leader Augusto Sandino and would reclaim the heroism and national identity bound up in that cultural icon.

This process of constructing and reconstructing cultural meanings occurred in each of the movements examined here. Drawing on cultural symbols to mobilize constituents was an integral strategy of all three. The Carapintada constructed their movements around the history and symbols of military heroism while simultaneously shedding the negative connotations attached to the Dirty War. The UDR mobilized around the heroism of the frontier period while disassociating itself from the violence associated with the period of the *coroneis* (regionally dominant and violent landlords).

In short, although I selected cases partly because of their primordial, instrumental, and constructivist criteria, the movements revealed much more than I had originally anticipated. I determined that the reasons for mobilizing explained less about a movement's political power than other factors did. Specifically, threats within the political environment had to be identified by movement leaders before they could be transformed into mobilizing factors. The cultural context contains within it the heroes, villains, and repertoires of political action that resonate with an uncivil movement's potential constituency and contribute to its emergence and political strength. And movement myths further strengthen the movement by allowing it to deflect negative associations with the past and with violent action.

Analyzing similar cases of uncivil movements outside the Latin American and transitional contexts further confirmed this explanatory model. Very different political contexts still generated a sense of threat that movements mobilized around. Diverse cultural contexts provided a set of symbols and meanings that uncivil movements exploited. And while the movements involved different constituents, they used similar myths to overcome negative images and develop support among constituents.

Tracing uncivil movements over time enabled me to explore not only their rise to political power but also their fall. Each movement followed a different evolutionary path. The Carapintada eventually became marginalized within the political system. The UDR closed its doors after it achieved major victories in the 1980 constitution and subsequent regulating legislation, only to reemerge in 1996. The Contras' guerrilla war ended with a cease-fire. They attempted to form a single political party but fragmented into various parties, factions, and paramilitary troops. Their demise is imminent. The evolutionary processes of institutionalization, latency, and disintegration are represented by these groups. But these outcomes do not reflect the transformative effect successful uncivil movements can have on the democratization process. Indeed, their disintegration may reflect their success, not their failure. Moreover, even when uncivil movements disappear, they set the stage for future movements that model their political strategies and goals on the successes (and failures) of their predecessors. The uncivil movements of today become part of the cultural stock upon which future uncivil movements build.

Uncivil movements' evolution follows a spiraling pattern. The shape that uncivil movements take resembles that of past movements—their predecessors' political action, discourse, and strategies. They depend on their association with the past to build a strong movement with resonance in society. But they do not follow the same path as their predecessors. The shape is distorted, expanded, or constrained by the negative associations of past violence, by the contemporary political environment, and by the movement's own internal crafting. The pace along the path may also change, responding to past and current political cues. The important point, however, is that because of the continued appeal of past movement activity, and perhaps also because of imaginative limitations, movements do not break with past patterns but adopt and adapt them in this spiraling pattern.

The three cases also allowed me to analyze the strategies new democratic governments have used when confronting uncivil movements. Although the movements evolved in the same geographical region and during a similar period of political transition, governments responded to them differently. I could assess, therefore, when democratic governments' strategies worked to reduce the power of these movements, why they worked, and whether they could be replicated in other countries. The non–Latin American cases included in this study further developed that analysis by allowing me to examine government strategies of dealing with uncivil movements in transitional democracies in other Third World countries (e.g., El Salvador, Haiti, South Africa), in Third World "consolidated" democracies (e.g., Israel), and in First World "consolidated" democracies (e.g., the United States and France).

Comparative analysis reveals that the same set of factors that empower uncivil movements—political, cultural, and movement—also undermine them. Uncivil movements plant the seeds of their own destruction. Yet because uncivil movements can have a profound impact on democratic stability before their demise, this book rejects an evolutionary approach in favor of active government intervention. There are ways in which willing democratic governments can reduce the power of uncivil movements.

I could not have mined this analytical framework and its implications for democratic stability from a single-case study. It was only by closely examining the three different paths and outcomes of similar groups at similar times, and comparing them with movements outside the region, that I could draw these conclusions about uncivil movements and democracy. But despite the richness of the comparative approach, it was not without its problems. The demands of a multi-case study (and the tenure system) limited the amount of time I could spend researching each country.

Researching uncivil movements, in particular, also proved problematic. Their semiclandestine nature made obtaining even basic information such as membership lists and phone numbers and addresses for leaders and members difficult. Lists were never complete or up to date. Background data on leaders and members were wrong. I also anticipated that even if I contacted movement members, they would be reluctant to talk with me, so I decided to try to interview the top leader first. Knowing how powerful these leaders were within the movement, I believed that they could open doors with the second- and third-tier leadership and members. This strategy worked. I interviewed nearly all of the key leaders in each movement. Not only did the interview with the key leader open doors, it also opened address books containing even cellular phone numbers that guaranteed communication. I do wonder every now and then what would have happened had I not made a favorable impression in the key interviews.

It is on this point of impression that I faced another difficulty in conducting research on uncivil movements. So much of my capacity to get interviews and hold them over hours and days depended on my relationship with these individuals. But no one could tell me about them or what to expect in advance. No one I knew in these countries had anything—or, I might add, *would* have anything—to do with members of such movements. Most of the scholars and political activists I talked to in-country warned me of the danger of conducting this research project. Some granting institutions also questioned the feasibility of the project and expressed reservations about its charged political content. One researcher who had conducted some similar work suggested that I follow his strategy and go undercover to conduct my research. Otherwise, he believed, I would end up either dead or with highly sanitized information.

Aside from the problem I would no doubt have with the university's Human Subjects Committee had I tried to deceive my informants, I simply could not disguise my identity. These are male patriarchal groups, and there are few roles that I, as a woman, could assume to gain access to them. I might have posed as a consultant, but I know too little about cattle and horse breeding to pass as a technical consultant for UDR ranchers. And neither the Carapintada nor the Contras had any interest in the findings of political opinion polls; they did not need a pollster to tell them which way the political winds blew. It became more and more obvious how entirely distinct my world was from the world of those I planned to interview.

And I was, I admit, afraid of being "found out." I walked to my first interview with my heart pounding. I was sure that my own politics would slip out and that I would thereby endanger myself. These people, after all, kill their adversaries. But no one viewed me as a threat. Perhaps because I was female? Or North American? Or a professor? I will never know the answer to all of these questions. Given passing comments made by those I interviewed, I think all of my identities played an important role in helping me get access to these leaders.

But perhaps more important, these informants wanted to talk and I wanted to listen. And I was perceived by them (because of my identities) to be a less biased listener than others. These movements generally get bad press. Indeed, because they don't like their public image, they try to avoid the media. But they believe in their mission, and they want to tell their side of the story. Giving that story to a North American professor seemed relatively risk-free.

They correctly perceive North American academics as less radical than their Latin American counterparts, even though in individual cases this is not always true. They certainly perceive North Americans as being less biased against them. Indeed, I rarely escaped an interview without some reference to how what they were doing was entirely consistent with—and therefore justified by—some practice, policy, law, or opinion in the United States. Furthermore, my informants' sexist attitudes no doubt shaped their perceptions of me. They seemed to view me as an apolitical recorder of their life stories. They seemed to believe that they could convince me of the correctness of their actions and their own spin on those actions.

I confess that my own political bias was not transparent to my informants. But then again, I never had to reveal where I stood, since nobody asked. It was extremely interesting what many informants assumed about me. Some suspected that I was from the CIA. This is often a problem for researchers attempting to study left-wing groups in the region. With my informants, however, the possibility that I might be from the CIA, or some other U.S. government agency, seemed to increase their desire to talk to me. One informant, for instance, explained that he was not bothered that the CIA had someone checking up on his group; he admired the United States' concern for national security and wished his own country shared that concern. I had the distinct impression that he and others were flattered by the notion that the CIA or some other U.S. government agency, and not just a university professor writing for a relatively small readership, was interested in them and their political role.

A phenomenon of reciprocity or exchange also played a role in securing interviews. One UDR leader agreed to an interview but insisted, once the interview had ended, on arguing against the U.S. tariff barriers on Brazilian oranges. Several Argentine military officers used the interview to explore how they might get their children scholarships to U.S. colleges and prep schools. Wounded Contra rebels politely answered my questions but seemed to see this as a medium of exchange for badly needed artificial limbs, glass eyes, and jobs. In one Felliniesque encounter, a young combatant put on shorts and circled me on the patio on his bicycle, peddling with his one leg to show me that the other one was missing, blown off in a landmine explosion. I felt as though I had unwittingly deceived these individuals into believing that I had the power, wealth, and political will to help them resolve their problems.

But I also felt, sometimes, like part of their public-relations stunts. These leaders wanted me to tell their side of the story—that is, the side that did not make it into what they considered to be the slanderous left-wing media. They wanted to convince me and my readership that they were the "good guys in the film," as one informant referred to his group. One Argentine military leader told me that he never accepted interviews with Argentine journalists, but he felt that I would do a careful job, and my work, published abroad, would be read and believed (even by Argentines) more than any article published in Argentina. One of the "hired-gun" prisoners I interviewed in Brazilian jails claimed that he had turned down interviews, even well-paid ones, because he felt that the reporters would distort his story. I suspected that he had agreed to the interview with me because I represented the interest of the United States in his case. His interview also gave him a chance to make a special request for employment within the prison. With the prison warden listening in on our conversation, it was at least worth a try.

Indeed, I often became suspicious of my informants' ulterior motives in agreeing to be interviewed. One scenario encapsulated this feeling. I spent a day with one of the most notoriously violent landholders in a particular region of Brazil. As we spoke, children, grandchildren, great-grandchildren, godparents, neighbors, sons-in-law, and mothers-in-law drifted in and out having coffee, ice cream, and cookies with us. I thought nothing of this level of sociability until the informant's daughter turned to me near the end of the interview and asked, "Leigh, you will not use any of the information we have given you to harm us, will you?" Even as I shook my head no, I wondered how they would react to being labeled part of an "uncivil movement."[5]

To this day I wonder why the Argentine military officer serving a life sentence called me to set up an interview outside the prison walls. Journalist friends had told me that they suspected that these "lifers" frequently left the prison. But I had already been given access to the prison. There was no reason for him to risk an interview on the outside. Moreover, the interview revealed nothing that an eavesdropping guard would have cared about. Why did he trust me not to tell about his freedom to travel home? Why didn't he care if I told? Why did he perhaps want me to tell? These questions were heightened in my mind a few days after this interview, when a bomb exploded in the Jewish Cultural Center in Buenos Aires. My informant had links with anti-Semitic groups. Reports in the newspaper revealed that he and other Carapintada lifers had been out of jail at the time of the bombing. I was not the source of these reports, but would my informant know that?

Most of my initial fears have subsided. I doubt that my informants betrayed any confidences with me. They did tell me their interpretation of the story: their "legitimating myths," their truths, or what they wanted me to hear. But despite their best efforts sometimes to whitewash or sanitize the stories and present a positive image, their rage was not difficult to provoke. Even in a controlled interview, a challenging question could set them off. Many times these individuals recognized later that they had revealed too much. It was not uncommon that in the postinterview setting these individuals tried to "take back," or explain away, some of the strong opinions they had expressed in the formal interview. By interviewing the individuals involved in these groups, I have tried to capture their own understanding of the movement, their reason for becoming involved, and their role in it. These interpretations clearly shaped my theoretical framework. I doubt, however, that any informant would recognize her or his interpretation in this model. It is thus consistent with the process-tracing approach developed by Alexander George and Timothy McKeown: "As we understand process-tracing, it involves both an attempt to reconstruct actors' definitions of the situation and an attempt to develop a theory of action. The framework within which actors' perceptions and actions are described is given by the researcher, not by the actors themselves."[6]

I believe that the honesty of the interviews was increased because I did not tape them. On the few occasions when I did record an interview, I found that the real, and less sanitized, interview began only after the recording stopped. I therefore preferred not to use a tape recorder and took copious notes instead. I have debated with myself and others whether to reveal informants' names as sources for the quotations I have used. In the end I decided to excise most names and even make a few individuals anonymous. While I never promised anonymity, I believe that these individuals are either particularly vulnerable or revealed more to me in the interview context than they would want to expose in the book context. In one case I assigned a pseudonym to protect the identity of an informant who played a central role in one chapter. Only the names of public figures, the top leaders of official organizations, remain attached to quotations, but nearly all participants in the project are listed in the bibliography.

I have some trepidations about the interview lists. Even after all the wonderful meals and coffee and conversations I enjoyed with these individuals, a small part of me continues to fear that they might not like what I say and retaliate against me. This fear was confirmed when I consulted a Brazilian researcher about removing the names of the interview respondents. He responded by saying, "It depends on whether you want to live to do another research project." My decision to list the participants' names is not merely a decision to share with readers the range of opinions I gathered in this research. It is also consistent with one of the main points I wish to make in this book: fear enhances uncivil movements' power. I thus undertake the policy I endorse in the book: to delegitimize movements by exposing who they are, what they do, and how they do it.

1 Defining Uncivil Movements

Uncivil movements are political groups within democracies that employ both civil and uncivil political action to promote exclusionary policies. They resemble other political groups—for example, political parties, interest groups, social movements, countermovements, and authoritarian movements. Indeed, uncivil movements form, participate in, and evolve into and out of these other types of political groups at different times. Despite commonalities with these other forms of political organization, however, uncivil movements constitute a unique political group deserving of analysis. The separate terms *uncivil* and *movements* signify their similarities with other political groups. But the combination *uncivil movements* highlights their distinctiveness from other political groups.

The term *uncivil* refers to the use of political violence by these movements to promote exclusionary objectives. Uncivil movements, in this regard, resemble the authoritarian movements of Latin America's past that engaged in coups or coup attempts, murdered political adversaries, and destroyed their property. Uncivil movements use violence, in other words, as a deliberate strategy to eliminate, intimidate, and silence political adversaries in other movements and within the government. Their violence therefore differs from the violence that might occur among "civil" movements attempting to defend themselves against aggression or that face violence as an unintended outcome of a "civil" political confrontation. Civil disobedience, for example, constitutes a form of rule breaking that sometimes involves violence, but it is intended to expand citizenship, political rights, and freedoms. Violence, in fact, is often the only weapon civil society actors possess to expand democratic rights and freedoms in an exclusionary state.[1] In contrast, uncivil movements' coup attempts, premeditated murders, and kidnappings fall outside any definition of civil disobedience. They use violence to expand their own political power and privileges while simultaneously eliminating the power and privileges of their adversaries. They seek to limit rather than advance the progress toward greater equality and freedom. In short, the "uncivil" aspects of uncivil movements include violent strategies against political adversaries to expand the exclusive rights and privileges of a particular group.

The term *movement* identifies the mobilizational style employed by uncivil movements. Indeed, uncivil movements, consciously or not, mimic social movements by mobilizing around identity, exclusion and marginalization, and unconventional political action. Uncivil movements do not pursue material interests alone but rather create new identities around culture and values that mobilize new and diverse members into their ranks. They claim to represent a constituency that is excluded from mainstream politics. Indeed, they consider mainstream politics to be corrupt, accommodated, and outmoded. And they offer, in contrast, a movement mobilized around meaningful political issues and unconventional political tactics.[2] But while opposing the mainstream, uncivil movements, like social movements, recognize the utility of working within the political system. They adopt a variation of social movements' "double-militancy" strategy by simultaneously maintaining their autonomy as a movement while working within the political institutional apparatus to promote their demands.[3] Uncivil movements therefore influence political outcomes in a civil manner through political parties, lobbies, electoral campaigns, and public office. But consistent with the idea of double militancy, uncivil movements also maintain their autonomy from the political system through unconventional political action, particularly through the use of violence against state and civil society adversaries. Both political strategies—civil and uncivil—seek to expand the rights and privileges of a particular group. In short, uncivil movements employ a social-mobilization style of politics, but they use it to defend and expand the power and privileges of an already privileged sector of society.

Uncivil movements constitute a distinct and unique type of political mobilization, as illustrated by the defining characteristics set forth above and summarized in figure 1.1. But uncivil movements are related to other political groups as well. They not only share characteristics with authoritarian movements and social movements, they also join or form political parties. Figure 1.2 illustrates the complex web of relationships between uncivil movements and other political groups.

Uncivil movements (*A*) constitute a separate type of political movement

UNCIVIL aspects
of uncivil movements

1. *Uncivil political action*

   a. Violence against social movement adversaries, e.g., kidnapping, murder, destruction of property

   b. Violence against the democratic government, e.g., kidnapping, murder, destruction of property, coups and coup attempts

2. *Uncivil political objectives*

   a. Eliminate competition from adversaries

   b. Perpetuate and expand political power and privileges of an exclusive sector

MOVEMENT aspects
of uncivil movements

1. *Social mobilization strategy*

   e.g., identity and symbolic politics, oppositional politics, unconventional political action

2. *Double-militancy*

   e.g., maintain movement autonomy while simultaneously participating in the political system through lobbies, political parties, and representation in government

FIGURE 1.1   Characteristics of Uncivil Movements

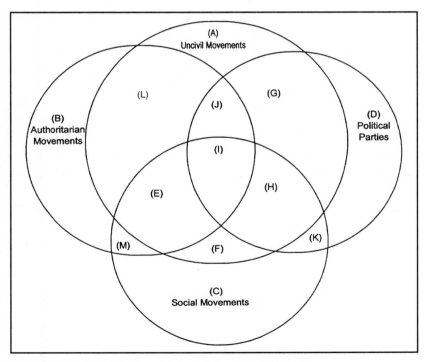

FIGURE 1.2   Relationship between Political Movements in Democracies

that sometimes acts alone, lacking a relationship with other political groups. Uncivil movements may prove either uninterested in or incapable of forming alliances with political parties, authoritarian movements, or social movements. The illustration also identifies authoritarian movements (*B*), social movements (*C*), and political parties (*D*) as separate political groups that do not always involve a relationship with uncivil movements. But the illustration also shows that uncivil movements overlap and share characteristics and political action with other political groups.

Uncivil movements diverge from authoritarian movements in that they accept and participate in democratic systems; they neither philosophically oppose democracy nor promote authoritarian ends. Yet in certain contexts uncivil movements ally with authoritarian movements to promote their political demands. The authoritarian coups of the 1960s and 1970s in Latin America provide an illustration of two of these alliances. At that time, uncivil movements of landholders, business leaders, and paramilitary and military groups conspired with political party leaders, right-wing women's and labor groups, the armed forces, and foreign governments to overthrow democratic regimes and implant authoritarian ones. Consider, for example, the involvement of an uncivil movement of landholders in Brazil. Before the 1964 coup these landholders were already involved in violence against rural labor activists. They opposed President João Goulart's government because it began a land redistribution program and, according to landowners, stimulated peasant mobilizations and land invasions. Clearly, then, landholder groups shared goals with the authoritarian movement and welcomed the coup and the favorable military regime that it installed. But landholders did not organize or lead the coup. In other words, they played a subsidiary role in the coup conspiracy and the authoritarian regime that it implanted, forming an alliance between an uncivil movement and a military authoritarian movement (*L*).

Uncivil movements had also begun organizing before the 1973 coup in Chile. The Patria y Libertad (Fatherland and Freedom) movement provides one example. The movement had used violence against leftist political leaders both inside and outside socialist President Salvador Allende's government. Evidence suggests that uncivil movements joined forces not only with the military but also with conservative political party leaders in the coup conspiracy that replaced Allende's government with the military authoritarian regime of General Augusto Pinochet. The Chilean case thus illustrates a union of uncivil movements, authoritarian movements, and political parties (*J*).

These two cases illustrate how authoritarian rule can result from such alliances. But not all coup conspirators necessarily share the goal of implanting an authoritarian regime. It is more likely, given the pattern of military intervention in Latin America up until that time, that uncivil movements expected the military simply to unseat the old president, restore order, and call new elections.[4] Authoritarian movements, and not uncivil movements, were the masterminds of the coups of the 1960s and 1970s. But the dramatic events of the coups and subsequent military regimes have overshadowed the distinction between different conspirators. This book will show that blurring the distinction between uncivil and authoritarian movements leads to political strategies that enhance uncivil movements' political power. For example, when uncivil movements reemerged and confronted the democratic regimes of the 1980s and 1990s, scholars and politicians alike feared the resurgence of coup coalitions. To avoid a coup, democratic governments sometimes capitulated to uncivil movements' demands. This book argues that uncivil movements won both concessions and institutional roles in the new democracies as a result of an exaggerated fear, stemming from a failure to distinguish uncivil from authoritarian movements.

Figure 1.2 illustrates that not all uncivil movements form alliances with authoritarian movements. Personalistic military leaders may act on their own, developing their own army of followers, like the caudillos of the nineteenth century in Latin America (B). Other types of alliances have also produced authoritarian results. The populist era in Latin America, particularly in Argentina from the 1940s to the 1970s, provides an example. Juan Perón's mobilization of the *descamisados* (the "shirtless," or popular sectors) contained some elements of social movement mobilization (C) but evolved into an alliance between the Peronist political party and social movement sectors (K). Uncivil movements also played a role in the Peronist alliances. The right wing of the Peronist movement formed the AAA (Argentine Anticommunist Alliance), a death squad comprised of military and civilian groups that kidnapped and murdered alleged subversives. Uncivil movements allied with a political party (G), and with the addition of the trade unionist movement, an alliance formed between uncivil movements, political parties, and social movements (H). The military coup of 1976 might be viewed as an extension of the alliance between the various uncivil, authoritarian, and social movements with political parties (I), but given that some of the social movements had left the alliance at this phase, it might provide a better illustration of a political party–uncivil movement–authoritarian movement alliance (J). The leftist factions of Peronism also formed alliances with uncivil movements. One example is the link between social movements and the uncivil Montonero movement (F). And the links between the *descamisados,* the Montoneros, and the Peronist Party reflect a left-wing variation of H.

This illustration confirms that uncivil movements are not always on the political right. The cases for this book, however, include only right-wing uncivil movements. In part that decision stems from a methodological attention to comparing similar uncivil movements in similar political moments. But it is also a bias that comes from a particular regional context. The right has overthrown democracies in Latin America's past, while the left has not. (The left has, however, overthrown right-wing dictatorships. Batista's Cuba and Somoza's Nicaragua provide the most compelling recent examples.) Perhaps because of this particular history, scholars continue to worry more about the overthrow of democracy by the historically powerful authoritarian right than about coups sponsored by the authoritarian left.

Nonetheless, the Montoneros in Argentina and other armed revolutionary movements suggest that uncivil movements do not carry a particular ideological banner. The only defining characteristic that might limit the number of left-wing violent movements that could be labeled "uncivil" is the exclusionary objective of uncivil movements. Even then left-wing guerrilla movements might use a discourse of expanding citizen rights while mobilizing around the elimination of their adversaries and extending rights and citizenship to one sector of society. Revolutionary movements that advocate overthrow, like the Sendero Luminoso of Peru, are not uncivil movements. Instead, such movements constitute authoritarian movements (B), an authoritarian movement allied with social movements (M), or an alliance of authoritarian, social, and uncivil movements (E). Similarly, armed left-wing groups that simultaneously use institutional politics and extralegal violence to extend rights to groups historically excluded from the political system do not fall under the uncivil movement definition. For example, the alliance between political parties and the EZLN (Zapatista Army for National Liberation) in southern Mexico and the armed indigenous groups currently grouped in the URNG (Guatemalan National Revolutionary Unity) in Guatemala still fit C or K more than A because they attempt to extend civil and human rights to excluded, rather than privileged, groups.

Understanding the relationship of uncivil movements to authoritarian movements, social movements, and political parties provides analytical precision as well as insights into threats to democracy. Uncivil movements have appeared in the discourse of political mobilization in Latin America only as authoritarian threats. This failure to understand uncivil movements as separate from authoritarian movements has created policies that inadvertently enhance, rather than reduce, their influence within democratic society. Moreover, mistaking uncivil movements for political parties, interest groups, or social movements ignores the profound impact they have on "normal" democratic politics. So while this book is concerned with the circumstances under which uncivil movements ally themselves with or transform into authoritarian ones, it is equally concerned about the less obvious and unexamined aspects of uncivil movement mobilization. That is, not when they intersect with authoritarian movements to overthrow democracies, but when acting independently, they subvert democracies through civil and uncivil means.

The Power of Uncivil Movements

Because uncivil movements are rarely differentiated from authoritarian movements, and authoritarian movements have overthrown democracies in the past, the mere mobilization of uncivil movements often appears as a threat to democracy. But uncivil movements' political power varies considerably.

The most obvious and dangerous indicator of uncivil movements' power is their capture of the state. But uncivil movements on their own usually lack sufficient electoral strength to elect their candidates to presidential office, much less overthrow the government. To succeed in a project to capture the state, uncivil movements rely on alliances. Uncivil movements, however, do not always seek government control. Instead, they hope to influence political outcomes, particularly those that directly affect them. Influence does not require control over the executive branch. Moreover, since successful movements can influence democratic politics without running the government, that objective is neither the only, the best, nor even the most important measure of uncivil movements' political power.

Winning political battles also proves problematic as a measure of uncivil movements' power. Not all political outcomes, for example, are equal. So while uncivil movements may achieve some policy goals, these may prove insignificant in terms of shaping democratic politics as a whole. Emphasizing these minor victories overstates and may even enhance their power. An accurate assessment of their power through political victories should focus on contested policy issues—that is, where uncivil movements override objections from their social movement and government adversaries. Shifting the policy debate in their favor or putting issues on the political agenda over the protest of government and civil society adversaries therefore provides important measures of uncivil movements' influence over democratic society.

Since influencing the political agenda and policy outcomes usually requires representatives in government, the election and appointment of uncivil movement leaders to government positions is another measure of the success of such movements. Exclusively focusing on the composition of legislatures and government agencies, however, ignores uncivil movements' capacity to influence government officials indirectly. In other words, without holding public office, uncivil movements may enjoy significant influence over public policy outcomes.

Uncivil movements could influence government officials' opinion through bribery and other forms of corruption. But they could also come by this support honestly: by winning significant public support. Government officials will be more responsive to pressure from uncivil movements if they sense growing support for them. Membership size determines the degree of public support, but the unique features of uncivil movements make this a problematic yardstick. It is often difficult to tell who belongs to an uncivil movement. A movement's rosters tend to be clandestine, and when they are public, many members will not openly join because of fear of the stigma associated with the movement. Official membership lists, in other words, can greatly underestimate the size of the movement. Uncivil movements, moreover, rarely form mass movements. But even without a large membership base, they often build powerful movements. They can compensate for their small membership with ample financial resources. By hiring "supporters" to lobby for them and to attend rallies, they can give the appearance of massive public support. They can pay to have public spaces plastered with posters and graffiti to create the illusion of widespread popular appeal. They may also use financial resources to purchase coverage in the mass media. But even financially poor uncivil movements can obtain the kind of media attention that compensates for, or disguises, their small size. Once their unconventional political action becomes "newsworthy," they gain the exposure they need to influence public opinion and government officials. Violent unconventional action thus plays a crucial role in attracting public attention to uncivil movements. Simultaneously, to the degree that uncivil movements' issues intersect with issues supported by a voting constituency, politicians may seek out the support of these uncivil movements, thus making them more politically powerful.

Figure 1.3 summarizes the seven indicators of uncivil movements' politi-

1. Overthrow the government in a coup coalition
2. Win contested policies
3. Shift policy debates in their favor
4. Get issues on the political agenda
5. Win direct representation in elected or appointed government positions
6. Win indirect representation in government through elected or appointed allies
7. Gain mass-media coverage

FIGURE 1.3   Indicators of Uncivil Movements' Political Power

cal power discussed above. Just how uncivil movements achieve political power in democracies is outlined in chapter 2. But before turning to that analysis, I will explore how the government policies and mobilizational strategies outlined in the existing democratization literature have enhanced uncivil movements' power, thereby transforming them into pathologies of democracy and civil society.

Pathologies

Because uncivil movements cross boundaries and merge with authoritarian movements, political parties, and social movements, we have had few analytical tools for understanding them as separate entities. This is nowhere more evident than in the redemocratization literature. Two trends dominate that literature. One emphasizes "democracy from above" and analyzes the strategies that newly democratic states might use to reduce the power of the old authoritarian elites over the democratic process. The uncertainty of the transition moment has led scholars to develop strategies to avoid authoritarian overthrows. The largely institutional remedies that scholars have proposed, however, have had the paradoxical effect of enhancing the power of uncivil movements over democracies. An institutions approach to democratization may inadvertently transform uncivil movements into a pathology of democracy.

The second trend within the democratization literature emphasizes the heroic efforts of civil society actors in breaking the silence imposed on them by authoritarian regimes and in struggling for greater democracy and freedom. These social movement mobilizations, however, do not have exclusive control over strategies of creating mobilizational identities, designing unconventional action, and confronting exclusionary and mainstream institutional structures. The uncivil movements analyzed in this book are engaged in similar activities. Accordingly, they form a pathology of civil society. They adopt social movement strategies but use them to empower themselves and eliminate social movements in civil society.

PATHOLOGIES OF DEMOCRACY

The institutions approach to redemocratization outlines the means by which transitional governments can survive and transform into democratic regimes that guarantee free and fair elections, universal suffrage, and broad protection of political and civil liberties. In developing their prescriptions, institutionalists draw heavily from lessons learned during the earlier period of "democratic breakdown" of the 1960s and 1970s. One of the major preoccupations for institutionalists is how to protect democracies from a resurgence by authoritarian actors, both the softliners, or *blandos,* and the hardliners, or *duros.* Uncivil movements are arguably the manifestation of a resurgence of *blandos* and *duros* in the postauthoritarian situation.

The original institutions approach within the democratization literature converged around a three-part strategy of moderation, institutionalization, and habituation to reduce the power of authoritarian movements and pave the way for democratic consolidation.[5] Moderation reassures authoritarian actors that democracy will not radically alter the rules of the political game. Institutionalization guarantees authoritarian actors a permanent role in the political apparatus, obviating the need for an extrainstitutional overthrow. And habituation allows authoritarian actors the necessary time to become sufficiently adept in democratic politics before they face the inevitable demands from the popular sector for economic and political reforms.

Uncivil movements illustrate some of the underlying problems with this strategy as a means of reducing the power of elites. While the uncivil movement approach concedes that the three-part strategy avoids an overthrow, it argues that this comes at a very high cost for democracies. The strategy enhances the power of uncivil movements over the political system and reduces the possibility of expanding democratic rights and freedoms to popular sectors.

Moderation, for example, does not necessarily appease extremists and end their violent rebellions. Even when democratic governments have adopted the kinds of moderation advocated in the institutions literature (i.e., policies that avoid contentious political or social justice issues) and have established a secure environment, uncivil movements have still mobilized. The first problem with the moderation strategy is subjective. Democratic governments and uncivil movements may not have the same opinion regarding what is moderate or radical. When Argentina's democratic government demonstrated what many considered to be moderation by ending the human rights trials of military officers, the Carapintada still rebelled. Because the government failed to acknowledge military heroism in the War against Subversion and the Malvinas War, the Carapintada continued to interpret the democratic government's policies as radical. Similarly, when the Brazilian democratic government adopted an agrarian reform law that was more moderate than that issued by the military regime, landholders still organized against the government and rural activists. They considered *any* agrarian reform to be radical. Similarly, the Contras viewed the Sandinistas' mixed economy program and the Chamorro government's unification policies as radical. They equated *any* form of expropriation and *any* role for the Sandinistas in government with provocation.

Moderation, in other words, does not guarantee democratic governments protection from uncivil movements. Movements can construe almost any policy that affects them negatively as radical and threatening. The only sure way for democratic governments to prevent uncivil movements from mobilizing is to give in to their demands altogether. While this kind of capitulation is likely to prevent uncivil actors from forming an authoritarian movement, it also provides them with de facto control over government policies. Moderation therefore protects against coups but enhances uncivil movements' political power.

Institutionalization also fails to check the threats uncivil movements pose to democracy. Institutions scholars assume that authoritarian elites used extrainstitutional coups in the 1960s and 1970s because the institutional apparatus had proved insufficient. Thus, the institutionalists advocate the development of particular institutional arrangements to avoid democratic breakdowns. Two overarching institutional concerns are (1) minimally ideological political parties and (2) nonpolarized political institutions capable of accommodating authoritarian elites and obviating the need for extrainstitutional assaults on democracy.[6] Yet historical examples challenge this view. Despite fairly stable and well-established democratic institutions in Chile and Uruguay in the 1970s, authoritarian conspiracies still toppled democratic regimes. Uncivil movements further call into question the role institutions play in safeguarding democracies from armed political groups. Even when uncivil movements form or join political parties, they do not abandon their extrainstitutional and uncivil acts. Indeed, uncivil movements depend on *both* institutional arrangements and extrainstitutional violence to enhance their political power. Institutions, in other words, become another weapon in uncivil movements' political arsenal; they do not replace the extrainstitutional or violent weapons. Thus, institution-building can actually increase the power of uncivil movements over democracy.

The cases in this book illustrate this problem. The Carapintada formed a powerful political party at the same time that they were engaged in coup attempts. The UDR formed a powerful political lobby and ran candidates for all levels of political office while still murdering rural leaders. And the Contras formed a political party and sponsored candidates for political office while simultaneously rearming and taking to the mountains as Recontras.

There is another problem with institutionalization that democratic theorists have noted, one that takes on particular importance in the analysis of uncivil movements' political power in new democracies. Robert Dahl argues that organized groups have a disproportionately greater impact over democracies than an equal or greater number of unorganized citizens. They shift the public agenda toward issues that concern them, elect representatives to the legislature, and distort the content of governments' policies.[7] But the problem is particularly grave in the case of uncivil movements in new democracies. Uncivil movements do not simply influence policies; they also shape the future democratic system. They are not just another organized movement in democratic society but a legacy of authoritarian rule. Their power over democracy can undermine faith in democratic institutions if citizens begin to view the executive, legislature, and judiciary as incapable of opposing powerful minority interests. Disillusionment with democratic government may emerge when executive branches make compromises to accommodate these movements, altering their policies to conform to their wishes; or when uncivil movements win legislative seats and shift legislative opinion toward their interests; or when they undermine the autonomous power of the judiciary by avoiding any investigation and prosecution of their criminal activities. But these movements also undermine democracy in less direct ways. Their presence and power can breed the kind of disenchantment that undermines democratic consolidation.[8] By accommodating uncivil movements, the democratic institutions not only appear "ineffective," a potentially destabilizing characteristic;[9] they also become vulnerable to accusations that the same authoritarian elites still run the government. In short, institutionalization enhances uncivil movements' power within the political system. And because they continue their extrainstitutional activity even after they form these institutions, they pervert the institutionalization process. They expand their power within the system while reducing the power of institutions of public authority to restrain them.

Institutionalization is not unimportant, however, in reducing the power of uncivil movements. It just does not play out in the way anticipated by the redemocratization scholars or with the same outcome for democratic stability. Institutionalization exacerbates the internal weaknesses of these movements, generally leading to their demise. It is not, therefore, the institutional channels of these movements that check their power, but rather their institutional weaknesses. But given that these movements often have a profound impact in an early period of time, institutionalization is not usually the best means of reducing their power.

The institutionalists' nearly exclusive focus on the legislative and executive branches also challenges the effectiveness of the institutions approach in building stable democracies. The institutions approach largely ignores the key role of the judiciary in the process of strengthening democracy. The uncivil movements examined here have operated with impunity. Unchecked by judicial authority, they have been free to pursue their two-pronged strategy of institutional and extrainstitutional political action. But the absence of an effective judiciary also undermines belief in the political system. As long as uncivil movements literally get away with murder, it is difficult to speak of a transition to rule by law.

The third component of the institutions strategy—habituation—builds on the other two. Unless authoritarian actors believe in institutions, they will not use them. According to the institutionalists, democratic beliefs and values develop with time and political learning.[10] Therefore, radical demands may stall the process of democratic development by confronting authoritarian elites before they have become habituated to democratic practice and process.[11] Building on the threats posed by popular unrest during the 1960s and 1970s, institutionalists urge popular sectors to hold back on radical and redistributive demands until after democracy becomes consolidated.[12]

Again, the case of the military coup in Chile in 1973 illustrates a challenge to the logic of the institutions approach. Even after habituation to democratic practice and procedures, authoritarian elites still used a coup to topple the democratic government and end the radical redistribution reforms. The Chilean case questions whether democracies are ever fully consolidated and whether authoritarian elites are ever fully habituated to democratic practices.[13] In addition, the emergence of uncivil movements in the so-called consolidated democracies—like the militia movement in the United States, religious fundamentalism in Israel, and nationalist movements in Europe—suggests that some groups may never become tolerant of reforms or accept the limitations imposed on them by the institutional apparatus.

Neither moderation, institutionalization, nor habituation reduces the power and privileges of uncivil movements. Uncivil movements' reaction to the political environment of a conservative transition is not what the institutionalists predicted. Rather than laying the groundwork for greater democracy, uncivil movements have exploited moderation, institutionalization, and habituation to their own uncivil ends. I argue that this process is endemic to democratization. By idealizing the redemocratization process, institutions scholars have failed to examine the pathologies of democracies, the ways in which uncivil movements exploit democratic institutions, discourse, and processes to enhance their power over the political system.[14]

PATHOLOGIES OF CIVIL SOCIETY

Uncivil movements also create pathologies of civil society. They use the discourse and practice of civil society movements, particularly social movements, to enhance their power in democratic society. But while social movements spearheaded the progressive reforms accompanying the political openings of the 1970s and 1980s,[15] uncivil movements attempted to check those reforms and protect their own power and privilege.

The social movement approach, like the institutions one, learned an important lesson from the breakdown of democracy in Latin America in the 1960s and 1970s, but it was a very different lesson. The social unrest that exploded during the earlier democratic era expressed a collective frustration with the constraints on the democratic project. Protest movements erupted because democratic governments proved unable to satisfy the social promises made during electoral campaigns. Elites perceived the grassroots mobilization from below and reformist governments as threats to their power and privilege. They thus staged overthrows and installed authoritarian regimes to protect their interests from perceived socioeconomic and political threats. The social movement approach, in sharp contrast to the institutions approach, concludes that by adopting a conservative strategy, the new democratic governments have increased their own vulnerability. Failing to bring about the much-needed and long-awaited socioeconomic reforms creates disenchantment with democratic governments and prompts greater mobilization from below to press for change. The social movement approach contends, in short, that democracy in Latin America will prove stable only when the gross inequalities of power and resources are resolved. Without reform, democracies will lack legitimacy in the eyes of the majority of their citizens. The social movement view of reform is thus very different from the view taken by institutions scholars, who claim that radical reform actually invites an authoritarian overthrow because it threatens and mobilizes elites.

The social movement approach also suggests that the kind of mobilization from below that occurs today is different from what happened during the 1960s, and that this shift alters the outcome for democratic politics and stability. The authoritarian era transformed popular movement politics. The movements of the 1960s and 1970s could be defined as groups mobilized by the left to bring about socioeconomic reform. With repression aimed at the left, such mobilization was highly constrained during the subsequent authoritarian period. Some left-wing parties continued to mobilize, but clandestinely.[16] And although some recent movements, like the new unionism in Brazil and neighborhood associations throughout the region, partially resembled the movements of the 1960s, the repressive environment meant that most movements did not have overt links with leftist parties. Instead, organizations sought help from the Catholic Church and local and international human rights organizations where possible. Although priests and nuns and international human rights activists faced repression, they had the organizational space, resources, international attention, and some limited liberty to help in organizational efforts. Through these alliances, social movements could partially disguise the political nature of their demands and focus on the regime's own contradictions. Thus, in the wage recovery campaign of the 1970s, Brazilian workers demanded not "labor rights" but rather the wages that were legally stipulated under the military regime's own policies.[17] Neighborhood associations throughout the region sought clean water, sewers, schools, and electricity consistent with the authoritarian regimes' own notions of development, growth, and progress. They did not publicly frame their interests as demands for an equitable distribution of wealth.

The social movement approach generally describes the shift in political action from the "interest and ideology"–based movements of the 1960s and 1970s to the "identity and culture"–based movements of the 1980s and 1990s. The movements organized by mothers and by indigenous peoples provide some examples. When women left their homes to protest the regimes' "disappearances" of their children, they acted out their socially constructed identities as mothers and thereby avoided being labeled "subversives" by the military regime. This identity as mothers partially shielded them from repression, since authoritarian regimes that emphasized the link between family and nation could not easily repress gatherings of mothers in public places in broad daylight.[18] Indigenous peoples had experienced state repression for centuries. But they mobilized during the authoritarian period, and they mobilized as indigenous peoples, not as an explicit social class of peasants or as an ideological group of communists. They used Indian symbols of dress, language, dance, and customs. And they demanded an end to the apartheid system that excluded them from citizenship. As indigenous peoples they could strengthen their alliances with cultural movements around the world, mobilizing international concern for human rights and cultural survival; one such activist, Rigoberta Menchú of Guatemala, even won the Nobel Peace Prize for her efforts in this area.

The emphasis on identity in social movement mobilization is not limited to repressive contexts. Indeed, European "new social movements" scholarship emphasizes identity and survival as sources of mobilization.[19] Groups have been mobilizing as women, indigenous peoples, environmentalists, gay activists, and neighborhood organizations not for reasons of instrumentality or political efficacy but because these movements have more meaning to individuals than mainstream political parties do. They identify a struggle that resonates with the values and lifestyles of their constituents in ways that mainstream politics do not. The constituents of these new social movements reject the accommodation and corruption of mainstream politics. They want to *do* politics in meaningful ways. Thus, the new social movements have engaged in unconventional and risky political action and called on constituents dedicated to the "cause" to carry out this action. Constituents have found in these new social movements a community of like-minded individuals, a shared identity and commitment to political change. While these movements have sometimes joined political parties to fight for particular concerns, they have maintained their autonomous identity, in accordance with social movements' double-militancy strategy.

The social movement approach, in short, exposes not only how popular mobilizations adapt and change because of political environments, but also how political environments are changed by these popular mobilizations. Under the military regimes, popular movements learned and implemented new grassroots mobilization tactics that proved successful even in the most inauspicious, indeed terrifying, conditions. Moreover, the victories won during the military regimes illustrate that popular mobilization for social distribution and justice does not always end in authoritarian coups, and can advance progressive political change.

Popular sectors, moreover, have not heeded the institutionalists' cautionary call to retract their demands in the interest of democratic stability. New social movements emerged during the inauspicious authoritarian period and proliferated with the expanded liberty and reduced repression of the transitions from authoritarian rule.[20] Having once risked their personal safety for their social and political demands, new social movements are unlikely to curtail their demands during the new democratic era. On the contrary, they should expect and demand even more from the new democracies than the limited reforms won under authoritarian rule. Indeed, the social movement approach suggests that the legitimacy of democratic governments depends on their capacity to overcome not only the political but also the structural roots of the repressive era.

The importance of government legitimacy bridges the social movement and institutions approaches. Juan Linz's seminal work on the institutional root of the breakdown of democratic regimes features efficacy and efficiency as the basis of democratic regimes' legitimacy and stability.[21] If new democracies prove incapable of guaranteeing basic material and security needs for the population, the popular base of their legitimacy will erode. In other words, the institutions and social movement approaches converge around the importance of legitimacy and the potentially destabilizing effect of popular disenchantment.[22]

This book offers insights into how right-wing uncivil movements prevent legitimation of the new democracies in Latin America. First, one of the most basic roles of any democratic state is the "monopoly of the legitimate use of physical force."[23] Armed right-wing groups, by virtue of their very existence, and certainly by their use of arms against their social movement and government adversaries, usually with impunity, challenge the legitimacy of the state. Second, the capacity of these uncivil movements to reverse social and political reforms further suggests the failure of democratic governments to gain legitimacy. In short, the convergence of social movement and institutions approaches points to the impact uncivil movements have on democratic legitimacy and stability.

The social movement approach, moreover, provides a curious vantage point for examining the mobilizational strategies uncivil movements use to influence democracies. Uncivil movements, just like their social movement adversaries, emphasize identity over interests. They use cultural symbols to empower new movements. They emphasize their political exclusion as a primary motivation for mobilizing. They draw on a "disenfranchised" constituency to engage in unconventional and meaningful political action. And they engage in the same type of double militancy of social movements by joining forces with political parties to achieve specific goals and enhance their success.

This book examines how uncivil movements exploit the mobilizing tools of social movements to enhance their power. The choice of tools depends largely on who they are (identities) but also on the set of cultural symbols and histories available to them to mobilize around those identities. The macro-level processes of breakdowns, transition, and consolidation generate a stock of cultural symbols upon which movements—social and uncivil—draw. Social and uncivil movements that find meaningful identities, political goals, and collective action strategies that resonate with a constituency will prove successful in mobilizing and influencing political outcomes. But uncivil movements represent the pathological side of civil society mobilization by subverting the tactics of mobilization around identity, culture, and empowerment to halt progress on social issues and to "disempower" popular movements.

This discussion of uncivil movements' capacity to expropriate social movement mobilization styles and strategies points to a larger question about civil society. Scholars tend to view civil society, like social movements, as inherently democratic, or at least as an agent of democratization. Yet many antidemocratic or nondemocratic actors fit into the parsimonious definition of civil society as nonstate, nonparty actors.[24] So too do uncivil movements. Most civil society scholars, however, reject that definition while also opposing the tendency to conflate civil society with democratic society. These scholars emphasize the "civil" and "civilizing" role of civil society. John Hall, for example, calls civil society a set of "social practices which make state-society interactions civilized."[25] Christopher G. A. Bryant refers to civil society as "a civilized or polished society in contrast to a rude, barbarous, or savage society."[26] In their classic treatment of civil society, Jean Cohen and Andrew Arato talk about social movements as building blocks of civil society, and civil society as a crucial ingredient in democracy. But their definition of social movements as "autonomous, voluntary, and indigenous associations within civil society using and expanding public discourse and public spaces for discourse"[27] could apply as well to uncivil movements.

Discussing uncivil movements and democracy brings out the ambiguity in definitions of social movements, civil society, and democracy. This book cannot hope to resolve that ambiguity. Instead, in Robert Dahl's tradition, it unpacks notions of democracy, avoiding simplistic dichotomies of democracies and nondemocracies, transitions and consolidations.[28] In particular, the study explores how uncivil movements manipulate democratic symbols, discourse, practices, and institutions to gain power within democratic societies and governments.

Conclusion

The uncivil movements approach developed here draws on the two broad literatures of the redemocratization field: the institutions approach and the social movements approach. But it also challenges those approaches. First, with regard to the institutions approach, this book argues that the strategies of moderation and institutionalization alone do not reduce the power of uncivil movements to threaten democracy. Indeed, moderation and institutionalization can enhance their power.

Second, this book challenges the assumption that democratic and civil values are inherent in social movement mobilization. Uncivil movements employ the same type of mobilization principles and strategies to advance their exclusionary politics. They aim to limit even the minimal democratic processes of free and fair elections, universal suffrage, and protection of political and civil liberties. Uncivil movements penetrate civil society, disguising some of their more uncivil aspects behind democratic institutional and social movement facades.

Third, this book rejects the division within the redemocratization literature between institutions and social movements and advocates a cultural-institutional approach. It employs an interactive model that identifies relationships among the political environment, the cultural context, and movement dynamics. It bridges the divide in the redemocratization literature by showing how institutional frameworks shape movements, movements shape institutional frameworks, and both institutions and movements shape, and are shaped by, cultural contexts.

Fourth, this book rejects the tendency to focus on the current global redemocratization process without historical and cultural nuance. While redemocratization does form a crucial backdrop for contemporary politics, it alone cannot explain political mobilization, nor can political mobilization alone explain redemocratization. The redemocratization process conditions, rather than determines, political mobilization. A country's unique political and cultural history also shapes political processes as movements adopt specific histories, repertoires of collective action, and mobilizational symbols and adapt them to critical political moments. In other words, redemocratization is not *the* set of political environmental factors that shape uncivil movements. It is *one* of the historical situations that condition the power uncivil movements will have over democracy.

Indeed, a fifth challenge this book makes to the redemocratization literature concerns dramatic events like democratic breakdowns and transitions from authoritarian rule. The problem with focusing on such events to examine politics is the inherent limitations they place on generating theory in comparative politics. By concentrating on breakdowns and transitions, political scientists develop snapshots and caricatures of political actors. We know little about who these actors are, who they were before the dramatic moment, and what they do after those dramatic political moments have passed. We also know little about how they think about politics or engage in politics during times of political normalcy. Such a limited understanding constrains our capacity to compare political change between countries or across regions. In addition, it leads to a tendency to generalize about political actors based on a crisis moment. That moment exaggerates certain characteristics and disguises others. This project seeks to untangle the political processes during dramatic breakdown and transition periods, to provide greater understanding of the postauthoritarian era.

Sixth, this book corrects one of the problems of crisis-driven political analysis by focusing on uncivil movements. Caricatures of armed right-wing groups have led social scientists and politicians to unwittingly exacerbate, rather than reduce, the power these groups wield and the threats they pose to democracy. Crisis-driven analysis has blinded social scientists and politicians to alternative strategies to contain threats to the redemocratization process. Through comparative analysis of uncivil movements, this book demystifies the threats to democracy from the armed right wing and proposes appropriate policies to defuse those threats and enhance democratic stability.

2 A Theoretical Approach
to Uncivil Movements

Having defined uncivil movements and their political power, let us now consider how they derive that political power within democracies. While uncivil movements resemble other political movements examined in the literature on political mobilization, their unique characteristics determine their particular mobilization tactics. Uncivil movements do not merely capitalize on insecurities or shared identities within a constituency and transform them into political resources. They also must persuade their constituents to join political movements that involve violence. This chapter examines how uncivil movements do so—how they frame political threats, use those threats to justify uncivil political action, and generate myths to counteract their own violent image. These three strategies reveal not only the mechanics of mobilization (the "how" of uncivil movements) but also the reason for their appeal (the "why"). This project thus marries mechanics with meaning.[1] But the strategies that build successful movements do not necessarily sustain them. The second part of this chapter examines the factors that limit uncivil movements' power: their political success, their inherent characteristics, and institutionalization. The chapter concludes by exploring strategies that willing democratic governments can employ to reduce the power of uncivil movements.

Mobilizational Strategies

Uncivil movements do not necessarily require dramatic structural or political change to mobilize constituents. They can generate political threats and opportunities out of fairly banal sets of events. They mobilize around catalyst threats that they frame as grave dangers. To effectively frame the political threat, uncivil movements draw on cultural cues. They relate the contemporary situation to past crises, an association that allows them to advocate the use of previously employed uncivil forms of political action to resolve the contemporary threat. But to avoid the stigma attached to past authoritarianism and violence, uncivil movements create legitimating myths, a means of simultaneously associating themselves (or "cuing up") with and distancing themselves from their predecessors and their uncivil acts. I treat the three-part process of framing, cuing, and mythmaking separately below, but implicit in the mobilization process is the interaction of these factors.

POLITICAL FRAMES

Much of the political mobilization literature assumes that structural and political changes generate movements. This assumption has prevailed through the grievance-based approaches and resource mobilization theories and into the current political process model.[2] There is little doubt that structural and political shifts generate new possibilities for mobilization. But grievances, political resources, and political opportunities do not simply emerge from such shifts. Instead, political agents must transform the threats created by these shifts into political action. Political agents frame contemporary events in a way that reflects how individuals feel and that mobilizes them around specific political action. In other words, even very dramatic shifts can fail to produce political movements if agents prove incapable of framing them in ways that generate collective action. Similarly, very moderate proposals for political reform can generate dramatic political movements if agents frame these reforms in ways that mobilize groups. Successful framing involves depicting contemporary events in ways that resonate with individuals' personal experiences or their perspectives on the world.[3]

Uncivil movements tend to use a four-level process to frame political threats: naming, blaming, aiming, and claiming. Movements must first identify, or "name," grievances. Although movement leaders face more challenges for mobilization when dramatic political and economic shifts have not occurred, grievances usually exist for uncivil movements' exploitation. Skillful naming involves uniting the broadest constituency possible under one set of grievances. The threat does not have to constitute the most serious threat the constituents have faced or even a more serious threat than other recent ones. The art of naming involves transforming even mild threats into catalysts for political action. Uncivil movements tend to use a universal discourse to recast the threat from a problem affecting a small minority to a threat with national and long-term, even cataclysmic, ramifications.

The second part of the framing process is "blaming," or identifying the source of the grievance. Uncivil movements do not usually blame structural forces over which individuals have little control. Instead, they tend to blame actors within the existing political system. This serves two purposes. First, it provides uncivil movements with a scapegoat for shared problems. Second, it allows uncivil movements to claim that these adversaries have excluded them from the political system. If uncivil movements already possessed power within the political system, they would have little reason to mobilize. By portraying themselves as powerless within the political system at a moment of crisis (even if it is a largely invented crisis), uncivil movements can generate support for extrainstitutional and violent political acts. Uncivil movements do not have to produce incontrovertible proof of exclusion from the political system. Instead, they frame the political situation, selecting evidence that supports their claim while ignoring conflicting data. Thus, even when uncivil movements have elected or appointed representatives, formed strong political party channels, or created powerful interest groups, they still claim exclusion from the political system.

The third part of the framing process is "aiming." Uncivil movements take aim at their target. They demonstrate to their potential constituents that the combination of severe threat and exclusion leaves the movement no alternative save radical political action. Exclusion, in other words, justifies violent action to overcome threat.

The fourth part of the framing process is "claiming." Assuming rationality among an uncivil movement's constituents, movement leaders have to show some payoff for engaging in uncivil (illegal and violent) political activity. They therefore claim victories over their adversaries. They select, or frame, events in a way that enables them to sustain the sense of threat and exclusion while also claiming that their past experience uniquely qualifies them to overcome threats and bring about change. The movements must convince constituents that they will reap rewards, but only with the active participation of individuals.

This four-part process suggests that political and economic contexts will facilitate or constrain the capacity of uncivil movements to frame threats and opportunities. Political and economic shifts, in other words, do not determine mobilization but rather provide a set of conditions that uncivil movements name, blame, take aim at, and claim victory over, to mobilize constituents. Democratic transitions therefore do not explain the rise of uncivil movements, but they do create uncertainties that uncivil movements can easily transform into catalyst threats.[4] Uncivil movements also take advantage of new opportunities provided by the democratic transitions—particularly political institutions—to claim success over their adversaries. Political transitions, in other words, facilitate uncivil movements' framing process.

But an examination of uncivil movements in so-called consolidated democracies shows that this four-part framing process is not peculiar to transitional situations. Routine democratic politics also offers uncivil movements opportunities to name, blame, aim, and claim. Discussions about relatively mild policy reforms, framed effectively, can generate a sense of threat to particular constituencies. Uncivil movements can blame an entrenched political system for failing to listen to excluded constituents. Closed out of discussions, uncivil movements can generate support for uncivil action, and with key electoral and political victories they can claim the movement's effectiveness. In short, the framing process works for uncivil movements in a variety of political contexts, transitional as well as stable. In either case, effective political framing unites a constituency around a shared understanding of the problem and the solution to that problem.[5] The creative process of framing is crucial, since as Carroll Smith-Rosenberg claims, individuals "seek through imagery and myth to mitigate their feelings of helplessness by deflecting and partially distorting change and thus bringing it within the control of the imagination."[6] Cultural cues and movement myths thus complement the political framing process.

CULTURAL CUES

To frame political threats and opportunities successfully, uncivil movements tend to draw on a stock of cultural symbols that "cue up" the movement with recognizable movements from the past, either domestic or foreign.[7] Uncivil movements draw on "foundational" threats, the kind of threats from the past that establish group identity or unity. Uncivil movements reclaim the past to evoke collective memories of fear, the danger of not acting, and the success of acting in a particular—that is, uncivil—way. These foundational threats resemble the mobilizational arguments found in cultural anthropology, particularly Clifford Geertz's seminal work on primordialism. Geertz describes situations that enhance threats to particular cultural groups, motivating them to act in "uncivil" ways. These identities, which Geertz defines as "givens of place, tongue, blood, looks, and way-of-life," provide a sense of belonging and security.[8] Threats to the group therefore threaten individuals within that group, prompting them to engage in collective action to defend themselves and their collective reality. Uncivil movements cue up contemporary events to past situations of threat to highlight the seriousness of those contemporary events and to motivate individuals to act in uncivil ways to resolve the threat.

Uncivil movements also frame events in a manner that is consistent with cultural stories, myths, and folktales. They draw on a stock of "cultural villains" from the past whom they can still blame for contemporary threats. Uncivil movements use the past to identify a shared symbol of evil, a single source of blame, a common enemy, a scapegoat, for contemporary feelings of insecurity, betrayal, and discrimination.[9] These villains may consist of adversarial groups or sectors within society, governments (or states), or even particular beliefs, ideologies, or practices that encroach on the rights and privileges of an uncivil movement's constituents. These cultural villains are invoked not only to alert members or potential members of an uncivil movement to the threat to themselves but also to evoke a sense of threat to the nation as a whole. Successful uncivil movements demonize culturally recognizable evils to mobilize support for uncivil political action.[10]

Part of the demonizing process involves the use of vitriolic language and symbols to provoke constituents' rage at the injustice they suffer at their enemies' hands. This often requires uncivil movements to counter prevailing images of their adversaries as weak or passive, particularly when their adversaries include popular sector social movements or fragile democratic governments. By creating this counter and demonic image of their adversaries, they can more easily convince their members and potential members that only collective action by the group can combat the threat the enemy poses. This imagery may seem unbelievable when uncivil movements enjoy more power within, and protection from, the state than their social movement adversaries do. Movements must therefore effectively manipulate cultural symbols, past crises, and contemporary information to convince their constituents of the threat. Rather than emasculate the enemy, they demonize it. But uncivil movements walk a fine line when they demonize the enemy. They must simultaneously convince their constituents that despite the demon's power, and the uncivil movements' alienation from mainstream politics, they still possess the potential to overcome the threat. They must claim power over the demon, since few individuals will waste their time on a hopeless proposition, and particularly one so fraught with stigmas of violence or authoritarianism. As Michael Rogin summarizes the point, "Demonization allows the counter-subversive, in the name of battling the subversive, to imitate his enemy."[11]

Demonizing and universalizing the threat allows uncivil movements to claim that only heroes and heroic acts can defeat the villains and save the nation (and, of course, the uncivil movements' constituency). And successful uncivil movements resurrect icons of heroism to identify their own struggle against evil. They draw parallels with past local, national, and even international symbols of heroic struggle to identify the justice of their uncivil mobilization and also to claim the likelihood of victory. Uncivil movements also cue up particular forms of political action. They draw from "repertoires of collective action" that symbolize a continuity of political traditions—a heroic tradition of acting for the collective good against evil.[12] In short, uncivil movements become "protagonists of the 'social drama' [who] respond to and clothe themselves in their culture's stock of sedimented symbols, archetypal characters, and rhetorical appeals."[13]

The mobilizational style employed by uncivil movements reflects their claim of exclusion from the political system. Regardless of the degree to which uncivil movements become institutionalized, they initially tend to employ high-profile, unconventional political action. They do not use organizational networks to recruit and sustain support. This unconventional type of political action is consistent with the "outsider" image such movements cultivate. Their exclusion from the centers of power forces them to resort to unconventional tactics to make themselves heard.

But there is another motivation behind this form of political action. Unconventional political action often captures media attention. Such attention is crucial to uncivil movement mobilization. Given the small size of these movements, face-to-face recruitment becomes impossible if the movement is to expand its membership beyond limited regions of the country. Media attention provides exposure in remote areas of the country; it provides free publicity. It also creates the impression that the movement has more strength than its small numbers suggest. As a movement's perceived power grows, so will its appeal to individuals who share the movement's goals but might not be willing to devote their time to a fringe movement. Thus, media attention to the movement provides members with the sense of being part of a national group that is frequently featured in the news. Consistent with the concept of an "imagined community,"[14] members of an uncivil movement need not actually take part in the movement's political activity, or even know those who are taking part, to feel united with the movement. Unconventional political acts therefore advance unity and collective identity as individuals come to see themselves as part of a collective rebellion against political complacency. Even bad press is better than no press at all. Once uncivil movements get press—often owing to their uncivil acts—they can spin justifications and denials of their violence using the legitimating myths discussed below.

Uncivil movements do not faithfully replicate past cultural icons, villains, and repertoires. Instead, they generally have to reinterpret/reframe them to suit contemporary needs and practices. The issues, constituencies, political environment, and even cultural context have changed. Thus, even a close approximation of the past by an uncivil movement is never simply a repetition of the same but rather involves innovation and adaptation.[15] Uncivil movements resurrect old ideas and styles selectively and recreate them to fit contemporary issues. They "draw upon cultural stock, but transform it."[16] This adaptation occurs with cultural villains and heroic icons as well as political actions. Charles Tilly's concept of repertoires of collective action emphasizes the cultural and transformative process of movement-making. Tilly contends that a "group has a heavy bias toward means it has previously used, but is not completely closed to innovation."[17] He contends that innovative movements produce continuous, gradual change by imitating other groups that have successfully used similar collective action or by "stretching the boundaries of forms of action that already belong to the repertoire."[18] Tilly's concept suggests that repertoires of collective action are not exclusively local. International conditions contribute to the cultural contexts in which uncivil movements succeed or fail. Uncivil movements borrow strategies from successful uncivil movements in other countries, gaining local legitimacy by modeling themselves on such movements. Uncivil movements can also heighten the sense of local threat by pointing to international events gone awry. They may even receive direct financial support from foreign uncivil movements or governments to increase their political power locally. So while uncivil movements tend to act locally, they often reflect global conditioning factors.

What transpires within successful uncivil movement mobilization is essentially the playing out of old ideas in new ways, but also new ideas in old ways.[19] Even slight alterations in activity can significantly change uncivil movements' discourse about their identity and political action. Similarly, uncivil movements may identify themselves with past heroic movements without in fact resembling them very closely. Culture therefore constitutes uncivil movements' "usefully manipulable tools."[20] The departure from the past is papered over with cultural labels. Both processes are facilitated by movement myths.

MOVEMENT MYTHS

Framing and cuing help mobilize a constituency by identifying the existing threat, the need to mobilize against it, and the success a particular uncivil form of mobilizing has enjoyed with respect to past threats and mobilizations. When movements frame or cue up contemporary movements with past uncivil or authoritarian movements, they generate support from the most radical elements, individuals with the violent passions of their predecessors. Such radical elements are necessary for the success of uncivil movements. They become the movements' storm troopers, the militant hard core, the individuals who tirelessly carry out the uncivil acts upon which the movements rely.

Social psychologists have attempted to explain this uncivil constituency. Among the most famous studies, of course, is the authoritarian personality (TAP) study, which found fascist propensities in individuals who shared similar early childhood experiences (i.e., excessively restrictive upbringing).[21] Such backgrounds created a set of conflicting personality traits that in combination would dispose an individual to follow fascist-style leaders and movements: conventionalism and submission to authority on one hand and repressed frustration with authority on the other, in both cases leading to aggression against out-groups.[22]

Subsequent social psychology experiments questioned early childhood socialization as the key to authoritarian personality types.[23] Situational factors convinced some scholars that authoritarian behavior could be triggered in seemingly well-balanced individuals from a variety of family backgrounds. The famous Milgram experiment, for example, established certain settings that could trigger aggressive behavior in seemingly nonaggressive individuals—in particular, where the authority figure was persuasive, the setting commanded respect, and personal responsibility could be negated in the face of scientific or technological sophistication.[24]

Even some rational actor approaches have attempted to explain radical movements of the uncivil variety.[25] Their small size and unconventional style of political action should undermine such approaches by failing to meet the criteria of self-interest (i.e., the pursuit of individual economic rewards, power, pleasure, and reputation) and efficiency (i.e., selecting from among a set of options the least costly and most beneficial strategy central to rational acting).[26] Nonetheless, self-identified rational choice scholars have explained the apparent nonrational cases of rebellious collective action.[27] They argue that individuals' self-interest must be broadened to include psychic rewards derived from collectivities, even when the political action is personally dangerous.[28]

Daniel Bell's seminal volume on the radical right in the United States attributed radicalism to collective frustration stemming from structural change.[29] Richard Hofstadter, for example, described a kind of reserve army of authoritarian personalities riddled with hate and submissiveness willing to follow any authoritarian leader who would press them into violent service.[30]

The "masculinities" literature attempts to explain the appeal of violence as part of cultural attributes of manliness, adventure, and even freedom and morality. Some of these studies claim a genetic or psychological predisposition toward violence in men, but even they recognize that this violent instinct has to be triggered by some context.[31] The "men's studies" approaches that I found most useful for this project examine the ways in which violence is constructed as part of the cultural understandings of male heroism. Cultural constructions of masculinity, in other words, feed and fuel violence in men.[32]

These various explanations for violence help explain uncivil movements in two important ways. First, they demonstrate that the kinds of militant storm troopers upon whom uncivil movements rely are normally plentiful. Indeed, every society may include a hard-core militant constituency that is constantly searching for uncivil movements within which to channel its violent tendencies. But uncivil movements rarely, if ever, gain political power in democracies if they rely exclusively on their militant following. This following can cost movements their legitimacy by identifying them with the radical, or "lunatic," fringe. Unless they gain numeric power, neither governments, the media, nor the general public will take them seriously as political players in the democratic system. Instead, they will be treated as criminal or terrorist organizations. Successful uncivil movements therefore have to appeal not only to the storm troopers who carry out the uncivil acts but also to constituents who do not openly support violence, because it is the latter who expand the size, appeal, and legitimacy of the movement. Therefore, the second way in which the literature summarized above contributes to the study of uncivil movements is by emphasizing the contextual factors that can provoke seemingly nonviolent individuals to join violent movements.

Particular forms of movement crafting can appeal to both the militant constituency and those who share the uncivil movement's goals but are hesitant to associate themselves with its violence—the "pragmatic" constituency.

Legitimating myths—defined as conflicting, and even contradictory, understandings of the movement and its goals that permit the movement's pragmatic members to deny or ignore its uncivil side—play a crucial role in uncivil movement mobilization. This myth creation involves outright denial as well as the use of images and stories that counter the movement's violent image. I adopt the definition of myth as a language designed to make what is political or contrived seem natural and inevitable.[33]

Symbols do not have uniform or obvious meaning. They are interpreted in different ways by different actors. Most symbols, for example, do not have a physical or visual expression but are ideas.[34] They are imprecise and need to be interpreted in specific ways by movement entrepreneurs in order to mobilize a constituency. Therefore, what is important is not so much the use of symbols but the meaning that the movement attaches to those symbols to generate the desired political outcome. As Anthony Cohen states, "So versatile are symbols they can often be bent into these idiosyncratic shapes of meanings without such distortions becoming visible to other people who use the same symbol at the same time."[35] The particular way in which uncivil movements manipulate symbols constitutes their "legitimating myths."

Legitimating myths provide a "civil" justification for pragmatic supporters to join uncivil movements. Pragmatic supporters point to legitimating myths to argue that the movements they endorse are misunderstood; they are actually neither violent nor extremist. Pragmatic supporters can remain blind to the uncivil aspects of the movement, because movements spin legitimating myths to mask those uncivil aspects behind general concepts of civility. Legitimating myths provide pragmatic supporters with the language they need to justify joining.[36]

But legitimating myths must also sustain support from hard-core militants—those who participate in the movement not despite its uncivil action but because of it. The myths are framed in such a way that hard-core militants can interpret them as "coding," a civil disguise for uncivil actions.[37] They recognize that the coding satisfies pragmatists and deflects democratic governments' attention away from the violent aspects of the uncivil movement.

Legitimating myths also help create cultural villains, heroes, and repertoires of political action. Because drawing on the past often links the movement with violence and authoritarianism, legitimating myths emerge to distance the movement from the past. Legitimating myths about leaders, the movement, and political action attempt to shed negative associations with the past while glorifying, and identifying with, positive images from the past.

The construction of myths around movement leaders suggests that leadership is more complex than the discussion in the social movement literature would suggest. That literature tends to treat leadership as a "resource" that movements exploit through the particular attributes of professional leaders or movement entrepreneurs.[38] Professionals bring to the movement managerial, communications, and recruitment skills and networks. Entrepreneurs, in contrast, lack these skills and networks but employ their unique personal attributes—or charisma—to centralize and assume personal control over it.[39]

Uncivil movements are dominated by entrepreneurs, not professional managers. The business metaphor effectively describes the roles these entrepreneurs play in creating successful uncivil movements. Movement entrepreneurs identify an opportunity in the political marketplace. They envision a movement-product that they can sell. They package that movement, using the frames and cuing discussed above. They create both the movement-product and consumer demand for that product. In other words, they are the founders, chief engineers, and marketing specialists of uncivil movements. Uncivil movement entrepreneurs initially tap an existing demand. But this demand is limited to a small "consumer base"—namely, the militant hard core seeking the adventure associated with violent iconoclastic movements. To increase demand, entrepreneurs modify the product to appeal to both the militant hard core and a pragmatic constituency of consumers. Indeed, entrepreneurs continue to alter the movement-product to sustain its appeal when consumer tastes change or the movement-product faces competition from other movements or political institutions.

To help sell their movement-product, entrepreneurs need the right image or spokesman. (I use the gendered form deliberately here to emphasize the significance and salience of uncivil movements' male leadership.) These spokesmen embody the movements; they become inextricably linked to them. Indeed, they become so closely associated with the movement that the entrepreneurs are rarely visible. They remain behind the scenes while the spokesmen take center stage. The entrepreneurs select these spokesmen from the founding entrepreneurial group. They recognize in them certain traits that can be used to market the movement effectively. While personal charisma is one such trait, entrepreneurs seek spokesmen with more than good speaking, sartorial, or physical style; coaching from public-relations experts can transform almost anyone into an effective communicator in those terms. What entrepreneurs particularly seek are spokesmen who can create an emotional bond with the movement's constituency.[40]

Constructing spokesmen is where the legitimating myths become relevant. The spokesman's past becomes the movement's past. His beliefs become the movement's beliefs. His identity becomes the movement's identity. Uncivil movements' spokesmen draw on and evoke images of past heroism. They use the language and symbols of heroic struggles, personifying the past and predicting future victories. Simultaneously, entrepreneurs shape the spokesmen's image to shield them from negative associations with past heroic struggles. As a result, spokesmen's look, language, and use of symbols evoke contradictory images. They expropriate much from former authoritarian warriors to appeal to the militant hard core. Yet they build into their image symbols of modernity, democracy, and professionalism to attract a broader constituency.

The movement's public transcript also forms part of the legitimating myths. The transcript contains universalistic language on democratic freedoms, rights, and values. So vague that any group could use it, the message permits the movement to shroud itself in a democratic cloak that obscures some of its undemocratic activity. An important part of the public transcript is the name of the movement. These labels create new positive identities that overshadow negative associations with the movement's past. In the context of redemocratization, for example, movements tend to adopt titles that include terms like *democracy, freedom, liberty,* or *independence.* Such names help broaden movements' appeal beyond a small sectoral constituency to include a "national" mission. In this way movements "legitimize" their activity by disguising it as a modern, democratic, national project.

In order to implement this democratic and national project, uncivil movements employ a universalizing myth. They claim to represent a wide constituency, portraying themselves as the vocal minority willing to stand up for the silent majority. This universal discourse often comes in the form of "antipolitics." Uncivil movements reject mainstream institutional politics as corrupt and exclusionary. They define their own task as putting excluded opinions on the agenda.

The antipolitics claim is used almost exclusively by right-wing, rather than left-wing, uncivil movements. Indeed, right-wing uncivil movements rarely refer to themselves as right-wing. While they mobilize around issues commonly associated with the right (e.g., the inviolability of private property rights, nationalist extremism, rigid morality, religious fundamentalism, and family values)[41] and attack their adversaries on the left, they also pay lip service to policies associated with the left (e.g., social justice and protection of national production). And in some cases they even attempt tactical alliances with left-wing movements. The antipolitics claim thus serves a number of legitimating functions for uncivil movements. For example, they can mask the power they actually possess within the mainstream political system by claiming that they constitute an excluded group that must operate outside the system by means of extrainstitutional and violent political action. They can present themselves as political mavericks, unbeholden to any "special interest group" and thus able to find nonpolitical solutions to national problems. They portray themselves as the authentic and "democratic" representatives of excluded voices, in contrast to back-room negotiators and elite politicians.

Perhaps the most crucial role of legitimating myths concerns violent political action. Violence is one of the defining characteristics of uncivil movements. It is also key to uncivil movements' success, since violence often works. Some studies claim that political actors who use violence have a higher-than-average success rate in achieving new advantages and gaining acceptance from their antagonists.[42] Others assert the efficacy of violence in more cautious terms: "It cannot be said that, in general, violation of the rules of pluralist politics is self-defeating for challengers."[43] Yet violence is rarely the only, or even the primary, tactic of political influence used by any group, uncivil movements included.[44] Uncivil movements mobilize within political systems through elected or appointed representatives, political parties, and lobbies. Frequently they engage in institutional efforts simultaneously with extrainstitutional, violent action. Uncivil movements therefore can easily spin myths about their civility by highlighting their work within the political system. They trumpet their participation and success within the institutional system to show that they are significant political actors.

This contradiction between civil and uncivil political action does not weaken uncivil movements; rather, movements exploit it to their advantage. Most uncivil movements, for example, deny that they use violence, but they benefit from rumors about their violence. These contradictory images permit uncivil movements to sustain support from both militant and pragmatic constituencies. As long as democratic governments fail to investigate or find evidence to link the movements to violence, this strategy works. Right-wing uncivil movements dismiss accusations of violence as left-wing propaganda spread by the media and the corrupt government—both of which they assume are controlled by the left—to destroy them. This denial of violence simultaneously satisfies the movements' pragmatic constituency and is interpreted by the militant constituency as "coding."

Because movements gain advantages from violence, their denials are not especially vigorous. Instead, they justify some of their violence. One such justification is a "relative-weight" defense. Movements claim that they reduce the level of violence by providing a peaceful channel for political expression. Without their control, they contend, anarchic forms of political violence would result. They also justify their violence as a form of civil disobedience. They further claim that they must use violence to protect the country and themselves from the more extreme violence used by their enemies. Another tactic used by uncivil movements is "blaming a few bad eggs." Movement leaders diffuse criticism from the group as a whole by asserting that they cannot control the individual violent acts of a few members.

When they do admit to using violence, uncivil movements frequently analogize to war. Like soldiers in a war, they are duty-bound to use violence to protect the country from enemies. The war metaphor emphasizes a just and responsible use of violence. It rejects the image of unprotected or innocent enemies, thus justifying violence against them. Transforming enemies into demons renders them legitimate targets of proportional violence.[45] The "just-war" analogy not only distinguishes the members of uncivil movements from murderers, psychopaths, and terrorists; it also enhances their image as soldiers sacrificing their personal security to fight a brutal and demonic enemy for the greater good of the nation.

The just-war analogy demonstrates the central role gendered discourse plays in uncivil movements' legitimating myths. Military symbols evoking manhood and heroism have limited appeal with women, however. And most uncivil movements recognize a need to attract support among women. At the very least, women fulfill traditionally defined gender roles within uncivil movements, such as charity and social work, clerical work, preparing and serving food and refreshments at meetings and rallies, fundraising, and accompanying their husbands at public events. But when movements attempt to expand their appeal beyond the militant hard core, women become an obvious group to target. Some pragmatic entrepreneurs advocate expanded roles for women within the movement. And when these roles include leadership positions or elected public office, they challenge traditional gendered roles. Female participation thus forms part of a movement's legitimating myths by countering the movements' bellicose, and extremist, male image.

By shattering traditional images of femininity, the expanded role of women in uncivil movements creates tensions between militant hard-core and pragmatic leaders. Hard-core militants within right-wing uncivil movements typically exalt women as mothers and nation builders, but not as political leaders.[46] Women's traditional responsibility is to produce, educate, and socialize their children for both the family and the nation. These militants consider the protection of women—as mothers or future mothers of loyal soldiers and patriotic citizens—to be part of their mission. While inviting women to stuff envelopes or serve coffee does not challenge this position, installing them in leadership positions does. Rather than provoke a conflict, however, uncivil movements simply present contrasting images: women are portrayed both as homemakers for the nation and as modern political leaders. Pragmatists "win" a modern image for themselves and the movement by supporting social change. The militant hard core continues to espouse a patriarchal view, which remains part of the movement's discourse. And because women's leadership positions are largely cosmetic and their activist husbands are really calling the shots behind the facade of female leadership, the militant hard core can attribute the contradiction to "coding."

This use of gender illustrates the process by which movements create legitimating myths. Movement entrepreneurs rarely consciously or deliberately adopt myths as a ruse to broaden their movement's appeal. Legitimating myths instead evolve out of power struggles among movement entrepreneurs, who include militants and pragmatists with diverging views. And while there are always a few pure militants and pure pragmatists among a movement's members and leaders, most are a bit of both: their pragmatism surfaces on some issues and their militancy on others. Legitimating myths accommodate the differences among them. Uncivil movements' loose organizational structure allows different leaders to take opposing positions on the same set of issues and to put out strident messages on those issues. Since usually no official line from the top leadership resolves the uncertainty regarding the position the movement takes on these issues, contradictory messages emerge. The top leadership tolerates, maybe even encourages, opposing views on issues. The multiplicity of messages provides members and potential members with a range of views from which they can select the one most consistent with their own. Pragmatic members may filter out the uncivil aspects of the movement and blame the government and left-wing media conspiracy for misrepresenting its views. Hard-core members interpret the moderate positions as "covers" designed to hide the authoritarian attitudes behind a democratic facade. Legitimating myths thus maintain loyalty and commitment from both camps.

But myths also emerge through trial and error and happenstance. Some work and others do not. Sometimes entrepreneurs accidentally hit a chord that resonates with a potential constituency. And myths are generated through a learning process developed by emulating social movements' or predecessors' successes. And perhaps most important, myths change as movements adapt and respond to new environments. When stigmatized for a particular message, movements alter that message, spin a new interpretation, or produce a conflicting one to limit damage to their public image.

In sum, entrepreneurial leaders generate legitimating myths around spokesmen, public transcripts, political action, and gender to help members and potential members make sense of the political environment. They generate these myths largely by drawing on cultural symbols but transforming them to fit a contemporary context. They allow constituents to deny, filter out, or justify aspects of the movement that they do not want to acknowledge or interrogate too thoroughly. They provide the means to bring together different individuals who share some, but not necessarily all, of the movement's tactics and ideas. They provide justification for individuals who might not otherwise join an overtly armed, right-wing, movement. They build on the vulnerability felt by certain sectors of the population, urging them to engage in collective action to end an urgent threat. They propose a possible solution to that threat that is recognizably similar to, but also distinct from, past uncivil solutions. They create a new identity that unites individuals with different views. And they broaden the appeal of the movement by casting it in terms of democratic, collective, and national goals rather than authoritarian, self-, or class interests. Movement entrepreneurs play a key role in creating these myths, but potential constituents "make sense" of them. Cohen brilliantly describes the process thus: "People can find common currency in behavior whilst still tailoring it subjectively (and interpretively) to their *own* needs."[47]

THE INTERACTION OF FRAMING, CUING, AND MYTHMAKING

The theoretical framework outlined in this book argues that no particular political or economic moment or cultural experience can explain the rise of uncivil movements, although that rise is often facilitated by transitional situations. Transitions thus do not explain but rather condition uncivil movements' emergence. What explains their emergence is the interaction between movement agency and context: the capacity of movements to exploit political and cultural contexts to their advantage.

Figure 2.1 summarizes the strategies that successful uncivil movements employ: political framing, cultural cues, and legitimating myths. The figure illustrates how these three strategies interact in the development of successful uncivil movements.

Uncivil movements capitalize on some sense of threat in the political and economic context. They identify, or name, this threat. To mobilize potential members around this threat, uncivil movements must spin narratives, or myths, around it. These narratives transform the threat from a relatively mild threat to a particular social sector into a universal threat. Framing and mythmaking thus interact. But to convince potential members of the movement of the gravity of the threat and mobilize them behind uncivil political action, uncivil movements evoke past crises. They blame villains from the past, linking framing, myths, and cues.

By demonizing and universalizing threats and framing themselves as excluded from the political system, uncivil movements justify unconventional and uncivil political action. They persuade potential members to join uncivil movements by resurrecting images of heroes and heroic movements that have defeated similar villains in the past. Uncivil movements incorporate symbols and patterns of political action to cue up to past heroic movements that overcame similar types of threats. Understanding that past movements often come with stigmas of authoritarianism and violence, uncivil movements do not simply replicate them. Instead, they create some distance between themselves and the unsavory past. They fabricate legitimating myths that conjure up positive images and suppress negative associations. Again, framing, cuing, and mythmaking interact.

In offering this discussion of framing, cuing, and mythmaking I might be

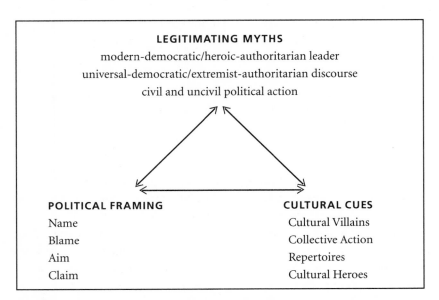

LEGITIMATING MYTHS
modern-democratic/heroic-authoritarian leader
universal-democratic/extremist-authoritarian discourse
civil and uncivil political action

POLITICAL FRAMING
Name
Blame
Aim
Claim

CULTURAL CUES
Cultural Villains
Collective Action
Repertoires
Cultural Heroes

FIGURE 2.1   Analytical Framework for Explaining Successful Uncivil Movements

accused of having prepared a veritable "How To" manual for uncivil movements. That is not my intention. On the contrary, I have sought to locate the sources of power for these movements in order to identify the means by which willing democratic governments and social movements can reduce their influence. To address those concerns, I turn to the second part of this analytical framework.

Limitations on the Power of Uncivil Movements

Limiting uncivil movements' power is not easy. The prevalence of threats and cultural symbols from which uncivil movements can draw provide multiple means of mobilization. Moreover, successful uncivil movements can radically transform the political system in a relatively short period of time. They can even continue to influence the political system after they have ceased to exist.

Despite their potential political power, however, uncivil movements display weaknesses resulting from three sets of conditions: (1) political success, (2) internal dynamics, and (3) democratic institution building. Ironically, these three factors also heighten uncivil movements' political power. Thus, successful uncivil movements tend to plant the seeds of their own destruction. As the discussion below makes clear, uncivil movements can, and often do, overcome these limitations and remain influential both within and outside the political system. These limitations therefore hint at ways in which democratic governments might reduce uncivil movements' power.

POLITICAL SUCCESS

Uncivil movements do not survive if they consistently fail to fulfill their goals. Members simply will not waste their time on a losing proposition. They will find some other way to achieve their goals. And without a base of support, uncivil movements eventually disintegrate without posing significant problems for democracies. Paradoxically, however, success can also weaken uncivil movements. If they eliminate the threat around which they have mobilized, they themselves should also disappear. Having accomplished their goals, they no longer have a role to play. This is particularly the case given the antipolitics sentiment within uncivil movements. Rather than searching for a permanent political role, uncivil movements generally are task-oriented, mandated only to fulfill a specific set of goals and to withdraw from politics after success.

Because of movement burnout, an uncivil movement's members usually lack the energy to sustain the movement after it has achieved its goals. Given their small size, uncivil movements repeatedly call on the same group of individuals to organize and carry out political action. And the kind of unconventional political action in which uncivil movements engage takes individuals away from their families, jobs, and homes. Leaders and members alike relinquish leisure time, income, and security for the sake of the movement. While individuals initially experience a "high" or sense of esprit de corps from such participation, the personal costs mount over time. Burnout is exacerbated by the public outrage that results from movements' uncivil actions. Victory over the purported threat therefore offers members the possibility of resuming their normal lives. Faced with this lack of sustained commitment from its members, the movement dwindles. Successful movements, just like the failed ones, tend to die of natural causes before they reach old age.

The short-livedness of uncivil movements, however, is not necessarily a measure of their political power. Uncivil movements maintain their political power even after they disband. As "latent movements" they can remobilize on short notice to confront future threats. They thus possess a form of veto power, guaranteeing that their victories will not be reversed lest they launch another uncivil initiative.

The influence of latent movements largely depends on continued popular perceptions of their power. Even when they have disbanded and lack the support to remobilize, the government, the media, and their civil society adversaries often perceive them as powerful enough to do so. This perception provides them with more power than they actually possess. Governments avoid redistribution policies, fearing a resurgence of uncivil movement violence. The media perceives mobilization of similar groups as the reemergence of uncivil movements. Popular sectors continue to blame these movements for uncivil actions, even when the movements no longer exist. Public perception of uncivil movements thus enables them to retain their political power and influence.

Successful uncivil movements also survive beyond their own lifetimes because they become models of heroism and form part of the repertoire of collective action upon which future uncivil movements rely. Subsequent uncivil movements both consciously and unconsciously resemble these precursor movements, in developing ideas, attracting a constituency, designing mobilization strategies, and carrying out political action. Remobilized latent uncivil movements rarely involve the same leaders, members, or networks. They rarely use the same name. Instead, uncivil movements emerge for different reasons at different times. Latent movements, in short, become part of the cultural context that shapes future uncivil mobilizations.[48]

Successful uncivil movements, in sum, have inherent strengths and weaknesses. The major weakness is that once they have accomplished their primary goals, they no longer have a direct role to play, and their membership pressures them to withdraw from politics. But their strengths generally outweigh this limitation. They can profoundly influence political outcomes even if they exist only briefly. They influence political outcomes even after they cease to exist because of public fear of remobilization. And they form part of the culture upon which future uncivil movements build.

INTERNAL DYNAMICS

The characteristics of uncivil movements that contribute to their successful emergence often fail to sustain them. Inherent tensions over leadership and political action surface over time and often lead to the demise of even successful uncivil movements.

A number of tensions arise when charismatic leaders emerge. Such leaders tend to become omnipotent (or perceive themselves as such). Movement entrepreneurs—those individuals who built the movement and promoted its charismatic leader—lose control of the movement as the leader amasses personal power. The charismatic leaders, rather than the entrepreneurs, come to represent the movement in media interviews, government negotiations, political campaigns, and other public forums. They become the glue that holds movements together.

Charismatic leaders form their own recruitment, organizational, and communication structures. Indeed, such leaders often actively resist a formalized structure. They prefer and cultivate ad hoc procedures, loose membership requirements, and a minimal division of labor. This provides them with greater personal control over the movement. Even when movements with charismatic leaders appear to be formal in structure, they are informal in practice. Movement constituents accept this idiosyncratic organizational and leadership structure because charismatic leaders do not simply exercise great authority; they inspire great devotion. Frequently, members and local leaders will not only gloss over the charismatic leaders' authoritarian style, they will defend it. They contend, for example, that because the leader is in touch with the people, decisions are in fact made democratically. They also claim that centralized leadership has advantages over rigid organizational networks, since it provides the kind of flexibility the movement needs to respond quickly to crises. The leader can easily shift the movement's message and tactics according to changes in the political and cultural context. Loose organizational structure also leaves room for local leaders to advance issues they care about, sometimes even in opposition to other movement leaders' views.

Charismatic leaders, in short, are not slaves to the program; they *are* the program. Uncivil movements therefore change with the leadership as it adapts to changing contexts. Little occurs within these movements without the direct oversight of their charismatic spokesmen. As a result, entrepreneurial leaders increasingly take roles subordinate to the charismatic leaders.

On the other hand, the charismatic leadership structure is inherently weak. The monopoly of power leads to tensions over succession, competition for second-tier leadership, and disagreements over future directions. It is not uncommon, for example, for charismatic spokesmen to become either unwilling or unable to lead the movement, creating succession crises. In some cases charismatic leaders die without an heir capable of filling their shoes. More typically, leaders tire of the movement. They look forward to more prestigious political positions. They may opt for the security of elected or appointed public office. As a result, uncivil movements often lose their charismatic leaders. And because of the cult of personality, movements can rarely generate new spokesmen who possess the same charisma.

But even when charismatic leaders remain in control of uncivil movements, they create problems. Competition over leadership emerges when entrepreneurial leaders seek their turn in power. In addition, new leaders emerge from below and compete with charismatic leaders. Charismatic leaders often react to such competition by purging their competitors from the ranks. They characterize the purges as necessary for the coherence and purity of the movement. And since neither the movement entrepreneurs nor the leaders emerging from below are visible because of the centralized control of the charismatic authority, their removal from the movement rarely causes a stir. The movement remains strong, and the leaders' control uncontested, at least for the short term. Frequent purges, however, undermine movements. Removed entrepreneurial and local leaders take with them not only their leadership skills but also followers and financial resources. In addition, public awareness of purges increases the perception that such movements are unstable, a perception that reduces their strength and appeal.

A natural tendency among radical movements toward moderation also increases tensions.[49] The burnout and success factors discussed above contribute to the desire on the part of the pragmatic members and leaders to move in a mainstream direction. This constituency begins to reject violent political action because of either government reprisals, stigma, or a desire for greater respectability within the political system. But hard-core militants remain attracted to the movement's tradition of high-profile violence. They reject moderation and push for intensified pressure through unconventional and violent political action, driving a wedge between themselves and the movement's pragmatic constituents. The common struggle had united the group, but victory over the threat breeds conflict over the use of violence as a political tactic and eventually undermines the coherence of the movement.

In sum, the internal factors that consolidate the power of uncivil movements also become their Achilles heel: charismatic leaders with entrepreneurial backing, a coalition of hard-core militants and pragmatic constituents, and programs that embrace both civil and uncivil political action. Ironically, the success of the movement exacerbates these vulnerabilities. Charismatic leaders seek more power, autonomy, and a mainstream political role. Entrepreneurial and second-tier leaders desire more power. Moderate members seek less unconventional tactics and more mainstream roles once the threat is resolved. And the hard-core members seek intensified violence to ensure that the threat does not reemerge. While these internal conflicts weaken an uncivil movement's political power, the change may come too late—that is, only after the movement has already successfully transformed the political system.

INSTITUTIONALIZATION

The gradual moderation mentioned above means that uncivil movements usually cannot resist the allure of institution building. During a period of urgency and danger, uncivil movements pursue radical action. But when the perceived threat has dissipated because of the movements' success, government retribution for violence, or waning popular appeal resulting from the stigma of violence, uncivil movements pursue lower-cost political action. Institutionalization becomes an obvious alternative. The impetus behind institutionalization may also come from charismatic leaders who fancy themselves as future national political leaders and transform their movements into political parties from which to launch a political career. Alternatively, charismatic leaders may begin to court an alliance with mainstream political parties in an effort to win nomination for political office within them.

When uncivil movements form or join political parties, they appear to follow the route institutions scholars predict. But it is precisely because they acquire power over the democratic government through the institutional path that this project partially challenges the institutions approach. When institution building eventually erodes uncivil movements' political power, it does so through a process unexamined by the institutions scholars.

Institutionalization enhances uncivil movements' power via "double militancy." Like social movements, uncivil movements recognize that remaining outside the political institutional structure limits their ability to influence political outcomes. But they also fear that they will be absorbed and become marginalized if they pursue an exclusively mainstream political party orientation. Double militancy allows uncivil movements to pursue their interests within the institutional framework through political parties and interest groups while maintaining their autonomy. The institutional prong of this double-militancy strategy usually involves allying with or forming antipolitics political parties.[50] These political parties resemble uncivil movements in their portrayal of mainstream politics as corrupt, self-interested, outmoded, and limited to inside players. Like uncivil movements, they portray themselves as political mavericks whose distance from the center of power affords them a unique, accurate, and unbiased understanding of the nation's problem, a vision for the future, and the capacity to implement it. Like uncivil movements, they claim that they are impartial, independent, and unbeholden to power brokers within the political system. They profess to represent ideas excluded from the mainstream. They contend that they are accountable only to their constituents, unmotivated by the material rewards of public office. Such claims link antipolitics parties with uncivil movements, providing uncivil movements with a vehicle for influencing political outcomes from within the political system without compromising their autonomy. Political parties allow uncivil movements to put issues on the political agenda, elect representatives, and increase their legitimacy from within the political system.

Double militancy challenges institutionalization as a means of controlling uncivil movements. Uncivil movements do not always fold when they form, or make alliances with, political parties. On the contrary, they maintain their uncivil activity as an alternative means of influencing political outcomes. They can strike from outside the system to reinvigorate stalled negotiations or reorient wayward political reforms. Unlike social movement action, the signature autonomous and extrainstitutional political action is uncivil—that is, illegal, violent, and aimed at checking rather than extending civil and political rights and public-policy reforms to the majority. In short, political parties become another weapon by which uncivil movements influence political outcomes. Institutionalization therefore has the opposite impact of that anticipated by the institutional approaches to redemocratization: rather than channeling political demands through the political system and thus moderating them, it becomes the source of their political power along with uncivil political actions.

Institutionalization can weaken the power of uncivil movements over democracies in some cases, albeit not in the way the institutions approach predicts. Uncivil movements derive much of their strength from their anti-system characteristics. Their icons of heroism, cultural villains, and repertoires of violent political action are built largely on an antipolitics ideology, and when they attempt to navigate the troubled waters that accompany a transition from movement to political party, their political power erodes. Shifting their orientation lessens their appeal. Pragmatic supporters might remain in these movements-cum-parties because they desire a less militant organization. But they are just as likely to abandon political activism altogether once the imminent threat, and the need for activism, disappears. Support from the militant hard core is also difficult to sustain during the transition from movement to party. Because these members most adamantly oppose mainstream politics, they view institutionalization as a "sellout" of the movement to corrupt parties and politicians.[51]

Uncivil movements' loose organizational structure complicates institutionalization. These movements rely on charismatic appeal and media attention to expand and unite their constituency. They do not build an organizational structure with networks throughout the country to recruit, expand, and centralize control. If they do attempt to build a more formal institutional structure, they must resolve their many internal weaknesses. Numbers of supporters pose a central problem. As long as they remain movements, they are less dependent on large numbers of supporters. But when they seek electoral power, the movement-cum-party must establish organizational and recruiting networks throughout the country to expand its support. An uncivil movement may be able to get the organizational network it needs by joining an existing political party. But charismatic leaders may feel constrained by the discipline of institutionalized political parties. And indeed, because uncivil movements are seen as anarchic, uncontrollable, and stigmatized, political parties may not even be willing to make alliances with them.

Institutionalization, in sum, does not uniformly impact uncivil movements' political power. The institutionalization process can exacerbate weaknesses inherent in uncivil movements, unraveling their political power. But it can also provide a dual weapon for uncivil movements. It permits them to continue their uncivil activity while creating a parallel civil and legal structure within the political system. This two-pronged strategy enhances the power of uncivil movements over the democratic process and contributes to the legitimating myths that attract a less militant following. Political institutions thus enable uncivil movements to achieve political power disproportionate to their relatively small size.

THE ROLE OF DEMOCRATIC GOVERNMENTS

Most of the new democracies in Latin America have adopted some version of the institutions approach, moderating their policies and opening channels within the political system to incorporate the former authoritarians. And while the new Latin American democracies have by and large avoided overthrows, it is not at all clear that political institutions have transformed authoritarians into democratic actors. However much the institutionalists may wish the case were otherwise, the fact remains that when uncivil movements form political institutions, they do not always abandon their extra-institutional violence. Such movements continue to threaten democracy.

The focus on institutionalization as the main strategy for stability is well illustrated by empirical cases. Uncivil movements usually move in a more moderate and institutional direction after they have already won victories over—or within—the political system. Institutionalization may come too late to check the power of uncivil movements. Uncivil movements have emerged and enjoyed considerable success in democracies with stable institutional structures as far-ranging as Chile in the 1970s, Israel, the United States, and Western Europe. Even the institutional argument that political parties should represent an array of ideological choices fails to hold. Adhering to the divide-and-conquer theory, institutions scholars contend that where political systems include a wide range of viewpoints, extremist positions become diluted, reducing their political power.[52] Again, a comparison of stable one- and two-party systems, like the United States and Japan, with the stable multiparty systems of Europe suggests that both types of system provide room for powerful uncivil movements. Indeed, multiparty systems provide more institutional channels for uncivil movements, enhancing their legitimacy within the political system. Uncivil movements formed part of the authoritarian coups that toppled both institutionally weak and fragmented political party systems, like Brazil and Argentina of the 1960s, and the institutionally strong two- and three-party systems of Uruguay and Chile of the 1970s. Uncivil movements appear insensitive to institutional frameworks largely because they act both within and outside these frameworks.

A second central assumption of the institutions approach is that ideological moderation by the government reduces the appeal of authoritarian movements. But scholarship on this issue produces contradictory findings. Some scholars claim that moderate right-wing governments are vulnerable to extreme-right mobilizations because they depend on the radical right for votes and funds. Yet other scholars have made the opposite claim: the radical right successfully mobilizes against leftist governments that seek accommodation to avoid confrontation.[53] Empirical analysis of uncivil movements supports neither claim. In Latin America alone, uncivil movements successfully mobilized against left-wing and left-leaning governments in Latin America in the 1960s and 1970s, but they have also mobilized successfully under the conservative governments of the 1980s and 1990s. This study of uncivil movements shows that effective framing can transform even moderate policy reforms proposed by conservative governments into universal threats requiring violent political action.

Although neither institutional frameworks nor ideology provide convincing explanations for when democratic governments will attempt to reduce the power of uncivil movements, democratic governments nevertheless play a critical role in that process. They do so through building institutions and strengthening democratic practices. Most important, democratic governments must decide to what extent they will tolerate uncivil movements. Uncivil movements can exploit policies of zero tolerance as well as policies of complete tolerance.

Democratic governments tolerant of uncivil movements ignore their violent acts, fail to enforce or enact laws against them, and encourage them to pursue their demands within the institutional apparatus. By failing to take legal measures against illegal acts, these democratic governments participate in uncivil movements' construction of legitimating myths. By failing to expose uncivil movements' actions, democratic governments miss the opportunity to counter legitimating myths, and thus they increase uncivil movements' appeal and legitimacy. As one scholar notes, "Insurgent groups do best when they succeed in gaining support from among influential groups in the system."[54] In addition, by ignoring the violent activity of uncivil movements, democratic governments lower the cost of such activity. As William Gamson has argued, movements use violence not when they are weak but when they are confident that they can avoid reprisal.[55] Under tolerant governments, in other words, uncivil movements literally get away with murder. Such tolerance not only strengthens uncivil movements, it also weakens democratic governments unable or unwilling to investigate and prosecute illegal and violent acts.

On the other hand, complete government intolerance can backfire, augmenting rather than reducing the power of uncivil movements. Where uncivil movements can claim that the government has used excessive force or exclusionary devices, they can actually win constituents. Through such claims, uncivil movements can portray themselves as martyrs to repression. The U.S. militia movement provides one example. The deaths of victims of military force employed by the U.S. government in Ruby Ridge, Idaho, and Waco, Texas, provoked a more widespread and ideologically coherent militia movement. This movement could claim that the U.S. government had used violence against patriots and democrats, conspired against individual rights, and silenced those attempting to defend democratic rights and freedoms.

Finding the optimal balance between tolerance and intolerance is not easy. It occurs only when democratic governments make an effort to inform, investigate, prosecute, and negotiate. These four strategies can help democratic governments reduce the power of uncivil movements.

Consider first the power of information. To avoid appearing excessively intolerant of uncivil movements, democratic governments may limit their efforts to tracking them. This strategy provides information that the government can use to thwart violence and to counter a movement's legitimating myths. When democratic governments can substantiate the types of violent activities in which uncivil movements engage, it becomes more difficult for those movements' supporters to ignore their uncivil side.

Not only can governments defuse support for uncivil movements by disseminating information about the movements' violent activities; they can achieve the same effect by disseminating information about the threat to which the uncivil movements are responding. John Sullivan and others point out that fear stimulates uncivil attitudes; it facilitates the mobilization of violence against scapegoats. Such fear can be generated by exaggerated media depictions of a threat—for example, depictions of particularly horrifying, unrepresentative forms of violence carried out against innocent individuals.[56] By providing more evenhanded information about the threat, governments can reduce unwarranted fear and so reduce the ability of uncivil movements to demonize enemies and mobilize uncivil action.

Other, longer-term, forms of information, or education, campaigns may also reduce the power of uncivil movements. Sullivan and his colleagues have suggested that democracies can protect themselves from uncivil behavior by inculcating democratic norms and values in the citizenry. They found that while nearly all individuals are intolerant of some group, those with a strong commitment to democratic norms and values refrain from acting out against the group they dislike.[57] Individuals who simply pay lip service to democratic norms and values, in contrast, are susceptible to authoritarian movements. So while education in democratic practice and values will not eliminate intolerant attitudes, it will reduce the predisposition to act on those attitudes.

Government investigation and prosecution are another tool for combating antidemocratic groups. The militant hard core exists in part because the costs of violent political action are relatively low compared with its thrill. Habituation to democracy is not likely to reduce the desire of the militant hard core to engage in aggressive acts. But as the cost of violence increases, the appeal should decline. By investigating the militant hard core of an uncivil movement, the government can avoid martyring the entire movement. Even pragmatic uncivil movement leaders recognize that they cannot control extremists. Democratic governments, in other words, can exploit the frictions between militants and pragmatists by taking legal action against the violence of the hard core. Militants may cast the government's response as excessive, thereby creating a martyred movement. But if the government has not used force, and if the pragmatists perceive the hard core as detrimental to the movement or its cause, the hard core is unlikely to succeed.

Governments can also use negotiations with particular factions or their leaders to weaken uncivil movements. Negotiations regarding material, status, or other interests of key leaders or factions are likely to draw the pragmatic leaders away from their uncivil movements, especially if these negotiations are coupled with measures taken against the hard core. Governments can negotiate with pragmatic leaders, drawing them into the political system while isolating the hard-core faction. As the hard-core members become estranged from the pragmatic members of the movement, the government enjoys greater liberty to investigate and prosecute the former for their involvement in radical, uncivil acts. The pragmatic members, in an attempt to save both themselves and the movement, will then dissociate from the hard core. They will continue to pursue their moderate policies with the guarantee of some protection from government investigation and prosecution.

By negotiating with an uncivil movement's leaders, the government can persuade a movement to relinquish some of its control in exchange for guarantees. Because uncivil movements rarely have aspirations to take political power (at least directly), governments do not need to make large concessions. While costly, government compensation for redistribution programs could provide the means by which greater equality could be achieved. The government could simultaneously remove the catalyst threat, at least among the pragmatic leadership of the movement. Redistribution with compensation thus paves the way toward counterbalancing the weight of uncivil movements with empowered social movements.

Information, investigation, prosecution, and negotiation provide democratic governments with the means to exploit uncivil movements' inherent weaknesses. All four mechanisms weaken the union between militant and pragmatic supporters of uncivil movements. As militants' control over the movement is exposed through informational and legal campaigns, and as pragmatic leadership wanes, democratic governments can accelerate the demise of uncivil movements.[58]

Conclusion

Uncivil movements do not evolve in a linear path. A movement may show signs of disintegration at one point, then catapult itself back to prominence by framing a new threat within the political environment. A movement that disbands may remain latent, forming part of the cultural and historical context that can later be resurrected in a new uncivil movement. Movements that have become institutionalized may revert to their uncivil orientation and pursue a two-pronged strategy of simultaneous civil and uncivil political action. International movements may also shape and reshape domestic movements. In short, uncivil movements' evolutionary process follows a "spiral of mobilization."[59]

The inherent weaknesses of uncivil movements do not necessarily reduce their power. Democratic governments seeking the demise of uncivil movements must proactively exploit those weaknesses at an early stage. However, if the government acts too aggressively, it will create a movement of martyrs capable of remobilizing broader public support.

Democratic governments can use information, investigation, prosecution, and negotiation to exploit the weaknesses of uncivil movements. At times, in particular during political transitions, democratic governments lack effective public security forces and judiciaries to check uncivil movements. But they often prove unwilling to use public authority even when they possess the power to do so. Uncivil movements sometimes provide "services" to democratic governments. Especially in newly emerging democratic regimes, the state may use the threat of an overthrow to keep popular sectors from making demands for social reforms. Democratic governments may also benefit from uncivil movements' violent repression of popular sector groups: dissent is squelched without the government having to dirty its hands.

Vigilante-style movements may also help the government maintain order in remote areas where official policing agencies are inadequate. Democratic governments generally do not publicly acknowledge or applaud the "services" uncivil movements provide; but privately they may be thankful. This may explain why governments are sometimes unwilling to suppress uncivil movements or stop their acts of violence.

Governments may also be unwilling to curb uncivil movements for fear of reprisal. Governments, just like potential constituents, assess the power of a movement on the basis of their past experiences with similar movements. Where uncivil movements have overthrown or subverted democratic politics in the past, governments are likely to view subsequent and similar movements as powerful and threatening. A history of successful uncivil movements will thus heighten a government's sense of vulnerability. But such a history will not necessarily determine a government's reaction to new uncivil movements. A government laboring under a sense of vulnerability may be provoked to enforce the law to stymie the activity of an uncivil movement; but such a government may also simply decide to capitulate.

History may also determine how social movement adversaries and the media view an uncivil movement.[60] If social movements associate uncivil movements with successful countermovements of the past, they are likely to exaggerate their power. They will see in the contemporary uncivil movement an authoritarian movement that may or may not in fact be there.

When democratic governments, the media, and social movements treat uncivil movements as potential coup plotters, they enhance the movements' power. Uncivil movements alone cannot stage successful coups. They do not generally desire an overthrow or even have the links with authoritarian groups necessary to launch a coup. By treating them as a conspiracy, democratic governments may actually be giving them more power to shape democratic politics. To avoid this outcome, democratic governments must determine the actual threat that uncivil movements pose.

In any event, democratic governments must defend themselves, their citizens, and the democratic system by prosecuting criminal activity. The chief form of institution building in which democratic governments must engage, therefore, is judicial reform.

3 The Argentine Carapintada

M ajor Martinez was the human catalyst for the Carapintada rebellions.[1] His role began in 1984 when, as a major in the army, Martinez was summoned to court for violating human rights. These violations occurred during the 1976–83 military regime, called the PRN (Process of National Reconstruction). The PRN was responsible for the War against Subversion, referred to as the Dirty War by its opponents, and for its estimated thirty thousand victims.[2] The democratic government that replaced the PRN, under President Raúl Alfonsín (1983–89), investigated and prosecuted military officers who had been involved in torture and murder during the Dirty War.

Martinez had served as an intelligence officer who supervised interrogations at La Perla detention center, one of the most notorious of the Dirty War's concentration camps. He was effective in this role, which, given the parameters of a dirty war, implied brutality in his treatment of prisoners. Indeed, twenty different torture survivors accused Martinez of torture, illegal detention, and homicide.[3] Even one of his political associates, requesting anonymity, described Martinez as the epitome of a sadistic intelligence officer, capable of continuing to torture those he had already tortured to death.[4]

When first summoned, Martinez told his superiors that he would not appear in court. Nearly a decade later he remembered his outrage at being called to trial and practically admitted to violent retribution:

I understand the civilian government's need to show its authority. But dishonor? Never. It was an act of service I was being accused of. I wasn't going to present myself. And I certainly wasn't going to appear without my shoelaces, without my belt. I wanted to be tried with decorum. . . . Ten days later the house of an official of the CONADEP [Argentine

Commission on the Disappeared] in Córdoba blew up. It was to show that we wouldn't put up with this.

To avert a crisis, Martinez's superiors postponed his trial and pursued more compliant human rights violators. But anticipating a second summons, Martinez joined forces with other military officers to plot a rebellion. He described the situation in this way: "In 1986 there were two thousand citations. This was a military debacle. We went and talked to people [in the military] about taking action. We decided that we would act on three cases. . . . We picked these three because [the individuals accused] accepted the operation, because we knew the dates for their trials, and because they were scheduled early in the process." This group drew up their plans while Martinez feigned willingness to stand trial. When summoned to trial for the second time, Martinez appeared as planned. But once the conspirators were in position, he fled from prosecution with the help of his co-conspirator and the lieutenant colonel in charge of him.

Simultaneously, the Carapintada launched their first rebellion. It occurred during Semana Santa (Holy Week) 1987 at a key army base in Buenos Aires, the Campo de Mayo Infantry School. The officers blackened their faces in combat style, whence the moniker Carapintada, or painted faces. The rebels demanded an end to the trials for the military's human rights violations during the War against Subversion, the replacement of the army chief of staff,[5] and an end to the delegitimizing campaigns conducted by the government and the media against the armed forces. The rebels called their uprising Operación Dignidad (Operation Dignity) to highlight their demand for the restoration of honor and respect to the armed forces.

An estimated two hundred thousand Argentines filled Buenos Aires' central Plaza de Mayo to protest the coup attempt against the newly formed democratic government.[6] Alfonsín had been elected to replace the most brutal military regime in Argentine history. He had campaigned for the presidency on a platform of exacting justice for the thousands of deaths, disappearances, and tortures suffered at the hands of the military regime. In one of his first acts in office, he named an official commission, CONADEP, to investigate human rights abuses by the military. In addition to investigating and prosecuting officers for military abuses during the Dirty War, he also began investigating the PRN's suicidal war to take back the Malvinas (or Falkland) Islands from British control. The PRN had staged this international war in a desperate effort to reassert the military's waning strength. By the Semana Santa uprising in 1987, the Malvinas and Dirty War investigations had led to the trial and imprisonment of the top leaders of the military junta and several middle-ranking officers.

President Alfonsín addressed the masses assembled in the Plaza de Mayo from the balcony of the Casa Rosada Presidential Palace. He promised them that he would resolve the conflict, then traveled to Campo de Mayo to talk with Aldo Rico, the lieutenant colonel in charge of the uprising. These negotiations led to the rebels' surrender on Easter Sunday (19 April 1987). Alfonsín then returned to the Plaza de Mayo to reassure the gathering of concerned citizens. In contrast to his earlier indictment of the rebels, he now referred to them as "heroes of the Malvinas War." He claimed that the democratic system was safe from threat, encouraged people to return to their homes, and wished them a happy Easter.

His optimistic message notwithstanding, Alfonsín had exacerbated civil-military tensions. His negotiations with the rebels drew criticism from both his supporters and his opponents. His supporters felt betrayed. In their opinion he had reversed his position with regard to human rights violations and capitulated to rebels' demands in the Semana Santa negotiations. The army chief of staff resigned, no doubt under pressure from Alfonsín and the rebel officers. But the opposition's strongest indictment of Alfonsín's negotiations with the rebels erupted over his Due Obedience Law, passed by Congress on 5 June 1987. The Due Obedience Law exempted from prosecution for human rights violations officers who had held the rank of lieutenant colonel or below during the PRN.[7] Alfonsín, sensitive to accusations of capitulating to the rebels, claimed that he had wanted to limit prosecutions of lower-ranking officers even before the rebellions began. He considered the trials of such officers potentially destabilizing to the democratic system and asserted that the Semana Santa uprising merely confirmed his view.[8] Nevertheless, this law severely limited the possibility of bringing torturers to justice.

In addition to drawing harsh criticism, Alfonsín's efforts to appease the rebels failed. The Carapintada led three subsequent uprisings in 1988 and 1990 (summarized in table 3.1). In January 1988 Rico seized the army regiment in Monte Caseros. The new army chief of staff, General José Dante Caridi, had issued orders that Rico be detained for insubordination. Rico refused to recognize Caridi's authority and escaped. In solidarity with Rico, six other regiments joined the uprising, which eventually totaled approximately 350 soldiers. Five days later Rico surrendered unconditionally. He was expelled from the armed forces and imprisoned. The High Command also forced into retirement, expelled, or exiled to remote locations other individuals identified as Carapintada.

TABLE 3.1   The Carapintada Rebellions

	Semana Santa (1987)	Virgen del Valle (1988)	Villa Martelli (1988)	Virgen de Luján (1990)
Leader	Rico	Rico	Seineldín	Seineldín
Location	Campo de Mayo, Buenos Aires	Monte Caseros, Corrientes	Villa Martelli base, Buenos Aires	Army head-quarters, Federal Capital
Support	6 lt. cols.; 30 officials; 23 subofficials; civilian and military moral support	300 rebels total, including 60 officials, 22 non-commis-sioned officers, and 6 regiments	1,000 sub-officials of various ranks	1,000 mainly lower-ranking officers; 574 detained, in-cluding 3 superior officials, 29 higher-ranking, 165 middle-ranking, 377 lower-ranking
Demands	End human rights trials; replace High Command chief; end government and media antimilitary campaign	Enforcement of Semana Santa accords; end to conflict between Rico and High Command	Reincorpora-tion of officers removed from service or forced to retire because of rebellion; increased mili-tary budget	Reinstatement of rebels; improved stan-dard of living for military personnel; Seineldín in command of armed forces
Outcome	Retirement of High Com-mand chief; Due Obedience Law passed; restructuring of armed forces; forced retirement of 9 rebel leaders	Rico surrenders; he is expelled from the mili-tary and impris-oned; Rico's associates forced to retire, fined, jailed, or sent to isolated outposts	Replacement of High Com-mand chief; 42% salary raise for armed forces; Seinel-dín charged with mutiny; Due Obedience Law expanded; trials ended; pardons granted	Rebels impris-oned and life sentence for Seineldín; 14 killed (5 civilians, 7 army, 2 navy prefect); 50 injured

Sources: Sain, *Los Levantamientos;* Norden, *Military Rebellion.*

The third rebellion occurred under the leadership of Colonel Mohammed Alí Seineldín in December 1988 in Villa Martelli. Probably the most important precipitating event was the High Command's failure to promote Seineldín to general. The rebels' stated demands, however, were similar to those that had presaged the Semana Santa rebellion: the resignation of General Caridi and installation of a general neutral to the Carapintada. They also demanded a full amnesty, more comprehensive than the Due Obedience Law, for human rights violations during the Dirty War. In addition, the rebels demanded reinstatement of those Carapintada whom the military High Command had forced to resign or retire or had expelled or exiled to remote outposts. They further demanded an increase in the military budget, particularly for salaries.

The rebellion ended with Seineldín's surrender. He claimed that he had reached an agreement with General Caridi. Although Caridi denied such an agreement,[9] shortly thereafter the rebels won two of their key demands. On 12 December the minister of defense announced a significant salary increase for military personnel, and on 21 December General Francisco Gassino replaced Caridi as army chief of staff.

Seineldín also led the fourth and most violent Carapintada uprising, on 3 December 1990, against the newly elected president, Carlos Saúl Menem (1990–99). The uprising made little sense, given the favorable civil-military relations that prevailed under Menem. Menem had granted presidential pardons to those punished for their involvement in the Dirty War, Malvinas War, and Carapintada uprisings. The Carapintada began to return to their original designations from their exiled outposts. The Menem government released Carapintada leaders, such as Rico and Seineldín, from prison and dropped charges against them. Menem further decreed in February 1990 that the armed forces could intervene in internal conflicts if required by the commander-in-chief. The military's dignity no longer seemed to be threatened. Nonetheless, Colonel Seineldín's uprising overtook eight different regiments, including the army headquarters in Buenos Aires, Edificio Libertador.[10]

The most persuasive explanation for the rebellion is Seineldín's personal vendetta against Menem. Seineldín had anticipated that Menem would promote him to general. After all, he had close personal ties with Menem: they were both Muslims of Middle Eastern descent who had converted to Catholicism, and Seineldín had developed a friendship with Menem's (subsequently estranged) wife, Zulema Yoma. Seineldín, moreover, had not merely endorsed Menem for president, he had actively prepared officers to defend

Menem militarily against a possible Radical Party maneuver to prevent Menem from assuming office after the elections. But precisely because of Seineldín's about-face on the Menem presidency, the personal and vindictive nature of the uprising, and the favorable civil-military relations Menem had cultivated, the uprising won little support among middle-ranking officers. Seineldín relied instead on lower-ranking officers to stage the rebellion.

Menem characterized the uprising as a coup attempt, declared martial law, and ordered his chiefs of staff to repress it forcefully. Within thirty-six hours, loyalist forces had combated their fellow Carapintada officers, the first time they had done so.[11] Fourteen people were killed in the uprising, including five civilians. Under the Law for the Defense of Democracy, the rebels faced charges of mutiny with bloodshed.[12] On 2 September 1991 Colonel Seineldín was imprisoned for life.[13]

Menem's harsh reaction to the 1990 uprising and the pardons he had granted to military officers involved in the War against Subversion, the Malvinas War, and earlier Carapintada uprisings effectively ended the rebellions. But the Carapintada did not disappear. Aldo Rico, the leader of the first two rebellions, and his followers joined forces with a small right-wing political party to form a new party called MODIN (Movement for Dignity and Independence). Seineldín, the leader of the last two rebellions, and his followers formed a political movement called MINeII (Movement for National Independence and Ibero-American Integration), which linked a number of extreme right-wing nationalist and Catholic movements and parties within Argentina and abroad.

The Carapintada's Political Success

There is little doubt that the Carapintada proved successful. They achieved a key goal in ending the military prosecutions. Indeed, their coup attempts not only ended the trials in Argentina, they also persuaded leaders of subsequent democratic transitions to avoid trials and adopt instead amnesties (e.g., Brazil and Uruguay) or truth commissions (e.g., Chile). They also achieved some minor goals of replacing members of the High Command with generals more favorable to them. In addition to achieving these early goals, Rico's MODIN became a powerful political force in Argentine government and society. It grew from a small rebel movement to a political party with representatives in Congress, the Senate, the Constituent Assembly (formed in 1994 to write the new democratic constitution), and provin-

TABLE 3.2   MODIN's Electoral Results, National and Buenos Aires, 1991–1997

	PJ	UCR	UCD	FREPASO[a]	MODIN
National					
1991 Congress					
Total	6,447,090	4,538,831	811,929	[b]	543,375
Percent	41.0	28.9	5.2	[b]	3.5
1993 Congress					
Total	6,631,344	4,711,214	417,726	530,724	911,412
Percent	42.4	30.1	2.7	3.4	5.8
1994 Constituent Assembly					
Total	6,092,335	3,114,166	n.a.	2,842,319	1,461,451
Percent	38.8	20.5	n.a.	16.7	9.2
1995 Congress					
Total	8,077,257	2,749,792	193,399[c]	4,795,479	289,167[c]
Percent	49.7	16.9	1.0	29.5	1.8
1997 Presidential					
Total	6,117,756	1,154,611	93,001	409,184	151,460
Percent	36.2	6.8	0.6	2.4	0.9
Buenos Aires					
1991 Gubernatorial					
Total	2,711,134	1,385,878	421,628	[b]	571,324
Percent	46.3	23.7	7.2	[b]	9.8
1992 Senate					
Total	572,005	897,313	n.a.	133,953	101,402
Percent	31.8	49.9	n.a.	7.4	5.6
1995 Gubernatorial					
Total	3,437,719	1,047,324	24,555	1,270,793	134,104
Percent	56.7	17.3	0.4	21.0	2.2

Sources: Pagina 12 and *El Clarín* articles on electoral results; Centro de Estudios Unión para la Nueva Mayoria; and "Argentina: Political Parties, 1996" and "Argentina: Party Distribution in Congress, 1996," in *Political Databases of the Americas* (on-line) (Washington, D.C.: Georgetown University/Organization of American States, 1999).

[a] FREPASO is the name of the party only after the 1995 elections. In the 1992 elections it joined an alliance with the Communist Party called Frente Grande.

[b] These dates predate the existence of FREPASO or Frente Grande.

[c] These figures were calculated based on total number of votes and percentage results for parties.

cial and municipal government. As table 3.2 illustrates, MODIN became, albeit for only a very brief period in 1993, the third most potent force in elections, trailing behind the two historically dominant political parties, the Peronists and the Radicals. It surpassed new political parties that had better funding and whose leaders had more political experience and historic visibility, such as the mainstream conservative party UCD (Union of the Democratic Center).

MODIN's meteoric rise alarmed its opposition. Political analysts feared that it might even be possible for Rico to win the presidency in the 1997 elections by capturing an untapped protest vote. As one analyst put it, "Rico never used the democratic rules of the game. But now he has to use them. He is a demagogue. He has fairly strong participation in Parliament. He has votes. He has influence. He is antisystem. It actually presents a terrifying possible future. People may grow increasingly sick of what is going on. They need an alternative, and Rico provides that alternative" [interview 13].

MODIN's rise challenges the idea that institutionalization reduces the power of authoritarians over the democratic system or transforms authoritarians into democrats. MODIN exemplifies the process by which authoritarians can disguise themselves as democrats, thus providing themselves with the political power to influence political outcomes from within and outside the institutional framework. MODIN's very existence erodes one of the greatest promises of the democratic transition: protection from arbitrary violence. While civilians disappeared at the hands of the military and are therefore unable to participate in the rebuilding of democracy, the torturers, through MODIN, have been free to shape that process.

Martinez provides one illustration. Given Martinez's record, I fully expected to find some identifying characteristic that would link him with the abuses he had committed: some indication of the blood he had spilled, of the lives lost at his hands. There was none. Martinez had remade himself.[14] This was obvious from his appearance. He had replaced his military uniform with fashionable Italian-style clothes and shoes, and his military haircut had given way to a stylishly long GQ look. Instead of military barracks, Martinez occupied a well-outfitted office in the exclusive Recoleta section of Buenos Aires. Having lost his military career, he had reinvented himself as a consultant for an environmental foundation and had begun working toward a Ph.D. in political science at the John F. Kennedy School for International Relations in Buenos Aires. Some might argue that Martinez is nothing more than a symbol of the banality of evil.[15] But he represents more than that. He symbolizes the way democratic processes can whitewash and legitimize antidemocratic groups and individuals. When I asked Martinez how he had become reconciled to his past, he answered, "Judging my role in the War against Subversion is a relative analysis. There are other things I know now. But honestly, I believe that what I did was correct and efficient. That was my analysis of the moment." The process of Due Obedience and presidential pardons have enabled Martinez to put the past behind him.[16] While he has not been able to progress within the military ranks, he has certainly landed on his feet even after committing atrocities during the Dirty War.

The immunity enjoyed by the institutionalized faction of the Carapintada raises the fundamental paradox of the institutional strategy. Should these individuals who were involved in human rights violations and attempted government overthrows be granted immunity from prosecution and incorporated into the democratic system? What are the implications of that process for the strength of democracy in Argentina?

Cynical views suggest that immunity from prosecution has always been and will always be part of Argentina's political system. Only partially joking, one military official described Argentines' resistance to life under rule by law:

We live in a civilized country without law. It is actually fun to live without law. It is happy. Imagine that I want to give my son a car. And along with the car I hand him a drivers' license. He didn't have to take a test, wait, or anything. They impose a restriction on cars one day a week via license plate numbers. So people just get several license plates. This country is a caricature of democracy, and it always has been. All of the institutions are false, because they exist artificially. They don't practice democracy. If Argentines woke up one morning and they were living with the laws of the United States, they would feel like they were in a dictatorship. Punishment for violating the system? That is standard operating procedure in the United States. In Argentina there are no sanctions. There are no punishments. There is no such thing as equality under the law. The constitution says that you should not deny to one what you give to another. But that is not practiced. [interview 14]

Continuing his account of "democracy Argentine style," this same retired military officer offered the following observation as an explanation of MODIN's appeal in democratic society: "There is no democracy in Argentina. That is a fantastic fallacy. It has all the formal attributes of a democracy, but it isn't one. We are all authoritarian and antidemocratic. Oriana Fallaci once said that there is a little fascist midget in all Argentines. She's wrong. There is a little democratic midget in all of us. The rest is fascist" [interview 14].

This version of "politics as usual" belies the hope shared by those who expected the democratic government to bring the human rights violators to justice. But disenchantment has not paralyzed the struggle for justice in Argentina. Nearly every day the newspaper *Página 12* publishes a small square or two with a picture of a disappeared person and a short message from his or her family or friends. Every Thursday afternoon the Madres (Mothers) and Abuelas (Grandmothers) de Plaza de Mayo continue to march in a silent vigil demanding the return of their disappeared children and grandchildren, just as they did during the military dictatorship. Public testimonies of the tortured or torturers resurrect feelings of outrage against injustices that remain unpunished. Efforts to produce public memorials and monuments and to maintain memory of repression in drama, song, and prose abound.[17] These public artifacts and events painfully confirm that repression is alive in the Argentine collective memory. The effort to bury the past has failed. The victims of repression have neither reconstructed their lives nor forgotten their past. They have not reached closure on the murders and disappearances. And the absence of closure may be due in part to the immunity that has allowed the torturers to remake themselves into respectable citizens and regain positions of authority in the new democratic society. Democracy thus provides the conditions for authoritarians—those who represent political views entirely antithetical to democracy—to compete in the political process.

The Carapintada in MODIN confirm that picture. Argentina's new democracy has pardoned not only torturers but also those who staged overthrows of the government. With those pardons torturers and subverters of the democratic process have remade themselves as democrats, become candidates for national office, and even won seats in government. Hebe de Bonafini, one of the founders of the Madres de Plaza de Mayo and a continuing activist, captured this irony:

> The worst thing about MODIN and Seineldín is not the groups themselves, but that the politicians share the table with them. . . . The government is making agreements with rapists, murderers, savage warriors. They treat them the same way they do other political figures. The government treats a governor of a province the same way it treats an assassin. In fact, assassins can become governors of a province. They are assassins, and they assassinate democracy. . . . The Carapintada phenomenon is really a black stain on our history. They are happy to be Carapintada. They are proud of it. They don't try to hide it. They are always willing to go paint their faces. The political leaders allow this.

Political leaders allow them to be in the marches. They shouldn't be there. [Bonafini, 26 July 1994]

Bonafini's comment illustrates a central criticism of the institutions approach: the government and political parties have provided the political space within which the Carapintada have gained political power and legitimacy. Her comment also raises the disturbing question of why individuals in civil society would support military torturers and coup leaders in the wake of the military regime's debacle. The Carapintada provide evidence of how political framing, cultural cuing, and movement mythmaking can enhance the power of these movements over democracy.

POLITICAL FRAMING

The Carapintada easily found a threat around which to mobilize: Alfonsín's investigation and prosecution of military violators of human rights. They interpreted Alfonsín's project as a crusade to imprison all of the Martinezes of the world. The threat was serious, since the nature of dirty war dictated that nearly all officers participate in some aspect of the repression.[18] In my interviews with the Carapintada, for example, only those posted outside the country during the Dirty War denied that they had participated in it. Because Alfonsín's policies affected so many in the military, it should have been a perfect "framing" device.

But the trials are not as simple an explanation of the Carapintada's successful framing as they might appear. A number of factors muddy the explanation. Very few of the officers who were scheduled for trial, for example, joined the Carapintada. Rather than mobilize against the investigations and trials, they seemed to accept them passively. In addition, Martinez was one of the only Carapintada members who appeared on the list of repressors compiled by the official government organ investigating human rights abuses, CONADEP, and the private human rights group CELS (Center for Legal and Social Studies).[19] Martinez claims that Aldo Rico and the other Carapintada leaders were equally involved in the Dirty War, but because of his position in intelligence (i.e., interrogations) he was more visible. Cristina Caiati of CELS confirmed this view, stating that most Carapintada were not involved in interrogation, reducing the likelihood that they could be identified by victims [Caiati, 8 August 1994].

Although the Carapintada may have feared future prosecution for their involvement in repression, these fears should have subsided with the Due

Obedience Law. The Carapintada consisted of middle- and lower-ranking officers whom the Due Obedience Law protected from investigation and prosecution. The fear of trials, therefore, does not explain support for the final three rebellions.

To clarify, the Carapintada did not mobilize against the trials because they harmed, or potentially harmed, some military officers and soldiers. Rather, they framed the trials as a threat to military dignity. And they linked the threat to the armed forces to national security concerns. The trials thus became the catalyst around which the Carapintada framed a universal threat to the nation.

The Carapintada subscribe to the view, not uncommon throughout the military, that the trials were unjust. They argue that an interim civilian president, Italo Luder (1975), had declared the war, not the military regime, and that the military had a duty to fulfill the order and defend the country from subversion. This version of the Dirty War is technically accurate; Luder did sign the declaration of war. But by most accounts, including Luder's, the military forced him to issue it. It was, without a doubt, the military regime's Dirty War.

Causation aside, the Carapintada view the trials as a form of "victors' justice." Almost without exception, the Carapintada believe that the military failed to achieve full victory in the war: they won the battles but lost the war. One version of victors' justice contends that the military failed to eliminate the subversives, so the subversives have remained politically powerful and are behind the trials. This version even claims that the "disappeared" are a propagandistic tool used by the subversives against the military. The following remarks made by civilian supporters of the Carapintada, who subsequently became leaders in MODIN, are illustrative:

> The military didn't win the war against subversion because the left and subversives won power in 1983. A lot of the so-called disappeared didn't disappear. [interview 11]

> There aren't as many disappeared as they say. They are in Europe or other parts of Latin America. [interview 24]

Interestingly, in my interviews with them military officers did not deny the disappearances. Instead, they tended to promote a different version of the PRN's defeat in the War against Subversion. They claimed that the PRN successfully conducted only the military side of the war, ignoring its crucial political side. Specifically, the PRN failed to win public support for the war.

Subversives, the Carapintada argued, were taking over the country, using excessive force and brutality. The military got involved to protect freedom and democracy from these subversives. But because the PRN did not explain the war well enough, only the military was blamed for brutality; the subversives' violence escaped reprimand, both in Argentina and abroad. To try to correct this interpretation of the past, Martinez helped organize a group called FAMUS (Relatives and Friends of those Killed by Subversion) to unite families affected by subversives' violence. One military wife echoed both this dismissal of the disappeared and her concern for military losses: "The Madres de Plaza de Mayo are wretched, intolerable. They don't respect me, I don't respect them. They are doing politics with their loss. I cry in silence. I am alone. They use their misery as a spectacle. They live very well. They get money from different places. They think that their pain is greater than anyone's. But mine is greater. They make a spectacle out of death" [interview 24].

Carapintada leaders blame the High Command's silence around the war for soldiers' diminishing popularity in Argentine society. By hiding the war before, during, and after the trials, the High Command robbed soldiers of the recognition they deserved for their heroic stand against the subversives. These military leaders defend the War against Subversion, but not the PRN's war strategy. Indeed, some Carapintada leaders even condemn the disappearances as part of that strategy: "It should have been clear who the enemies in the war were. Take them to justice. Even give them a life sentence or death sentence. But not disappearances" [interview 39].

The Carapintada, in sum, believe that the trials eroded military dignity. They undermined respect for the chain of command, which requires obedience to superiors' orders. They challenged the military's duty to defend the nation from threat and demeaned its heroic efforts to combat subversion. Without dignity, the military could not maintain the esprit de corps necessary to fulfill its patriotic duty. The loss of military dignity, in other words, contributed to national vulnerability.

But the Carapintada also used the trials to point to another problem of military defense: the military command structure. The Carapintada publicly indicted the military High Command for its incapacity to defend the armed forces (and the nation) from the human rights trials. They framed the issue in terms that resonated with officers and soldiers who had fought in both the Dirty War and the Malvinas War. Just as the Carapintada blamed defeat in the Dirty War on the High Command's failure to understand or win the political side of the war, they also attributed the Malvinas War debacle to the "desk generals" in the High Command who were incapable of developing a combat strategy. Consider the following remark by one of the Malvinas veterans:

> I agree with the intention to recover a part of our nation. But the moment was wrong. There was a lack of awareness of the history of the world. Britain is not going to abandon a colony without a fight. The United States is not going to do battle against Britain. So it ended up being a fight against NATO. And the way it was run—the first thing the [commanding] general took over was his car. A car! To drive around the island! Meanwhile, the soldiers arrived without combat gear. It was criminal. [interview 39]

In the Carapintada view, the military defeat in the Malvinas allowed Alfonsín to prosecute the PRN junta leaders who led the nation into the debacle and robbed the soldiers who had fought the war of their dignity and hero status. Alfonsín's trials, in their opinion, reinforced a mistaken view in Argentine society about the Malvinas War. The initial strong national support for the war disintegrated into protests over the slaughter of military conscripts. One Carapintada veteran of Malvinas dismissed the public outcry against the war: "Soldiers died in Malvinas, not boys" [interview 1]. But the widespread criticism of the war and protests about human rights violations discredited the military, reduced its morale, and eroded its dignity and capacity to protect the nation from threat.

Against this backdrop, the Carapintada launched their attack on Alfonsín's promotion policies. According to the Carapintada, Alfonsín promoted generals loyal to him without evaluating their military expertise. He bypassed military leaders who had seniority and respect in the officer corps and advanced the careers of those who lacked the reputation for military heroism that many middle- and lower-ranking officers admired. These were considered within the military at the time to be the least prepared of the officer corps, the quintessential desk generals. Concerned only about their own careers, the desk generals did not challenge the prosecutions and the impact they had on military dignity and national defense.

The Carapintada viewed these promotions as, at best, misled; Alfonsín was perpetuating a history of poor military leadership within the High Command. At worst, however, his promotion policy constituted a deliberate attempt to undermine the strength of the armed forces. This latter view fit a version of Argentine political history, prevalent in the armed forces, according to which the Radical Party is antimilitary, predisposed to undermine the armed forces. The Carapintada could tap into officers' interpretations of Alfonsín's policies in this historical context, leading them to conclude that the military faced a serious threat.

The Carapintada, in short, transformed the catalyst threat provided by the trials into a universal threat. The trials provided a concrete focus, symbolizing a deeper and more universal sense of threat. By linking military dignity with national defense, the Carapintada captured a mood within the military. Of course, not all of the military supported the Carapintada. In the wake of the PRN's political, economic, and military debacle, most military officers feared that armed insurrection would backfire, heightening civilian hostility toward the military and civilian fears of a coup. But even these officers shared the Carapintada's desire to restore military dignity and national security. One civilian analyst of the military whom I interviewed acknowledged that the Carapintada were harming democracy with their "anticonstitutionality, fascism, and justification of the Dirty War," but he applauded their effort to identify the danger to the armed forces posed by Alfonsín's policies. He claimed that the Carapintada understood and gave voice to the anxiety within the military about the humiliating Malvinas defeat, corruption within the armed forces, and the desk generals' practical ignorance of defense [interview 5]. One top military official, who will remain anonymous, summed up his opinion of the Carapintada in this way: "Their ultimate goals were not wrong; they just used dishonorable means." A former military officer who had served in the same unit as many of the Carapintada, but who rejected the rebellions, identified the Carapintada as the only representatives of an opinion that was unspoken but widespread within the military at the time:

> Rios Ereñú [the head of the High Command] didn't have either support or prestige within the armed forces. There was resentment in the armed forces because others better qualified were passed over. Everyone knew something would happen. . . . Alfonsín was convinced that the armed forces had a party. So he forgot the interests of the nation. He created a weak defense. . . . I share the motivations [of the Carapintada]. They love the army more than anything else. We gave the best of our lives to the army. . . . The American public hanged Calley, not the whole army, for problems in Vietnam. In Argentina they wanted to punish everyone. This couldn't happen. Someone had to stop it. And no general was there to stop it. So it had to be a lieutenant colonel: Rico. [interview 11]

The Carapintada's message reached beyond the military, attracting significant civilian support as well. Right-wing nationalists offered the most obvious source of support. They shared the Carapintada's view that Alfonsín's military policies threatened national security. These nationalists provided moral and material support for the Carapintada, whom they considered to be dedicated military officers attempting to protect the nation from Alfonsín's destructive policies. They shared the rebels' sense of exclusion. They believed that Alfonsín's government listened only to certain voices. Rebellion was the only way to get attention in a political environment dominated by international and domestic human rights groups in which hostility toward the military had replaced concern for national defense. These nationalists also shared the rebels' desire to proclaim the heroism of the War against Subversion and the Malvinas War, condemn subversive violence, and restore Argentina's international prominence and reputation. They viewed Alfonsín as fixated on the nation's failures rather than its promise, and thus as incapable of fulfilling national goals.

The Carapintada completed the four parts of the framing process effectively. By naming the threat to military dignity and national defense, they identified a universal threat, not simply one that would mobilize support from a narrow, materially motivated interest group. They blamed the threat not on the amorphous transition process but rather on specific political actors: the Alfonsín government, the desk generals in the military, and subversives. They aimed their political action against these enemies, contending that the gravity of the threat and their own exclusion from the political process left them no alternative but to use force to overcome the threat. And as the last step of the framing process, the Carapintada claimed that despite the odds against them, they could overcome that threat.

The Carapintada's claim emerged from their (no doubt inflated) sense of their own power and position within the military. They saw themselves as uniquely qualified and trained to lead the nation. Their background in the infantry had provided them with combat training. Their relatively humble socioeconomic origins and their socialization within the armed forces imbued them with a strong sense of patriotism and duty to the nation: "Infantry represents the middle class in society. It is humble. It doesn't have aristocratic aspirations. It is a group willing to sacrifice, risk, do anything for the nation. . . . It is an intellectually charged, curious group" [interview 45]. The claims of heroism in the War against Subversion and the Malvinas War further developed the Carapintada's sense of themselves as the most effective and heroic military leaders. And, by extension, they saw themselves as the only group in Argentine society courageous enough to take the lead and stand up to the misled civilian authorities: "In all modesty, I must say that we were good military men. We were all future generals. We were the ones with the most courses, with the most decorations. We were real soldiers, not desk soldiers. But we were also unconventional. We didn't accept the norms. And we had enough freedom to act. So we weren't very typical of the military to begin with" [interview 39]. The self-importance shared by the leaders of the Carapintada gave them a sense of exalted mission and de facto leadership of the military movement. And once they had tasted power after the first rebellion, no commanding officer could control them.

Part of the Carapintada's claim to overcome obstacles took institutional shape. When the Carapintada formed MODIN, they seized a political moment. Recognizing that the political context had changed, reducing support for armed insurgency, they saw that the institutional route provided the only method for sustaining power over the political process. This interpretation of the political context was confirmed when Seineldín and his supporters faced life sentences. The institutional route also provided political careers for officers who had few prospects in the military. Those who had been expelled were unlikely to be reinstated. Those who remained in the military had little hope for promotions. They had to pursue other careers. The Independence Party's search for new direction offered the Carapintada leaders a new opportunity. Using the Independence Party's institutional structure, and that party's acceptance of Rico's leadership, MODIN took off.

MODIN quickly found a political niche. It became an opposition party, claiming to represent the unheard voices of the military and civilian nationalists. MODIN's unconventional style became its political cache. It projected itself as a movement with a strong militaristic figure at its helm that could find pragmatic solutions to political messes. MODIN ran against the traditional parties, back-room negotiations, and mainstream exclusion. It claimed to remain true to its principles. And Rico, to prove that point, refused on several occasions even to sit with "corrupt politicians." He stormed out of government negotiation sessions in disgust. And he taunted the government with his warrior imagery. In the 1994 Constituent Assembly, for example, Rico threatened to paint his face again.

CULTURAL CUES

The preceding discussion of political framing suggests the ways in which the Carapintada cued up their movement with past threats from particular villains and modeled it after the cultural heroes and repertoires of political action that had overcome those threats in the past. The Carapintada skill-fully tapped a number of fears that resonated deeply with their potential constituency and resurrected cultural icons that could overcome those fears.

To capitalize on the pervasive sense of national vulnerability, the Cara-pintada drew on foundational threats. The military, since its origins in the Independence era, had forged the nation and defended its borders. The Carapintada linked their rebellions in the contemporary era to the military's original national project by frequently referring to, and quoting from, José de San Martín, the Argentine military hero of the Independence era. It was not uncommon to find his portrait hanging in offices occupied by Cara-pintada and MODIN leaders. The Carapintada used the historical threat to national borders and national identity, and the historic role of the military to protect the nation from such threats, to strike a deep cultural chord that resonated not only with the military itself but also with civilian nationalists.

The Carapintada also drew on military *caudillismo*. The role of the caudillo, or military strongman, originated just after the Latin American Wars of In-dependence. While widely reviled for the dictatorships they established throughout the region, caudillos nonetheless still appealed to Carapintada followers. The caudillo, in their view, has a national vision, offers pragmatic solutions, and possesses sufficient force and autonomy to implement them. The caudillo personifies the antipolitics ideology rampant within right-wing uncivil movements. Not only are they unbeholden to any particular groups, caudillos make their own laws and establish their own systems of control. One MODIN leader hinted at the conscious crafting of Rico as a caudillo: "The caudillo of the party is military. . . . The public image [of Rico] is a military caudillo, and it works very well" [interview 2]. Again, the Carapintada linked their movement with caudillos by frequently referring to Argentina's famous caudillo (and infamous dictator) of the early 1800s, Juan Manuel de Rosas. He also occupies hallowed space on Carapintada office walls.

But the contemporary military caudillo after whom the Carapintada model themselves is General Juan Perón. Rico and MODIN actively cultivated his image, building on the continued strong support for Perón and Peronism. MODIN leaders even hinted at the conscious construction of Rico in Perón's image: "Being military, [the military leaders of MODIN] are antipolitics, anticorruption. They don't have a political past that attaches them to cor-ruption. People love the military image of standing up to corrupt politi-cians: Peronism. They love the general as a national leader" [interview 7]. Rico flaunted his identification with Perón. He proudly donned military clothing in his initial campaigns. He dressed in fatigues or camouflage and rode atop the MODIN-mobile throughout the country. He used the force-ful, populist Peronist style to speak to gathered masses. And he embellished his military caudillo image with nationalist symbols: he posed sipping *mate* out of the traditional gourd while tangos, military marches, and national hymns blared from loudspeakers. These deliberate attempts to model him-self on Perón had the desired outcome, as this fan attests: "I had been caught up in Rico since Semana Santa. When you see him in the caravans he looks just like Perón" [interview 9].

The association with Peronism also indirectly distanced the Carapintada from the Radical Party. As I mentioned above, a large portion of the military distrusted the Radical Party on the basis of the historical view that the party had actively attempted to erode the military's national power. Peronism thus offered an alternative foundation upon which to build opposition to Alfonsín.

Counterinsurgency provided another foundational threat upon which the Carapintada built their movement. Infantry training in Argentina drew heav-ily from the counterinsurgency tactics used in the French war with Algeria and subsequently adopted U.S. counterinsurgency tactics.[20] Indeed, the pride of the infantry division originated with this specialized and intense psycho-logical and military training. The Seineldín group symbolized this counter-insurgency past more directly than the Rico group. Prior to the 1976 coup, after all, Seineldín had been the military liaison to the secret Argentine Anti-communist Association, or Triple A, under the directorship of José López Rega, a right-wing (civilian) Peronist.[21] The AAA eliminated subversion through death-squad activity, assassinating key leaders on the left. Seineldín also participated in the 1975 dirty war in Tucumán under Antonio Domingo Bussi's command. Both of these events served as precursors to the dirty-war activities conducted after the military assumed power.

Seineldín resurrects not only a military cultural icon but also a religious one. He cultivates his relationship with the extreme right wing of the con-servative Argentine Catholic Church. He reportedly has links to extreme-right members of the conservative Catholic Church in Argentina.[22] But Seineldín also cultivates a religious mysticism. He claims to converse directly with the Virgin and has adopted an ascetic lifestyle reminiscent of the most devout clerics.

During the PRN, Seineldín wove together these religious and military strands. According to an anonymous source, he founded and commanded a right-wing Catholic and nationalist secret society within the military called Orden (The Order) that followed three principles: antiliberalism, anti-Marxism, and Catholicism.[23] The group eschewed direct involvement in politics, but the anonymous source described a scenario that contradicted this claim. He recounted that the five directors of Orden voted after the Malvinas War on staging a coup. The group was split down the middle until Seineldín cast the deciding vote against a coup attempt. Orden lasted about ten years, dissolving with the Semana Santa uprising. Orden officers, like the military at large, split over the question of armed insurrection. Only a small faction of Orden officers joined the Carapintada. The top leaders of the movement (e.g., Seineldín and Rico), however, had participated in Orden.

This split in Orden represents tension over selecting particular repertoires of collective, and particularly uncivil, political action. The Carapintada drew on the most obvious repertoire of collective action available to them: the military coup. The Argentine military has staged frequent coups and coup attempts. Just since World War II, for example, the military staged coups in 1943, 1955, 1966, and 1976. The military has not only directly intervened in Argentine politics, it has maintained a de facto veto power over government decisions. Certainly the Carapintada followed in its predecessors' footsteps by vetoing Alfonsín's trials and promotions.

But the Carapintada did not adopt this repertoire of collective action exclusively. Other repertoires also existed within Argentina that the Carapintada appropriated. Specifically Peronism, the populist-style political party that Perón constructed to include various constituencies, provided a model for Rico. While Seineldín continued to use the coup attempt to influence politics, Rico's Carapintada evolved in a more institutional direction. The Peronist model became increasingly advantageous to Rico as Menem dropped the traditional Peronist mantle, opting for a less populist and more neoliberal economic strategy. As one MODIN leader remarked, "We raise the flag of Peronism that was dropped [by Menem], . . . Peronism of Perón" [interview 7]. Rico and MODIN attracted away from Menem those Peronists who rejected Menem's "neoliberalism." MODIN, for example, opposed Menem's shrinking of public spending, arguing that such a strategy weakens Argentina's national industrial structure and impoverishes the population. The MODIN economic program emphasizes development over debt repayment, and national investment over privatization and direct foreign investment. Referring to Menem's neoliberal policies, MODIN opposed "savage capitalism" and advocated a strong role for the state. It argued that the state is necessary to fulfill the nation's historic commitment to social justice. MODIN's policies are thus reminiscent of Perón's right-wing populism. It is not surprising, therefore, that MODIN's won its strongest support in the periphery of Buenos Aires among Peronist trade unionists. MODIN found a powerful discourse with broad appeal among a previously mobilized constituency.

The Carapintada thus drew on cultural icons of heroism and villainy and repertoires of uncivil political action to build their powerful movement. But the Carapintada did not simply mimic these cultural artifacts and action. They adapted them to the contemporary moment and even spun contradictory myths about them to appeal to the widest constituency possible.

LEGITIMATING MYTHS

The contrast between Rico's and Seineldín's movements is most evident on the question of legitimating myths. Both movements' appeal depended on creating political fears and convincing constituents that they could overcome those threats, building on past events. Rico's movement achieved more political power than Seineldín's because the former spun myths to unite a broad constituency.

Seineldín represents an unadulterated authoritarian pattern. Seineldín himself appeals to fanatical elements only: right-wing nationalists, extremists in the security forces (i.e., private security companies, the military, and the police), fundamentalist Catholics, fascists, and open defenders of the Dirty War. Seineldín remains true to himself and his authoritarian background. His small fanatical following knows exactly what it supports. Its members do not change, soften, or disguise their traditional, authoritarian values. The message shocks because of its retrograde authoritarianism.

An episode that occurred at a book signing sponsored by Seineldín's supporters, which I attended, illustrates the movement's views. One speaker told a fictitious story involving a mother who had allowed her oldest sons to fight a patriotic war with the Indians on the frontier. After the first two sons die, she sends her youngest son, Angel, to the front to fight for the nation. When little Angel is killed, she mounts a horse, rides to the frontier, and avenges his death by killing an Indian with her bare hands. At a fevered pitch, the speaker thundered out a thinly veiled criticism of the Madres de Plaza de Mayo: "THESE ARE THE KINDS OF MOTHERS WE NEED IN THIS COUNTRY." Only a few reporters and I continued to sit quietly in our seats while the rest of the audience rose in fervent applause with feet stamping and screams of "Viva Argentina." It was clear that the message was not intended for the unconverted.

Seineldín remains concerned with national security issues. While this concern was formerly manifested in his anticommunism, today his movement advocates national security through regional defense, particularly alliances between Latin American militaries. This strategy assumes both the absence of border or other conflicts between Latin American nations and a transnational threat that national armies cannot defeat alone. In a perversion of the "democracies don't make war on each other" adage, Seineldín's first overtures linked his group with Venezuelan Lieutenant Colonel Hugo Chavez, who backed two coup attempts in 1992 against the democratic government (and was elected president of Venezuela in 1998).[24] Alliances with coup plotters resemble Operación Condor, in which the Southern Cone militaries collaborated in their common war against subversion.

Like most right-wing nationalist movements in Argentina, Seineldín's movement attracts fascist support. His name shares wall space throughout Buenos Aires with mainstream political figures of the graffiti world, but it usually appears beside a swastika. Seineldín's political adviser, Gustavo Breide Obeid, claims that Seineldín rejects fascism and anti-Semitism. But I found no evidence that Seineldín had publicly or privately done so. Moreover, even Breide Obeid admits that fascists are attracted to Seineldín because they share the same, presumably anticommunist, ideology. The strong anti-Semitic strain within the Argentine military, from which Seineldín draws substantial support, is well documented in testimonies and studies of the Dirty War.[25]

Seineldín's movement casts itself as a moral and religious crusade against the evils of democracy, modernity, and secularism, backed by military force. It participates in the political system only indirectly through its alliances with small right-wing nationalist political parties. It does not attempt to shed its association with the past authoritarian system. Legitimating myths, in other words, do not play a role in the Seineldín movement. And as a result, its appeal is limited to the hard-core militants and the open supporters of uncivil political action.

Rico's faction of the Carapintada contrasts sharply with Seineldín's movement. Rico studied under Seineldín, admired him, shared leadership of the Carapintada with him, and formed part of Orden. Yet he abandoned Seineldín in favor of a distinctly modern political image. A less packaged movement, for example, might have put Martinez, not Rico, at the helm of the Carapintada after Semana Santa. Martinez had, after all, masterminded the Carapintada rebellions and initiated the creation of MODIN. He used his significant social contacts in Buenos Aires to forge alliances with leaders of the Independence Party. Martinez charted the course that the Carapintada would later take. But Martinez's political instincts led him to refuse the MODIN leadership. According to MODIN's former and current leaders, Martinez recognized the liability his human rights record brought to the party. Instead, he became one of the movement entrepreneurs who worked behind the scenes to transform Aldo Rico the military officer into Aldo Rico the political leader. Rico was not burdened by Martinez's past. Indeed, he had no political profile prior to the Semana Santa uprising. According to several sources, Martinez had to persuade a reluctant and politically unambitious Rico to make this move. Martinez attributes Rico's conversion to politics to his pragmatic realization that he lacked options within the military. Martinez recounted to me a conversation he had with Rico while the latter was detained for the Carapintada rebellion, in which Rico articulated this realization: "MODIN brought out certain things. What were people like when they were out of the [military] corporation? What is left of someone in their new world? Rico is fatalistic. He said to me, 'I'm a prisoner. What am I going to do when I get out? I can't just go out and get a job. What am I going to live as? I don't have any other place where I can go . . . except politics.'"

Martinez refuses credit for transforming Rico into a political leader. Instead, he describes that transformation as a process whereby a group of movement entrepreneurs, including Rico, recognized in Rico critical leadership characteristics: "Saying we invented Rico is unjust. We all invested in Rico . . . even Rico himself. You can't make a leader. You can provide incentives, projects, and help build a leader." These entrepreneurs transformed the unknown Rico into Rico the military hero, the caudillo. They spun legitimating myths around him to increase his public appeal not only to hard-core militants but also to those uncomfortable—at least publicly—with violence and authoritarianism.

Perón might have been a perfect model for the movement, but its entrepreneurs recognized that too close an association with Perón might limit the movement's appeal since Peronism had enemies among the groups MODIN courted. Thus, Rico maintained a subliminal link with Peronism, manifested in his image, use of symbols, and speaking style. While numerous MODIN leaders considered the party to embody Peronism, the party had not so labeled itself. MODIN hoped to appeal to passionate Peronists and passionate anti-Peronists alike. One does not find, therefore, photographs of Juan or Eva Perón in the offices of any MODIN leaders, although such photographs adorn the walls of most nationalist party leaders in the country. The following statement by Rico attests to his desire to build appeal around a universal set of Argentine icons and heroes:

[MODIN] doesn't offer anything new. It offers national objectives that have been alive throughout Argentine history in the Radical Party and in the PJ [Peronist Party]. . . . The party has a doctrine, just like the other parties: that the solution to the problem is a national solution. It is a party in formation. It wants to end partisan struggles and search for common solutions. To put order in politics. To fight corruption. To have loyalty—loyalty to the nation. [Rico, 24 June 1994]

This view was echoed by one of Rico's closest advisers in the party, who also described the movement and the party as growing out of a cultural history of both Peronism and anti-Peronism: "From PJ we took social justice. From UCR [the Radical Party] we took rescuing the regime. From [former president Arturo] Frondizi we took development. We are closest to PJ in our doctrine" [interview 39].

The MODIN symbols—tangos, national hymns, military marches, the *mate* bowl and straw, the Argentine flag, and military heroes like San Martín and Rosas—appeal to Peronists and anti-Peronists alike, though each group interprets them in its own way. They evoke national pride without suggesting partisan sectarianism. As this MODIN leader states, the party was unabashed in its appropriation and adaptation of past cultural symbols:

We want to save what was good from the past. We are not bitter. A future should have some of the old in it. Eva Perón might not work today. Who knows? But we need to be in a country where the shoes we wear are made here, where people aren't hungry because the factories are working. [We need] to have what we once had: our dreams. That people don't steal from us; that we keep getting more, not less; that the government works for the people. [interview 24]

MODIN even began to distance itself from its military image. Rico, over time, shifted his sartorial style from military fatigues to fine suits and ties or a casual Ralph Lauren look. Religious and populist symbols and discourse replaced military references. Rico's MODIN proved so effective in its legitimating myths that its archenemy, Hebe de Bonafini, founder of the Madres de Plaza de Mayo, charged it with disguising a right-wing agenda with left-wing discourse to win working-class votes [Bonafini, 26 July 1994]. Of course, Perón had used the same "trick." Indeed, one MODIN leader argued that the party was building "a nonclass party—like Peronism in the sense of nationalism, but without having the demagoguery of working for the lower echelon of society" [interview 2].

The legitimating myths spun around Rico's image were often conscious. Rico, for example, hired a "cultural adviser," rather than a political adviser, to assist with his image. At first blush, Rico and his cultural adviser could not have less in common. The adviser represents much that Rico despises. He cultivates a "counterculture" image with his imposing height draped completely in black and his flowing blond hair worn shoulder-length. He is a painter who uses naked women as his canvases and a poet and essayist published in both Spanish and English. He dedicated one of his recent publications to a well-known U.S. playwright, his son's godfather. Although only in his early forties, Rico's imagemaker claims that he has been married four times, and that his latest wife is almost twenty years his junior. This track record is not surprising, given his obsession with picking up women (which I observed firsthand).

Despite these striking differences, Rico and his adviser are kindred spirits. They both are megalomaniacs, are risk takers, believe that they can do whatever they desire, and like to provoke reaction. They are self-conscious "bad boys" who come from wildly different subcultures in Argentine society. The adviser says that Rico appealed to him because he believed Rico could shake up traditional politics and concepts in Argentina. He admits to a nihilistic streak that Rico satisfied. But once MODIN became more than a protest party, battering ram, or lightning rod and began to move in more mainstream directions, the adviser lost interest in it—and Rico.

The cultural adviser had planned to ally Rico and the left, and he did set up one meeting between Rico and leaders from the left before MODIN party leaders thwarted his efforts.[26] Rico liked the idea of a left alliance. It would have been consistent with the legitimating myths he spun around his own ideology. He sidestepped ideological polarization by rejecting labels of left and right. He claimed to share the left's philosophy but not its solutions. Rico professed himself "anti-ideology," since, as he put it, "ideology obscures things. It's like a cloud. It hides the way things are" [Rico, 24 June 1994].

Rico's associates reflect his ideological ambiguity. Some of them refer to him as a "socialist" or "anarcho-socialist." Others link him with right-wing extremism. A fellow right-wing nationalist from a different party commented that "MODIN is filled with extreme rightists like Rico. He is extreme right in his ideology, behavior, and discourse" [interview 17].

Myths about his past also obscure Rico's ideological orientation. Rico refers to his father as a Spanish immigrant who came to Argentina, met his wife, worked as a waiter, had two sons, and eventually amassed sufficient funds to buy some bars. Rico's party associates embellish the story. In some versions Rico's father is an anarchist who fought in the Spanish Civil War and imbued his children with a revolutionary spirit. Those versions glorify

Rico's humble origins and commitment to social justice. Other versions spin a Horatio Alger story in which Rico's father begins with a couple of pubs but eventually becomes an influential restaurateur. By refusing to enter into these debates, Rico has allowed his followers to construct a variety of images about him from which they can select the most appealing. The ambiguity about his background and ideology unite diverse individuals around Rico, even though they hold different, and sometimes contradictory, views of him.

But why would Rico and MODIN flirt with the left when they had no illusion of winning its votes or members? Indeed, their appeal is built around representing a silenced right wing. And when they backed particular policies, as in the Constituent Assembly, they endorsed issues generally associated with the political right—for example, a requirement that the president of Argentina be Catholic, the outlawing of abortion and the IUD, the prohibition of divorce, and the denial of rights to homosexuals. Their right-wing and exclusionary attitudes also surfaced when they compared themselves with other political parties and movements around the world. The following statement was fairly typical: "There are parties being created around the world [similar to MODIN], but I couldn't say what they are. These are parties that have returned to fundamental values—foundational concepts. They are against ideologies of the left and right. They are against foreign concepts of social democracy or liberalism. One example is the semifascist parties in Italy" [interview 38]. Another leader compared MODIN's ideology with that of Charles DeGaulle in France, Partido Popular in Spain, Silvio Berlusconi in Italy, and Germany's Helmut Kohl, all of whom advocated "capitalism with a social content" [interview 16].

MODIN obscured its ideology to create a new movement unburdened by negative associations with the past. MODIN leaders recited a refrain to me so often that it could have been their mantra. The party, they claimed, emphasized nationalism with a c (*nacionalismo*) and not with a z (*nazismo*). Nazism, they argued, had no place in Argentina, a country free of racial and ethnic prejudice. Such inclusionary rhetoric notwithstanding, I rarely made it through an interview without MODIN leaders making at least one disparaging comment about non-Caucasian, non-Catholic Argentines, or non-Argentine Latin Americans living in Argentina.[27] The contradiction is perhaps best illustrated by this Carapintada leader's comment: "*Argentinismo* doesn't have traits of exclusion. It is a rejection of European ideas, like Marxism" [interview 33].

MODIN's implication in anti-Semitic activities belies this inclusionary discourse. In May 1994, for example, three young men were arrested for painting "RICO 95" inside swastikas on a number of walls in the tradition-ally Jewish neighborhood of Onze.[28] MODIN leaders condemned the act, blaming it on agents provocateurs. Moreover, they rejected the image of the party as anti-Semitic and claimed to have Jewish members, although none of the party leaders could name one. No one has ever identified those al-leged agents provocateurs. One confidential informant accused Rico's con-fidant in the party, Morello, of organizing the act, but he failed to provide proof. Morello is also under investigation for his involvement in the 1994 bombing of the Jewish Cultural Center, but to date no proof directly links him or any other individual or group to the 1994 bombing, or to the 1992 bombing of the Israeli embassy.[29]

Denying their right-wing attitudes and flirting with the left comprised part of the movement's legitimating myths. By promoting an antipolitics ideology, the movement built support among individuals who considered themselves to be politically iconoclastic or "nonideological." This strategy also furthered the movement's goal of winning the "protest vote" against Menemism. In July 1994, for example, MODIN participated in a march op-posing Menem's economic policies organized by a number of trade unions, human rights organizations, environmentalists, and left-wing political par-ties and party factions. Most of these groups accepted, and even welcomed, MODIN's presence as an indication of opposition to Menem's policies by both the left and the right.[30] And Rico and MODIN cultivated this idea, constructing Menem's economic policy as the real legacy of authoritarian rule and their own ideas as the only acceptable alternative. Thus, MODIN responded to Menem's reduced government spending policies by advocat-ing social justice. Against Menem's adoption of free trade, MODIN pro-moted protection of national industry and national jobs. MODIN confronted Menem's amorous and financial scandals with an anticorruption and mo-rality campaign. The party pinned a retrograde and antisocial label on Menem's policies, identifying him with the military regime:

> Perhaps the [PRN's] most serious problem was the choice of minister of the economy. He didn't think about national, but rather international, interests. The same politics as today. That's why [former] Economic Minister José Martínez de Hoz wrote a book about the [last] ten years of [Argentine] politics. Because it is the same now as under him. The bosses of the bosses care more about who is picked for minister of the economy than who is the president. [interview 39]

MODIN, in sum, simultaneously criticized the widely discredited economic polices of the PRN and Menem and presented itself as an alternative to those policies in order to lure supporters away from its mainstream competitors.[31]

MODIN not only distanced itself from the negative aspects of the PRN, it even attempted to overcome its own violent image as Carapintada. MODIN denied that the Carapintada had led coup attempts, used violence, or otherwise tried to overthrow the government. Instead, these military officers argued that they had rebelled in "*gremial*" actions, nonviolent protests within the military. In the absence of a capable High Command, these officers claimed, uprisings offered the only means for responsible military officers to carry out their duty to defend the nation. They designed the uprisings not to overthrow the democratic government but rather to signal to the High Command that the Alfonsín government threatened the future of the armed forces and the nation's defense. Denying the coup aspects of the uprisings, one of Rico's followers stated, "A coup does not take place in a barracks" [interview 1]. Martinez also claimed, "We never had the idea of organizing a coup. . . . If you study the pictures, you'll see that there was never a time when Rico appeared armed." The Carapintada in MODIN further deflect accusations of coup conspiracies by distinguishing themselves from Seineldín's coup-oriented Carapintada. MODIN's military leaders claim that they rejected Seineldín's last uprising because it constituted a coup attempt.[32] The following account reflects that view:

> Before the third of December, there was no sense of the group being involved in coups. It was clear. These were relationships between the army and society that had to be addressed. The third of December [uprising] began to sound like a coup. It was taking a clearly political tone. . . . We had gotten pretty much everything we had asked for. We had unconditional acceptance within the armed forces and government. And now [Seineldín] was imposing a political project on us, and it was an authoritarian political project. I don't touch these themes. I'm not going to tell my forces how to think politically. I deal with military themes, not political themes. I deal with professional themes. [interview 12]

Most observers—even sympathetic military ones—considered the Semana Santa uprising a coup attempt. While Rico did not take up arms, the other leaders did. The only factor that kept the uprising from becoming a coup was the Carapintada's inability to arouse sufficient support within the military:

It was a coup attempt. Rico wanted and wants power. Justifying it as *gremial* action is a smokescreen. He didn't go forward with the coup because [his superiors in the Carapintada] stopped him. They invented him, and they told him to stop. They sensed that there was not enough support in the armed forces, in the population, or in the international community for a successful coup. [interview 12]

Evidence contradicts MODIN's coup denials. First, several MODIN leaders had participated in Seineldín's final coup attempt. And those who did not explained that they had suspected a government trap. These officers did not consider Seineldín's final uprising different from the others in its design, but only in the government's willingness to crush it. Unlike the earlier uprisings under Alfonsín, the Menem government knew in advance about the coup attempt. Elimination of disloyal leaders within the military provided a strong motivation to retaliate. And after substantially improving civil-military relations, Menem could count on loyal troops to retaliate. Not only did officers generally refuse to participate in the coup, they agreed to crush it:

It was almost unanimous that we [officers] were going to say no to the uprising. What was not unanimous was how we were going to deal with the uprising. I said I would repress it. But we were divided. I was against how it was conducted. We felt used. They played with our friendship. They pressured us. This was not ethical. That is what broke it. They didn't respect leadership. About one hundred officials stayed, compared with three hundred subofficials. Those officers who stayed felt like they had an obligation to do so—for the sake of their role and their fondness for their subofficials. There was an exploitation of relationships of camaraderie. We had sweated together. . . . I know only one lieutenant who stayed willingly, but he was a fundamentalist. [interview 12]

In addition to denying its involvement in coups, MODIN used a "relative-weight" argument to counter its negative and violent image. MODIN leaders claimed that they had reduced the violence in the country by providing an outlet within the system for the party's members to express their political demands and their frustrations. Without such an outlet, those members would have engaged in extrainstitutional and violent protests, as this remark by a MODIN leader suggests: "We became a recognized force. We became part of the mind set. We were able to channel political aspirations through MODIN. If MODIN weren't there, there might have been a social explosion: a coup or riots. But we provided an institutional channel, a means within the system—a route" [interview 38].

But MODIN's role in eliminating coup attempts is questionable. MODIN formed simultaneous with, and included leaders who participated in, uprisings. The most violent Carapintada uprising occurred *after* MODIN had formed; indeed, some of MODIN's leaders participated in it. MODIN did not end the coup attempts. They ended only when the government imprisoned the coup leaders.

MODIN also deflected criticism by changing its image. Dogged by its association with the military regime, MODIN sought ways of distancing itself from that regime. Regarding human rights abuses, for example, Rico's MODIN advocated compassion for losses on both sides of the war. One MODIN leader reflected this shared understanding in her comments on the Dirty War: "I understand the Mothers of the Plaza de Mayo as mothers. There were losses. We all had losses. But we are not all out there blaming, doing more harm. It is over. We must act like after World War II. Japan could not have moved forward if it had kept looking back at Hiroshima. We must look toward the future. It was painful on both sides" [interview 28].

Rico used his own past as a metaphor for Argentina's losses on both sides of the Dirty War. He asserts that subversives killed his brother, a medical doctor, in Central America, and that the Argentine army killed his wife's brother, a Montonero guerrilla and childhood friend of Rico. Rico's associates in the party, however, circulate contrasting versions of his past. In some versions Rico's brother is killed by the Salvadoran army (not by subversives) because of his involvement with the Salvadoran guerrillas. In others he is killed while fighting for the Sandinistas in Nicaragua. Questions also arise regarding Rico's brother-in-law. Was Crocco really a Montonero guerrilla murdered by the military for his involvement in kidnapping the anti-Peronist General Aramburu? Or was he a Montonero on the ultra-right allied with the military?[33] Rico's wife Noemí burst into tears when I pressed for details.

Some MODIN leaders go even further to distinguish Rico and the party from the PRN. For example, some claim that Rico had protested the Dirty War and spent time in a military prison for refusing to participate. According to one anonymous civilian informant, Rico told his commanding officer that he would fight subversives in combat but would not go into a house and drag families out. None of MODIN's military leaders confirmed that story. Martinez, implying firsthand knowledge of Rico's involvement in the Dirty War, claimed that "quite the contrary" was true. One can only conclude that the anonymous source of the story invented it to humanize Rico and soften his involvement in the war. The following remark by a MODIN leader shows that the party consciously countered its negative association with the PRN: "MODIN has an image problem. The cupola [of the party] is military. And this is seen badly in the eyes of the public. The public doesn't distinguish Rico from the PRN. He was a nationalist and opposed the liberal bent of the PRN. The PRN undermined the image of the military in the eyes of the public. But the armed forces were not running the country—the junta was" [interview 41].

This "image problem" drove MODIN to seek representatives outside the military establishment. For example, MODIN frequently flagged one of its party leaders whose parents were among the disappeared. MODIN did not intend to attract other children of the disappeared with this emphasis; the leader clearly provided the exception that confirmed the rule of MODIN's right-wing appeal. But the leader did provide a legitimating myth for members trying to reconcile their participation in a party run by alleged torturers. A quota law passed in 1993 provided another opportunity to alter the party's image. The law required political parties to include women candidates on their electoral slates.[34] Woefully unable to attract women's votes, MODIN pragmatists saw in this law the means to overcome their gender gap. Nonetheless, party leaders disagreed over the issue. Some considered women's votes a lost cause. They argued that women do not vote for MODIN because, in the words of one MODIN leader, "they are looking for a pretty face, and Rico does not have a pretty face." Another top leader in MODIN argued that the only way party candidates could win the female vote was to run naked through the Plaza de Mayo. He added, "The Argentine woman is too turned on to television. She equates a good leader with a seducer" [interview 39].

Most MODIN leaders showed more restraint in insulting women. They recognized that the party's bellicose image repelled female voters. As one leader explained, "Women want a strong leader who will put order in the country. But they don't want military leaders. They are afraid of war. They are concerned first about their children, and they don't realize that politicians, and not military personnel, decide war policy. When they realize that MODIN is not a military party, then they will vote for it. That can be done only by getting out proposals and candidates" [interview 38].

The quota law forced MODIN to increase the role of women in the party, consistent with some of its pragmatists' concerns. MODIN claimed to have exceeded the legal requirements, including a higher proportion of female candidates on their electoral lists than any other party in the 1994 Constituent Assembly elections. But who were these women? Almost without exception, MODIN activists' wives occupied MODIN's leadership posts. These women confessed to me that they had had little to do with the party before their nomination. Indeed, two of them asked me to interview their husbands, citing their limited experience in the party. And while female leaders frequently mentioned the party's strong support for them fulfilling their dual duties as mothers and politicians, all but one female leader I interviewed had live-in help—not common for the contemporary middle class in Argentina—to care for children and households. And this "support" from the party appeared to be insufficient to sustain women's involvement in the party. Reflecting a sentiment widespread among the women leaders I interviewed, one said she would quit at the end of her term, because, in her words, "I refuse to run my home by cellular phone" [interview 25].

Even before the quota law, MODIN had attempted to demilitarize its image and thus appeal to women. But these efforts often echoed authoritarian attitudes about women's roles as mothers of soldiers and citizens. For example:

> The woman has become a sexual object for consumers. We need to recover her dignity. We need to say no to selling products by using the female anatomy. She is the future. She is the family. She educates our children. There isn't a future without the woman. She reproduces our species. Teaching our children to love our country is the woman's job. [interview 16]

> Civilization is monstrous, and we only realize it afterward. If it happened suddenly we would see it, but it happens slowly, and we don't realize what is going on. Woman is sacred. She is a mystery. And they use her for marketing strategies. Everything they want to sell on television they sell with a breast, or a leg, or some other part of the female anatomy. This is not right. [interview 2]

While opposing the objectification of women, such views are patronizing and antifeminist. But MODIN did not attempt to attract feminists. None of its women leaders considered themselves to be feminists. Some even professed themselves "antifeminist" while still demanding equal rights for women. This confusion was expressed most eloquently by the wife of one Carapintada leader:

> I am not a feminist. I am feminine. . . . My husband has always respected my way, my personality, the space that I occupy. . . . The sixteenth of July is our anniversary, and I asked him for a signed

photograph. . . . On it he inscribed [my name], not "to my beloved wife" or "my adoring wife." He wrote my name. I thanked him for that—for recognizing me as an independent woman. . . . Feminists are extreme. . . . They think that men enslave us. Machismo doesn't work, and neither does feminism. These are both extreme attitudes. Respect works, and being respected. . . . Women have a space in MODIN. Some have come to me and said, "When are we going to form a feminine branch of MODIN? The Peronist Party has one." But we don't need one. We are the trunk of the party—not the branch. We work together in the party. We are the impetus. We sustain the party. . . . My role is a service role. I try to be with [my husband] when he is campaigning. It is important that women see and understand that [MODIN men] are like everyone. They are there with their wives. This makes their image a little less rigid. I try to go with my husband whenever I can. [interview 24]

This attitude about women reflects MODIN's efforts to alter its image. Unlike Seineldín's movement, MODIN was not satisfied representing only the military hard core, fundamentalist Catholics, and extreme right-wing nationalists. Thus, it disseminated images that softened or even contradicted its armed right-wing past.

On the other hand, MODIN recognized that it derived most of its support from its uncivil image. It had more influence and power as a group of potential coup plotters than as a fringe political party. Legitimating myths allowed it to present an array of messages, often contradictory, from which a fairly broad spectrum of constituents could choose. These messages not only constituted a deliberate attempt to deceive but also reflected the diverse viewpoints held by the eclectic group of party leaders. They emerged from the interaction of political framing, cultural cuing, and legitimating myths. They appropriated and glorified old cultural icons, unifying constituents against a common enemy, but they also adapted the past to a contemporary situation. Rico and MODIN secured support not solely by mimicking Perón's dynamic (i.e., mobilizing, crowd-pleasing oratory style), but also by spinning competing versions of Rico's personal stories, ideology, and image that permitted diverse individuals to construct images of Rico in keeping with their own ideologies and tastes. Rico carefully avoided providing facts that might privilege one interpretation over another. He wanted to be whatever his followers desired: a left-wing sympathizer caught on the wrong side of a war, a right-wing totalitarian attempting to shape a new Argentine identity, a Peronist, an anti-Peronist, or an apolitical man of the people with pragmatic solutions to the nation's problems. In short, Rico's image had broader appeal than Seineldín's narrow military and right-wing Catholic nationalism.

Despite its mythmaking, MODIN could not afford to dissociate itself completely from the past. MODIN's antisubversive, Catholic, and social conservatism meant that it would appeal only to individuals who shared those right-wing values. The party designed legitimating myths not to attract its adversaries but rather to provide a justification to persuade fellow travelers to join a party run by Dirty War officers. Myths allowed the party to extend its appeal beyond just the militant hard core. As one MODIN leader admitted, "Myth is important. Without myth, the party doesn't go forward" [interview 2].

Spinning these myths allowed MODIN to attract a following unavailable to the Seineldín group. One of MODIN's major achievements, for example, was winning support among youths voting for the first time. Party leaders attributed this success to the antipolitics campaign: "The strength of MODIN is with young people. In the last elections, 70 percent of those who voted for MODIN were under twenty-five. They see something that is romantic and heroic. They don't value politicians but rather see them as corrupt" [interview 38]. MODIN did not actively cultivate youth support. It had a youth branch, but party leaders had great difficulty naming even one leader of that branch whom I could interview. The "youth leader" they eventually identified and whom I interviewed had left the youth movement, had no idea what kinds of activities the youth movement engaged in, could name no other youth leader, and could not explain to me why MODIN had formed a youth branch, since he perceived no generational differences or conflicts, or any advantages a youth branch could provide.

MODIN attracted youths through image, not effort. The Argentine "Generation X" seemed to find in MODIN a viable alternative to status quo politics. Some label the appeal "Rambo politics," since MODIN attracts youth support partly through its militaristic style. But perhaps more significant, MODIN embodied an antisystem orientation, a kind of right-wing counterculture. Because of their age and lack of experience with the PRN, these youths may have had fewer negative associations with the military than older voters had. They heard MODIN's message of change and believed in it.

Rico's MODIN appealed to a broad, though predominantly right-wing, constituency. Individuals already inclined toward its message could read into it what they wanted. So while security forces saw MODIN as the only group that represented them against subversives in government, the working-class periphery saw it as the only viable alternative to neoliberalism, and Generation X saw it as a nonideological, non-class-based postmaterialist solution to national angst. Seineldín received support only from the security forces and right-wing Peronists. His limited economic program failed to win support from trade unionists, and he offered too little that was new to captivate Generation X. He was, and remains, an authoritarian retread, because of his failure to spin the legitimating myths that would draw in a broader constituency.

Limitations on the Carapintada's Power

Both Carapintada factions acquired significant political power during their initial phases, allowing them to transform Argentine democratic politics and indirectly shape postauthoritarian politics in other countries of the region. But despite this profound impact, the Carapintada could not sustain their political power. The Seineldín and Rico groups provide evidence of uncivil movements' inherent weakness, though the two cases point to different sets of vulnerabilities.

Seineldín's group represents the limitations of unreconstructed authoritarianism, or the danger of appealing exclusively to a militant hard core. Seineldín continued using the coup as his weapon against the democratic government, even when the catalyst threat of the trials had ceased to exist, civil-military relations had improved, and institutional options for shaping politics from within the political system had become available. All of these factors reduced the cost to the Menem government of crushing Seineldín's faction. Seineldín could not even claim martyrdom, despite his life sentence. By pardoning the generals for their human rights violations and the Carapintada for their earlier rebellions, by staging parades to honor Malvinas veterans, and by establishing a role for the military in civilian government, Menem avoided charges that he had singled out military rebels for exceptional punishment. Menem's response to Seineldín illustrates the role democratic governments can play in reducing the power of uncivil movements, through artful negotiation with pragmatists coupled with investigation and prosecution of the militant hard core.

Menem's policies ended the rebellions, but not Seineldín's political mobilization. From his country-club-style internment he formed MINeII and has managed to sustain a limited political following and political exposure.[35] In 1994, for example, officers handed out leaflets at barracks calling for Seineldín's liberty. In addition, shortly before his death former president Arturo Frondizi (1958–62) called on Menem to grant a pardon to Seineldín.[36]

Moreover, a number of small nationalist parties continually call for Seineldín's freedom and propose him as a presidential candidate for right-wing nationalist blocks.[37] In 1998 even Rico joined this chorus for a presidential pardon.

Those who call for Seineldín's pardon and candidacy for the presidency recognize his political limitations. What they find appealing about him is not his political acumen. On the contrary, his supporters question his capacity to lead a political movement, as the following words from one of his strongest backers attest: "He really doesn't understand anything about politics, not even the most obvious things. He is an excellent person but is an 'anti-Perón' in the sense of his understanding of politics" [interview 36].

While Seineldín's fundamentalist Catholicism and right-wing nationalism garnered support in the past, his age, style, and imprisonment cast doubt on whether he can sustain that support over time. He had a profound impact on the last generation of military officers through his mentoring and his leadership of the AAA and Orden. But many of the officers he trained have left the military through retirement or expulsion. His own imprisonment has prevented him from training or mentoring any new officers, although he is allegedly teaching military training courses in the prison. His traditional authoritarian style also fails to resonate with more than an obsolete political constituency. While his unreconstructed authoritarianism might appeal to a militant hard core, without legitimating myths Seineldín will not build a broader base. His movement will disappear over time, or become latent, deriving future political power only as a minority movement in alliance with other political movements, or by remaking the movement with modern and democratic myths. As one political observer wrote, "Like a dinosaur, he has not found a way to survive with the changes that democracy has brought. He has ended up being a caricature of himself: he was thrown out of the army by Menem, he's still in jail, and his political message does not even provoke outrage any more."[38]

It is somewhat artificial to draw too stark a contrast between the Seineldín and Rico factions, since Seineldín mentored Rico and his followers. Nonetheless, the two groups chose different routes to adapt to a new political environment, and the institutional route selected by Rico yielded greater success, at least temporarily. Over time, however, even MODIN's institutional route demonstrated its limitations. A rapid drop in political power followed MODIN's peak in the 1993 national elections, as table 3.2 illustrates. Rico's MODIN illustrates how institutionalization plants the seeds of an uncivil movement's destruction. Rico's charismatic leadership, the weakness of the party's program, and the opposition role that initially won the party significant support led to its demise over time.

Rico amassed an extraordinary amount of personal power and autonomy in the party. It was not long before "Rico" became synonymous with "MODIN." Not one of the MODIN leaders I interviewed believed that the political party could survive without Rico. And Rico, despite his earlier reluctance, grew to adore his political power. As he put it, "I love what I do. I have a passion for what I do. I love the contact I have with other people. It's like a drug. It's an environment without limits" [Rico, 24 June 1994].

With his political power increasing, Rico began to reject party entrepreneurs' control over him. Indeed, the party's frequent purges suggest that Rico did not tolerate any independence from or competition with him in the party. In 1992, for example, he purged Martinez and one of his closest associates from the party, despite their critical roles in creating both Rico and MODIN.[39] In 1993 MODIN purged its only two senators and one of its three congressmen. In 1994 Rico's top leaders in Buenos Aires Province, both of them personal friends of his, Luis Polo and Julio Carreto, left MODIN. In addition to these high-profile purges, MODIN lost over seventeen provincial deputies and sixteen town assembly people from 1992 to 1994. These departures usually appeared voluntary; without exception, however, purged leaders claimed that Rico had made conditions within the party so unbearable that they saw no option but to leave.

Party leaders tried to explain away the purges. One explanation focused on the party's need to eliminate leaders with tarnished legal records. But I found no correlation between criminal records and purges. While some of those purged had criminal records, others did not. And many with criminal records remained with the party. Indeed, most of the top leaders, including Rico, had engaged in criminal activity in Semana Santa, although the Due Obedience Law cleansed most Carapintada leaders' records.

This legalistic justification contradicted another explanation for the purges: the party's need to improve its image and particularly to shed its association with the PRN and human rights abuses. Among the purged leaders, only Martinez and his closest associate had human rights records. Rico's supporters contend that Rico agonized and debated with other leaders over his decision to purge his close personal friends and colleagues-in-arms. They conclude that his devotion to the party forced him to ignore his own personal anguish and do what was best for the party. In his interview with me, Rico pointedly avoided answering questions regarding Martinez's dismissal.

Instead, he spoke generally about personally painful, but politically necessary, decisions to remove people from the party who could not accept party rules and norms. He did not mention past human rights abuses as an explanation for purges. Martinez also rejected this explanation: "[Rico] has an exaggerated sense of pragmatism. . . . He defines himself as tactical. He is rigid. . . . There is no fair play. He has to win. . . . He is willing to make alliances with anyone, . . . so he wouldn't have any trouble with me and my past." Given that the vast majority of the purges involved civilians without involvement in the Dirty War, this explanation does not hold up against the evidence.

Corruption constituted another explanation for purges. The party hoped to avoid the vices that infected other political parties in the country by eliminating corruption, even the mere suspicion of corruption:

> For the first elections in 1991 we let in candidates from other parties. But they were suspected of corruption, so we had to dismiss them: seventeen town assemblymen, one congressman, and two provincial senators. You could tell [they were corrupt] because they would first show up in old clothes and broken shoes, getting off the bus. Then you would see them a year later in new clothes. The next year they would be driving a new car. Or you could tell because of their votes. They were voting in such a way that you had to conclude that they were getting paid off—[that is, they were voting] in ways that were not consistent with the party. [interview 39]

If the criteria of new clothes and cars had been consistently applied, most of the top leaders of MODIN would be out of the party today. Despite their humble military backgrounds, these leaders have quickly assumed the material well-being of the Argentine upper middle class. Moreover, MODIN's right-wing party competitors have frequently criticized MODIN's tolerance for corruption. As one critic stated, "MODIN talks about a fight against corruption, but it hasn't made one denouncement of corruption—not even verbally. And they have voted in favor of situations where there are confirmed cases of corruption in Buenos Aires Province. Montiel [the MODIN representative on the Buenos Aires city council] has kept corrupt Peronist Party members in power by failing to vote against them" [interview 20].

The most compelling explanation for the purges is competition within the party. Rico purged Martinez and his closest associate not despite their critical role in the party's formation, but because of it. He had to wrest control away from them to secure his own autonomy and power. Rico also purged party leaders with a strong commitment to Peronism, presumably because they lacked loyalty to his personal control. One prominent legislator purged from MODIN stated, "I just felt that I could not express my Peronist feelings [in MODIN]. . . . I am a Peronist but not a Menemist" [interview 23]. Another explained that he had joined the party because he thought it would resemble Peronism, and he left when it fell short of those ideals:

> Menem didn't have anything to do with Peronism. The Peronist doctrine emphasizes the common good. That is a fundamental principle. Menem is a liberal. He advocates free-market politics, without any popular sentiment. I wouldn't have voted for him if he had made this clear in his campaign. So in the beginning of '91 Rico was looking for people in La Matanza. He seemed to have the historical expression of Peronism down. It looked like he was going to wave the Peronist flag. He was very much like Perón in 1943: colonel of the army, responsive to the demands of the population. But these were beliefs without a party structure that supported them. . . . There was too little space within the party. There were too many restrictions. There were no openings to popular democratic demands. It turned out to be a party that was just like the others. They were criticizing Menem, but without posing an alternative. They didn't have a plan for governing. I came from a different party. I expected things to be different. I had a few conversations with Rico. He is capricious. He makes his own demands. He is a Rambo type. . . . He is looking for a certain amount of power and a certain lifestyle. The conversations didn't lead anywhere. We ended up in a screaming match where I shouted back. I finally had to leave the party. [interview 3]

While the party claimed to tolerate different political directions, too close an identification with Peronism seemed to threaten Rico's authority over candidates. In other words, the more programmatic the leaders, the more likely they would be purged.

Disagreement with Rico and his small clique of followers also resulted in purges. One purged leader claimed that in the absence of any internal party democracy, Rico made all decisions and even hand-picked candidates for political slates. Loyalty to Rico, and not the capacity to win votes or represent a district, was the main criterion for selection. Another purged member made the following observations:

Rico just decided who would go on the list [of candidates] and where.
. . . Orders went from Rico down. No one could express their opinion.
And what they had from the Peronist Party were the worst—
marginals—nothing from the middle class. . . . There were no internal
elections. . . . It didn't matter to [the party leadership] that we left. They
said, "Rico has the votes for the party. If you're bothered by something,
leave. If you don't like the way the party is, leave. We don't need you.
Rico has the votes." [interview 9]

MODIN leaders who remained with the party rejected this criticism of
Rico's personal control. They praised the party for its participatory democracy, arguing that all opinions were heard and respected and that decisions
were reached collectively. Yet these leaders could not back up their defense.
They provided no examples of cases in which the party had overturned Rico's
decision. The only examples of internal democracy involved cases in which
Rico had accepted opinions other than those everyone believed he held but
that he had not openly expressed. By implication, these leaders suggested
that party members could shape party policies only on issues about which
Rico either had no opinion or had not yet expressed one.

Rico's personality offers additional contradictory evidence. He can, on
occasion, appear calm, thoughtful, even timid. But he has an explosive tem-
per and can easily be provoked, by the slightest question or event, into committing irrational acts. His pride is easily wounded, making it impossible for
him to admit his own errors. When put in a position in which he feels that
he lacks the upper hand, he attempts to scare or intimidate. In this way he
has irritated innumerable journalists and fellow-politicians of all political
stripes. Even members of his own party express frustration with his aggressive personality.

The most recent purge of the two provincial leaders perhaps best illustrates Rico's autocratic style. These leaders' loyalty to Rico and MODIN
seemed unquestioned. Indeed, they had carried out many of the earlier party
purges to protect Rico and MODIN. When they disagreed with Rico, however, they were purged. Even they could not challenge him. And they could
not even challenge him on the party's own terms. Rico's decision to support
the Peronist Party governor's second term conflicted, they argued, with the
party's policy against corruption, back-room pacts, and Menemism. They
learned that when the party program clashed with Rico's goals, Rico would
win even at the cost of fragmenting the party, losing his friends, and eliminating powerful political leaders.[40]

While Rico could justify his first purge on a number of grounds, subsequent purges began to erode the party's strength. Even his supporters wondered about Rico's leadership style and the impact it might have on the party. One leader commented, "He is a military man—authoritarian. He controls too much. He doesn't allow for diverging opinions. And we lose good leaders like the provincial senators" [interview 41]. One of Rico's former associates in the Carapintada explained his own decision to stay out of MODIN: "[Rico] can't let anyone be in the party who might be a better leader than he is. That limits the party" [interview 34].

Concerns also arose over Rico's ulterior motives. Some leaders suggested that Rico used the purges for personal financial gain. Since parties receive funds according to the number of seats they win, the party continues to receive funds even after it loses its politicians to other party affiliations. And since it has fewer politicians to whom it must distribute those funds, the party and its leaders benefit financially from the purges. These critics contend that Rico is investing his "savings" from the purges in some business ventures that will support him when he leaves politics.[41]

One former MODIN leader believed that material motivations explained his own purge. MODIN had accused him of voting for three laws that the party opposed, and even proof to the contrary did not change the party's opinion. This leader assumed that the party had trumped up false accusations, the real motivation for the purge being financial. He had put up his own money to campaign, won public office, and paid for the MODIN headquarters in his district. While this money was technically loaned by him to the party, he assumes that the party never had any intention of paying him back and purged him instead.

Rico's material and political goals seem compatible. His political strategy focused on what was good for Aldo Rico. He betrayed his allies and supporters in the party. He violated the party's principles when they proved inconvenient. He even rejected the movement's commitment to unconventional politics by adopting comfortable and conventional institutional politics. As Rico's imagemaker described the situation, "Rico is no longer antisystem. Rico wants power. He is within the system. He is not the opposition."

In short, Rico typifies a situation common to uncivil movements. He attracted a loyal following as a result of a charismatic bond. The party depended not on a program but on his charismatic leadership. Over time Rico sought more political power within the movement. He grew distant from the movement entrepreneurs who had put him in power. He also distanced himself from the base of supporters who had sustained that power. This allowed him to look after his own political ambitions, unconstrained by the party.

But MODIN did not fragment because of Rico alone. The contradictions that had once provided members of the movement with an array of positions from which to choose were now, as a result of institutionalization, transformed into party frictions. MODIN had to develop party platforms to compete in elections and influence political outcomes. The institutionalization process thus exacerbated existing schisms between the hard-core militants and the pragmatists. For example, MODIN tried to take advantage of Menem's loose morality to create a family-values agenda. The entire party supported the agenda in its broad strokes, but consensus broke down over specific policy reforms. The only policy proposal that came close to winning a consensus within the party was the antiabortion position. Even in that case one leader remarked that he felt uncomfortable telling a woman that she must carry an unwanted child to term, and a few other leaders made exceptions to allow abortion in the cases of rape or incest. An overwhelming majority, however, felt strongly that as tragic as the pregnancies from such violations were, the fetus was a person, and human rights required protection of that person. It is cruelly ironic that this group, comprised of leaders accused of violating adults' human rights, used a human rights argument against aborting a fetus.

In contrast to wide support for the antiabortion stance, MODIN leaders split on every other "family-values" issue. A few leaders in the party, for example, organized an anti-IUD campaign, arguing that "the IUD works like an abortion and should be prohibited" [interview 26]. They firmly believed that the party backed their campaign. But dissent, and not consensus, emerged in my conversations about birth control with both women and men in the party. One party leader stated, "You can't impose the rhythm method on the population. One sector within the party is more orthodox Catholic than others" [interview 25]. But like legitimating myths, this opposition to the anti-IUD campaign did not become public within or outside the party. Perhaps they helped to test public support for an extreme profamily position, even when few of them endorsed it. The end result, however, is that MODIN became labeled an extreme-right party.

Divorce also generated disagreements within the party. Most of the MODIN leaders I interviewed pointed to the divorce of one of MODIN's few congressman as the difficulty in endorsing such a position. Those behind the antidivorce position continued to defend it adamantly, however, arguing that divorced members of MODIN would have to live with their own conscience on the subject. Most MODIN leaders preferred a position on sexual morality and used Rico's marriage as emblematic of the ideal marriage. A MODIN leader described this old-fashioned love story in the following way: "He is still in love with his wife and she admires him. This is something that is so antiquated in today's age. And he has even said in public that she is his first woman. And everyone says, 'This isn't something you publicly admit'" [interview 38]. But in stark contrast to this public image, party leaders admitted to me in confidence that Rico and his intimate group of top advisers engaged in frequent indiscretions with party secretaries. Legitimating myths simultaneously present Rico as playboy and faithful husband.

Party leaders also disputed MODIN's position on sexual orientation. A few party leaders issued a statement that called homosexuality a mental health issue that required medical intervention. As one of them put it, "Homosexuals are ill. Their practices must stop. We must modify their behavior. We don't accept them. They are human beings, but they threaten the importance of the family" [interview 26]. Contradicting this view, another MODIN leader stated that gay rights "is a complex theme. But there shouldn't be discrimination. We even want them to participate in our political party" [interview 18].

In addition to the family-values agenda, MODIN also endorsed a Catholic agenda. Specifically, MODIN mobilized within the Constituent Assembly (and against the majority) to retain the constitutional mandate requiring that the president of the republic be Catholic. The party even went so far as to chastise the Catholic Church hierarchy for failing to mobilize on that issue. A majority of MODIN leaders agreed with the position, asserting that only a Catholic president could maintain the national spirit and identity of a country that is 80 percent Catholic. When I suggested that the democratic system of voting would allow the majority to protect itself against an individual who might threaten those cultural traditions, the following reaction from a self-professed nationalist was typical: "I can imagine Argentines voting for a Shiite because they don't see any problem; they don't want to appear to be racist. But this presents problems of double nationality. The Shiites feel more Shiite than Argentine" [interview 20].

These strong opinions did not come from religious leaders. Indeed, only two of MODIN's top leaders even belonged to a church and attended it with any regularity. The vast majority could not remember when they had last attended mass. And only one individual produced a nonideological argument for the position. He stated that the constitution was being produced at an enormous speed that did not permit the kind of in-depth discussion necessary for changing traditional laws in the nation, therefore MODIN should leave intact as many laws as possible for later discussion and possible amendment [interview 18].

The point of this discussion of MODIN's fragmented and incoherent policies is that Rico frequently harangued the press for refusing to cover the party's policy proposals and positions. But my own efforts to uncover consensus positions revealed little more than vague guiding principles without solid backing for any specific policies to implement those principles. As a protest movement, MODIN had generated contradictory positions to increase its support. But as an institutional party, MODIN was hurt by these divisions. It appeared incapable of reaching any consensus.

The process of institutionalization highlighted the fragmentation within the party and weakened its political power. Without consensus on policy issues, the party suffered doubly. First, it appeared incoherent and weak, incapable of taking bold leadership. Second, when it did take bold policy initiatives, the militants set the agenda. In short, the movement could not disguise its radical views behind legitimating myths.

MODIN's demise is also traceable to political factors external to the movement. MODIN's success resulted from its monopoly over the opposition to Menem's Peronist Party, but over time it lost that role because of competition from other, more viable, opposition parties. MODIN leaders believed that the party would grow as long as Menem remained in power. Rico expected that Menem's economic program would self-destruct during his second term, sending voters to seek refuge under MODIN's protection. What MODIN had not anticipated is that it would compete with other viable alternatives.

The Frente Grande (Broad Front) emerged shortly before the Constituent Assembly elections in 1994 to oppose Menem's efforts to rewrite the constitution to allow him to run for a second term in office. Menem's bid for reelection tore apart the already fragile alliances within the Peronist Party. Carlos "Chacho" Alvarez and a number of left-of-center Peronist dissidents abandoned Menem to form the Frente, joining forces with leftist parties, most significantly Federico "Pino" Solanas's Communist Party.

Frente Grande soon surpassed MODIN and took over as the third force in Argentine party politics. MODIN leaders attempted to discredit the victory, arguing that the front would be torn apart by ideological and programmatic differences within the top leadership and voter antipathy toward the Communist Party. They further argued that the Frente Grande had no support outside the capital city of Buenos Aires and thus would break up before the 1995 elections.

In part these predictions came true. The Frente Grande, as originally designed, did break up shortly after the 1994 Constituent Assembly elections. This fragmentation, however, strengthened rather than weakened Chacho Alvarez's electoral support. He lost his greatest impediment to forming a broad centrist coalition (Communist Party leader Solanas) and subsequently formed an alliance with dissident Peronists and dissident Radical Party leaders, called FREPASO (National Solidarity Front). Alvarez also gained support from some of the purged MODIN leaders. As a protest against Menem, these seasoned leaders led the charge over Rico's small and inexperienced group. In the 1995 presidential elections, FREPASO achieved second place behind Menem's Peronist Party.

FREPASO's competitive edge over MODIN is not surprising. In addition to their political experience, FREPASO leaders have stronger credentials as Peronists and defenders of the working class. Given a choice between Rico and Alvarez, anti-Menemist Peronists sided with Alvarez. MODIN could not secure the working- and middle-class vote. FREPASO, in other words, sealed MODIN's fate as a marginal opposition party, as this quote suggests: "[Rico] wanted a personal structure . . . and that means that he will win votes from the pockets of the most marginal areas—areas where there has been rapid population growth due to internal migration, lack of work, and the search for a caudillo as part of the cultural authoritarianism that prevails there" [interview 15].

MODIN's hopes that the FREPASO coalition would collapse became increasingly unlikely with the 1997 elections. FREPASO joined together in an even stronger coalition, Alianza (Alliance). Alianza provided a centrist alternative to Menem's corruption and the serious problem of unemployment, without threatening the middle class with radical economic reform. It began leading in elections, reducing MODIN to a fifth-place position.

The "loser" image does not fit Rico's personality. As one of his colleagues described him, "He'll do anything not to lose. He is proud, vain, and arrogant. He doesn't ever want to be defeated. And he is incapable of ethical conduct" [interview 14]. Moreover, Rico is impatient. In the military academy this cost him a year of his training, forcing him to repeat it. In Malvinas he urged Seineldín to reject the existing authority and take control. The reactions that led to the military uprisings are part of this impatience, as were the party purges and pacts he masterminded. One of Rico's non-Carapintada military colleagues described his psychological profile in this way: "He has a breakdown every five years" [interview 19]. Whether because of a breakdown, pride, or impatience, Rico abandoned MODIN in 1998 and joined forces with his former rivals in the Peronist Party. He also abandoned national politics, accepting a position as mayor of a Buenos Aires Province town, San Miguel.[42] Without Rico, the party has lost its political power. Rico, in short, became both the cause of the party's demise and one of its greatest casualties.

As the Carapintada shifted from movement to institution, therefore, they lost much of their original base of support. Some radical elements rejected the mainstream direction of the MODIN leadership. But MODIN also failed to win any support from new constituents because it was perceived as being politically incoherent or too closely linked to radicalism. Neither FREPASO nor Alianza shared MODIN's stigma of authoritarianism and violence. Neither suffered from class and gender gaps like MODIN. While MODIN appeared increasingly radical on policy positions, FREPASO and Alianza became more centrist. Rico's attempts to brand FREPASO and Alianza as radical backfired. For example, he remarked that Alvarez's wife was alive only because "she gave up many comrades" during the dictatorship.[43] And reacting to the possible presidency of Alianza candidate Graciela Fernández Meijide, mother of a disappeared son, Rico stated, "I can assure you that many of the disappeared will reappear."[44] Rather than impugning FREPASO or Alianza, these comments simply branded Rico a right-wing radical.

The changing political environment brought new challenges to which the movement failed to adapt. The unconventional politics of an institutionalized political party lost some of its original appeal over time and in the wake of moderate successes. Having become just another party with a caudillo-style leadership and almost no program, MODIN could not sustain itself. On the other hand, sustaining its unconventional political action would not have helped MODIN grow. It faced serious impediments in building support for its movement as long as it was perceived as an armed right-wing authoritarian movement, particularly at a time when other more viable and less stigmatized protest parties had emerged. In short, the movement's success and its inherent limitations led to its eventual demise.

Conclusion

The Carapintada offer an interesting perspective on the institutions approach and the measures that democratic governments should pursue to reduce the power of uncivil movements. The Alfonsín government can serve as an example of what the institutions approach warned against. It provoked a military coup by adopting the radical policy of investigating and prosecuting officers for human rights abuses and the Malvinas War debacle. Without the trials, the Carapintada never would have emerged. Moreover, Menem restored order only after granting amnesties and pardons for human rights abuses. The Argentine case thus appears to confirm the importance of moderation for democratic stability.[45]

The Argentine case also seems to confirm the institutionalization and habituation components of the institutions approach. The Carapintada formed a political party and began to work within the political system to pursue their political goals. This suggests that institutionalization transforms authoritarians into democrats, guaranteeing democratic stability.

But counterfactuals question the success of the institutions approach in explaining the Argentine case. What might have happened, for instance, if after the first Carapintada rebellion Alfonsín had not passed the Due Obedience Law but had used the force of law to harshly prosecute the rebels for threatening democracy? The institutions approach suggests that such a strategy would have united even the moderate forces within the military and brought about an overthrow. Alfonsín may have envisioned this scenario. But it seems, at least in retrospect, an unlikely outcome. The military lacked internal and external cohesion owing to the PRN's governing disasters and the Malvinas War defeat. The military High Command was loyal to Alfonsín and not the Carapintada. Moreover, most military officers—even those who shared the Carapintada's goals—considered an armed uprising an inappropriate, even deleterious, course of action. Rather than rally behind the rebellious officers, they would have acted as they did in 1987: keeping a low profile, acknowledging the Carapintada's goals, and rejecting their methods. For these reasons I cannot imagine that prosecutions for rebellion would have triggered an overthrow. Indeed, it is more probable that military officers, fearing prosecution, would have decided against leading any more uprisings.

The Argentine case further challenges moderation as a means of avoiding uncivil movements' threats. Even after moderating its policies and capitulating to the rebels, the Alfonsín government still faced two more rebellions and Menem another. The Carapintada faction of the military refused to be easily bought off by moderate policies. Instead, these military officers used the Alfonsín government's moderate treatment to launch not only more rebellions but political careers. Moderation enhanced their political power.

The Carapintada case also raises questions about whether institutionalization can serve as a mechanism for transforming authoritarians into democrats. MODIN demonstrated that former authoritarians can play the democratic game. But even after they formed a political party, they continued to engage in military uprisings. Institutionalization simply provided them with an additional political tool—one they could use along with violence—to achieve their political goals. The Carapintada became a movement that paid lip service to democratic ideals but whose lack of commitment to democracy liberated them from constraints on acting undemocratically.[46]

Moreover, the example of the Carapintada shows that uncivil movements can become institutional players, thereby increasing, rather than reducing, their power in democracies. The Rico group that formed the political institution MODIN had a more profound impact on democracy than the less institutionalized Seineldín group. While MODIN achieved national electoral prominence, Seineldín's movement remained an extreme-right fringe movement without significant influence. Clearly Seineldín's limited power had something to do with his life sentence. The comparison between the two cases suggests, therefore, that legal authority, and not institutionalization, might prove the more appropriate means of reducing the power of these movements. The comparison also suggests that movements that remain outside the institutional structure may lose power more quickly. They lack the authority that institutionalization affords and that constitutes a powerful legitimating myth. Relegated to the marginal and extremist fringe, they face more difficulties in securing support from pragmatists. In short, institutionalization legitimates uncivil movements, providing them with not only a forum but also an image that enhances their appeal.

These caveats notwithstanding, the Carapintada case shows how institutionalization can exacerbate uncivil movements' inherent weaknesses. Rico's personal power, so crucial to the movement's rise, contributed to its demise. His purges undermined the movement. He sacrificed party principles to save his own political hide. Contradictory views, critical to the legitimating myths that initially expanded the movement, ultimately limited the movement's appeal to radicals.

But the vulnerabilities that accompany institutionalization often come too late, after the damage has been done—a fact that challenges gradualism as a strategy for limiting the power of uncivil movements. The Carapintada had a profound impact on the nature of the democratic regime in its early years. The Semana Santa uprising virtually ended the possibility of trials for human rights abuses. So while institutionalization eroded the Carapintada's political power, that erosion happened after the movement had already shaped the democratic system and the judiciary's capacity to redress past grievances.

Rather than confirming the institutions approach, therefore, the Argentine case suggests an alternative. Menem adopted a different strategy that ended the rebellions. The pardons and amnesties he authorized may look like moderation, but they constitute a broader policy of compromise with the military. Menem "negotiated" with the pragmatists. I do not mean that he sat at the bargaining table with them, but rather he developed a face-saving strategy. Menem appeased the Carapintada and other military officers who felt insecure about the trials by granting a pardon. He extended the pardon, however, to the military's adversaries, the guerrilla movements on the left. Although the levels of atrocities were not parallel, Menem claimed to have meted out equal treatment to both sides. He also valorized the Malvinas War with parades and declarations. Moreover, he recognized the political institutions that represented the Carapintada. In addition to this negotiated strategy, however, Menem imposed harsh penalties for violent opposition. His no-tolerance policy for military rebellions crushed the militant hardline. By employing negotiation and prosecution, Menem divided the pragmatists from the militants and prevented the martyred militants from rebelling by conquering them.

For the moment, Menem has both Carapintada groups where he needs them. Neither Seineldín nor Rico has much chance of gaining electoral ground or extrainstitutional power. While the fragmentation of the movement has weakened them, they retain enough power and income to save face and refrain from the extrainstitutional political acts that will draw increased media attention. They also lack sufficient support within the military or society to carry off those kinds of political acts. They therefore fail to pose a threat to the democratic government.

With the rebellions buried in the past and the Carapintada only weakly represented in political institutions, Argentina becomes a test case for revisiting the cautious policies of the past. Along the lines of the institutions approach, democratic governments should now feel sufficiently stable to adopt substantive policies to strengthen democracy without provoking a coup. Specifically, the democratic government could now investigate the human rights abuses and bring justice to the victims of the Dirty War. I have no doubt that the government could fulfill this responsibility without provoking a coup.

Even if some small group of military officers mobilized, the Argentine democratic government now has experience in suppressing coup attempts, surviving them, and restoring order without capitulating to rebels' demands or sacrificing democratic ideals. It can use the legal system to prosecute rebels for threatening democracy. To prepare for a possible uprising, however, democratic governments must investigate uncivil movements. They must be aware that at times these movements do form alliances with authoritarian movements to topple the government. And democratic governments have the responsibility to know when that might happen.

The recent investigations into former junta leaders General Videla and Admiral Massera provide the test case. Both face accusations for involvement in the kidnapping of children of political prisoners. These prosecutions do not violate pardons or amnesty laws, since military officers did not receive immunity for this type of kidnapping. Indeed, rather than eroding the legal system, such prosecutions could enhance the power of the judiciary by providing it with a powerful autonomous role in democracy.

These prosecutions also provide a form of delegitimating myth to stifle support for existing and future uncivil movements. Public disclosures of the military regime's atrocities inform new generations of voters about the military's role in the Dirty War. While Generation X may look for iconoclast politicians, they may hesitate to support those who commit arbitrary assassinations, like throwing drugged men, women, and children from planes and stealing children from their families. This is hardly the kind of "heroism" the Carapintada hoped to claim from the Dirty War. The democratic government (and media) can reduce the appeal of the movement by providing information that challenges the image the movement hopes to promote.

4 The Brazilian Rural
Democratic Union

On 22 December 1988 Francisco (Chico) Mendes was murdered. Chico Mendes was a Brazilian rubber tapper in the Amazonian state of Acre. His background was like most rubber tappers': he was poor, lacked formal education, had lived most of his life deep in the Brazilian rain forest. But unlike most rubber tappers, Chico Mendes achieved international acclaim. He had led rubber tappers to link arms in front of bulldozers to prevent clear-cutting of the forest. Driven first by defense of rubber tappers' livelihood—without rubber trees, they could not tap for latex—Chico Mendes's objective paralleled international concerns over the destruction of the rain forest. Mendes thus became a spokesperson for the international environmental movement. He won the United Nations' Global 500 award for his defense of the environment. He became a witness in international hearings on the Brazilian rain forest. As a result of his testimony, the World Bank and the Inter-American Development Bank made funding to Brazil contingent upon environmental protections.[1]

His assassination provoked outrage, but not surprise. For years Chico Mendes had been receiving death threats from landholders. He had bodyguards who accompanied him constantly. He was killed stepping out his back door, on the way to his shower, with two armed bodyguards in his house just a few feet away from him.

His murderer was Darci Alves, the son of an Acre landholder. Darci turned himself in to the police. He and his father, Darli Alves, were arrested, investigated, prosecuted, and imprisoned. This made Brazilian history, since despite high levels of landholder violence against rural workers, not one landlord had ever faced prosecution. It was only when pressure from powerful foreign governments, nongovernmental organizations, and citizens came to bear that rural justice was won. And even in this case the culprits escaped from prison, once international attention had subsided.

This event catapulted the UDR (Rural Democratic Union) onto the international political stage. The UDR had already captured domestic attention since its formation in 1985. Formed by a group of wealthy ranchers, the UDR was widely viewed in Brazil as the modern reincarnation of the rural *coroneis,* or colonels. These historic figures, popularized in Jorge Amado novels and soap-opera adaptations,[2] maintained absolute power in their rural domains by using violence against enemies and traitors, lavishing financial rewards on loyal local authorities, and exploiting and intimidating rural workers to keep them in line. The UDR differed from these archetypical rural landlords in breaking out of the constraints of local politics. Its members hoped to shape national politics. And Chico Mendes's efforts on the international level threatened to reduce their power. He was therefore an obvious target.

Progressive rural and political organizations and the media condemned the UDR for its involvement in the Chico Mendes murder. The UDR's response was characteristically equivocal. At first the president of the UDR branch in Acre acknowledged Alves's involvement. He considered Alves a "pinned bull" because of his history of violence.[3] The UDR's national president, Ronaldo Caiado, recognizing the potentially grave repercussions for the UDR, appeared to accept the blame and promised to expel from the movement any members officially involved in violence. "We must demonstrate to society that violence is not part of the UDR program," he said.[4] But denials soon followed. The UDR-Acre president retracted earlier statements and denied that Alves was a member of UDR. He created an image of Alves as a recluse who had isolated himself on his ranch and together with his multitude of children formed a Protestant sect [interview 61]. Some UDR supporters argued that the three generations of violence in his family provided evidence that Alves had acted alone. Others suggested that Alves's son had acted alone, without his father's knowledge, or any understanding of Chico Mendes's fame. He acted with a myopic vision of improving the situation for his family. Some landholders argued that the UDR would not have been involved, since landholders trusted Mendes and did not want to lose him. Or they claimed that fear of stigma would have prevented landholders from murdering him: "Darli didn't do any good for us. We don't want this type of person in our movement. But there are these types of people in every segment of society: journalists always have one of their own harm them" [interview 16].

Some government bureaucrats also questioned whether the UDR had played a role in the murder. The UDR-Acre is viewed by these leaders as extremely weak. As one government bureaucrat put it, "If it was the UDR [behind the murder], it was the only act that the organization committed. Nothing was ever proven, and it was their only public act. They really didn't have much action here. I really doubt they were behind it" [interview 80].

Rural progressive groups also disagreed over the level of UDR involvement. According to one of the foremost religious figures of Acre, an active defender of rural movements, "The UDR was never strong. They had everything in their hands. They didn't need to use violence. The issue with Chico Mendes was personal anger. Chico had reacted, and Darli wasn't used to opposition" [interview 60]. One of the key organizers for Acre's progressive Catholic Church's Pastoral Land Commission argued, however, that the UDR had to be involved: "The task of murdering Chico Mendes fell into the hands of Darli. It was convenient. There was already a link between Darci and Chico. And Darli had a criminal past. Using Darli was a way to save the skin of the others. He wouldn't sell them down the river like *pistoleiros* [hired guns]. Using Darli was very well thought out" [anonymous]. In my interview with her, Mendes's widow also blames a movement of landholders for the murder. She claims that the assassination was a victory not only for the Alves family but for all the others who were behind the murder. The victory consisted not only in Mendes's death but also in the legal immunity the murders and co-conspirators enjoyed and the destruction of the rubber tappers' union. The union movement lost its leadership and purpose [Ilzamar Gadelha Mendes, 19 November 1995].

The whole story behind the Chico Mendes murder will probably never be known, a fact that lends it beautifully to conspiracy theories on both sides of the political divide. Practically speaking, the case is closed. It ended with the imprisonment and later escape by a landlord and his son. While the father was returned to prison, his son, the confessed murderer, remains at large. In most people's minds the case is over, even if unresolved. Leaving cases of rural violence like this one open to interpretation allows facts to be rewritten, different tales to be told. And an uncivil movement like the UDR benefits from this ambiguity.

The UDR's Political Success

Landholders are, and have historically been, a powerful group in Brazil, especially when compared with the rural poor and working class. Landholders have repeatedly resisted any change to the inegalitarian land-tenure system in Brazil that they benefit from and that is widely touted as a central source of poverty in the country. The United Nations' FIDA (International Fund for Agricultural Development), for example, reported in 1994 that 28.8 million rural Brazilians, 73 percent of the rural population, live below the poverty line. FIDA found that eighty-five of every one thousand children born in rural areas die before reaching five years of age. And 88 percent of the land belongs to the richest 20 percent of the population, with the poorest 40 percent holding only 1 percent of the land. The report concludes that "Brazil is the Latin American country with the greatest number of poor in rural areas." FIDA found the source of the problem in economic and institutional policies that exclude the rural poor, and in policies that ignore the productive potential of small producers. Other statistics-gathering institutions placed 73 percent of Brazil's rural population below the poverty line. Table 4.1 provides additional information to demonstrate the relative economic power of Brazilian landholders.

The inegalitarian land-tenure system in Brazil prompted the emergence of rural social movements. The progressive wing of the Catholic Church founded its Pastoral Land Commission (CPT). Left-wing parties and politicians helped form the Landless Peasant Movement (MST). And these movements shared the goals of raising public and government awareness of the relationship between land-tenure patterns and poverty, organizing unemployed and underemployed rural workers to fight for reform, and stimulating land invasions to carry out land distribution.[5] The government partially heeded their call by initiating some agrarian reform programs. To combat these reforms, UDR mobilized. And it proved extremely successful.

The UDR's first victory was over the National Plan for Agrarian Reform (PNRA). The PNRA was introduced at the end of the military regime by Tancredo Neves. Neves, the head of the official opposition party—the Brazilian Democratic Movement (MDB), later Party of the Brazilian Democratic Movement (PMDB)—to the military regime, defeated the military regime's candidate in the 1985 presidential elections. One of his campaign promises was agrarian reform. Neves died before he could take office, however, leaving his vice president, José Sarney, in charge of the challenging democratic transition. Sarney had been the president of the military regime's own political party, the National Alliance for Renewal (ARENA), and broke with the military regime only after the transition from authoritarian rule. Even then he was the head of a conservative political party that allied with the

TABLE 4.1   Land Distribution in Brazil

Size of Property	Number of Properties	Total Number (%)	Total Area (hectares)	Total Area (%)
Less than 10 ha.				
1970	2,519,630	51.2	9,083,495	3.1
1980	2,598,019	50.4	9,004,259	2.5
1985	3,085,841	52.9	10,029,780	2.6
Between 10 and 100 ha.				
1970	1,934,392	39.3	60,069,704	20.4
1980	2,016,774	39.1	64,494,343	17.7
1985	2,166,424	37.1	69,678,938	18.5
Between 100 and 1,000 ha.				
1970	414,746	8.4	108,742,676	37.0
1980	488,521	9.5	126,799,188	34.8
1985	518,618	8.9	131,893,557	35.1
Between 1,000 and 10,000 ha.				
1970	35,425	0.7	80,059,162	27.2
1980	45,496	0.9	104,548,849	28.7
1985	47,931	0.8	108,397,132	28.8
Over 10,000 ha.				
1970	1,449	0.02	36,190,429	12.3
1980	2,345	0.04	60,007,780	16.4
1985	2,174	0.04	56,287,168	15.0

Sources: IBGE, Censo agropecuario, 1980 (Brazil: IBGE, 1985), and IBGE, Anuário estatístico, 1986 (Brazil: IBGE, 1987); reprinted in Biorn Maybury-Lewis, "The Debate over Agrarian Reform in Brazil," Columbia University, Institute of Latin American and Iberian Studies, Papers on Latin America #14, 1990, 2–3.

official opposition party to create a broad democratic coalition for the 1985 elections.

Despite his solid conservative credentials, Sarney began carrying out Neves's campaign promises, including agrarian reform. Sarney announced the PNRA in May 1985. The plan called for the distribution of both state and privately owned lands to ameliorate the problems of rural poverty. But, as demonstrated in table 4.2, by the time the PNRA was put into law, it bore little resemblance to the original program. Landholders organized to protest the PNRA, and, fearing an uprising, the Sarney government took the teeth out of the program.

In addition to emasculating the PNRA, the UDR also influenced the appointment of public officials in agriculture. Landholders noted that Brazil's

TABLE 4.2   Agrarian Reform Programs in Brazil

Program	Dates	Description	Total Area (hectares)	Number of Families (thousands)
Goulart reform	1960–63	Land next to highways and railways		
Land statute/ military regime	1964–85	Rural enterprises; colonization; agrarian reform		
PNRA proposal/ Sarney plan	May 1985	Expropriation/ redistribution of state and nonproductive private lands	372 million by the year 2000	710 by the year 2000
PNRA I law/ Sarney plan	October 1985	See above	16.3 million by 1989	140 by 1989
PNRA II law/ Sarney plan	1986	See above	1,746	45.3
Collor plan	1992	See above	6 million	118
Cardoso plan	1997	See above	4.9 million	287 (1995–98)

Sources: Americas Watch, *The Struggle for Land in Brazil: Rural Violence Continues* (New York: Human Rights Watch, May 1992), 19–21; *Agencia Folha* 22.12.97; 21h12 de Brasília; *Agencia Folha* 21.12.98; 18h34 de Brasília.

recent democratic governments had favored the UDR in the Ministry of Agriculture and rural social movements in the agrarian reform agencies, MIRAD (Ministry of Agrarian Reform and Development) and INCRA (Institute for Colonization and Agrarian Reform). But there is no consistent pattern. The UDR did win a powerful representative in the ministry under President Fernando Collor de Mello.[6] Nevertheless, it has also won representation in INCRA under President Fernando Henrique Cardoso.[7] His INCRA appointment went to Brasílio de Araujo Neto, a large landholder well entrenched in the Rural Society of the State of Paraná and allegedly tied to the UDR.[8] Both the government and the UDR deny any direct pressure over appointments and resignations; nonetheless, the UDR won significant representation in government agencies tied to agriculture and agrarian reform.

UDR leaders also won elected positions in local, state, and national government. The tremendous support shown in the 1990 legislative elections for Ronaldo Caiado, the charismatic president of the UDR, was only the most obvious sign of the group's electoral power. In addition, a number of UDR leaders and UDR sympathizers took office as governors during the 1985–95 era. One of the most colorful of these figures is the governor who ran on the campaign of providing a "chainsaw for every home" to clear the rain forest. UDR leaders and sympathizers also cut their teeth on local politics, taking positions as mayors.

In the legislature, the UDR also played a significant role. Its heavy lobbying made it a formidable source of pressure. News articles highlighted the role the "Agro-boys"—a term intended to link them to the right-wing orthodox economics of the "Chicago-boys"—played in their aggressive lobbying in the Constituent Assembly. These articles accused the UDR of violence and intimidation in their lobbying tactics. But the UDR was not investigated for its aggression; instead the Regional Electoral Tribunal investigated the movement for engaging in political campaigns and assuming the role of a political party without having registered as one.[9] The head of MIRAD also criticized the movement for undermining political parties and eroding democratic stability.[10] The concern arose because of the UDR's tremendous power. To win support within the National Constituent Assembly (ANC), the body charged with drafting the new constitution after the transition from authoritarian rule, the UDR mobilized on the grassroots level to elect members. It published posters defaming its enemies and encouraging the electorate to vote for its friends. Those friends included legislators who had supported the free-enterprise system and the protection of private property. By appearing on the poster, these friends could count on receiving free publicity and electoral support from UDR members, as well as substantial financial contributions. The enemies feared violent retribution. By electing new representatives to the Constituent Assembly and lobbying existing members of the ANC, the UDR claimed to have secured 290 representatives (out of 559) dedicated to defending private property from agrarian reform.[11]

This bloc comprised the Centrão, or broad center, a conservative "free-enterprise" block within the Constituent Assembly. As one UDR leader described it, "The Centrão was the great creation of the UDR. It was our salvation in the Constituent Assembly" [interview 26]. A particular faction within the Centrão specifically defended rural property and became known as the *bancada ruralista* (ruralists' bloc), or the Parliamentary Front for Agriculture (FPA). By the mid-1990s the *bancada ruralista* possessed close to a simple majority in Congress (140 solid votes—with 40 more it would have a majority). It has used its power, and some say guerrilla tactics, to win some concessions on agricultural policy, particularly rural credit. Caiado claims credit for forming the front. In his words, "The *bancada ruralista* was created by me between 1990 and 1994. I proposed the idea, when I was in the legislature, of creating a superparty organization—without any link to parties— to support farming and ranching. We achieved some victories. We stood our ground" [Caiado, 17 August 1995]. In this statement Caiado clearly understates the power of the Centrão and the FPA. Journalists and pundits alike believed that these lobbies possessed more power than the political parties in the country did.

But certainly the UDR's greatest victory was its defeat of the agrarian reform amendment to the 1988 constitution. All of the preliminary drafts of the constitution included agrarian reform. Opinion polls suggested that both the broad public and the Constituent Assembly favored reform. But the UDR overturned this strong support and limited the amendment to expropriation of idle property, property that does not fulfill a "social function." The UDR recognized its victory but remained mobilized to determine how this "social function" would be defined in ordinary law. That law was established in 1993 and further protected UDR landholders' interests.[12] With the virtual defeat of the agrarian reform, the UDR removed some of the legitimacy and legality of rural social movements' efforts to ameliorate the skewed land-tenure situation in the country, rural poverty, and the weak electoral base of rural workers.

UDR pressure around agrarian reform came through its populist-style mobilizations. It blocked traffic in Brasília in 1987 with trucks and farm machinery to protest the agrarian reform legislation. The press called this the largest protest rally since Brasília's creation in the 1960s. The police put the numbers at fifteen thousand, but the UDR estimated twenty to twenty-five thousand. Simultaneous eruptions occurred locally throughout the country.[13] UDR members also camped out, filled the congressional halls, and joined massive rallies in Brasília during the key votes in the Constituent Assembly. One of these rallies in July 1987 was estimated at forty thousand. The UDR thus beat its own record for mobilizing the largest rally in Brasília's history.[14]

The UDR supported these "lobbying" efforts through its famous cattle auctions. Local UDR branches sometimes auctioned off as many as six thousand head of cattle, with some members buying cattle and then redonating them to the auction on the spot. These auctions not only generated substantial funds used to avoid charging dues and to support the aggressive and populist lobby that allowed the movement to bring trucks, tractors, and other farm machinery to block the streets in Brasília. They also catalyzed solidarity among landholders and demonstrated that the movement was not beholden to the government.

The judiciary provided further evidence of the UDR's ability to weaken or control democratic institutions. As table 4.3 illustrates, Chico Mendes was not the only victim of rural violence in the 1980s. Murders of environmentalists, leaders of rural worker and landless peasant movements, and their supporters in the progressive Catholic Church and legal community proliferated in rural Brazil during that era. The UDR got away with murder. To date, and despite the escalating levels of rural violence, not one landholder has served a sentence for rural violence. Indeed, landholders are rarely investigated or prosecuted. The judiciary has done very little to limit the role and power of landholders in rural violence. This has led students of the Brazilian judiciary and its relationship to land conflict to conclude that "the judiciary has consistently favored the land owners."[15]

Much of the literature on human rights in Brazil assumes that landholders' economic and political power protects them from investigation and prosecution. Not unlike a "privileged-position" argument,[16] these approaches assume that because the members of the UDR share the same socioeconomic background and values with lawyers and judges, they therefore receive more favorable treatment. One leader within the MST succinctly summarized this view by stating that landholders "have control over the judiciary

TABLE 4.3   Rural Violence in Brazil

Year	Number Killed	Increase (%)
1983	17	—
1984	100	488
1985	125	25
1986	105	−16
1987	109	4
1988	93	−15
1989	56	−40
1990	75	34
1991	49	−35
1992	46	−6
1993	52	13
1994	47	−10
1995	41	−13
1996	54	32

Sources: Comissão Pastoral da Terra (CPT), "Conflitos no campo: Brasil 97" (Brazil: Gráfica e Editora Pe. Berthier, 1998), 15; CPT, "Rompendo o cerco e a cerca: Conflitos no campo 1989" (Goiânia, GO: Comissão Pastoral da Terra, 1990), 28.

because they are the only ones, along with the business class, who are able to send their kids to the kinds of schools that get you judgeships" [anonymous].

This social class argument is undoubtedly crucial to understanding the power of landholders in the judiciary. But their immunity is further reinforced by the inadequate system of investigation and prosecution. The first stage of this process rests with the police who are charged with the duty of investigating crimes. There are a number of problems at this stage that tend to prejudice investigation in favor of landholders. Police in Brazil are notoriously overworked, undertrained, and underpaid. They have many more cases than they can possibly handle. And even if they had the time, they often lack the skills to conduct the kind of investigation necessary for determining guilt or innocence. In addition, studies of Brazilian police operations have documented their bias in investigations. If the police consider the individual involved in a crime to be a "marginal," they are less likely to pursue a rigorous investigation that might determine the individual's innocence. Instead, they only provide evidence of the individual's guilt. Cases abound in which police have worked for landholders. This service provides them with the extra income they need to support their families. And many cases suggest that such arrangements often involve police violence against peasants. In sum, it is very difficult to get a fair investigation from the police, especially in remote rural areas. As Jorge Amado describes landholders' immunity, "Any of today's living might tomorrow be lying dead in the street, a bullet-hole in his chest. For over and above the court of justice, the judge, the prosecutor, and the citizen jury was the law of the trigger, which in Ilhéus was the court of final appeal."[17]

A few illustrations from actual cases support these arguments. The individual charged as the hired gun for a UDR leader in the murder of a rural labor union leader, Expedito de Souza, had this to say about the case against him: "The whole thing was bought. The detective knows what he did. They had to get somebody, and they got me, not the person who did it. . . . And the delegate [from the police] won an award for this case. . . . Put electric shocks to me to get a confession . . . and got rewarded" [interview 88].[18]

The following description by the head of the police in the Pontal de Paranapanema hints at the cozy relationship between the police and landholders:

Our wages have always been low. But today we're not doing so badly. Some get five minimum wages [i.e., five times the minimum wage]— $500 a month. But there are some people who can live with $500 and others who need $5,000. So they do double time. Our commander said it was possible to supplement our wages with extra work. So they work as drivers. They always have guaranteed work because everyone would rather have a trained policeman working for them than a guy off the street. Now our wages satisfy our basic needs. But as long as it doesn't interfere with your work, you're entitled to take another job. I've had only two cases where this has been a problem. They were working as tractor drivers at dawn in Rancharia. They were kidnapped, with their uniforms and their guns. [interview 63]

It is possible that these off-duty police were driving tractors at dawn. Given that they were in uniform and armed, however, it is more likely that they were guarding the ranch against invasion.

The rural murders in 1995 in Rondônia also suggest that landholders have benefited from police protection. In that case landholders' hired help had apparently dressed in police uniforms and bolstered the police force to carry out a raid on a settlement in the middle of the night. An unknown number of settlers died in the raid, including small children. The involvement of the police on the side of landholders in conflicts brings their neutrality into question. Consider, for example, the comment by this MST leader:

[Landowners] don't really have much need for hired guns any more because they are protected by the state. The military police are their hired guns. They have institutional protection. There are a lot of confrontations, and often the landholders are the people who direct the military police in these confrontations. There can be as many as four hundred soldiers within a ranch. So the landholders don't need to form their own militias. [anonymous]

Problems with rural justice do not end with these questionable practices. After the police conduct their investigations, they send their reports to the prosecutor. The prosecutor then determines which of the cases she or he will try. The prosecutor has the power to, and frequently does, shelve the case. This means either that the case is never tried or that it is delayed so long that no credible witnesses or other forms of evidence can be presented. The prosecutor shelves the case because she or he has too many cases to try all of them, the police reports are too weak to go forward with a case, the prosecutor has some personal bias toward the defendant, or any combination of these factors.[19] Thus, in addition to bias, structural constraints keep prosecutors from convicting murderous landholders.

One example of these kinds of constraints in the judicial system is the murder of a Maranhão priest, Padre Josimo Morais Tavares, in 1985, one of the first cases in which the UDR was implicated. Nearly fifteen years later the case has not progressed. After such a long time, the possibility of gathering witnesses with any credible memory of the case is slim. The case has been shelved.

A further complication in investigating and prosecuting landholders is that they generally do not carry out these crimes themselves. A system of hired guns protects them. They do not commit the murders; they do not usually even know who pulled the trigger, since they use intermediaries to hire the assassin. The assassin also does not know who contracted him to kill the victim or why. Indeed, several landholders may be behind a murder. The murder can be traced to the hired gun, but usually no further. This system makes it particularly difficult to implicate an organization like the UDR in rural violence. As one CPT leader stated, "It is difficult to link these crimes to the UDR. The UDR is a corporate entity [*pessoa jurídica*], not a person [*pessoa física*]. . . . I've seen the statutes of the UDR. There is nothing in them saying that they are going to kill people. It is a class organ; it is not the same as a death squad. But they have the same philosophy as a death squad" [anonymous].

The delays in any case within the judicial system in Brazil give ample time for powerful individuals, even the hired guns who understand the system, to flee from the law or manipulate evidence. Landholders, who can meet bail or convince the judge that their economic responsibilities will keep them from fleeing, are not among the individuals who sit in Brazilian jails for years waiting for their trials to begin. This was clearly the case in the murder of Pará rural labor organizer Expedito Ribeiro de Souza in 1991. The landholder accused of murder posted bail and subsequently "disappeared," never to stand trial.

The prison system also allows individuals to avoid their punishment. In numerous cases documented by human rights organizations, individuals have "escaped" from prison. This sometimes appears to involve little more than walking out the gate. Thus, even in the rare cases in which individuals are convicted of rural crimes, they generally do not serve time. In the Chico Mendes murder, the guilty landholders "escaped" from prison. The international outcry, instrumental in imprisoning them, was barely a murmur when they escaped. One prison guard commented on the prison's security system in this way: "The only people who stay in this prison are the ones who want to."[20]

This evidence about the UDR's power over the executive, the legislature, and the judiciary does not imply that the UDR hoped to assume authoritarian control over the democratic state. On the contrary, the UDR had no reason to pursue such action. It found democratic institutions extremely malleable in promoting its agenda. The UDR promoted itself as democratic by forming a democratic lobby and pressuring for change within the democratic system. Simultaneously, the movement's power enabled it to elect and influence legislators and government decisions. Rather than directly controlling the government, the UDR used democratic institutions to control political outcomes. Its members defeated proposals to distribute land. They avoided prosecution for involvement in violence. And they assumed a democratic veneer to hide their uncivil actions. In short, while institutional mechanisms no doubt played a role in preventing coup conspiracies from developing, these institutions failed to insulate themselves from a powerful uncivil movement.

Even UDR leaders admit that they beat the system. An attorney who had successfully defended landholders from government expropriation of their land attested that "the judicial system is becoming more in favor of the landholder" [interview 78]. One landholder praised the judicial system for recognizing the danger of an invasion of his land and effectively ending it: "I had the beginning of an invasion on my land, and I immediately had the justice system put a stop to it. I didn't have to shoot anyone. There was respect through the justice system" [interview 10].

The growing power of landholders in Brazil has had grave consequences for the development of a democratic political culture. After twenty-one years of authoritarian rule, Brazilian civil society had great expectations for the democratic transition. Principally, however, the democratic opposition to authoritarian rule hoped for two types of protections: protection from violence and protection from poverty. These were the democratic values for which those in the democratic opposition had risked their lives confronting the authoritarian regime.[21]

The UDR symbolized for the democratic opposition the main obstacles to bringing about transformations in the structure of violence and poverty. The UDR proved capable of penetrating democratic institutions and controlling their decisions. Members of the UDR used rural violence with impunity against those who promoted land distribution. The democratic government seemed, simply, to look the other way except in high-profile cases, like the Chico Mendes murder. Even then the government's resolve to punish the murderers diminished with the lack of international and domestic attention to the case. And by taking the teeth out of the agrarian reform proposal, the UDR succeeded in eliminating one crucial way of resolving problems of rural and urban property, skewed land distribution patterns, food production, and employment. The MST sees the UDR's success as having limited any possibility for the country to move forward in distributing land and power: "The UDR was formed for three different reasons: the PNRA, the constitution, and the progressive block in Congress. It wanted to avoid any advances in the constitution. It succeeded. The law that it passed was very backward—more backward than the military regime's land statute" [anonymous]. Discontent with the new democratic government's incapacity or unwillingness to end rural violence has led Human Rights Watch to consider new definitions of human rights violations. Human rights violators can include not only governments that perpetrate the violence but also governments that fail to properly investigate and prosecute criminal cases [Cavallaro, 30 November 1995].

The progressive Catholic Church and the CPT continue to press for land distribution and contend that they have the pope's support in this endeavor. As one of the top religious leaders for Acre states, "In this specific topic of land, the pope is very sensitive. He always supports us when he talks, when he comes here, when I go there. He thinks that without agrarian reform Brazil will not be democratic" [anonymous].

The MST has continued its land invasions to bring pressure against the democratic governments' intransigence on agrarian reform. The MST sees these invasions as acts of civil disobedience, the only means of bringing more democracy to the country. One of the squatters on a land settlement described the process as the only chance of ending the cycle of political and economic inequality in Brazil:

> People in my family, in the city, say, "How can you do that? How can you take land? People have rights to their land." To the religious people I say this: "Do you think God made the land for only a few, or for everyone?" And they say, "For everyone." And then I say, "Then why is so much land in the hands of a few and we have nothing?" And they say, "Well, they worked harder." And I say, "Did they really work that much harder to have that much land?" [interview 49]

Another leader in the same settlement described the invasions as a political strategy to keep the government aware of the need for agrarian reform [interview 84]. To bring about change in such an intransigent political climate sometimes requires breaking the law, as the following comment by an MST national coordinator attests:

> The claim that the UDR makes about the legality of its defense of private property and the illegality of our land occupations is technically correct. But we make a distinction between legal and legitimate. Not everything that is legal is legitimate. We believe that what we do is legitimate given the inequality. The struggle is illegal but legitimate. Land must be expropriated. Property is not sacred. It has to be productive. [anonymous]

In sum, the UDR overcame its social movement and state adversaries to gain substantial political ground during the democratic transition of the 1980s and 1990s. How it succeeded in this polarized and fragile political moment depended on its political framing, cultural cues, and movement myths.

POLITICAL FRAMING

The UDR had an easy task mobilizing landholders behind an identifiable threat. It named the threat as the expropriation of private property. And it blamed that threat on the left-wing and rural social movements sponsoring land invasions, the new democratic governments engaged in land reform programs, and even state reformers. But many of the threats to private property had begun before the transition from authoritarian rule, when rural social movements mobilized as part of the opposition to the military regime. Even the military regime itself had initiated an agrarian reform program, and individual state governments implemented agrarian reforms under the dictatorship. São Paulo's governor, Franco Montoro, for example, declared land in the western region of Pontal de Paranapanema *terra devoluta,* or land belonging to the state, and eligible for expropriation and redistribution. Montoro argued that the land titles for ranches in that particular area were invalid.[22] Landholders claimed that they had bought their land and possessed legal titles. The state countered that only the state had the right to sell the land. Those who claimed ownership either had bought the land under false pretexts or had falsified documents.[23] Landholders, unwilling to forgo their claims to the land, argued that under Brazilian "squatters'" law they possess legal rights to the land if they have used it for ten years. While this is generally true, the squatters' law does not protect *terra devoluta.* Landholders in the Pontal de Paranapanema therefore began mobilizing even before the end of the military regime to combat government expropriation of "their" land. These landholders in western São Paulo State eventually joined the Goiás group in founding the UDR in 1985. This initial group of affected landholders began a publicity campaign that spread throughout the country warning of imminent threats to other landholders as a result of national and local reforms and social movement mobilization:

> We began to mobilize because we were worried about the changes in the constitution. The class of rural producers was totally uninformed. We needed to have the right to own property guaranteed in law. There had been various invasions in 1985, like today. These created the moment to make rural producers aware of the dangers of expropriation of productive lands. There had been various expropriations of productive lands that shouldn't have taken place. These were fertile, productive lands in São Paulo and in northern Paraná. There were also areas of expropriations in the Pontal, where INCRA had even given out prizes. These expropriations increased awareness. We began to meet. We organized. We set out to change the law. Our objective was to make people aware of the problem. This was difficult because people were self-sufficient, uninformed, and without any collective consciousness. Eventually we struggled together for representation in the Constituent Assembly. [interview 75]

But the UDR's primary task was to make the threat credible even to those landholders who would not be affected by the reforms. All landholders, even those who owned only small plots of land, had to believe that the threat would eventually affect them. It was only in this way that UDR leaders could transform the movement from a radical group of a few large landholders protecting their power and privilege into a national movement of landholders combating a threat to the nation. They did this by framing the movement as the fortress against a universal threat to the private-property system upon which the nation was founded. They emphasized the urgent need to act at that particular political juncture. And they claimed to possess the moral authority and organizational capacity to defeat this threat to the nation.

The UDR used personal testimonies as part of its framing process to foster a sense of insecurity among landholders. Plínio Junqueira, a property owner in the Pontal de Paranapanema, generated the first of these stories. He had lost part of his land during Montoro's agrarian reform program. Junqueira became a founding member and entrepreneurial leader of the UDR. Indeed, the UDR became his personal crusade. Armed with slides of his property taken before and after expropriation and with the awards he had won for the improvements he had made on his land, he left his home and family to travel around the country, mainly at his own expense, to mobilize a passive and isolated rural elite behind a protest movement.

Junqueira's story resonated with landholders. It played on their insecurities about a lack of government protection from land invasions and agrarian reform. The story contended that Junqueira's land should have been protected from expropriation. After all, he had legal title and had not left the land idle. Indeed, he had even won awards for his ranching achievements. If the government could expropriate Junqueira's property, what would stop it from expropriating all private land? Only by organizing could landholders protect themselves.

Junqueira's story mobilized landholders who anticipated or had already faced expropriation and those who ideologically opposed any agrarian reform. But the injustice mined from Junqueira's experience stimulated mobilization even among landholders who had not feared agrarian reform. Some of them saw themselves in Junqueira; they had legal title and used their land productively, not for speculation. Others interpreted Junqueira's story as a warning against believing that even if they had only a small plot of land, they might face expropriation. Impelled to action by Junqueira's story, various regional entities formed their own UDR and became part of a national UDR headquartered in Brasília in 1986.

The UDR did not blame specific state-level reforms or even the PNRA for expropriation. Instead it viewed these policies as emblematic of the democratic government's leftist tendencies. The policy changes merely set the stage for the total eradication of the private-property system that would become fully embodied in the constitution. Thus, preparing for the Constituent Assembly became a crucial goal for the UDR, not only in battling each individual threat to private property but also in getting representatives elected to office to defend the private-property system and to combat the left in the legislature, in the streets, and in rural communities. The UDR argued that landholders could no longer assume that their property had protection under titles or the law, because the expropriation-oriented government, out to undermine the rural elite sector, would seize any land.

The UDR pointed to the impressive gains the left had made in electoral politics with the end of the military regime. The legislative elections of 1986 had provided them with a progressive bloc in Congress. And a number of these progressive legislators had cut their political teeth in the CPT and MST. The coincidence of left-wing electoral victories and government agrarian reform programs allowed the UDR to spin conspiracy theories about the attack on the private-property system: "In 1985 there was expropriation terrorism in the country and land invasions. The UDR was born to defend liberty, the right to property, [and] free enterprise, and to counter terrorism" [interview 43].

The UDR even accused conservative President Sarney of adopting "radical," "ultraradical," and "socialist" agrarian reform programs to cater to the left:

> The Sarney government was putting forward a socialist radical agrarian reform. And there were other radical programs as well. So this [the formation of the UDR] was a reaction against it—the first and only reaction against it in the country. [interview 12]

> Everyone was concerned about Sarney's first agrarian reform law. It was ultraradical. It was absurd. Russia didn't even have anything like this. It was absurd for a democratic country. [interview 19]

> The main reason I founded UDR was to defend my land. And to defend a principle, the principle of private property—a democratic principle. In 1920 we had a communist government in Brazil. The left had always existed. In 1988 both the left and the democrats were in power. That's when things began. . . . I never faced a direct threat. But I was sure I could be expropriated and I would lose my property. . . . I believe in the absolute right of property. We have to get rid of the communist trash in Brazil. [interview 47]

The UDR thus transformed the catalyst threat to a small group of privileged landholders into a threat to the nation's very foundation: the capitalist system, individual freedoms, and the right to private property. It even linked the threat to private property to the threat to democracy and rule by law. The message was simple. The totalitarian left had infiltrated the democratic government, the church, and rural movements. As a result, no private property was safe from government expropriation. Laws did not protect private property. Indeed, the constitution would enshrine the antidemocratic right to expropriate private property. The UDR sent out the message that landholders needed to act urgently and collectively before the left undermined the free-enterprise system and democratic rights.

By framing individual action as ineffective in the face of such a universal threat, the UDR catalyzed a movement. The UDR portrayed the threat in such a way that it drew in not only landholders directly affected by the PNRA or by government reforms and landholders with large idle tracts, but also landholders who would not ever be directly affected by the agrarian reforms. The UDR attracted landholders from different regions, different size farms, and different sectors of production. The movement appealed to landholders with different ideologies, educational backgrounds, and ages. It even resonated with small landholders who had little to fear from either the rural social movement or the government: "I did not personally feel threatened. I had 250 hectares. I didn't have any fear of expropriation. But if protection for property disappeared, then I would. And I also believed in defending the principle of property rights" [interview 18].

The UDR also had to argue that it was uniquely capable of defending landholders and Brazil from this universal threat. It did this through a two-part strategy. It had to show that it had a viable alternative to the left's (and the government's) agrarian reform program. And it had to convince landholders that it was the only entity that could implement this alternative. The UDR's discourse therefore advocated agrarian reform but rejected the "outmoded" leftist type of agrarian reform adopted by the government as undermining agricultural production in the country. The UDR's agrarian reform program, the group's leaders argued, would overcome the backward model proposed by the left and adopted by the government by making efficient use of technology and capital: "The attitude about land is often based more on passion than reason. Our left is stupid. They want more land. They don't think about capital and technology. Land doesn't have any power. It doesn't pay for anything. Production does. We need more production in the country" [interview 74].

Upon close examination, however, the UDR did not have an agrarian reform plan at all. It simply advocated, in the name of agrarian reform, protection for private property and favorable agricultural policies. The first principle of the UDR's agrarian reform project, for example, involved the inviolability of private property. The only land available for distribution under the UDR's plan was state-owned land. Over the objection of UDR extremists, the movement paid lip service to the social function of land. Its conception of that social function, however, included fallow land. The UDR contended that if landholders had plans to use land at a later date, it could not be deemed idle. The UDR, in other words, considered only land expressly held for speculation purposes as subject to expropriation on social grounds. Moreover, when the government expropriated land, the landholder would receive the fair market value of that land, paid in money, rather than bonds.

Only this type of "market-based" agrarian reform, the UDR claimed, would increase agricultural production, rural employment, and the supply of inexpensive agricultural products. UDR leaders referred to their reform as a "social project within a capitalist structure." Caiado offered this summary of the UDR's rejection of the left's agrarian reform program:

> The UDR wasn't created because of agrarian reform; it was created to defend private property. These are two different things. What we disputed was the right of private property. In 1988 the Berlin Wall had not yet come down. And here in Brazil, the left believed that communism was the best thing in the world, that statism was the best thing in the world. And so what they were trying to do in 1984 was undermine the right to private property. No one would own anything. Property belonged to everyone, as in the Soviet Union. A democratic country cannot accept an authoritarian state, especially one without respect for private property. Should private property fulfill a social function? Yes, it should. You can't hold on to rural property only for land values. It has to be used for the public good: feeding and employing people. But the agrarian reform law was formed more along ideological lines than with rationality. Many people hid behind it to win money or votes. It became good business in Brazil: selling heaven, paradise. It is the Chicago style: I'm Al Capone, and if you want to do business you have to pay me for protection. . . . What is the agrarian reform problem? There isn't a shortage of land. All of the ranches are for sale, because of the economic crisis. Only the government has land. The struggle has a solution. There isn't any shortage. The government just doesn't want to implement agrarian policy. [Caiado, 17 August 1995]

To convince landholders that it could and should defend them against the leftist agrarian reform plan, the UDR had to compete with the official entities set up within the political system to defend agrarian interests. During the 1930s and 1940s President Getúlio Vargas had formed official landholders' "unions." Each state had an official agricultural federation to represent landholders. At the national level, these federations were united in the National Confederation of Agriculture (CNA). Vargas designed this top-down corporatist model to vertically integrate sectors of society into the government apparatus, and to control conflict among those sectors and between them and the government. In addition to official channels, landholders had also formed "parallel" organizations. These parallel organizations were designed primarily to defend the interests of particular subsectors of agriculture. The rural societies, united in the powerful Brazilian Rural Society (SRB), formed to represent the coffee barons. Associations of cattle breeders, orange growers, rice growers, and other types of producers also organized specific campaigns for their sectors. Cooperatives also developed in the agroindustry area as a means of generating funds for agricultural investment.

The UDR characterized these entities as ineffective because they were developed by the state and dependent on it for resources, reducing their autonomy and combativeness. The UDR argued that such corporatist entities could not aggressively defend the interests of their constituents; they were simply too tied up with the government: "It is extremely hard to build class consciousness. It is a congenital debility. Our entities were born by a law imposed on us. They were not built out of necessity. They were created by the state, by the central public authority. This creates an important difference. They have to be born from the base. They need to be. The difference is how well you can get participation" [interview 16].

These official entities had resources provided to them from the obligatory dues paid by the landholders, but they lacked leadership. By the mid-1980s the leaders of the most powerful official entities had been in office for two decades. According to the UDR, these leaders had grown used to compliance with the military regime. They hoped to retain their positions of authority, and the power and privileges associated with them. They therefore accepted government decisions. They lacked the experience, the independence, the skills, and the political style to combat the government's agrarian reform. The UDR, in contrast, was the kind of confrontational entity that could defend landholders in their struggle with the state.

To promote its effectiveness, the UDR drew on parallels with the "new unionism" in Brazil, the opposition movement to the coopted union leadership structure that had thwarted labor reforms.[24] The UDR used the term *pelego*—a term generally employed to describe labor leaders controlled by the government—to refer to the leadership of the official entities.[25] It also employed other language typically associated with the opposition labor movement. One UDR leader I interviewed referred to the state federations as "reactionary"; another called them "fascistic" [interview 4]. Further echoing the new unionism movement, the UDR called for an authentic and combative leadership, responsive to the grassroots. Ronaldo Caiado and Altair Veloso, two of the founders of the movement, openly admitted that they had modeled the UDR on these leftist movements. The similarity was not lost on the media; they referred to Caiado as the "Lula on the right," associating him with the president of the metalworkers union who broke away from *pelego* control, formed the new union movement, headed the Workers' Party (PT), won a seat in Congress, and only narrowly lost his bid for the presidency against Collor. The media also referred to the UDR as the "CUT on the right," after the combative, authentic, independent, and grassroots-oriented labor confederation. The authenticity, combative style, and grass-roots orientation of this type of organization had a lot of appeal to land-holders, who viewed the official entities as "artificial" [interview 52] and "incompetent and nonfunctioning" [interview 79]. One UDR leader de-scribed the weakness of his own agricultural federation in this way:

> FARSUL [Federation of Agriculture of Rio Grande do Sul] was mainly an organization that represented cattle producers. But their power was slowly deteriorating. They were a traditional group involved in diplo-matic negotiations. But we needed a political movement that was stronger—not just pretty boys in top government positions [*gabinete de salto alto*]. We needed a strong movement. [The traditional entities] began to lose ground in the press and in society. They had political power. . . . Our great enemy was not the MST. It was these traditional producers—their envy, their easy-chair style, their tied hands. [inter-view 46]

The UDR did not limit itself to expressing mild frustration over lost po-tential; it indicted the leaders of the official entities for corruption. Taking landholders' money and performing no services in exchange formed part of those accusations. But so too did tendencies to accept bribes and payoffs. Consider, for example, this landlord's harsh appraisal of the official repre-sentative entities:

> This was all unreal. Until society reached a crisis, these organizations were umbilically tied to the government. The government gave them their financing through a mandatory tax. It was like a tap. Whenever the entities got too demanding, the government turned off the tap, and they wouldn't have their benefits. As a result, the entities were run by people who were preoccupied with resolving their own personal problems. It was anachronistic. Group after group, it was always the same. They liked the idea of running these entities. It gave them some importance. Oh, Dr. Joe Schmo [*Fulano*] is the head of this or that. They didn't feel in their skin the problems of the rural producer. . . . These are bureau-crats [*lideranza de gabinete*]; they don't relate to the farmer. There is so much nepotism in FEAG [Federation of Agriculture of Goiás]. The son

of the treasurer gets the position of secretary. They take trips abroad and never report back to us—not one comparative statistic, not one bit of information that we can learn from. In the UDR we were great about putting together statistics. We had men who had lots of international experience, who were educated, vigorous, not timid. We developed a cold and rational discourse. We were called aggressive, criticized for not playing by the rules. [interview 64]

The UDR also offered a product different from what the official entities offered. The UDR was organized, its leaders argued, not to defend the interests of a particular sector but rather to defend the interests of all owners of private property. Its value-added, in other words, was solidarity across diverse sectors to defend the free-enterprise system from a common threat: "The CNA, federations, SRB, and others are all concerned with agricultural policies. Only the UDR was concerned with property.... It is only the UDR that has the independence to do this work" [interview 90].

The UDR thus created an urgent need for itself. There was an obvious threat to private property. There was no other organization capable of representing landholders and defending them from this threat. And important decisions that affected private-property owners were about to be made. Participation in the UDR was the only means of addressing this serious situation.

In sum, the UDR's political framing process involved the four-part strategy of naming, blaming, aiming, and claiming. The UDR identified a universal threat—the challenge to private property and democratic rights—that extended beyond the support of the narrow group of landholders directly affected by proposed reforms. It blamed the left and its infiltration of the government, rural movements, and the church for the threat. It contended that the exclusion of the rural sector in the democratic process, the magnitude of the threat, and the ongoing political processes justified urgent collective political action to eliminate the threat. And it claimed to be the only movement capable of combating this threat.

CULTURAL CUES

As mentioned above, the cultural icon most closely linked to Brazilian landholders is the violent rural *coronel,* capable of raw brutality against any threats to his interests. Jorge Amado describes these *coroneis* as "indomitable, titanic men of unlimited courage, for whom life had no value. It was worth exactly the price of a swig of rum, sufficient to pay for the hired gunman who hid behind a guava or breadfruit tree, waiting for his designated victim to come into the sights of his repeating rifle."[26] Certain individual members of the UDR evoked the image of the *coroneis* to heighten fears of the movement. But the *coroneis* generally operated independently and only to protect their own individual interests. The UDR, in contrast, saw itself as a collective movement working to defend the nation against broad threats. It had to draw on other cultural icons of rural heroism to resonate with potential constituents.

An obvious set of predecessor movements were the landholder mobilizations that occurred during the government of President João Goulart (1961–64). They provided a stock of cultural heroes and villains and a repertoire of political action upon which the movement could build. Landholders argued that Goulart had stimulated land invasions by rural social movements. Among the most notable of these rural social movements were the Peasant Leagues led by Francisco Julião in the Northeast, but an estimated 2,181 leagues in twenty states had proliferated by the Goulart era.[27] Landholders viewed these rural social movements as inspired, if not directly orchestrated, by communists. Goulart had also designed an agrarian reform program that threatened to expropriate private land. Landholders reacted by organizing armed militias. These militias not only combated land invasions by the rural social movements, they also sent a message to the national government that landholders would not passively accept threats to their landownership. This political moment is captured in the following remarks:

> The mobilization of landholders to defend their land began in the 1960s. João Goulart made a decree that all of the land around the highways and railways would be expropriated. That is when armed militias of landholders began to form in Pará, Goiás, Minas Gerais. . . . That was the climate. . . . At the time, João Pinheiro Neto was the president of INDA, the predecessor to INCRA. He was from a traditional family in Minas, but he had some revolutionary ideas. He had proposed this idea to Goulart: to take over productive and unproductive lands. That is when the first groups of reaction began. They never had a name or became that important, because the military stepped in. [interview 81]

While unknown by name to most Brazilians, even landholders, these armed militias were legendary both as contemporary *coroneis* to their adversaries and as a "collective defense" against leftist subversion to their supporters. One UDR president admitted that the original impetus behind the UDR was the reorganization of armed militias to defend private land (Roosevelt

Roque dos Santos, 18 August 1992).[28] Just as in the 1960s, landholders began arming in "collective defense" against CPT and MST land occupations and against government expropriations of private land. *Gaucho* landholders, for example, formed the PURR (Pact of Rural Unity) in Rio Grande do Sul. The PURR president referred to the organization as an agile and capable communication network that permitted rapid relocation of men, arms, and ammunition to defend land. Groups like the Association of Ranchers of Alto Xingú (AFAX) and the Association of Rural Producers in Southern Pará also formed paramilitary-type groups to fight threats to private property [interview 66]. Landholders in the Center-West contracted a private security firm, called Solução (the Solution), to help them defend their land. The press linked murders of rural organizers and massacres of peasants to Solução.[29] One of the first groups to join the UDR grew out of the militia movement in Goiás.

The anti-Goulart and antileft mobilization by landlords in the 1960s culminated in their active support for the military coup that ousted Goulart. They helped install the military dictatorship (1964–85) that imposed "order" on the countryside with repression against rural organizers. According to *Brasil: Nunca mais,* rural organizers constituted a large proportion of the victims of the regime's human rights violations.[30] Thus, while landholders cannot be held solely responsible for the military coup, they played an instrumental role in extending support for it to the countryside.

But aside from eliminating rural "subversion," the military's attitude toward landholders remained ambiguous. The regime adopted a land statute (*estatuto de terra*) that many landholders considered extremely radical. One UDR leader I interviewed considered it "more communist than the Russian agrarian reform" [interview 77]. Despite these strong emotions, landholders did not mobilize against the land statute. One government official believed that landholders felt they had no recourse under the authoritarian state [interview 37]. But more commonly landholders remarked that the military regime's policy affected few private properties, compensated expropriation with a fair price, and complemented agrarian reform with extremely favorable agricultural policies. Indeed, most of the landholders considered the military regime exceptionally good for agriculture. Particularly under the most repressive president, General Emílio Médici (1969–74), landholders received incentives to colonize new lands, ample investment opportunities, cheap and plentiful credit, and good terms of trade for agricultural products. In short, landholders did not feel threatened by the military regime's agrarian reform: "The 1970s did harm some producers, but without a major trauma. It was more of a technical than a political reform. And there wasn't any organization by landholders" [interview 16].

Moreover, landholders cite positive outcomes of the military regime, particularly its protection of private property from rural social movements. Indeed, in interviews several UDR landholders hinted at the close cooperation between the military regime and landholders in finding and eliminating threats from rural leaders. And they contended that because the leftist threat had resurfaced in the 1980s, the close relationship between the UDR and the military continued. One UDR leader hinted that the military regime's intelligence apparatus (SNI) helped his movement target leaders of rural social movements: "I could go to the SNI and ask them for information on anyone I wanted, anyone I had to talk to. We had our channels within the military. We had links within the army in Brasília. But without any compromises. They supported what we were doing" [interview 18]. The UDR's close relationship with the military is further evidenced by its use of the Superior War College (ESG)—the military academy famous for training officers who participated in the coup conspiracy in 1964—to provide leadership training to UDR-Youth [interview 12]. And one of the professed ideologues behind the UDR told me that the military viewed the UDR as the "continuation of the 1964 Revolution" [interview 67].

Cuing up its movement with the 1964 coup allowed the UDR to construct an image of the contemporary left as a legacy of subversion. The UDR drew on fear of social disorder from the 1960s. It also cued itself up to the heroism of the coup plotters who risked their lives to save the nation from the villains on the left.

In its efforts to demonize the left, the UDR had to counter a widespread image of the left and rural workers as victims of oppression or exploitation, and portray them instead as criminals and subversives attempting to undermine democratic stability in the country. The UDR drew its "left as subversives" image from the CPT- and MST-inspired invasions. The UDR frequently condemned the left for acting outside the law. It called on the democratic government to end the lawlessness that threatened democratic stability. As one UDR leader stated, "The left is upsetting order in the country. Someone is going to die.... The MST and PT are going to destabilize the country" [interview 74]. But the UDR went even further: it claimed that the landless peasants were after not just land but control. UDR leaders frequently recited a version of the following litany: "The landless [sem terra] of today will be the houseless [sem casa], the carless [sem auto], and the BMW-less [sem BMW] of tomorrow" [interview 50]. This lawbreaking, in other words, had a more subversive intent, in their view. According to the UDR, the left in the 1980s, just like its predecessors in the 1960s, hoped to supplant democratic rule with a totalitarian project that would undermine capitalist democracy: "The CPT, the parties on the left . . . they are all very active and stimulate invasions. They aren't really oriented toward the problem called *sem terra* [landlessness]. They are instead oriented toward weakening the government. They invade land, and no one stays there. They just move on to invade more land" [interview 10].

The UDR further demonized the left by associating it with international conspiracies. One UDR leader, for example, claimed that "only communists support [the left], like Castro in Cuba, Russia" [interview 43]. Another claimed that communism had infiltrated the country so thoroughly that even the church was affected: "Priests . . . wore the crucifix on top of their robes and the hammer and sickle underneath" [interview 64]. In short, the UDR evoked familiar fears of a leftist revolution, fears instilled in Brazilians during the 1960s, by drawing parallels between the landless peasant movement and the threat of national and international conspiracies to implant a socialist revolution in Brazil.[31]

But the threat from the left, according to the UDR, was not only subversion reminiscent of earlier unstable moments. The left also threatened to undermine Brazil's development and economic progress. The UDR thus drew on a strong cultural pull: the goal of transforming Brazil into an economic superpower. The obsolete, inefficient agrarian reform proposed by the left and adopted by the democratic government undermined that goal. One UDR leader, for example, compared leftist agrarian reforms endorsed by the landless peasant movement with capitalist reforms endorsed by the UDR: "Agrarian reform has failed in China, Russia, Mexico, Portugal, Nicaragua, Chile. Where it has occurred democratically, in the United States, it has succeeded" [interview 43]. Another leader made broader claims about agrarian reform in general: "Agrarian reform has failed throughout the world. Russia imports food because communism finished off agriculture" [interview 27]. The collapse of the Soviet bloc further fueled UDR criticisms of the left's agrarian reform project: "The Berlin Wall came down, changing things. It showed that communism was incompetent. Cuba is still producing tobacco and sugar the same way it did during colonial times. Brazil produces what it does because of capitalism. . . . We don't talk about left and right anymore. I'm using an old language. Today we talk about competent and incompetent" [interview 74].

The UDR views the MST and CPT agrarian reform as stemming agricultural development by perpetuating the small-landholding system, ignoring the collective agriculture projects the MST had implemented on its settlements. The small farmer, the UDR claimed, is an antiquated notion that contradicts the left's professed goals. These small plots have negative consequences for rural production: fewer jobs, higher prices for agricultural products, and higher government expenditures in rural areas. Dividing up land into small plots would ultimately transfer to rural areas the urban problems of unemployment, poverty, and lack of social services. Two UDR presidents commented on the impoverishment associated with the dividing up of farms:

> In the United States there aren't family farms any more. Land is concentrated, and concentrated in the hands of those who produce.... [So what do they want to do here?] Take the shantytowns away from the seaside where the tourists have to see them and take malaria, tuberculosis, leprosy, to the countryside. Is this just? Is this agrarian reform? [Caiado, 17 August 1995]

> The [left's] idea is that expropriation will produce cheaper agricultural products. But of course the reality of the situation is that those who would occupy the land don't know how to farm. They don't have the information, the resources, or the education to do so. This is not a rational agricultural policy. It is one that responds to emotional needs and demands. [interview 4]

The UDR attributed the inefficiency of the left's agrarian program partly to its dependence on foreign supporters, particularly Germany, Belgium, and Holland, that do not understand Brazilian agriculture. Indeed, one radical UDR version depicts the Brazilian left as a dupe in a foreign conspiracy against Brazilian development. In this version, Germany especially but also the United States deliberately stimulated leftist land conflicts to keep Brazilian exports from competing with their own. Hence this comment: "The land conflict doesn't really exist. It is ideological. It is financed from abroad—from Germany" [interview 6]. This conspiracy theory is most developed on the environmental issue. UDR leaders complain that the United States, having already destroyed its own forests for the sake of progress, is now trying to prevent Brazil from developing its own frontier. As one landholder stated, "We also have the right to get rich" [interview 16].

The UDR built on the strong goal of national development that the military regime had also emphasized. The military regime's nationalist and patriotic discourse promoted an image of itself as capable of finding a pragmatic solution to national underdevelopment. Similarly, in the 1980s the UDR cast itself as the ultimate group of patriots, the only group willing to make sacrifices for the national good. The following remark is typical of the kinds of nationalistic images the UDR evoked to vilify the left and claim the moral high ground: "There was a division in the halls of the constitution with PT on one side and UDR on the other. PT had thrown the Brazilian flag on the floor. And Caiado joined hands with all of the UDR members there, and we began to sing the national anthem. That was an emotional moment. It showed the civic spirit of the UDR, the love for our country" [interview 28].

In a clever, although perhaps unconscious, twist, the UDR even attacked the left in language the left itself had used to attack the military regime. The UDR portrayed those on the left as coup-minded authoritarians nostalgic for past models of production and dependent on foreign allies to promote their project. Through this criticism the UDR cast itself both as the antithesis of the left but also as committed to the cause historically associated with the left: the UDR would save the nation from the grip of dictatorial rule, underdevelopment, and foreign domination.

Landowners in the UDR drew heavily on the 1960s for their cultural heroes, villains, and repertoires of political action. They drew on a threat that had catalyzed similar movements in the past: leftist subversion. They demonized the left to demonstrate the need for urgent collective action. And they identified themselves as descendants of past heroes, willing and able to mobilize to effectively eliminate the threat and save Brazil.

But the UDR recognized some of the limitations of drawing so heavily on the discourse and action of the 1960s. They had to be careful to distance themselves from the 1964 coup:

> The Revolution of 1964 occurred partly because of threats to private property. Conservative forces in the country overthrew the government and implanted a military regime. Society wouldn't accept this kind of change now. One of the reasons [for the 1964 coup] was to avoid a civil war over landownership. And it implanted a dictatorship. There isn't any climate for that kind of government now. [interview 90]

But a depleted stock of positive cultural images and symbols left UDR leaders with few options. They attempted to transform the *coroneis* into benevolent caregivers: "The great feeling of *compadres,* affective links, family, doesn't exist any more. There is no relationship between workers and owners. There is no feeling of the second father, the godfather [*padrinho*]" [interview 50].

The UDR attempted to reimagine the conquering land grabbers as pioneers and frontiersmen:

> My father arrived from Italy and didn't speak a word of Portuguese. By night he was a sharecropper. By day he was a day-laborer [*colono*]. This is the way he lived until he could put together a little money to buy a bit of his own land in São Paulo. And this is what I had always believed in. There are opportunities; some have more than others, but if you make an effort and struggle, you can win. My friend was a pioneer in this area of São Luis: Constantino Cunha Guimaraes. He's seventy-five years old. It used to take him an entire day by jeep to get to his land. And now that there are roads and you can get there in a few hours, they can take it away from him? Now it's mine, they say? [interview 64]

But most UDR leaders seemed to realize that reimagining the role of landholders in Brazilian history was a hopeless cause. Negative stereotypes of landholders were simply too deeply embedded to change. The image of landholders as national heroes was contested in folktales and literatures by counterimages of violent *coroneis*, ruthless local power brokers, and antidemocratic coup plotters. Indeed, in some cases UDR leaders had to draw on positive landholding images from outside Brazil. They found in U.S. pioneers, farmers, and ranchers a more favorable image to promote. And the U.S. images they used were not limited to the rural sector. Landholders made frequent references to U.S. history and politics as models for their movement. UDR leaders often cited Abraham Lincoln, Franklin Delano Roosevelt, and John Fitzgerald Kennedy as their inspiration. Ultimately, however, the UDR had problems using cultural images. It had to resort instead to spinning legitimating myths that would sustain support from both the old-style militants and the new class of landholders.

LEGITIMATING MYTHS

The UDR had guaranteed backing from the militant landlords, the descendants of rural *coroneis*, rural militias, and coup plotters. These constituents believed that it was their continuing mission to protect private landholding in Brazil and the free-enterprise system throughout the world against leftist threats. But not all UDR supporters shared this vision of landholders' historical political mission. Many of them were second- or third-generation landlords with urban professions. They rejected the image of landholders as uneducated rednecks who used violence to get their way. As one landholder described this new generation, "The rural class today consists of doctor-landholders, businessman-landholders, lawyer-landholders, taxi driver–land-holders, etc. . . . A landholder-landholder is hard to find" [interview 64]. These new landholders hoped to shed the association with the rural *coroneis*, an image that simply didn't have cachet in the modern democratic world. They saw in the UDR the means to do this, but their vision was almost diametrically opposed to the militant hard core's version of the UDR. For the new landlords, the UDR struggle was only partially about restoring land to the Junqueiras of Brazil. For them, the UDR's most important role involved creating a new identity for landholders as modern entrepreneurs and building a political entity to defend that identity.

An obvious tension arose between these two constituencies, but the UDR successfully forged an alliance between them. It did so partially by finding the right leader, one who could bridge the gap between the two. It also spun a series of legitimating myths to persuade the new class of landholders to participate in the UDR while using coding to sustain support from the traditional militants.

Junqueira might have been a natural leader for the movement. He had the personal story that catalyzed support. He had the personal finances to invest in a national campaign against agrarian reform. And he had the energy and the sense of mission to devote his time to this enterprise. But the UDR did not select Junqueira as its leader. Like many of the other founders and entrepreneurs who worked tirelessly behind the scenes to build the movement, Junqueira was simply too rural to run the national organization. He was introverted, uneducated, and rough. While this style resonated with the traditional landholders, he lacked the modern democratic image the UDR needed to capture national attention during the transition from authoritarian rule.

Ronaldo Caiado fit that bill. Caiado was the obvious choice among the original founders in Goiás and São Paulo because of his background and personal characteristics. He appealed to the traditional landholding authoritarian elite because of his lineage of Goiás landholders. So prominent was his family in Goiás that many of his ancestors had held powerful political positions in state and federal government. The family still owned extensive tracts of land and wielded considerable political power in Goiás. The prominence of Goiás in the movement no doubt catapulted Caiado to the presidency. But even beyond the regional appeal, Caiado represented a familiar historical figure: the powerful landholder-politician. He was the modern incarnation of rural politics that had dominated Brazilian history. As one UDR leader put it, "Ronaldo Caiado's presence was important. He was charismatic, intelligent, from an agricultural family. . . . He knew how to say things in a way that people could respond to. He was an ideal leader" [interview 75].

Yet it is precisely because Caiado was more than rural-politics-as-usual that he attracted strong support. He represented a new kind of rural politics that differentiated him from the old images. He was sophisticated, urbane, educated, and modern. He had a degree in medicine and a thriving medical practice in Goiânia. He had won scholarships to study for an advanced degree in medicine in France. His well-tailored clothes, his good looks, his cosmopolitan demeanor, could not have contrasted more with the old image of the authoritarian landholder. He was articulate. He spoke to the new generation of landholders. Caiado attracted those who had rural roots and still benefited from the prestige and power of their family's landholdings, but who thought of themselves as urban, modern, and democratic. Not wanting to be associated with an old authoritarian movement in the new democratic Brazil, these landholders responded to the "new-ruralism" image that Caiado projected: "The UDR appeared with new leadership and a good argument—through Caiado—that could counter the MST. I'm a doctor, articulate, and I'm part of a new ruralism like Caiado. We are landholders by choice. We are the children of successful landholders; we were able to study and learn a profession. We don't live off the ranch. The traditional landholder doesn't have this choice" [interview 46].

These new ruralists should not be mistaken for "technocratic" landholders of the agribusiness variety. The offspring of traditional landholders, they had not become agribusiness owners and even held such corporate enterprises in disdain. They had left behind their rural lifestyle, become highly educated, and pursued urban careers, but they also held on to the status and privileges of their rural heritage. While they did not live on the land or even necessarily rely on it for their income, they identified with, and had a lot of nostalgia for, the rural lifestyle. They constituted a group as distinct from agribusiness as from traditional landholding. But because of their separate identity, they were unlikely to openly join a movement headed by a traditional landholder like Junqueira. They eschewed the negative images of the authoritarian rural politics of the past. They were attracted to the UDR because it provided a charismatic leader who was both modern and capable— one who could protect land and change the image of the landholding elite. Because of his distinctive background and personal style, Caiado was one of the only individuals in the movement who would appeal to the new ruralists while sustaining support from the traditional rural elite.

It is not surprising, therefore, that the UDR became inextricably linked to Caiado. As one of the landholders I interviewed stated, "The organization wasn't structured. It was simply based on Ronaldo Caiado" [interview 34]. His personal appeal and charismatic style attracted individuals to him and to the movement. The devotion he inspired was profound:

Dr. Caiado won me over. Everyone was willing to do whatever he wanted. [interview 12]

Ronaldo . . . became a demigod. That was his image. People wanted to touch him, to kiss him. I remember one time an old man came up to him and said, "You really exist!" and passed his hand over him. [interview 35]

Ronaldo Caiado was charismatic. He had passion [garra], a love for what he was doing, and this was contagious. [interview 28]

Caiado grew important not only in the movement but in national politics as well. The press was attracted to him, and vice versa. He thus brought the movement the media exposure that helped it expand beyond Goiás and São Paulo. Landholders around the country began to see Caiado in the newspapers, in magazines, and on television. They were attracted to him and to his message, even though the media attention was not always positive.

One of the greatest challenges the movement faced was overcoming the violent image that associated it with rural *coroneis* and the authoritarian regime. The stigma of its violent origins as a militia became harder to shed as the UDR faced accusations of murder in high-profile cases like those of Chico Mendes and others: the Maranhão priest, Padre Josimo Morais Tavares (1985); Paulo Fontelles, an attorney for rural workers in southern Pará (1987); and Expedito Ribeiro de Souza, a Pará rural labor organizer (1991). The movement also faced accusations of death threats and assassinations of countless other less well known rural citizens. Indeed, the UDR was widely perceived as being responsible for the escalation of rural violence that had occurred since its inception in 1985 (see table 4.3). A number of scandals linked the movement to massive arms purchasing.[32] The UDR was also implicated in the use of the security firm Solução, associated with the previous military regime, to violently defend landholders' property.[33]

Because these claims were never fully investigated, the UDR could simply deny them. Yet its leaders admitted the movement's involvement in violence. One of its founders, for example, volunteered information about the UDR's involvement in the 1993 murder of Dom Patrick Hanhanhan, bishop of Conceição de Araguaia. While his death had been attributed to an intestinal thrombosis, UDR leader Jairo Andrade stated that "he didn't die [of natural causes]; we sent people to poison him."[34] Another UDR founder and top leader allegedly confessed to the press that the movement used its famous cattle auctions to raise money to buy arms.[35]

Moreover, the UDR's right-wing radicalism seemed positive to some of the movement's leaders, like this founder and professed UDR ideologue: "The UDR was a pressure group like many others—like the PT, like Hitler's movement. Just change the names and you have the same kind of group.... They are similar because they are very radical. There are two things that make people radical: women and land" [interview 67].

To maintain support from both modern landholders reluctant to admit to violence and the traditional landholders who joined the movement because of its violence, the UDR generated myths, both denying and justifying the violence. The UDR floated various "explanations" for the violence. "Offense is the best form of defense" was one such argument. The use of violence was justified in terms of protecting rights: when private-property rights are violated, citizens have a duty, a moral imperative, to defend those rights by any means, even violence: "Property is a right. And people have a right to defend their land.... There is a right to defend your land with weapons. But why kill the ant? Instead you should kill the queen ant or the anthill. Go for the head, not the tail" [anonymous].[36] This type of justification frequently came in the form of the mantra "If a man does not defend his land, he has no right to keep it."

But another group of landholders justified violence using a "fairness principle." Since the land invasions were illegal, they argued, they had the right to defend themselves. Some, like this UDR leader, likened themselves to other groups that typically used armed protection, particularly banks and industries: "I am in favor of forming militias. Banks have guards to protect them. Why shouldn't we also have our security systems?" [interview 90]. Another UDR leader claimed that armed defense should be understood by citizens. "How do you think they would react," he questioned, "if their houses were invaded?" [interview 18].

The UDR further claimed legal justification for the use of arms. The UDR first developed this legal argument in early 1986. The UDR used the findings by two lawyers contracted by the extreme-right Catholic organization TFP (Tradition, Family, and Property) to claim that under the civil code, landholders have the right to defend their property with arms.[37] This led some UDR leaders to make statements like this one: "The civil code allows me to defend what is mine. If someone attacks my land, I'm not going to greet him with flowers in my hand. I have the right to defend my land. If anyone's land is invaded, I'm going to defend their right to defend their land.... The civil code gives us the right—like the right in the United States—to form militias" [interview 4]. The parallel with the United States is an appropriate one, since just as with the case of militias in the United States, the right to an armed defense of the land remains highly contested within the Brazilian legal community.

But most UDR leaders attempted, at least in public, to shed this violent image. They generally denied the movement's association with violence. This denial took various forms. The most common defense was to blame the media for negative propaganda: "If a lie is repeated a million times, it is eventually accepted as the truth. That is what happened with the UDR and its violent image" [interview 10]. Movement leaders implied that they could not possibly combat the UDR's violent image because of the falsehoods launched at them from what they considered to be the two dominant leftist forces in the country: the media and the church. These leaders argued that the left was using the stigma of violence to reduce the UDR's political power.

Denial also came in the form of legalistic arguments, such as "None of the accusations of violence have ever been proved" [interview 4]. Such a statement could mean that the UDR was indeed involved in violence but proof did not exist. Or it could mean that the UDR was not involved in violence, otherwise legal proof would exist. This "innocent until proven guilty" type of argument, however, requires faith in the legal system, a faith that few Brazilians share. Since the government has not investigated any of the cases in which the UDR was allegedly involved, neither its guilt nor its innocence has been established.

Some UDR leaders admitted that members of the movement were involved in violence. Rather than deny the violence, they used a "bad-egg" defense, arguing that the organization as a whole could not be blamed for the actions of a few members. One leader said, "If a Presbyterian or a Catholic, let's say a Catholic, commits a murder, does everyone say, 'Catholics commit murder?' Those people who committed those murders just happened to be in the UDR" [interview 10]. Another leader said, "Some group within PT assaulted a bank. That doesn't make PT a band of thieves. These are individuals [not the movement] who have been accused" [interview 4].

The bad-egg defense assumed regional dimensions. Landholders from the Southeast implied that violence occurred more frequently in the North or

Northeast. A landholder from Rio Grande do Sul, for example, stated, "Our adversaries concentrated on the arms issue. This was true only in a few of the UDRs. Here we used discussion and argument as our ammunition" [interview 46]. Leaders from the eastern region of São Paulo State blamed the UDR's violent image on the landholders in the western part of the state, who faced particular regional conditions. Referring to the problems in the Pontal de Paranapanema, one leader stated:

> There is a difference between the UDR and *uderistas* [UDR members].
> Many *uderistas* are on the frontier, and they have been involved in a
> constant battle. They have title to their land on paper, but they are still
> not secure. They use different methods than we do. Here, we use justice.
> On the frontier, it is the law of survival of the fittest. But the violence is
> on both sides. The church stimulates the violence. . . . We believe in
> democracy. As democrats we have to respect the judiciary and what it is
> doing. We believe in the judiciary. On the frontier they do not. [interview 70]

Violence would be pinned on particular regions on the basis of the size of farm and the type of production typical of those regions. Landholders from extensive ranches or farms, particularly in the North (e.g., Pará) were believed to be more violent than those from smaller, primarily agricultural, properties in the South (e.g., Rio Grande do Sul). There is little doubt that cattle ranchers who owned extensive territories that they left fallow for pasture land were more vulnerable to expropriation than those who planted their land. The same can be said of the cattle ranchers in the relatively new territories in the North, who had not even completed the task of clearing their extensive frontier land to turn it into pasture or agricultural plots. And the sheer size of these properties made them difficult to police or fence in, leaving such landholders even more vulnerable to rural invasions.

But ideological divisions did not fall neatly along regional, farm-size, or sectoral lines. UDR leaders from the relatively small, agriculture-based South shared the ideology of the extreme faction associated with northern cattle ranchers. Moreover, some of the most moderate or pragmatic UDR leaders held extensive land in the North, oriented their production toward cattle and horse breeding, and had a high percentage of idle land.

Among landholders who acknowledged the movement's involvement in violence were those who used a "relative-weight" defense. These landholders argued that both rural and urban violence were products of Brazil's violent culture, and rural violence should not be held to a different standard than urban violence: "[Rural violence] is the same as violence in the city. Maybe it isn't even as serious as violence in the city. It is due to the destruction of the state, politics, judiciary, wherever it occurs. [Brazilian rural areas] are like the Far West, where there is no law, no justice. But this is true in areas of Rio [de Janeiro]. The police just don't enter certain areas" [interview 41].

The relative-weight argument also underlay UDR leaders' claims that the left generated more violence than the UDR. The UDR believed that the press, and Brazilian society as a whole, ignored violence against landholders perpetrated by the left: "There were a lot of landholders who were murdered. But there is no press coverage of them. They don't get any emphasis" [interview 10]. The left's violence, in the UDR's opinion, matched landlords'. Moreover, the UDR contended that landholders were justified in using violence to protect their land, whereas invaders were not:

Who produces more violence: the invader or the UDR member who defends his land? The UDR's use of violence is left-wing propaganda. But if someone invades my land, I will kill him to defend it. [interview 18]

The landholder goes to the courts to get people off the land. And violence on the land is considered the landholder's fault. But who invaded the land? In the press the judges order them to vacate the land. The police fulfill the order. The landholder has called them. And the invaders are viewed as saints, without faults! . . . Violence is from the invaders. The political parties need a new flag to wave, and this is it. It pays their salaries. Really, the countryside is peaceful. These conflicts are fabricated. The violence of these invasions is not an accident like the crazy snipers in the United States. . . . These are created, administered. [interview 86]

Carrying this relative-weight argument even further, some UDR leaders claimed that the UDR had in fact limited rather than escalated rural violence. Without the UDR, they argued, rural violence would have been much greater:

The violence would be worse without the UDR. Without the UDR, landholders would not have an organ fighting for their legal rights and would take matters into their own hands. [They would] use violence rather than laws to protect their lands. The legal statute allows landholders to use physical force to defend their private property from invasion. But the UDR is organized to use the law to defend private property. [interview 4]

We felt protected when the UDR existed. . . . When the UDR existed, no one planned invasions. The MST was afraid of the UDR—not the ones who really wanted land, but the ones who were making all the noise about it, the ones who were provoking the invasions. It was the image of the UDR that they feared. The UDR was never a group of hired guns, a militia, or any other type of armed group. It never provided physical protection for any ranch. It didn't need to, because there weren't any invasions. The UDR also never had protection from the police. Here the justice system and the police are *very* slow. [Justice] . . . crawls here. The justice system doesn't work for either side. It's too slow. So we have had to find our own private justice system. [interview 26]

I found no evidence that these mixed messages on UDR's involvement in violence were deliberately and consciously generated by the movement's leaders. Rather, they were generated out of the diverse reactions of landholders. Indeed, even within the UDR few leaders knew who held what position on violence. As one leader explained it to me, "I don't know who might be a liberal [in the UDR leadership]. You would think someone was, from their private conversations with you, and then they would take a more extreme line in meetings" [interview 18]. Ambiguity, both deliberate and accidental, allowed the movement to win support from a number of different sectors. On the one hand there were the authoritarian landowners who were comfortable with the idea of violence and had been attracted to the UDR precisely because of its violent image. When UDR leaders advocated violence or failed to punish members who engaged in it, it reassured these landholders that the movement would protect their interests by any means, even violence. And when UDR leaders denied any involvement in violence or attributed it to a few "bad eggs" in the movement, they could interpret it as strategy, the movement's way of protecting itself from government reprisal. The ambiguity could appeal equally well to the more moderate landholders who deplored the use of violence and supported the UDR for its other activities. When UDR leaders spoke out against violence and invoked the bad-egg defense, these landholders were reassured that they had not, after all, cast their lot with an uncivil movement. And when UDR leaders projected a violent image, they too could interpret it as strategy, the movement's way of enhancing its power. One of the pragmatists put it this way: "Maybe our image did discourage invasions. If you said you had guards on the property, they didn't know whether you did or didn't, but they knew they better not take the chance—they better respect that property" [interview 10].

The ambiguity surrounding the UDR's association with arms proved useful to the movement. As a minority movement, the UDR's power depended in large part on its capacity to evoke fear. It needed to be viewed as a radical movement that could and would use arms to defend its interests. It succeeded in projecting that image. Yet it had to avoid any direct association with violence, lest the government outlaw the movement. Moreover, the movement could not sustain either its membership or its formal organization if it were linked to violence. The use of violence, therefore, had to be both clandestine and yet known, rumored and yet real. The failure of the judiciary to investigate the UDR allowed the movement to float different interpretations of its links to violence, retaining both militant and pragmatic supporters.

Legitimating myths also emerged around the UDR's commitment to democracy. Most UDR leaders unabashedly admitted support for the military regime and even considered the military presidents to be the best presidents the country had ever had.[38] But they did not consider themselves authoritarians. Even the hardline members of the UDR accepted democracy, as long as it provided the same protections of private property and agricultural production that the military regime had provided. Besides, even if the UDR, or some group within the UDR, wanted another coup and another military regime, it was not likely to happen, and the UDR appeared cognizant of that fact. There simply was not enough support from the military or other key coup conspirators for another round of authoritarian rule. For this reason the UDR did not support an authoritarian reversal but rather sought to increase its political power within the democratic system.

To function in the democratic context, the UDR needed to play by the rules, and so it built a "democratic" lobby. In other words, it worked through democratic institutions while simultaneously carrying out uncivil acts of violence against rural political organizers. Indeed, the peak of the UDR's institutional strength coincided with the peak of rural violence.

Language played an integral role in the UDR's presentation of itself as a democratic force. It included the word *democracy* in its name. Its leaders frequently talked about the loss of privileges in strongly democratic terms—in terms of "rights" and "freedoms." They often referred to the "sacred right" of private property and to landholders' "right" to defend it. Their discussion of leftist totalitarianism presented the UDR's political mobilization as a liberationist movement for democratic freedoms. The following remark epitomizes the "democratic" offensive used by the UDR: "Our image is a radical right group. . . . We aren't afraid to admit what we are. We're open about what we want. . . . We are the democratic right. And there should be a democratic left, but not an authoritarian one" [interview 4].

The UDR also used language to promote an image of itself as a modern and efficient organization. For example, it began a campaign to shed references to landholders as *fazendeiros,* or plantation owners, a term that evoked images of exploitative, authoritarian, and feudal *coroneis.* The term was replaced with *productores rurais,* or rural producers. This new term associated the UDR with modern entrepreneurial farmers oriented toward cost-efficient agricultural production for the good of the nation. UDR leaders claimed that, unlike the left, their movement produced jobs and food despite government policies that worked against them: "We produce and provide jobs. But our left is thirty or forty years behind the times. They want to destroy our image, destroy capitalism. Industry, on the other hand, is the hero. It is demoralizing. The country needs food. And Brazil is one of the last countries based on agriculture that doesn't have subsidies" [interview 74].

The UDR parlayed this argument about modernity and efficiency into a political statement. Like most political actors, the UDR avoided too close an association with the former military regime during the new democratic era. It also avoided the label "right wing."[39] The UDR tried to claim that it was "neither left nor right." Not one UDR leader I interviewed defined himself or herself as right wing.[40] Instead, UDR leaders avoided the term and referred to their ideology as "centrist," "liberal," or "conservative." Some also argued that the terms *right* and *left* have lost their meaning in the contemporary world: "The leftist is the man who opposes. The rightist is the man who supports. If the left opposes poverty, misery, and injustice and is in favor of income distribution and more justice, then I am on the left. If the right is in favor of private property, rights and obligations, law and order, then I am on the right" [interview 64]. But not all of the UDR leaders I interviewed were so adept at avoiding the right-wing label. Many initially rejected the label but nearly always "slipped" and identified themselves eventually as right wing. For example: "The left and the right don't exist anymore. The world is on the right. There is no middle. It's like being pregnant. You're either pregnant or not; you can't be sort of pregnant. There is no middle in ideology, either. And the left doesn't have support" [interview 80].

The UDR also employed gender to project an alternative image of itself.

The movement banked on a widely held misperception that women do not participate in radical and violent movements. By creating UDR-Woman (UDR-Mulher), the UDR consciously attempted to soften its image and expand its appeal. UDR-Woman carried out most of the UDR's social projects, fulfilling an auxiliary function. These social projects involved local-level services, such as financing mobile health service units in remote rural areas, providing rural police patrol cars to deter theft in such areas, and implementing civic action projects in the schools. One of UDR-Woman's national projects involved a campaign to provide Rio de Janeiro flood victims with food and clothing. The group also did much of the fundraising, envelope stuffing, and backstage work for the cattle auctions. This view of UDR-Woman's function was confirmed in a number of UDR leaders' statements:

> UDR-Woman was mainly a social group, like Rotary or Lions. They worked in that way: food campaigns. [interview 69]

> We had the same set of goals as the UDR, the same objectives, which were to protect land and private property. We just had a different kind of action. Our action was about changing the image. The men did the political side, the lobby, and we worked on the social side. We wanted to show society that we weren't so bad—that we work hard, that we struggle. [interview 28]

UDR-Woman thus played a dual role of providing both support service to the movement and public relations. The group's members attempted to shatter the image of the UDR as a movement of violent and self-interested landlords by projecting an alternative image of patriotism and commitment to national development. Their charity work received little press attention, however, and therefore did little to change the UDR's image. Indeed, the most mileage the UDR got out of UDR-Woman was the subliminal message of a photograph and blurb in the popular news magazine *Veja*. The photo captured a group of beautiful wealthy women lobbying for the UDR in the Constituent Assembly. The caption read, "The Muses of the UDR." The short article perhaps unwittingly presented the modern entrepreneurial and democratic image that most UDR leaders hoped to project to fight the authoritarian image of the past.

In short, the UDR generated myths to fulfill the complicated task of both cuing itself up with successful traditional authoritarian movements from the past and distancing itself from that authoritarian past. The association with that old style of movement provided the UDR with the militant support of the hard core. It also provided the movement with political power; the UDR drew on its predecessors' involvement in coup conspiracies to pose potential threats to the democratic government. The UDR's public transcript, in contrast, emphasized its commitment to democratic change and defeating the totalitarian threat from the left. Its charismatic leaders and contradictory discourse held together a fragile alliance of traditional militants and modern landholders.

Limitations on the UDR's Power

Despite its successful use of political framing, cultural cuing, and legitimating myths, on 29 November 1994 the UDR closed its doors. The movement faced inherent limitations that prevented it from remaining politically active. While these limitations surfaced only after the UDR had already won its most immediate demands—the end of the agrarian reform program—they still point to weaknesses upon which future democratic governments might play to reduce the political power of uncivil movements. These limitations further plagued the movement when it tried to reemerge in 1996.

The majority of UDR leaders blamed the demise of the movement on Caiado's leadership. This criticism surfaced after Caiado's bid for the presidency in 1989. The adamant antipolitics contingent within the movement saw his bid as a betrayal of the movement's goal of remaining outside (or above) mainstream politics (which the typical UDR member equated with corruption). Such members became politically active in the UDR only because of the movement's message of urgency and threat. They saw themselves as solving problems, not "doing politics": "I had never been involved in politics. I didn't like politics. I had a clean ideal. UDR shared that. It stood behind a principle, and it brought together honest men, without political or personal ambition" [interview 18].

When Caiado entered the race, many UDR leaders criticized him for having become "a typical politician," out for his own narrow self-interest and self-aggrandizement at the expense of the movement and its constituents. He had entered the world of "dirty politics" and "deal making." And his critics within the movement accused him of going back on his promise to keep the movement separate from politics, tricking the landholding class, and exploiting the movement for his own personal gain.

But some UDR leaders understood Caiado's bid not as a betrayal but as a natural outcome of the cult of personality. The devotion he inspired within the movement, the hero-worship, had filled Caiado's head with illusions of power, transforming him from an honest movement leader into an egocentric politician. The hero-worshipers within the movement and Caiado himself had lost sight of the movement's more modest political program. Indeed, enthusiasm for Caiado had simply taken over, leading UDR leaders and Caiado himself to believe that he could even win the presidency:

> The UDR had always been against getting involved in politics. . . . We wanted the UDR to have influence in politics, to defend our interests, but not to run candidates. . . . [But] when [Caiado] said he was going to run for president, everyone thought that he was the law. . . . There was a lot of fanaticism around Caiado at the time. No one was using common sense. They actually thought he could win. I knew he didn't have a chance, but . . . once it was decided that he would run, I had to lend my support. . . . Caiado would have had much more influence in the Congress. He would have had even more influence as the head of the organization. Just like Lula, he has more strength as the president of PT than as a deputy. . . . His running for office undermined the entity's sense of purpose, at least in the South. The movement had gone more in a political direction. Many people felt disillusioned and used. It wasn't just Caiado. Others [in the UDR] also ran for positions: Abelardo Lupião. The members felt manipulated by these political quests. [interview 79]

Even more damaging to the movement than Caiado's run for the presidency was his embarrassing defeat. He received so little support that it was obvious that not even the movement's own members had voted for him. In their defense, Caiado's supporters in the UDR claimed that they could not afford to cast their ballot for Caiado because of the urgent need to defeat the leftist candidate, Lula. Since Caiado had not come even close to defeating Lula in the preelection polls, they had to vote for Collor over Caiado.

But these supporters also felt that Caiado had misunderstood the political campaign process. They continued to defend him against criticism for having run in the first place; after all, his decision had been endorsed by the UDR leadership.[41] But the plan, they claimed, had been a publicity stunt, not a serious bid for the presidency. This is what Caiado had failed to understand. Caiado was supposed to enter the race only to gain media exposure for the movement. The UDR could take advantage of the free advertising provided to candidates by the Brazilian government. Caiado would then withdraw his candidacy before the election, to avoid the embarrassment of losing and to ensure the left's defeat:

The UDR should have been apolitical, without any compromises. . . . We needed to have media coverage to get our message across. But the media is expensive, and the UDR just didn't have those kinds of resources. So the free hour on television for candidates was one way to use the media without having to pay for it. Our agreement was that Caiado would run for president until a certain day and then drop out of the race. He would use his candidacy to have a serious dialogue with the public about rural problems. But that agreement wasn't followed. He didn't drop out after that certain day. . . . The movement had little enthusiasm for a presidential campaign. [interview 6]

Resentment of Caiado heightened when he failed to learn his lesson from the defeat. Disregarding the fallout for the movement, Caiado attempted political suicide once again in 1994 when he ran for governor of Goiás against a popular incumbent. One UDR leader explained the problem for the movement:

Caiado was a good congressman, a good legislator. But he is not a good executive. He is a great spokesperson, and he did a great job in Congress. We were well represented. But then he ran for governor. I said, "My dear little man, are you crazy?" He was running against a great governor, a good friend. This was really too bad. It ended everything. He would have been a great leader in rural politics. He would have been able to modernize agrarian policies in the areas of credit, banks, interests, stocks, decisions, and future harvests. [interview 6]

Caiado's electoral defeats did not simply damage the UDR's political power; they also ruled him out as a future leader of the movement. Disillusioned, the UDR membership withdrew their support for him, and for the movement. Caiado himself was disillusioned as well, not just with the movement whose members had failed to support him but with Brazilian politics in general. His poor showing in the elections convinced him that he had no political future, and he returned to his small clinic in Goiânia. This UDR member summed up the disappointment on both sides:

Caiado committed a grave error: he ran for president. Most of us were against that decision, but we accepted his choice. This was a great disillusionment for him. He has charisma, he knows how to speak, he is good-looking, he is very appealing. But if he hadn't gotten mixed up in politics, the UDR would be stronger now than ever. He is too disillusioned to return. He was the federal deputy who got the highest votes in

Goiás. When he ran for governor, we told him, "Don't do that. Run for senator; you'll have eight years." And so he lost, and now he is doing medicine. He is a good doctor, but he is a natural politician. [interview 27]

Ultimately, Caiado's bid weakened the movement by leaving it leaderless. Those who tried to fill Caiado's shoes lacked his charismatic appeal. His first successor, Nagib Abude, fell ill shortly after taking office and stepped down. The subsequent leader, Roosevelt Roque dos Santos, was organizationally capable but lacked Caiado's fire and passion. As one UDR leader commented, "Another Caiado is not likely to appear" [interview 28]. No one had the personal qualifications or the background to forge unity between the traditional and the modern landlords.

The succession issue, moreover, revealed smoldering jealousies within the movement. Some of the founders and entrepreneurs believed that Caiado had weakened the movement by amassing personal power and closing out those who had contributed their hard work and passion to building it. These jealousies were most often expressed by the traditional landholders. They recognized that they did not have the modern image that the charismatic Caiado embodied; they resembled the old *coroneis*. But this did not stop them from expressing their frustration at being closed out of the movement because of Caiado's personal leadership style. The following diatribe against Caiado, by one of the movement entrepreneurs, illustrates the animosity that some felt toward him because of his monopoly over the movement:

Mr. Ronaldo Caiado was a disaster for the organization. He was making fun of our message. He manipulated everything to make himself president of an organization that wasn't supposed to have a president. We had planned to just have coordinators. He made himself out to be the visionary behind the group, the founder, when really we were all visionaries. We all—forty men—worked concurrently to found the organization. . . . The UDR was capable, but it was manipulated by Ronaldo. He didn't earn his bread working on the land. He was a doctor, educated in France, intelligent, who spoke well and was a pretty boy.

. . . I realized early, before he ran for president, [that Caiado was going after his own interests]. But everyone said I was just against him: a competitor. He had already created a myth around himself. I left the UDR in 1987 or 1988, before he ran for president. I just felt I was powerless in trying to convince the rest of the movement where he was

taking it. Why stay with the leadership? People were joining because of
what they could get out of the UDR. It was cute to be in the UDR.

Mr. Ronaldo Caiado created a mystique around himself. He used the
UDR for his own personal advancement. He ran for president and that
destroyed the group. He didn't even get 1 percent of the rural vote. He
threw it all away. The power that we had was destroyed. It looked like
we didn't represent anyone, not even the rural sector—not even the
sector we said we were defending. We didn't have force. [interview 64]

Most of the sniping within the UDR was less personal than this, and UDR
leaders viewed it as a symptom of a movement already in decline rather
than as a cause of that decline. As one leader stated, "There are some people
who blame Caiado's candidacy for the demise of the UDR. But . . . producers
had already started leaving the movement before his candidacy. Those who
didn't want to participate any more used this as a pretext" [interview 86].

Some UDR leaders mentioned burnout as contributing to the demise of
the movement. The long hours, travel, and stress that the movement's
high-profile activities involved drove leaders and members to look for reasons to abandon the movement and get back to their lives. Consider these
comments by UDR activists:

In 1988 the law was approved. There had been a national crisis, and
then our objectives were achieved. The original leaders were worn out.
. . . I stepped down because I needed to get back to my family life and
my business. I had sacrificed a lot. I had stimulated new leaders. I had
done my part. [interview 18]

There is a certain amount of burnout in this type of work, and people
want to return to their normal lives, their family life. [interview 50]

Caiado himself was not immune to burnout. He used these words to describe the pace associated with UDR activism: "It's tiring work. You don't
stop anywhere, not even in your own state. You don't stay with your family.
You work twenty-four hours a day at an accelerated rhythm" [Caiado, 17
August 1995]. After years as the charismatic leader of an uncivil movement,
it is not surprising that he sought the relative comfort of public office.

The UDR's success in eliminating the threat of agrarian reform exacerbated both burnout and factionalism. For some UDR members, this victory
marked the end of the movement: it had accomplished its goals, had no
more reason to exist, and should close its doors. This view stemmed as much

from burnout as from a philosophical position on the movement's function. In contrast, other members saw the victory over agrarian reform as only the beginning. They viewed the UDR as an enduring expression of a new political consciousness among landholders and a commitment to combat any future threats to them. For these members, the UDR had failed to accomplish its goals. As one UDR-Youth leader lamented, the UDR was "a dream that was never fulfilled" [interview 12]. Caiado also believed that the movement had fallen short of its goal of building a new rural producer consciousness. This led one UDR leader to conclude that the succession problem was what ended the movement: "There is interest in forming another UDR, but there is no leader to form it" [interview 26]. The factionalism that contributed to the movement's demise surfaced only after the movement had accomplished its goals: "After the ratification of the constitution, the rural producers were calmer. The level of participation in the UDR fell off. There wasn't that uncertainty; there was more security. Participation began falling off, and the petty differences began. No one focused on these differences in the beginning" [interview 86].

The very success of the UDR, in other words, hastened its demise. The headiness of the movement's political power provoked Caiado to make a bid for president and governor, urged on by his devout followers. The personal political power he wielded created jealousies. And once the movement achieved its goal of defeating agrarian reform, tensions surfaced over the future direction the movement should take.

National and international politics also played a role in limiting the movement's future. The threat from the left, upon which the UDR was built, diminished when the right won the presidential elections of 1990. And the collapse of the Soviet bloc made claims of an international leftist conspiracy ring hollow:

And we achieved our goals. In October 1988 the constitution was ratified. In March 1990 Collor won. We began to see this as the last fight between the left and the right on the planet. The Berlin Wall had already fallen. There was a [political] opening in the Soviet Union. The left didn't have a flag to wave. In the only place where it had established a government, it had failed. The left was finished. We had won. We had gotten protections in the constitution, and we had gotten Collor elected. Collor appeared to be—*appeared* to be—honest, young, strong. Everyone thought, "No one's going to lay a hand on me ever again." This was our sweet illusion. [interview 1]

The movement ended, in other words, when it lost the leadership, unity, energy, and purpose it needed to survive. Some leaders rested on their laurels, satisfied with the transformations the UDR had brought about to guard against future threats to landholders. Even with the 1995 election of Fernando Henrique Cardoso, once feared by the right as a dangerous leftist, landholders felt secure in the movement's achievements. They considered Cardoso too "intelligent" and "balanced" to threaten their interests. They felt that they had made an indelible mark on Brazilian democracy. Consider, for example, the remarks of this prominent UDR leader:

> All of the UDR's ideas—privatization, reducing the size of the state, ending trade barriers—were all adopted by Fernando Henrique. So there was no reason to exist. . . . When Fernando Henrique won, the left had lost. Fernando Henrique was making an alliance with the landholders. . . . If Lula had won, I have no doubt that the UDR would still be around, defending the constitution. [interview 4]

But not all UDR leaders shared this sense of security, of safety from the left and agrarian reform. A significant minority believed that it was not enough merely to have secured legislation; the UDR needed to remain active to enforce that legislation. The tranquility that followed the legislative victory had lulled landholders into a false sense of security. As one UDR leader stated, "They think that because the law exists, their property is safe. They think they are assured protection. They don't think we need a UDR any more" [interview 90]. Yet even the UDR's representatives in the legislature, according to several UDR leaders, "left much to be desired" [interview 75].

Indeed, UDR leaders began to recognize warning signs in the increase in land invasions in the Pontal and elsewhere in the mid-1990s. To them these signs suggested that the UDR had closed prematurely, before it had eliminated the threat to private property. Several of the landholders I interviewed expressed this sense of alarm:

> Today there is no respect for land. Look what is happening in the Pontal—that mess there. And the landholders are thinking of starting a movement. When danger strikes, everyone remembers the UDR. [interview 10]

> A civil war could begin. We accept things only up to a certain point. When it becomes robbery, we won't accept it. It could happen here [Rio Grande do Sul], or in the Pontal, or in Paraná. [interview 46]

The UDR's directors believed that exclusion from government further threatened the interests of landholders. The left had again found representation in government while landholders had lost their voice and influence. In other words, the events that had prompted the emergence of the UDR in the mid-1980s were resurfacing: a powerful rural social movement with a voice and influence in government, land invasions, waning landholder influence in government, and a government unwilling or unable to end the conflict over land. Consider these landlords' descriptions of the mid-1990s:

Things are as bad as they were in 1985. In fact, they may be worse. The landless are more violent, more aggressive. . . . There is representation on the left that the president speaks with, but we do not have a representative. [interview 75]

Today we're facing the same problems we had ten years ago. But before, we had a chain of command, a hierarchy with municipal, regional, state, and national organizations. This hierarchy of support doesn't exist anymore. Everyone is isolated again. And armed conflict is beginning again. . . . The government isn't taking control. It's not enforcing the law. The judicial system is too slow. It's not worth going through [judicial channels], because by the time a judgment is reached, it's too late. . . . The press portrays the landless as the poor people who are hungry. They don't show our level of production. They shape opinions against us. [interview 90]

Among this set of alarmed landholders were some fervent anticommunists. These extremists felt that the lack of vigilance in the "post–Cold War era" had provided the left with room to mobilize a virulent global attack on the private-enterprise system. They saw Brazil as a prime target through the local operatives in the MST. Conspiracy theories abounded:

In the 1990s we are facing a rural guerrilla movement. They are occupying strategic points: where they can cut off electricity through high-tensions wires, where they have support. They are characteristic of the other types of rural guerrilla movements like the Shining Path, Tupamaros, Chiapas. They are making a ring around the most strategically important areas to cut them off. They want to take power. This is written in their documents. We seized their documents from them. And they say openly, "We are the last radicals in the country." [interview 43]

Echoing some of the same indictments that had been leveled against former president Sarney, landholders referred to Cardoso as a leftist. As one commented, "He is a Marxist. And he has card-carrying Marxists as his advisers" [interview 77]. Some of these extremists even made thinly veiled suggestions that Cardoso and his supporters should have been eliminated by the military regime:

> The [Cardoso] government is on the left. This doesn't exist in other countries. In Paraguay, the left is dead. We won't talk about whether violating human rights is right or wrong. Stroessner lined up the leftists and shot them. They don't exist anymore. In Argentina, they liquidated ten thousand communists. Those mothers who march around the Plaza de Mayo know very well that their children are dead . . . thrown into the sea, all of them into the sea. It was a war without prisoners. . . . A political movement without the support of the president can't do much. The federal government is stimulating invasions. The great majority here, and throughout the world, is silent. So the *sem vergonha* [shameless, a play on the *sem terra* or landless] have invaded three properties, have three to invade, and eleven more planned. [interview 27]

The tension between the extremists and the pragmatists had been kept under wraps during the period of urgency, when the landholding sector was united behind the goal of defeating agrarian reform. The pragmatists ignored or denied the UDR's violence at the time. But after the UDR defeated the agrarian reform movement and closed its doors, Cardoso was elected to office, and the extremists began to mobilize again, moderate UDR leaders lost interest in the movement. They saw the stigma of violence and extremism as more threatening to landholders than the events transpiring at the time. Indeed, several leaders cited the violence and the stigma of violence as the reason for the demise of the movement, and not Caiado's leadership style. They believed that the violence associated with the movement led pragmatists to abandon it: "[Violence] was one of the issues that brought the movement to an end. I'd say [it was] the principal reason. The movement turned into a guerrilla group" [interview 40]. There is no evidence that landholders abandoned the movement because of this stigma of violence until after the defeat of agrarian reform. Violence seems to have been considered by the pragmatists the price of uniting landholders behind a successful movement.

UDR violence did not end after the movement closed its doors. When new land invasions erupted in the Pontal de Paranapanema in 1995, the press suggested that the UDR had formed an armed militia to combat them. On one of the evening news programs, a Pontal landholder opened up his weapons cache for filming.[42] Doubting that the movement had really closed, the media saw the UDR behind a number of rural organizations.[43] The UDR's enemies also doubted that the movement had ended its reign of terror by officially closing its doors. One political leader on the left expressed that skepticism in these terms:

> The UDR changed names, but it still exists. Their name was giving them a bad feeling, so they changed it. Now they are the *bancada ruralista,* the S.O.S. Fazendeiro, the TFP. They have 140 deputies now. This is the biggest section within Congress. And it comes from all of the parties, except PT, PCdoB [Communist Party of Brazil], and other parties on the left. . . . The Rondônia massacre last night . . . —there is little doubt that the UDR was behind it. [interview 56]

And, living up to the expectations of its enemies and the media, the movement did reemerge in 1996 in response to continued land invasions and the government's failure to end them. This reemergence fulfilled its members' expectations as well. As one UDR leader put it, "From the embers it left burning, it will only take a spark to reignite it" [interview 69]. UDR leaders widely believed that the spirit remained alive among landholders. Caiado remarked, "The spirit of UDR did not die. I wasn't the organizer of the mentality, the institution, the class organization" [Caiado, 17 August 1995]. And because of this enduring spirit, UDR leaders felt certain that the movement would remobilize: "In thirty days the UDR could be built again. That is our temperament. If there is danger, we mobilize. If things are fine, we don't mobilize" [interview 6]. Indeed, certain local UDR branches remained intact, poised to take up the torch against future threats even after the national UDR office closed: "We never extinguished the UDR here. We are still registered. We are still a legal entity. We only deactivated the entity temporarily. . . . If there were a need, we would reopen: if there were invasions or unjust expropriations or bad-faith expropriations, and if the existing entities didn't act with the necessary force—if the government didn't respond to our demands" [interview 43].

But the remobilized UDR had more power in the imaginations of its members, its enemies, and the media than it actually developed. The limitations it faced during its final stages had not disappeared with reorganization. In fact, they became more obvious. The movement's leaders and members remained divided on the type of organization it should become: civil or uncivil. They also could not decide what threat or threats they should organize around. And they never found the charismatic leader who might have overcome these tensions.

The president of the reorganized UDR had been behind a failed effort to transform the UDR into a political party. These efforts were stymied by the antipolitics feelings within the landholding class, as described by this top leader:

> We were on our way to forming a new party called the PLI [Free Enterprise Party], that we later agreed to call the PDN [National Democratic Party]. The idea was to have a party to defend free enterprise. The UDR would still be an organization of the rural class, but there would also be a political party. . . . The idea of the political party never got off the ground. One of the problems with this party, and any party that represents class interests, is mixing politics with those interests. Politicians have to make too many compromises to stay in office. [interview 4]

But even if landholders had endorsed this shift from movement to party, they had no social sector with which they might ally to create a viable party. Political parties and politicians in general were unwilling to identify openly with the UDR. When Caiado sought a political party to support his candidacy for president, for example, he found few takers. Even the financial incentives the UDR offered to members of the political class who supported UDR views proved insufficient to persuade politicians to lend open support for the movement. UDR founder Salvador Farina, for example, went public with a list of UDR supporters in Congress, but those on the list denied the association. They would only support the movement in private.

The closest the UDR came to a broad alliance was its association with an urban movement to protect private property. The UDR made inroads into an alliance with the right-wing politician Guillerme Afif Domingos. The UDR even backed an urban UDR, called the MDU (Urban Democratic Movement), but the initiative failed partly because of the UDR's reputation for violence and partly because of Caiado's impolitic attack on the most powerful leader within the MDU, Eduardo da Rocha Azevedo, the head of the São Paulo Stock Exchange.

The UDR had more success linking up with extremist movements. It considered, for example, an alliance with the radical fundamentalist Catholic movement TFP. The TFP, founded in Brazil but having branches throughout the world, closely resembles the Spanish Falange movement, famous for its support of General Francisco Franco's dictatorship. It is rumored to train soldiers to fight wars against the left. Indeed, two of the top leaders in the UDR, who asked to remain anonymous, confirmed that the TFP had offered the UDR an army of sixteen hundred men, free of charge, to fight land invasions. But while the two movements share a common ideology centered around private property and leftist threats, UDR leaders believed that an alliance with such an extreme movement would undermine, rather than enhance, their movement's political power. Ironically, leaders within the TFP claim that the alliance fell through because the TFP considered the UDR too radical. The alliance seems to have been limited to mutual support on issues. The TFP provided the UDR with legal doctrines they had solicited to support armed protection of private property. In addition, individual UDR members are also TFP members and sympathizers. And during the UDR's brief withdrawal, the TFP founded S.O.S. Fazendeiro, a militant landholders' self-defense unit, to fill the vacuum.

Some former UDR leaders tried to remobilize around the UDR's lobbying successes. Rather than emphasizing the threat of land invasions, they attacked President Cardoso's economic policies as embodied in his Plano Real. They claimed that these economic policies threatened farmers even more than the expropriations and invasions of the 1980s had done because of reduced access to credit, high interest rates on borrowing, low prices for agricultural products, high prices for agricultural inputs, inadequate storage facilities, unfair competition from foreign producers, inadequate trade policy on agricultural goods, and a host of other agricultural concerns. Farmers began to default, incapable of paying their debts to the Bank of Brazil. As a UDR president stated, "Few people are aware that losing your land to the bank has become a more serious threat to landholders than land invasions" [Roosevelt Roque dos Santos, 18 August 1992]. Landholders claimed that these agricultural policies had had a universal impact on producers: "The crisis is now universal. It doesn't affect only small producers or producers of a specific product. You can't just explain it away as incompetence anymore. The cattle rancher always rented land to agricultural producers. In Rio Grande do Sul, 80 percent of the farmers rent land. But they are broke now and are renting less land. That affects even the cattle ranchers" [interview 17].

Despite these claims of a universal threat to rural producers, the UDR could not mobilize around agricultural policy. This failure points to some of the intrinsic weaknesses of uncivil movements. The threat never achieved the resonance with landholders that land invasions had. In part this was the result of the capacity of individual farmers to negotiate solutions. While producers could agree that the policies harmed them, they had different resources available to them to overcome threats. The UDR had avoided agricultural issues because of the wide diversity of rural sectors included in the movement. This had proved to be a constant source of frustration to the agricultural producers in the movement:

> The UDR, unhappily, did not make agricultural policy its central concern. It was more oriented toward defense of property. That was also one of our concerns [in Rio Grande do Sul]. But I felt strongly, and I talked to Caiado about this, that an entity like the UDR could not survive if it focused only on property issues. Its mobilization and articulation depended on the threat. That's what gave the UDR its support. It grew extremely rapidly. But the land issue would eventually be resolved. The issue of agricultural policy was important to continue to sustain the movement. [interview 79]

But the UDR also lacked the expertise to deal with the range of issues embodied in agricultural policies. Other entities had a competitive advantage over the UDR on that score. The Confederation of Agriculture, the federations of agriculture, the rural societies, and the cooperatives defended particular sectoral interests. And the *bancada ruralista* that the UDR helped establish also represented and protected agricultural production in the government. As already mentioned, official organs' corruption, cooptation, and accommodation have limited the appeal of these traditional entities among landholders. The criticisms of the *bancada* stem from the antipolitics sentiment among landholders. They accuse the *bancada* of having distanced itself from its agricultural base, thereby failing to comprehend the gravity of farmers' problems and to design effective solutions. Like other politicians, landholders view the *bancada* as out for personal gain. They believe that it is susceptible to bribes and corruption: "The president has begun to use [the *bancada ruralista*] for his own ends: an exchange of votes, manipulation, corruption. This is not illegal, but it is immoral. The *bancada* is not listening to its base" [interview 44].

Criticisms of these official and legislative organs suggest that the UDR may have been able to create a need for itself around agricultural policy issues. But a new organization of landholders filled that void. The "We Can't Plant" movement in 1995 mobilized around the country to raise consciousness about the plight of farmers. In July the movement blocked streets in Brasília, bringing in trucks, tractors, and farm machinery from various parts of the country. The event received phenomenal news coverage in which the movement was identified as an offshoot of the UDR, the reporters having no doubt picked up on the similarity in political tactics. Even some UDR leaders perceived the movement as a legacy of the UDR: "The spirit of the UDR still exists. The march . . . led by the Federation of Agriculture of Rio Grande do Sul was carrying the flag of the UDR. It had the unity and mobilization spirit of the UDR" [interview 4].

The link existed not only in tactics; some of the movement's leaders had been involved in the UDR. But the movement's organizers rejected any direct association with the UDR. And even some UDR leaders lamented the movement and its failure to have learned political strategy from the UDR. They criticized the movement for resorting to an outmoded, pre-UDR style of regional- and sectoral-based political action, rather than uniting the landholding class behind a common struggle:

> Now we've returned to the time pre-UDR: the bureaucrats [*lideranza de gabinete*]. The farmers' protest [*caminhonaço*] shows this. It was led by a civic group. The heads of it were those who feel agriculture in their bones. No one called these people together. These are men who are suffering. This is a base movement, a movement that the UDR once led. Now there is no leadership. The leaders went along in the farmers' protest—they didn't lead. [interview 64]

The limitations in the UDR case are instructive with regard to reducing the power of uncivil movements. The case points to the fragile unity forged during a period of emergency. While the UDR's charismatic leadership, political framing of the threat, and legitimating myths drew militant and moderate landholders together, it could not sustain that alliance. The Achilles heel of the movement was its dependence on Caiado and its link to violence. Once Caiado left the movement without a leader and the urgency behind the movement dissipated, feelings of exhaustion, betrayal, and revulsion over the violence surfaced. The UDR case hints at ways in which democratic governments can hasten the demise of uncivil movements, rather than waiting until after the movements achieve their victories for their appeal to dissipate.

Conclusion

The UDR is a good test case for the institutions approach to democratic stability. In a certain light it can be viewed as a confirmation of that approach. Landholders who had engaged in violent activities during the early years of the democratic period accepted the very moderate agrarian reform adopted in the 1988 constitution. They used a semi-institutional lobby to help shape political outcomes, obviating the need for extrainstitutional overthrows to protect their interests. Gradually, therefore, landholders became more confident of their ability to use the political system to confront future threats. They even tolerated the election of President Fernando Henrique Cardoso despite his leftist past and stated commitment to agrarian reform. Thus, moderation, institutionalization, and gradualism effectively ended the threat of authoritarian coups in the Brazilian UDR case.

While not entirely wrong, such an interpretation glosses over important implications of the institutions strategy for the future of democracy in Brazil. With regard to moderation, for example, the UDR used force not only to moderate but actually to reverse agrarian reform. The reform adopted in the constitution was less powerful than that instituted by the military regime. The democratic government avoided a potential coup conspiracy of threatened landholders, but it also eliminated the possibility for overcoming rural poverty and the gross inequality of land distribution in the country.

What would have happened, for example, if the government had implemented a progressive agrarian reform rather than the "moderate" one in the 1988 constitution? Of course we will never know the answer to this question. There is little evidence to suggest, however, that the UDR could have formed a coup conspiracy. It needed support within the military and some parts of the urban sector at the very least. It needed some support within civil society. But the UDR had not succeeded in expanding its base to include those sectors. Indeed, the UDR was widely viewed as an extremist movement out for its own narrow self-interest. Its radicalism was widely rejected by mainstream political society. Indeed, its radicalism even cost it support within its own rural community. The UDR played a very effective media game of pressure politics by bringing in truckloads of supporters, raising massive amounts of money, and hinting at the amassing of arms. But little support existed even within the movement for a coup. And the lack of support outside the movement for UDR goals brings into question its capacity to deliver on that threat.

Another problem with the moderation part of the institutions strategy is that the UDR mobilized against a moderate, actually conservative, government. Sarney should have been immune to overthrow. He had solid credentials on the right. He did not have the profile that should have threatened the right or prompted a rebellion. The UDR framed Sarney's agrarian reform as leftist to catalyze a right-wing reaction against it. This strategy demonstrates two points. First, the UDR's support was limited by the lack of a broad threat to democratic society. It could catalyze support from landholders, but urban and military sectors did not find the UDR's accusations against Sarney credible. Second, the UDR demonstrated that uncivil movements can mobilize against even moderate reforms. Therefore, a moderate approach to social reform will not necessarily prevent uncivil movements from emerging. Government action in limiting the power of these movements is therefore critical.

The UDR case also points to a weakness in institutionalization as a means of limiting uncivil movements. Even after the movement had formed a powerful lobby, landholder violence continued. Indeed, the peak of the UDR's lobbying activity coincided with the peak in rural violence. Rather than channeling political demands exclusively through the political system, institutions simply provided another weapon in addition to violence in the UDR's arsenal for promoting landholders' objectives.

Clearly the UDR had a democratic right to organize and lobby the executive and legislature. Institutionalization in itself therefore did not pose a problem for the democratic government, but the democratic government's inability to protect rural activists from enjoying the same political rights and personal security did pose problems. The judiciary's failure to investigate and prosecute cases of rural violence gave the UDR and other landholders carte blanche to eliminate the most powerful rural labor leaders in the country as well as less famous leaders. Whether the democratic governments deliberately and conspiratorially avoided these investigations and prosecutions or simply failed to provide adequate resources, they tolerated violations of human rights and undermined democratic institutions and authority.

Given the system of hired guns and middlemen, the government might have had a difficult time proving beyond a shadow of a doubt that UDR landholders were involved in violence against rural leaders. Making such a case would have required allocating more resources to the judiciary. It would also have required that the investigation and sentencing be unbiased, something that could not have been guaranteed. Clearly, the obstacles to overcoming the vicious cycle of landholder immunity are great. A concerted commitment to democratic justice and effective government, however, requires that the effort be made to overcome them.

Would UDR landholders indicted, prosecuted, and sentenced for rural violence become martyrs and so escalate the threat to the democratic government? This seems highly unlikely. First, those who did face the prospect of investigation have gone underground. The UDR has not championed their cause. On the contrary, it has used either denial or the bad-egg defense to

distance itself from these landholders' acts of violence. The UDR has justified the use of violence only in general principle (the right to defend property), not in individual cases.

Counterevidence suggests that the UDR would have met its demise much
sooner with careful investigation and prosecution of its members' involvement in violence. The pragmatists did not totally reject the movement's association with violence, but they were clearly uncomfortable with it. Government exposure of individual UDR members' involvement in murders
would have made it more difficult for the pragmatists to ignore the violence
and the movement's support of it. And the militant hard core lacked sufficient support to run the movement on their own; they needed the pragmatists. With the government involved in proving the UDR's violent streak, the
UDR would be hard pressed to remain even a latent movement. If it reemerged, it would have to shed its name, its leaders, and every association
with its past. Indeed, even without incontrovertible proof of violence, rural
leaders often eschewed association with the UDR for fear of stigma.

These criticisms of the institutions argument aside, the UDR case suggests ways in which institutionalization can erode a powerful movement. At
the height of the movement's struggle, the charismatic leadership, unconventional political action, and message of solidarity unified and mobilized a
powerful movement of landholders aimed at ending threats to private property. Ironically, this successful mobilization limited the UDR's future as a
movement. Attempts by some UDR leaders to transform the movement into
a permanent, semi-institutionalized lobby or institutionalized political party
brought out some of the contradictions that could be ignored at the height
of the struggle. Most members and leaders saw the movement as being about
a single issue: defeating agrarian reform. With their mission accomplished
in the 1988 constitution, they saw no point in remaining politically active.
This view was not shared by the hard core, who had much broader objectives than the constitutional protections. They distrusted government authorities to enforce the law and rural social movements to comply with it.
They saw a future for the UDR in vigilant protection of their gains in the
constitution. These hard-core leaders hinted at a readiness for violence to
enforce the law. Pragmatic leaders had overlooked the militia mentality in
the UDR at the height of struggle. After the UDR's victory, they looked forward to distancing themselves from this type of political action by with-
drawing from the movement.

A different group of pragmatic landholders also had a vision for the UDR's
future. The threat of agrarian reform was over, they claimed, but new threats

around economic and agricultural policy had surfaced that the UDR should combat with its message of injustice and solidarity, charismatic leadership, and unconventional political action. The new threat also indicated the tenuous alliance within the UDR. Some UDR leaders were so wealthy that the economic policies simply did not affect them. Others were not dependent upon agricultural production and therefore had no interest in forming part of a permanent lobby to defend those interests. Still others felt that agriculture was largely sectoral and adequately defended by the existing agricultural entities. In short, there was little enthusiasm behind a permanent lobby to defend changing landholding interests.

Part of the reluctance arose from the antipolitics strain within the movement. The institutional future of the movement disappeared because some leaders did not want to be part of a mainstream political movement. While they would mobilize to fight specific threats, they wanted no part of a permanent lobby. Indeed, these individuals began to view the charismatic Caiado with suspicion because of his evident taste for political life.

In short, the UDR was undermined by the combination of its initial success, its inability to develop into a permanent institution, and its factionalism. The loss of the charismatic leader, message of threat, and urgency further unraveled the movement. Yet, borrowing from Mark Twain, rumors of the UDR's death were greatly exaggerated. The UDR, an example of a latent uncivil movement, neither disappeared altogether nor transformed into a permanent political institution. This raises some questions about the habituation argument in the institutions strategy. The UDR, despite its successful foray into semi-institutional politics, never became the kind of political institution imagined in the institutions strategy. The UDR learned to use the democratic system, but without becoming democratic along the institutions strategy lines. It does not seem to be any more willing to compromise and accept reforms than before its experience in democratic politics. Instead, it remains poised to combat future land conflicts in Brazil. The UDR's legacy is one of combative politics, not compromise. It is one that continues to involve violence as a means of resolving rural conflicts.

The legacy of the UDR has affected democratic political culture. The UDR's capacity to shape political outcomes on the land issue has heightened land conflicts. The skewed distribution of land persists. Rural popular groups have mobilized in a more radical direction to try to end the social injustice. And landholders' hired guns have retaliated, along with public authorities, to end this radical political action. Far from reducing the sources of social tension in the new democracies, the institutions strategy in the Brazilian case has exacerbated them. In addition, the institutions strategy has weakened faith in the ability of democratic institutions to ensure basic democratic rights of equality, legal recourse, and personal security. The UDR has shaped political appointments, elections, and outcomes while representing a much smaller proportion of the Brazilian electorate than the landless peasants and their advocates. The democratic institutions have tended to protect landholders, perhaps fearing violent retaliation if they do not. The legitimacy of the executive, legislature, and judiciary, already weak in Brazil, is further undermined by the land issue.

The Brazilian case thus poses an alternative to the institutions strategy for controlling authoritarian groups. The institutions strategy in Brazil views contemporary politics through myopic lenses dating from the Goulart period. When Goulart implemented an agrarian reform, he provoked a wave of rural violence that ultimately escalated into an authoritarian overthrow. Sarney saw in the UDR's emergence a potential threat to his government. But the Sarney government might have learned more from the military regime's strategy than from Goulart's agrarian reform. Sarney was, after all, part of that regime. The military regime did not use force (although it might have done so) to implement its agrarian reform program. Instead it used inducements: payment for expropriation, compensatory colonization programs, and stimulation of the private-property sector to appease landholders. The Sarney government could have copied this strategy of compensating the private sector for its losses, thus preempting a landholders' mobilization. Recognizing the emotional and symbolic power of land redistribution, Sarney needed to demonstrate that he was not against landholders or private property. This kind of "moderation" does not involve capitulating to uncivil movements but is rather "artful negotiation."

Compensation might have been enough to diffuse the mobilization of the UDR. A fair number of the UDR's pragmatic leaders wanted little more than an assurance that agrarian reform did not mean socialization of private property. Negotiating adequate compensation could have resolved that concern. It might not have been an option, however, given the economic situation in Brazil at the time of the transition. Moreover, the insecurity felt by many on the right at the time of the transition still might have generated support for the UDR's leadership, message, and action. But the movement would have faced more difficulty attracting the pragmatists.

There is a twist to the UDR case that identifies one way in which institutionalization reduces the power of uncivil movements. Caiado could not resist the allure of public office, and the launch of his political career accelerated the demise of the movement; his political ambitions alienated the antipolitics faction of the movement, his embarrassing defeat eroded support for the movement even further, and the entire episode left the UDR without a charismatic leader. Negotiating an exit for leaders of uncivil movements, therefore, can weaken the movement's power by provoking factions, frustrations, and succession struggles.

There is another aspect of the UDR case that points to ways in which democratic governments can reduce the power of uncivil movements: the power of legitimating myths to generate support from moderate sectors. Moderates need such myths to justify their participation in uncivil movements. By investigating and prosecuting particular UDR leaders who were involved in violence, the democratic government could have made it much more difficult for the movement to spin myths around violence. By presenting the pragmatists with evidence of the UDR's use of violence, the government could have eroded their interest in joining the movement and so hastened its demise.

All of these strategies would have required political will on the part of the government. While I am sure that none of the democratic governments enjoyed the UDR thorn in their side, they may have found the landholders preferable to, and effective at controlling, the leftist CPT and MST. But political will is different from political stability. By failing to prosecute and capitulating to landholders, the democratic governments may have heightened political polarization, armed conflict, and disenchantment with the government. By failing to act, the government allowed landholders to get away with murder. Given the state of rural politics in Brazil, it is doubtful that much has changed with the transition from authoritarian rule. It is not surprising that leaders of popular rural movements refer to the democratic government as a recreation of authoritarian rule in democratic guise.

5 The Nicaraguan Contras

El arbolito is a landmark in Managua, Nicaragua, used to help locate addresses in a city in which street names and numbers are virtually nonexistent. This "little tree" stands defiantly in the middle of a busy street. Its story, like that of the Contras, is one of endurance if not strength. The city planners had tried to kill the tree to make the road. But the tree sprang back to life. They tried to kill it again, but the tree blossomed once more. Finally the planners had to accept the tree; it just wouldn't go away. And so they built a tiny monument around it. The tree never grew very big, but it persisted and formed part of the Nicaraguan consciousness.

The Contras tell a similar tale. Despite numerous efforts in recent years to rid the country of the Contras, they keep coming back. They emerged with the 1979 Nicaraguan Revolution, initially comprised of the Somoza dynasty's National Guard. The U.S. government had created the National Guard during its military intervention in Nicaragua in the 1920s. When the United States pulled out, it left the head of the guard, Anastacio Somoza Debayle, in charge of the country. He soon assumed dictatorial control over the country. National Guard repression, backed by U.S. support, helped sustain a Somoza dynasty. His control passed to his sons after his death. But in the 1970s a coalition of forces mobilized against the Somozas, culminating in the 1979 revolution.

Shortly after the revolution, the Marxist FSLN (Sandinista National Liberation Front) consolidated power. The Sandinistas took their name from Augusto Sandino, the peasant leader who had led a struggle for national liberation. Somoza's National Guard ambushed and murdered Sandino in 1934. The Sandinistas adopted the Sandino struggle for social change, targeting Somocistas and guardsmen as the enemies of the revolution.

Faced with imprisonment in postrevolutionary Nicaragua, guardsmen and

Somoza sympathizers generally chose exile. But one group of guardsmen joined a counterrevolutionary war against the Sandinistas. The following personal history of an ex-guardsman describes his path into the Contra war:

> I had been in the military since 1973. I had traveled to West Point and to Argentina for training. I had taken some courses in accounting, but I was basically a military man. In 1979 [after the revolution] I was told I should leave the country. The Red Cross met us to lift us out, but we were surrounded. I went to jail, but then I escaped and went to Honduras. I fought [with the Contras] between 1984 and 1987. I was head of intelligence. [interview 18]

Like him, most of the guardsmen joined the Contra forces organizing on the Honduran border, first in MILPAS (the People's Anti-Sandinista Militias) and then in the FDN (Nicaraguan Democratic Front). The FDN proliferated from 1979 to the mid-1980s with the help of U.S. training, funding, and direction.

The FSLN's elite trained army, the EPS (Sandinista People's Army), fought a civil war against the Contras but failed to defeat them. Indeed, the Contra forces began to swell, incorporating, along with the Somocistas and guardsmen, peasants, indigenous peoples, and even former revolutionaries. This shift in the composition of the Contra forces allowed the Reagan administration to portray the group not as the personal army of the former dictatorship but rather as "freedom fighters" and "the moral equivalent of our founding fathers." The United States even renamed the Contras the Resistance to capture this image of a Nicaraguan people standing up to the Sandinistas' repressive regime.

The story of the Contras is much more complex than the "Resistance" designation connotes. Among the peasants who joined the Contras were some who had defended the Somoza regime and attacked the "Sandinista dictatorship," as in the following case:

> I was with the Resistance since the beginning. The Sandinistas arrived, and I was with the Resistance. I was 100 percent against their communist, Marxist, Leninist ideologies. I was a member of the Liberal Party— the National Liberal Party—with Somoza. I'm not embarrassed to say it. We lived a very peaceful life in those days . . . [unlike] the dark nights of the Sandinista era. . . . The Sandinistas used grotesque pressure. There was rationing of food. We were forced to do vigilance from block to block. We had to be in lines for everything. We were warned that if

we didn't collaborate with them we would go to prison. . . . Above all,
the Sandinistas were anti-Christian. In the name of Christ I must reject
them in the deepest place in my heart. [interview 48]

Other peasants joined the Contras for instrumental rather than ideological reasons. Peasants struggling to survive in the war zone found some relief
in the U.S.-sponsored war. They received desperately needed food, health
care, and spending money once they began fighting with the Contras. An
OAS (Organization of American States) officer working in the Managua
peacekeeping mission explained that peasants, unable to produce or sell their
agricultural products because of the war, ironically found some protection
by fighting on the Contra side: "During the war they were taken care of.
They ate well. They were healthy. . . . They even had mosquito repellent! One
told me that when he was with the Contras he ate meat two or three times a
week. Since the end of the war he has gone two or three months without
eating a piece of meat" [anonymous].

Joining the Contra side of the war made logical sense; after all, how could
the Contras lose with their U.S. backing? A surprising lack of political passion characterized many Contras' explanations for joining the war. For example: "I was thirteen years old when I entered MILPAS. I didn't like the
[Sandinista] government, but I can't really say why. My family had land. The
Sandinistas said that it was given to us from Somoza. You had to be against
them, because things were bad" [interview 24].

Evidence suggests that it was only after the peasant-Contras had begun
their training that their explanations for joining the Contras acquired an
ideological patina. In interviews they frequently repeated, verbatim, the same
line: "We were the containment wall against international communism."
Those who had not entered the war for ideological reasons, in other words,
learned such reasons shortly after entering the war.

The Sandinistas' policy errors further explain the Contras' rise. Peasants
and revolutionaries joined the Contras to oppose the Sandinista government's
monopoly of power, political exclusion, and distorted agrarian policies. The
story of one such Contra and his brothers illustrates how peasants who had
supported the revolution began to turn against the FSLN:

In 1977–79 we had been with the Sandinistas. Two of my brothers died
fighting for the revolution. . . . We had come from a peasant family. In
1979 my family was rewarded for everything we had done for the
revolution: I was given a scholarship to study in Cuba. I studied
agricultural techniques for growing coffee and cocoa. I came back from

Cuba as a young revolutionary with a communist spirit. I was excited about living in the new democracy. But we lived in one of the most war-torn zones in the country. Peasants were at war. I began to hear a lot of negative things from the peasants. They began to call the Sandinistas *piricuaco*. This was a term invented by the Sandinistas in 1979 to refer to the National Guard. It means a dog out for blood. But now people were using it against the Sandinistas: Sandinista *piricuaco*. The Sandinistas stole from people. They were killing peasants. . . . I began to attend the assemblies of the Sandinista Youth and to criticize things. I talked about the things that were going on. And one person, a person who I know had been a Somocista and later became a Sandinista, called me a reactionary. *He* was calling *me* a reactionary! . . . Then my brothers were called for military service. And they opted to fight for the Contras instead of fighting for the EPS. . . . So in 1983 we began our anti-Sandinista activity. We joined MILPAS. We wanted to overcome the errors of the revolution. We wanted to make our dreams of the revolution come true: for the people of the countryside to be treated with respect. This was the way of our father. On 4 February 1988 my father was killed by the EPS for being the father of Resistance fighters. [interview 13]

This story conveys some of the excesses and abuses local FSLN leaders carried out in rural areas. It also illustrates the highly unpopular conscription of teenagers into the EPS. Both issues turned peasants against the Sandinistas. But peasant-Contras also criticized the FSLN for its agrarian programs of collectivized agriculture, price controls, and state control over the purchase of agriculture products. Disillusionment with the FSLN, and particularly its consolidation of power after the revolution, spread throughout the country, provoking revolutionary leaders to defect from it.[1] One revolutionary hero, Eden Pastora (Comandante Zero), organized a group of ex-revolutionaries to fight against the Sandinistas on the Costa Rican border. Under Pastora's leadership these ex-revolutionaries maintained an ambiguous relationship with the other Contras. They denied involvement in the Contra movement while still using U.S. funds to fight the Sandinistas, as this leader of the Southern Command explained: "There was a struggle against fascism and totalitarianism. We weren't Contras; we were revolutionaries. We were for change; we were for honesty, liberty, democracy, a dignified foreign policy. That's why we were ready to die, to fight. In the North [the Contras] wanted the status quo ante, subordination, the people as an instrument, revenge, hatred" [interview 62]. Eventually Pastora left the Southern Command, contributing to a closer alliance between the Northern and Southern Commands in the war.

The ex-revolutionary branch of the Contras also included indigenous peoples of Nicaragua's Atlantic Coast, primarily Miskito. The indigenous peoples had initially formed an alliance with the Sandinista government, believing that the Sandinistas would recognize the historical rights of the indigenous peoples and end the repression, exploitation, and poverty they had experienced under Somoza. But when they perceived the Sandinistas as not only reneging on the promises of cultural rights and autonomy in the region but also imposing their own repressive rule, they soured on the FSLN and mobilized against it:

> As indigenous people we had hoped that 1979 would bring a change in Managua's attitude about the region. Many of us supported Sandinismo. I did, too. However, the nature of the totalitarian system that was implanted did not allow the struggle for change that has been going on here for five hundred years. They were the solution. They would bring equality between people. They would bring the new man. They would make all of the properties part of the state. The state would organize people. . . . It's too bad that we had to fight, for our land and our culture. And I don't mean culture in the sense of going out there and beating a drum. I mean the survival of our people and our nation as we have developed it over thousands of years. What we wanted was recognition of our economic relations, our health system, the right to govern ourselves, to elect our own authorities in our area. We wanted to realize these objectives after so many years of domination, racism, apartheid. [interview 8]

> [The Sandinistas] told us they were going to restore our historic rights, and we trusted them. We have always been poor. And because we are indigenous people, we felt especially oppressed. The Sandinistas said they were going to recognize our lands. We formed Misurasata, a union of the Miskito, Sumo, and Rama peoples with the Sandinistas. . . . Up until this point we hadn't really had any war. But we sympathized with the Sandinistas. On 18 February 1981 we were all going to sign the agreement to recognize the Miskito land. We were all very happy. But on 17 February 1981 they ordered our capture. Brooklin, Stedman, the leaders of the community, were captured. We were accused of being

counterrevolutionaries, of being people of the CIA. But we didn't even know what the CIA was! And we had never gotten along with the guard. They said that we were trying to separate the Atlantic Coast from the rest of the country and this was part of a CIA project. This is when the conflict occurred. We were all surprised. . . . One of our leaders was assassinated. And the pressure was great. By the middle of March 1981 we were involved in conflict. There was persecution by the state security apparatus. . . . The Sandinistas wanted to use us like instruments. . . . We started to think it was time to go. Some of us went to Honduras. And then more groups left, and then more. We became militarized because there was no liberty. . . . We could see that things were getting more conflictual. So we started to train. We didn't have any shoes, but we were going to fight the Sandinistas. [interview 44]

The Sandinistas recognized the errors they had made on the Atlantic Coast and tried to correct them.[2] But by the time the Sandinistas granted an autonomy law for the Atlantic Coast, it was too late; massive numbers of indigenous people had joined the armed struggle against the Sandinistas. Even Atlantic Coast Sandinistas faulted the FSLN for failing to understand the indigenous culture, committing errors that could have been avoided and that led to Contra support among the indigenous peoples:

There was one flight a week to Managua. We would say, "Let's go to Nicaragua." It seemed like another country to us. Here the climate is different: tropical and humid. The churches are different: Moravian and Protestant. We were taught in English. . . . My memory is still fresh. We remember, but with a little less passion, the war. After the revolution there was a utopia. The USSR and Cuba were still able to help us out. There was a Sandinista government in Nicaragua. There was a war going on against our rights. The war never should have begun. The indigenous peoples were poor. The theoreticians of the revolution didn't recognize indigenous people. Cuba didn't serve as a model: [in Cuba] the indigenous peoples had already been eradicated. . . . The theory was political and military. Somocismo, like other dictatorships, didn't provide any space for us. The revolution began with good intentions. There would be participation, democracy, etc. But the policies were not always implemented very well in all places. The propaganda produced fear in people. [interview 67]

Other Sandinistas, while recognizing FSLN errors in rural and indigenous areas, contend that the FSLN never had a chance to succeed; U.S. propaganda and the counterrevolutionary war undermined it before it could bring solutions to peasants and indigenous peoples:

> There was little the revolution could do in one year; it would take many years. How could you enjoy the revolution in such a short time? So the Contras were invented. Communism was going to eat the children. And these are very humble people. Communism is going to take away your land. We had always believed in God, and the propaganda said that communism would eliminate the church. The United States did here what it has done in Grenada, Panama, and elsewhere. That is, it made the revolution hostage in a protracted war. The obligatory military service is what made the most enemies of the revolution, and that only existed because of the war. . . . The criticism [of the Sandinistas] is around the problems of scarcity. But there was a blockade. There was plenty of money, but no food to buy because of the blockade. [interview 73]

But others suggest that the FSLN's ideology was incompatible with peasant and indigenous cultures, both of which historically distrusted the state. Prior to the revolution, the state rarely interacted with either peasants or indigenous peoples. Few state services extended to isolated rural and indigenous areas. And when the state intervened, it often used repressive force to control or manipulate rural areas. Failing to appreciate this history, the Sandinistas blindly played into the image of a coercive state.[3] While conscription probably could not have been avoided, given the Contra war, some Sandinistas later realized that they had moved too far, too quickly in land tenure, production, and marketing reforms that stimulated support for the Contras: "The peasants joined the Contras because of the church and the strong dose of anticommunism. They didn't have much education. And there were abuses. Instead of Leninism, we needed to keep looking for Sandino. We committed errors. We were dogmatic, more pope than the pope. It was capitalism by the state" [interview 5].

U.S. support and Sandinista policy errors, in other words, forged an alliance of Somocistas, ex-revolutionaries, peasants, and indigenous peoples prepared to fight against the FSLN. While fighting for different reasons and often in independent operations, the Northern, Southern, and Atlantic Coast Commands eventually consolidated under the direction of the FDN's Enrique Bermúdez, a former National Guardsman.

Despite working together for nearly a decade, the Contras failed to militarily defeat the EPS. Of course, the well-trained EPS never defeated the Contras, either. Several international peace negotiation efforts during the decade of war failed. The Contadora peacemaking process involved five Latin American countries and promised the Contras amnesty and a negotiated settlement, to no avail. Different conferences, involving the Central American presidents, advanced the prospects for peace but did not end the conflict. The Contras endured despite the surprising electoral defeat of the Frente Sandinista in February 1990. And even after Violeta Chamorro took office as the new Nicaraguan president, backed by a coalition of forces favorable to the Contras, they remained mobilized. And even though the Contra war ended with the Chamorro government's diplomatic assurances, resettlement camps (development poles), and amnesties to disarm and reincorporate the Contras into Nicaraguan life, the Contras endured. They even survived assassinations of their leaders. Rather than disbanding, one group of Contras formed a political party, the PRN (Party of Nicaraguan Resistance). Another group rearmed and returned to the mountains as "Recontras" to pressure the government to fulfill the peace agreements and provide former Contra combatants with land, housing, jobs, and social services such as health care and education. Through a series of military operations and government buy-offs, or rewards for loyalty, the Chamorro government nearly eliminated the Recontras. Nonetheless, rural criminal bands, left over from the Recontras, continue to prey on rural communities and battle government troops. And the PRN, despite its divisions over leadership and its failure to win any seats in the local Atlantic Coast elections in 1994, survived and competed in local and national elections in 1996.

The Contras, like the *arbolito*, have endured despite concerted efforts to eliminate them. Their persistence has made them part of a contemporary Nicaraguan reality. But they are not a powerful movement. Like the *arbolito*, they are tenacious, yet small and weak. And their relative weakness provides insights into the factors that can limit uncivil movements' political power in democratic systems.

The Contras' Political Success

While weak compared with the other uncivil movements examined in this book, the Contras have influenced Nicaraguan politics. The left and the right concur that the Contra war contributed to the Sandinistas' demise, particularly their defeat in the 1990 presidential elections. The Contras and the right contend that their moral suasion won over the Nicaraguan people and their military prowess provided the electorate with the backing they needed to vote their conscience. The left, in contrast, blames the Contra war for preventing the FSLN from carrying out its social revolution to reduce inequality and poverty. The FSLN was forced to divert scarce resources from fighting poverty, illness, and illiteracy in order to battle the Contras. What Nicaraguans voted for in the 1990 elections was not an end to the Sandinistas but an end to the Contra war, its violence, and the misery it inflicted on the country. Even some Sandinistas voted against the FSLN candidate and incumbent president Daniel Ortega in 1990 because they believed that his victory would prolong and perhaps even escalate the war. Both the Contra and FSLN versions confirm that the Contras achieved their primary goal: the Sandinistas' defeat.

The Contras also succeeded in returning to Nicaragua. The victorious President Chamorro and her UNO (National Opposition Union) party negotiated cease-fire agreements to disarm and resettle Contra combatants. As table 5.1 shows, the peacemaking process began well before the 1990 elections. But only after the 1990 elections did the Contras accept disarmament. In the 1990 agreements, the Contras won their goals of "development poles," land distribution, jobs, and social services to assist in their reintegration into Nicaraguan society.

The Contras could also count among their political victories the removal of top Sandinistas from government positions. Chamorro had tried to avoid polarization, and to ease the transition, by retaining some Sandinistas in their government positions, although the U.S. government and the Contras pressured Chamorro to remove them. Under duress, Humberto Ortega, head of the EPS, resigned from Chamorro's government, signifying a Contra and U.S. political victory.

These political successes notwithstanding, the Contras never proved capable of gaining the same kind of victories in legislation or in branches of government as the other uncivil movements examined in this book. The PRN elected only one congressman. It had finished fourth in the 1994 local elections on the Atlantic Coast but won no political seats as a result. Most important, the Contras failed to achieve their most significant postwar demand: fulfillment of the 1990 peace accords. In other words, despite some limited success, the Contras provide an example of weak political framing, cultural cuing, and mythmaking.

TABLE 5.1   Evolution of Cease-Fire Agreements in Nicaragua

Agreement	Year	Goals	Outcomes
Contadora Group Mexico, Venezuela, Colombia, Panama	1983	Avoid war between Nicaragua and Honduras	(1984) Nicaragua agrees; Reagan administration urges Honduras, El Salvador, and Costa Rica to demand changes in accord
Arias Plan: *Esquipulas I* Presidents of Costa Rica, El Salvador, Guatemala, Honduras	1987 (Feb)	Establish legitimate rule in Nicaragua through association with other Central American countries; establish internal democracy; end aid to Contras	Rejected because of prohibition of aid to Contras and internal democratization clause
Arias Plan: *Esquipulas II* Presidents of Costa Rica, El Salvador, Guatemala, Honduras, Nicaragua	1987 (Aug)	Establish procedure for a firm and lasting peace in Central America	Nicaragua government sets up National Reconciliation Commission; Contra-government dialogue begins
Sapoá Nicaraguan government and Contras	1988	Cease-fire	Contras break off talks
El Salvador Summit Central American presidents	1989 (Feb)	Disband Contra army	U.S. approves nonlethal aid to maintain Contras; peace process on hold
Tela Summit Central American presidents	1989 (Apr)	Prepare for Nicaraguan elections; deploy international peacemakers; dismantle Contras	Contras reinfiltrate Nicaragua; Ortega cancels cease-fire
San Isidro Emergency Summit Central American presidents	1989 (Dec)	Reconsideration of cease-fire and Contra demobilization	Expand international peacekeeping apparatus
Resettlement Chamorro government and Contras	1990	Disarmament and reintegration of Contras	23 development poles (3,280 square miles) for rural economic development with security forces, social services, job creation and extension

Sources: Walker, *Revolution*; Martí i Puig, *La Revolución*.

POLITICAL FRAMING

The political environment in which the Contras evolved is different from the other cases analyzed in this book. They mobilized shortly after the 1979 revolution and before the Sandinista regime had become what most scholars would label "democratic." The revolution marked a first phase in the transition from authoritarian rule, but the war that ensued shortly thereafter posed a unique set of problems for guaranteeing democratic rights and freedoms. Even the 1984 elections, widely considered to be democratic, failed to end the war. Thus, for the purposes of this study the post-1990 period, when the Contras returned to Nicaragua from war, provides more insight into their impact on democratic politics.[4]

The end of the war surprised the Contras. They had not expected fair elections, freedom for Nicaraguans to vote for the FSLN's opposition, or the FSLN's withdrawal from government. When Chamorro not only won but assumed office, the Contras lost their raison d'être. The commanding officers for each Contra unit signed the cease-fire agreement with the Chamorro government, and Contras turned in their arms and returned to civilian life in Nicaragua.

Tired of war and exile, most Contras eagerly anticipated restarting their lives in their own country. And they felt sure that the Chamorro government and the United States would fulfill the cease-fire agreements. It was a rude awakening, therefore, when the agreements fell through, the Contras lost leverage over President Chamorro, and the United States abandoned Nicaragua and the Contra struggle. In this context, Contras mobilized against the Chamorro government:

> The agreements were lamentable. They were based on disarming without getting anything in exchange, elections without any guarantees. We didn't participate at all [in the elections or in the agreements]. We were treated poorly. The UNO [Chamorro's political party] became an obstacle to peace. There is frustration—so much blood was spilled in the war. The elections would not have been possible without the war. There could at least be something to help out the people. But there is not even any effort to talk to them. There is no answer for them. [interview 32]

The Chamorro government admitted that it could not fulfill its promises to the Contras. The government had anticipated eight thousand returning Contras, not the twenty thousand who actually turned in their arms in exchange for land. The government, woefully inexperienced and administratively overwhelmed, could not satisfy even the basic needs of these individuals. An anonymous member of the Tripartite Commission overseeing the peace accords stated that the government fulfilled only about 40 percent of its agreements.

This political environment produced an abundance of potential catalyst threats. The Contras faced poverty, landlessness, unemployment, violence, and a lack of social services as the result of the Chamorro government's failure to fulfill the cease-fire agreements. They faced a grave situation, but they did not unite behind the argument that the government was ignoring Contras while satisfying the ex-EPS members' needs. According to government statistics, for example, Contras received more of the resettlement benefits than EPS combatants. The Nicaraguan Agrarian Reform Institute (INRA) distributed land to 6,374 ex-combatants. Of those, 5,309 (83%) were ex-members of the Resistance and 1,065 (17%) were ex-members of the EPS.[5] The Contras therefore received substantially more land than the demobilized EPS soldiers. But the 5,309 who received land comprise only about 25 percent of the 20,000 Contras who officially disarmed in 1990. In short, only a small portion of the Contras actually received land from the government.

Those Contras who received land were forced to fight for legal title to it. Bureaucratic inefficiency created most of these delays, though some resulted from competing claims. These conflicts arose, ironically, when the Chamorro government distributed land to Contras that the Sandinistas had confiscated. The prior owners, Nicaraguan exiles in Miami, contested the redistribution of their land.[6] Thus, peasant-Contras clashed with the so-called *confiscados*, their former allies during the war. The *confiscados* have demanded that the Chamorro government either return their property to them or compensate them in dollars for its market value.

Peasant-Contras who received land also had difficulty making the land productive. They could not afford seeds, fertilizers, or other agricultural inputs. And without land titles, they were unable to obtain credit. Many ex-combatants, having spent their entire adult lives at war rather than on the land, lacked farming experience.[7] As one Contra explained, "Ninety-five percent of the Resistance were peasants, and some were very young. So even if they used to work the land, they've forgotten how. We have to readapt them [to agricultural production]. But this is not easy when people have lived their entire lives watching their backs" [interview 13]. Without the minimal conditions to produce, many Contras sold the land they received from the resettlement programs. One anonymous government official, formerly a Contra combatant, estimates that 70–80 percent have done so. Lacking a regular source of income, the multitude joined the ranks of the urban un- or under-employed.

Not all of the land was sold out of desperation, however. Even Contra leaders criticize ex-Contra combatants for "cheating" on the government's land distribution program. One leader involved in the reincorporation process claimed that ex-combatants sold the land they were given to make a profit and then turned around and "squatted" on new lands:

> We have to begin to change the mentality. Historically there has been a paternalistic mentality here. People don't understand that they have rights but also responsibilities. They are selling off the land that they were given [as a result of the peace accords]. They must learn to be honest. Land is a problem. There were four thousand lots in Managua handed out. These lots have been sold, and then the people go on to invade new lands. They are doing business off of the agreements. Nicaraguans have to learn to help themselves. We need to organize ourselves and get stronger. We need to evolve. We need to develop trust, to develop serious people. [interview 32]

The development poles illustrate another set of problems associated with the land distribution programs. The Contras criticize the poles for locating people on land in regions in which they lacked family, farming experience, and support networks. Sandinistas in the development poles, according to the Contras, created a hostile environment. So while some Contras remained in these zones and eventually became part of the community, others sold their land and moved to the city or to other rural areas where they had relatives.

Socioeconomic conditions exacerbated the land problems and heightened Contras' sense of abandonment. With 60 percent unemployment in the country and 70 percent of the population living below the poverty line, most Nicaraguans live in misery. Because of their limited education and peasant background, the Contras are perhaps penalized more than the demobilized EPS. The EPS, drawn primarily from urban backgrounds and trained in urban areas, had greater access to education during the war. As one Contra leader stated, "The [Sandinista] army was largely drawn from urban groups. They had better access to schools. Many in the Resistance don't know how to read or write" [interview 32]. Another commented that "the Sandinistas are professionals, but we've lost time. We're behind" [interview 46]. Contras expressed great frustration with their limited marketability in the postwar era:

> I am forty-five years old. I lost fifteen years of my life in politics. It is only now that I am able to study. [interview 79]

> Men who are thirty or forty years old are just now beginning to study. All of those lost years! So they really have to put in the effort to stay with it. Some commanders think only of the stars they earned in battle. "I managed one hundred people," they think. "What am I doing back here without work?" This is really hard. I earned a B.A. in war, but it isn't something I can put on my résumé. [interview 46]

In short, Contras' limited access to land, skills, jobs, and education created bleak prospects for their resettlement. In this situation, ex-combatants sought out their former commanding officers for help in solving their problems. But now, in peacetime, these commanders no longer had access to money, food, or medicine:

> We came [back to the country] with a certain mentality from the mountains. Those of us in the High Command had ex-combatants coming to us as if we were still their commanders. They were looking to us to take care of them. Money could keep them content. Everything was resolved with money. But we had to tell them, "This isn't the war. It's very different. There isn't money to give out." This was a hard lesson to learn. It wasn't their fault. In the war, whatever we wanted we asked for and an airlift brought it to us. The programs that were set up to help the ex-combatants have failed completely. [interview 18]

Both the commanders who formed the PRN and those who became Recontras explained their postwar political involvement as a sense of duty to their troops: "We have a responsibility to them. We want to live to see the day that men who fought against communism aren't hungry. Because that is our reality" [interview 75]. This responsibility sometimes even drove commanders to give up their dreams of leading a "normal" life again. Instead, they felt compelled to remain involved in the Contra struggle:

> In 1991 I returned to Managua. I had two different sets of feelings. One was happiness to be back in the country where I thought I would never be again. I met up with old friends; I could remember the old places, the old things we did. But the other feeling was facing life without any

support, without anything. Poverty, assassinations, injustice. There are still people in jail for things they didn't do. So I went to the West—to León—where there was never any war. And I disappeared from the war. I learned to live with a low profile. . . . But as a commander, even if I wanted to I could not give up on the struggle. I had to find an answer for all of those people I had commanded. I had a moral responsibility for these troops. I needed to make those demands for which we had fought. [interview 66]

Contras have received veterans pensions to partially compensate for the time and opportunities they lost because of the war. But even these pensions have left them feeling discriminated against and bitter. They claim that EPS veterans receive higher pensions than Contra veterans. The Contra director of an agency designed to assist veterans and victims of the war contends that actually the opposite is probably true. In his assessment, both groups receive miserable pensions, and he even suggests that the Contras may have benefited more than the Sandinistas [interview 32].

Contras also consider themselves to be uniquely targeted for violence in the postwar period. Enrique Bermúdez was just one of the top Contra leaders murdered after returning to Nicaragua. The investigation never turned up any suspects for his murder, committed in broad daylight in the parking lot of the exclusive Hotel Intercontinental.[8] Bermúdez's second in command, "Comandante Fernando," was murdered in 1992 in front of a bar where he had been enjoying a drink with his brother-in-law. Two agents of the state security apparatus were found guilty and sentenced for this murder, but Fernando's widow claimed in her interview with me that they were released from prison before completing their sentences.

Although only top leaders seemed targeted for murder,[9] a climate of insecurity prevailed in the postwar era that threatened Contras at all different levels. The government's failure to investigate or punish rampant violence throughout the country heightened the sense of insecurity, particularly acute in the rural areas, where few government agencies of any type provide protection or justice. In the highly polarized postwar environment, Contras interpreted these crimes as deliberate: "The reinsertion has been difficult. On average, about one demobilized Resistance fighter is murdered per week, sometimes more, sometimes less. And 95–98 percent of those who are to blame for these murders have total immunity. This is in large part due to police negligence. There is no investigation. Indeed, the police and the army are involved in most of these murders" [interview 59]. Contras believe that they have been the target of more violence than Sandinistas: "More Contras died than Sandinistas [after the war]. I once heard a Sandinista say, 'Our plan is to kill them off, one by one, until there is not one left'" [interview 57].

Yet Sandinistas claim that they have suffered a disproportionate share of the postwar violence, as well as being unfairly accused of causing violence:

> [The Contras] have a mercenary attitude, something like "I fought in the war, so I have a right to something." This is ignorance. . . . The only explanation for the lack of armed conflict here is the behavior of the FSLN. Because there are a lot of provocations. We just don't respond to them. There is a car accident and someone dies, and everyone says, "The FSLN caused the accident to kill the person." Someone goes crazy and begins shooting, and people say, "They were sent by the FSLN." [interview 73]

Both the Contras and the Sandinistas have their own human rights agencies, which have documented violence against each faction. It is impossible to judge which side has suffered more.[10] And the nature of the violence has changed over the years. In the current context of widespread distrust of state security organs ostensibly designed to provide physical safety, investigate crimes, and prosecute the guilty, Nicaraguans on both political sides have resorted to private forms of security. Lawlessness prevails both in terms of increased numbers of violent crimes and in terms of the failure to prosecute them. As one representative of the Organization of American States involved in the demobilization remarked, "The lack of a state is not just in infrastructure. Communities do not have judges or police, and what [security apparatus] does exist is insufficient. Violence becomes privatized. Everyone takes the law into their own hands. Armed groups establish their own order" [anonymous].

In short, the Contras had ample opportunity to mobilize around several potential catalyst threats: little land, little possibility of producing on that land, few jobs and low pensions, and violence directed against them. Faced with such threats, Contras felt abandoned and excluded from the democratic process. They felt betrayed by their former supporters and compatriots in the government who, after the war, ignored them and their serious problems: "There is a democratic government [in Nicaragua today]. We are not represented in it, but it is democratic. And it is the result of our efforts. Without the Contras, this would be a totalitarian country, like Cuba" [interview 33].

Contras also felt betrayed by the U.S. government. Contras believed that the United States had prevented a military defeat of the FSLN by negotiating the end of the war. Many contended that they could have militarily defeated the Sandinistas with U.S. help, and the victory would have provided them with the protections they needed in the postwar era. Instead, the U.S. government, the Chamorro government, and the Contras negotiated a peace agreement that promised much on paper but delivered little in reality:

> I was never in agreement with the demobilization. I wanted to fight for a military victory. But the circumstances didn't permit it. We could have won the war if our allies had supported us. But the United States only wanted to give enough support to pressure the government, not to win the war. I was against the Esquipulas agreements, the peace agreements. I thought [the cease-fire agreement] was a death sentence. I was against it. We disarmed, but the EPS stayed the same—the structure of the EPS remained the same. We handed in our arms because of elections, and then we returned. [interview 22]

An angrier view of the U.S. deception was articulated by this Contra leader:

> We returned believing in their lie. The situation had been negotiated by Washington. We realized we were going to have to begin preparing ourselves once the negotiations began. And this meant preparing ourselves psychologically for when we would go back to Nicaragua. But we had no idea about what we would actually face. If we had known, we would still be armed. The hunger, the poverty, the unemployment, the dislocation, the assaults on the highways. There is nothing for people to do. They don't have work. We taught them how to do carpentry and other types of semiskilled labor. But when we came back, of course, there wasn't anything for them to do. But there were arms for killing and robbing. That was the easiest way to make money. The government and its ally are to blame. They provided the guns and did away with our youth. And we didn't agree with the decision to disarm. But there wasn't any option. The people didn't want any more war. The war was won in Washington, whether we accepted it or not, whether we thought it was wrong or right. The government was still elected. We couldn't oppose it. We had to accept the decision. We had fought for the people. And they were tired of all the blood. [interview 1]

Contras also felt abandoned by the cadre of Nicaraguan politicians who had supported them in Washington during the war. After the war these politicians returned to their former political lives within their old political parties, unconcerned about the fate of ex-combatants. As one Contra commander put it, "We fought and fought, and then others took power. There is a lot of feeling against the politicians" [interview 44]. When these politicians did meet with Contras, they offered them handouts or bribed them with money or positions to join their political party. Some Contras recognized that only by mobilizing themselves could they overcome their political exclusion:

> The politicians never come down to the village to discover what it's like. We, the leaders who live in the community, know what it's like. . . . Whoever seems to be able to put a finger in the dike is going to get support. What is Arnaldo Alemán good for? He is the maximum leader for a strong political current. He is only going to solve the problems of the bourgeoisie. There aren't any presidents who are going to come down and talk to us—of these there are very few. . . . The base that elected them is forgotten. We know this now from experience. It doesn't matter how nicely they talk; we don't get anything from talk. [interview 10]

Why weren't the Contras able to mobilize successfully, given the ample supply of catalyst threats available? Part of their weakness resulted from ineffective framing. They had little difficulty identifying the threat given the inequitable land distribution and rural poverty that plagued ex-Contra combatants. Ex-Contras faced rampant unemployment, along with ex-EPS combatants and the noncombatant rural and urban poor. The contemporary poor's struggle, moreover, was linked to a history of political exclusion around which the Contras mobilized.

Blaming and aiming, however, proved more difficult. The Contras' key enemy—the Sandinistas—could not be held responsible for the failure to fulfill the cease-fire agreements. They had not created the agreements, nor were they in a position to stall or advance them. Instead, the Contras had to blame the Chamorro government and, to a lesser extent, the U.S. government. But how could they demonize the only two forces likely and able to defend them? Without a scapegoat for their problem, the Contras could not effectively unite behind uncivil action.

Moreover, the Contras could not credibly claim success in overcoming the threat. In most Nicaraguans' minds the Contras were associated with the National Guard, which had historically perpetuated, rather than ameliorated, systems of inequality and injustice. While a military victory over the Sandinistas might have established the Contras as national heroes, at least in some eyes, the FSLN left after an electoral defeat. The Contras could claim, at best, only an indirect victory over the Sandinistas—hardly the stuff of which heroes are made.

In short, history and circumstance prevented the Contras from framing the situation to unite a broad constituency around an urgent and universal threat. And their efforts were further hampered by the absence of strong cultural cues upon which they could build the movement.

CULTURAL CUES

The Contras tried to foster unity around the cultural symbol of the peasantry, and particularly the heroic icon of Augusto Sandino. Sandino had led a peasant rebellion in the 1920s to end the inegalitarian distribution of land and political power, and the imperialism and dictatorship that perpetuated it. His Robin Hood–style social programs, the brave stand he took against the United States, and his eventual martyrdom transformed him into Nicaragua's undisputed political hero. Thus, following the defeat of the Sandinistas and after the Chamorro government removed from public spaces most other symbols erected by the FSLN, Sandino's enormous silhouette statue, complete with his signature peasant hat and bandanna, remains standing on a hill overlooking Managua.

Sandino posed complications as a Contra cultural icon. For starters, the FSLN had already claimed Sandino as its own hero, even adopting his name. With his image so bound up with the Sandinistas, Contras could neither use Sandino's name, dress like him, nor adorn their party headquarters with his picture. What the Contras tried to do instead was portray the Sandinistas as betraying Sandino and the Nicaraguan revolution. They appropriated the Sandinistas discourse against Somocismo and turned it against the FSLN. In this way they demonized their enemy, transforming the Sandinistas into a political regime against which Sandino himself would have fought for national liberation. They blamed the FSLN for Soviet and Cuban imperialist domination of Nicaragua, a charge the FSLN and Sandino had successfully launched against the United States. They labeled the FSLN power-hungry and corrupt, echoing a key criticism of Somoza, especially when he profited off the international relief aid provided for the 1972 earthquake victims. The Contras capitalized on the FSLN's piñata scandal, in which the FSLN distributed land and property to its top leadership before leaving office. In the Contra discourse, the piñata provided incontrovertible proof that the

FSLN was no more committed to the people or social justice than Somoza's "kleptocracy" had been. Both were cut from the same corrupt cloth:

> The FSLN . . . showed their corruption with the piñata. Their leaders were undermined with the piñata. While the peasants and workers are hungry and living with scarcity, these guys are dividing up the riches. [interview 46]

> There is no national consensus. There are different interests: Sandinistas vs. democrats. Among the Sandinistas, there is no sense of justice. . . . Right now you're seen as either revolutionary or counterrevolutionary. That will continue until the children of revolutionary parents aren't afraid of seeing reason, seeing the revolution that could have been. Instead there was the piñata, an enormous harm to the country. Everyone who participated in it looks like a thief. [interview 16]

The Contras also linked Sandinismo to Somocismo in the matter of repression. The Contras accused the FSLN, and particularly the EPS, of staging a reign of terror against their political opposition, real or suspected. Again the Contras utilized leftist discourse previously directed against Somoza to attack the FSLN: the Contras had to mobilize against the Sandinistas to protect the revolution's objectives and to defend peasants' rights. Consider this Contra leader's autobiographical sketch:

> I joined the Resistance in 1980. I was one of the founders of MILPAS. This was only nine months after the triumph. I was already armed. My motive was that we were the object of repression. If you didn't join them you were considered reactionary, a Somocista—even if you weren't friends with the [National] Guard. If you didn't go with the Sandinistas you had two choices: join the Contras or leave the country. These were the only options. So I decided to join the Contras and try to pressure [the Sandinistas] for change. They were trying to radicalize the country and spread this radicalism throughout the rest of Latin America. There were assassinations of farmers. This is what hurt me the most. I am from a peasant background. I am a farmer. And they killed two farmers in my community who happened both to be my very close friends. [interview 72]

The Contras thus cued up the Sandinistas with cultural villains. They not only portrayed the Sandinistas as a left-wing version of the Somocistas but also likened their tactics to those of repressive military regimes in other parts of Latin America in the 1980s:

> I am an anti-Sandinista by conviction. I was before the revolution and after. . . . In 1979 I got involved [in the war]. My family supported Somoza. This cost my father his life. We suffered a lot. There were a massive number of assassinations. He was killed on 8 August 1979. He was kidnapped and nine days later taken . . . to a clandestine slaughter-house [*matador*] and killed. I had to collect the body. And I saw a lot of bodies there. This had a strong impact on me. . . . So when MILPAS was formed, it was like a dream come true. We had been so frightened. We were silenced by fear. We thought only about survival. But MILPAS brought together the Somocistas, those who had fought with the Frente Sandinista but who left it, and the families of the assassinated, and those who had no politics. [interview 53]

Transforming the revolutionary heroes in the FSLN into villains worked during the Contra war, but afterward the Sandinistas had lost much of their political power. Chamorro electorally defeated the Sandinista presidential candidate and figurehead for the party, Daniel Ortega. The Chamorro government then purged FSLN leaders from government positions. Moreover, the party split into two broad factions. Daniel Ortega and his brother Humberto led the "orthodox" faction comprising the EPS hardcore. Writer and intellectual Sergio Ramirez led the "renovation" faction, which founded a new political party called the MRS (Sandinista Renewal Movement). This party attracted the "soft core" of the FSLN, those committed to social change and critical of the militarization of the FSLN. Each faction competed for the grassroots Sandinista vote and considered their own movement the legitimate offspring of Sandino and bearer of the revolution's true spirit and ideals.

But the Contras dismissed these signs of weakness in the FSLN. They viewed the FSLN split as artificial and assumed that the factions would overlook their differences and unite to win elections over a right-wing candidate. Moreover, Chamorro's purge did not satisfy the Contras, since they believed that the FSLN continued to manipulate political outcomes behind the scenes: "[The Chamorro government] was flexible with the Frente. But it was too flexible. It gave it too much oxygen. That was its error. It also managed resources very poorly. Resources were spent according to the dictates of the Frente—well, the government. It's the same now" [interview 37].

The second difficulty Contras faced in adopting Sandino as their symbol was their previous close association with Somoza and the National Guard.

The Contras knew they must distance themselves from the negative imagery associated with Somoza and the guard. One former commander described the Contras as "the most discriminated against group" in Nicaraguan history because of their association with Somoza [interview 66]. And as one former guardsman admitted in an interview with me, there were *no* positive associations with Somoza and the guard:

> When we were thinking about what to call our group, we realized that Sandino was a nationalist. He had fought for the sovereignty of the country. He was a national hero. As the National Guard, we had a handicap: we had supported Somoza. How could we persuade people to like us? We decided that we needed to identify ourselves with the struggle of Sandino to defend Central America from communism. We also began to think about the military of the past and we thought about . . . the Legionnaires. The legion had appeal even to foreigners. So we used this image. We called ourselves the Fifteenth of September Legion. "Legion" represented the past military heroism, "Fifteenth of September" represented the independence of Central America. So we brought together both the liberation of Central America and the image of Sandino. . . . We made some statements to try to eliminate the stigma that we were Somocistas. We said we didn't want anything to do with Somoza. . . . The Nicaraguan Democratic Union–Armed Revolutionary Forces [UDN-FARN] were anti-Somocistas. They said that having the group in the hands of the National Guard was too harmful for the operation. [interview 42]

Contras generally dismissed the relationship between their movement and Somoza's National Guard by arguing that while the guardsmen had played a founding role for the Contras, most had gradually left the country during the war, become U.S. citizens, and settled into civilian life in Miami. One top leader of the Southern Command, for example, stated, "In the beginning the North was the guard. But they began to die or get tired of the war, or left, or got kicked out, and then they weren't there anymore" [interview 62]. One leader of a Contra defense group made a similar observation: "The FDN was the backbone of the Contras. These were peasants, not the guard. Actually, there were all different political stripes in the group. A study of the Contras in 1989 put their average age at eighteen. Well, if that was the average age in 1989, the majority would have been too young to be guardsmen in 1979" [interview 59]. Contras also distanced themselves from the guardsmen by accusing them of Somocismo. Consider this view of the differences between the guard and the "reconstructed" Contras: "The guard all ended up in Miami. They think we are all either Sandinista or progovernment. They really are Somocistas. They talk a lot, but they don't ever do anything or help anyone. The worst thing is that they don't even help out the rearmed groups. They just talk" [interview 37]. Indeed, the Contras made a concerted effort to distinguish between the "old" Somocista Contras and the "new" Contras committed to social and democratic change:

> The Sandinistas have done a good propaganda job abroad saying that the Resistance was against the revolution, that we're Somocistas. But we are genuinely peasants. We never bothered anyone. We're against arbitrary rule. The National Guard wanted things to be like they were. But there were two groups of Contras. One was against the Sandinistas' abuses, the genuine Contras. We wanted a democratic country. The other Contra was the guard, the Somocistas, who wanted to return the country to the past. This included Enrique Bermúdez and others. The Sandinistas took advantage of that image. [interview 33]

But such an image belied the evidence of guardsman leadership, although often disguised, within the Contras even after the war. In my interviews with guardsmen, not one openly admitted his role in the National Guard or his support for Somoza. Instead, they tried to hide their identity. One, for example, referred to himself as a member of the "army." Only after I questioned what he meant did he use the phrase "National Guard." Another guardsman explained away his background in the guard as a product of youthful naiveté rather than an ideological commitment: "I was too young when I went to Mexico [for National Guard officer training]—I was seventeen—to know much about politics. But I did know that the Sandinistas were the bad guys in the movie, and we were the good guys. And like the movies, the good guys won" [interview 68]. Similarly, many Contras associated with Somoza claimed that they were falsely accused:

> We've always had restaurants. And we had "Plancha I" when the government changed [from the Somocistas to the Sandinistas]. A lot of officers ate there because of its location, including Somoza's son and top officials. So the Sandinistas accused us of being pro-Somoza. They captured me on 2 October 1979. They said I was a member of the regime. But I just had a restaurant. I went into exile [and joined the Contras] after I spent seven months in jail. I saw assassinations in the prison. I was tortured—here are the marks that are still with me. [interview 75]

These denials were so intense that one could leave these interviews with the impression that no one had supported Somoza. The only interviewees who openly admitted to me that they had supported Somoza were peasant-Contras, the very group that the Contra leadership utilized to build a political-cultural link to Sandino and distance the movement from Somocismo. Peasant-Contras expressed nostalgia for the jobs and security they had enjoyed under Somoza: "Under Somoza there was employment. There was less delinquency. There was education. Yes, it was private, but everyone had a better economic situation, so they could afford it. Today you see this extreme poverty. Somoza gave things back to the people. He wasn't just out for himself" [interview 57].

The U.S. alliance presented the Contras with a third obstacle to cuing up with Sandino. Sandino had demonized the United States as the enemy of Nicaragua's peasants. Most Contras would not go that far but claimed their movement's independence from the United States. As one Contra combatant stated, "Some say we were used by the gringos. But we really fought for our convictions—from the heart" [interview 57]. While anti-Sandinista rebels would have emerged without U.S. support, they would not have had the numbers, training, longevity, or success that the U.S.-backed Contras enjoyed. So, rather than denying the U.S. role in the war, the Contras engaged in a strategy of remaking it. They transformed the United States from the imperial power that Sandino had condemned into a liberating force fighting for freedom and democracy.

Despite the obstacles impeding a credible link to Sandino—the Contras' competition with the FSLN for Sandino symbolism, their previous support for Somoza and guardsmen, and their association with the United States—the Contras effectively claimed Sandino's form of political action: armed insurrection. Contras likened the peasant uprising for social justice and political power of the 1920s to the similar situation of the 1980s under the Sandinista government. The historical link to armed peasant uprising proved particularly useful, since it reflected not only the formation of the Contras but also the emergence of the Recontras, those remobilized Contras who fought for the fulfillment of peace accord promises to ex-combatants.

The Recontras staged their first attack in October 1990. From an initially small base, their numbers grew to an estimated three thousand at their peak in 1993. The Recontras were led by several different commanders, comprised different troops, and operated independently in different areas of the country. They seized highways, kidnapped politicians, and took over public buildings.[11]

The Recontras claimed to be continuing Sandino's struggle on behalf of Nicaraguan peasants. They rearmed because of the violence against Contras in the postwar era, the inability or unwillingness of the Chamorro government to end that violence, the impossible conditions for rural production due to unfulfilled resettlement agreements, and the Contras' exclusion from government. One Recontra leader described the factors that had led him and his brothers to rearm:

> After the negotiations we returned [to Nicaragua] in 1991. But we had never turned in our arms. . . . Under the cease-fire agreements, we bought a farm and the government facilitated our payment for the land. It was in León. . . . We were working in the rice fields one day when an official from the police tried to kill us—while we were working on our own farm! That was at the end of 1991. It was our first warning. But we realized we might not get a second one. We might be dead. . . . It was our right to protect ourselves. So in January 1992 we headed for the mountains. We had a noble cause: self-defense and a way to save the government. We wanted to create justice. [interview 13]

Even Contras who did not rearm understood that without basic conditions for survival, an increasing number of peasants would join the roving bands of Recontras in the mountains. As during the Contra war, these bands provided their members with a sense of security and well-being: "If we were producing in the countryside, we wouldn't be armed today. But there aren't resources there. . . . Those who rearmed were motivated by the government's failure to keep its promises. How do you give up your gun when you are threatened? The government put money into other areas—not into the areas where it should have put money" [interview 37].

In an effort to address ex-combatants' complaints about public security, the Chamorro government employed Contras in the police force. Initially the ex-Contra police assumed the lowest-level positions, because of a lack of specific police training.[12] Their marginalized, powerless, and disdained positions within the police force did nothing to ameliorate the Contras' sense of material and physical insecurity, and may even have exacerbated it. Because of their lack of experience and training, Contras in police positions often abused their role, and lost their jobs as a result.[13] To avoid this outcome, the Frente Norte 3-80 negotiated high-level training for Recontra police as part of its cease-fire agreement with the Chamorro government.

But Sandinista human rights groups and Contras alike criticized the incorporation of Contras into the police force. Sandinistas viewed Contras in the police as the proverbial fox guarding the chicken coop:

> The government treats the Recontras with less aggression than the ex-Sandinistas. They have negotiated jobs for some of these Recontras: Chacal [the head of Frente Norte 3-80]. They have put them in police positions. It is strategic. It is no coincidence that Sandinista groups are murdered. This is not right. You cannot give assassins responsible positions in the police or government. [interview 11]

Surprisingly, even some Contras criticized the involvement of Recontras in public security, albeit for different reasons. As the following remark suggests, some Contras believed that if the Contra police became too well trained, they might fail to act in the interest of the Contras, thus defeating the very purpose of having them on the police force: "Here in the countryside the police commit assaults, they abuse their power. Some of the police are from the Resistance. But they are no longer Resistance. They now have to follow the orders of their superiors. And their superiors are the Sandinistas. They have to obey and do what they tell them" [interview 48].

These criticisms around ideological polarization ignored a more fundamental problem with ex-combatants serving in public-security forces: their fitness for the job. Skills for war do not necessarily translate into public-security skills. They involve different mentalities and techniques. The use of weapons constitutes only a small component of public security, and experience in that regard hardly qualifies an individual for the job.

Chamorro's opponents did not limit their criticism to complaints about incorporating Recontras into the police force. They contended that by negotiating with Contras over land, police security, and positions in government, Chamorro had compelled more Recontras to mobilize.[14] But Chamorro's use of force against the Recontras contradicted this point. She negotiated only with the politically oriented Recontras, and she ceased those negotiations once they demobilized. She then employed the EPS to eliminate the remaining Recontras, whom she labeled "rural delinquents."

By rearming, the Contras certainly continued the Sandino style of collective action. But not all Contras considered such actions appropriate in the postwar era. Nicaraguans wanted peace. Thus, simultaneous with the Recontra mobilization, Contras formed a political party, the PRN.[15] In the Nicaraguan political context, party formation also constituted a repertoire of political action, or even a national sport. In the 1996 presidential elections, for example, forty different political parties and party factions registered a candidate. The Nicaraguan passion for party formation prompted this comment from an informant: "A gringo told me this joke, and it surprised and impressed me that our national spirit could be captured so well by a foreigner. Four Nicaraguans go into a room, and they come out with six different political parties" [interview 7].

As in the case of other uncivil movements, the decision to form a political party generated tensions. Political parties and politicians are widely discredited within the Nicaraguan peasantry. The peasant-Contras I interviewed viewed politicians as corrupt, unresponsive to their needs, and interested only in reelection and self-aggrandizement. One PRN president summarized this attitude: "Everyone is used to handouts here. People who get jobs get them because they are the political followers of the person in charge. We are manufacturing dictatorships. And there is a big cost. Everything is propaganda, fraud, from Somoza to the Sandinistas. . . . José Martí once said, 'Maybe someday honor will become the fashion'" [Fabio Gadea, 10 March 1995]. To counter this widespread perception, party leaders sought to portray the PRN as a party of difference, a true alternative. PRN leaders argued that unlike other political parties, this one would listen to and represent the real interests of its peasant constituency. It would be accountable. As one PRN leader explained, the party would fill a vacuum and capitalize on the tendency of other political parties to sell out to enrich their leaders:

> It's important to point out to the [other political] parties that we exist only because of their poor performance in the past. [Political parties in Nicaragua] always encounter leadership problems. The leadership never concerns itself about the party's base. . . . The Sandinistas are a result of the poor performance of earlier political parties. None of those parties were concerned with social issues. All they worried about was personal enrichment. . . . The political parties are full of caudillos who betray the country and those they make agreements with. Chamorro, Somoza, Ortega—they're all alike. [interview 33]

The PRN intended to break away from the prevailing pattern in Nicaragua's political party structure. It would be not a personalistic party formed around a caudillo like the elite patronage parties that dominated Nicaraguan politics, but rather a participatory party rooted in the popular base of the movement:

We all have to prepare ourselves. We don't want to be armchair politicians, but rather grassroots politicians. We want to work hard. And we don't want to make mistakes. . . . We've got to get rid of the type of leaders who win and then go to sleep and wake up only when it's time to eat again. [interview 46]

The other parties are made up of conservative families from the upper class, the business class. They are sellouts. [interview 13]

In this spirit, the PRN attempted to turn its main political liability—its lack of experience—into an asset. Party ties, party vices, and party culture would not corrupt the PRN political novices. They had a clean slate. Moreover, they had a commitment, tested during ten years of war, to serve the interests of the peasants. The war experience distinguished the PRN from other political parties, so they argued, because they had proved that they were willing to sacrifice themselves for the Nicaraguan peasantry. Most Contras proudly referred to themselves as Contras, even after the movement adopted the name Resistance, to distinguish themselves from the pseudo-Resistance politicians who had not made sacrifices for the Nicaraguan people. The following comment reflects this attitude: "The Liberals say they are the Resistance. But this is an error. They are not Resistance. They didn't shed tears, give their blood, go to jail or into exile for the Resistance. They don't know what it means to be Resistance. They won the Atlantic Coast in 1994 by lying. The PRN is the Resistance" [interview 48].

But Contras recognized that appealing to combatants alone would greatly limit the party's size and scope. The PRN thus attempted to broaden its support by capitalizing on its Resistance label. This Resistance umbrella included noncombatants who had struggled against the Sandinista government in their own way: widows and orphans of combatants, exiles, and peasants who had endured Sandinista rule.[16] By 1995 this appeal appeared to be working; the PRN claimed 350,000 members, including combatants of every rank, combatant family members, and members of the civilian Resistance. The following excerpts illustrate the conscious packaging of the movement to attract a broader base:

And finally we became a party, the PRN. We aren't the party of "the Resistance," because there are others in our party who were not part of the Resistance. We are the party of resistance. We include anyone who is against the totalitarian system. We are all Nicaraguans. We are all against totalitarianism. [interview 37]

The Resistance should include not only combatants but everyone who opposed the Sandinista regime. That is the Resistance: those who were in exile. Even though they were not maltreated, they still formed the Resistance. Because they supported us. Other countries are also Resistance because of their help. [interview 72]

The PRN might have been able to use its distinctive identity as a Resistance and peasant party to win at least some political power. But all of the other conservative parties also adopted the Resistance label and highlighted support they had received from commandos, combatants, family members of ex-combatants, members of the civilian Resistance, and anti-Sandinistas in general. Moreover, the two Sandinista parties capitalized on their peasant base and their commitment to social change and rural development. The PRN, in other words, lost its identity; by entering mainstream politics, it became just another amorphous party in the political system, losing its competitive edge.

In sum, the Contras followed the uncivil movement pattern of cuing up with the past, but they did so unsuccessfully. They selected an appropriate cultural icon, Sandino, but had to compete with their archenemy to appropriate that image for themselves. The enemy they sought to demonize had lost most of its power. They simultaneously pursued two repertoires of collective action, a civil-political-party route and an uncivil-armed-insurrection path. But both strategies failed to win significant support. In the final analysis, the Contras could not generate the unity and passion around a cultural icon, villain, or political action that has been critical to the success of other uncivil movements. This failure resulted in large part from the movement's weakness in mythmaking.

LEGITIMATING MYTHS

The Contras tried to maintain their eclectic origins and tactics by spinning myths around the movement. These myths provided contradictory stories about the movement's violence, its ideology, and its leadership. Indeed, the Contras' emphasis on their peasant roots, which detracted from their National Guard image, bolstered movement myths. It provided a coherent story line explaining the Contras' political attitudes and actions over time. It linked the Contras to Sandino and his armed struggle to defend the peasantry. It distanced them from Somocistas and guardsmen who had oppressed peasants. And it suggested that Contras did not oppose social revolution, but only authoritarian controls and political exclusion. Their peasant ori-

gins also distinguished the Contras' political party, the PRN, from the traditional, elite political parties that had historically courted peasants during
campaigns and ignored them after the elections.

The Contras' peasant base is undeniable. The legitimating myth merely
emphasized this origin over the prevailing view of the movement as a group
of Somocistas and guardsmen. In this way the movement attracted individuals reluctant to identify openly with Somoza or the guard. Somocistas
and guardsmen alike recognized that a close identification with Somocismo
could limit the movement's development. Therefore, they accepted even
prorevolution and "sons of Sandino" myths, as long as the anti-Sandinista
message remained clear.

Regardless of how the Contras constructed their identity, they were compelled to address their involvement in a violent war. Rather than deny their
involvement, they justified it. Their peasant origin helped in that regard. To
counter the prevailing image of Contras—as National Guardsmen defending the power and privilege of the authoritarian elite and the United States—
they spun myths about defending the rights of the Nicaraguan people, a
peasant people. The Contra war in this scenario became a just war. And the
Contras, who had sacrificed their security for justice and freedom from oppression, became war heroes. As one Contra combatant argued, "We were
fighting for democracy, freedom—to not be persecuted. I am proud of being free and of freeing the Nicaraguan people. We achieved our objectives"
[interview 25].

The Contras also constructed relative-weight arguments to defend their
involvement in a violent war. They claimed that the war ended Sandinista
state repression, likening the Sandinistas to Central American authoritarian
regimes of the 1980s. However, there is no evidence confirming FSLN involvement in massacres or scorched-earth tactics used by Central American
military regimes. Moreover, some domestic and international human rights
agencies cited the Contras for violating the Geneva Convention by raping,
kidnapping, and murdering Nicaraguan civilians.[17] Rather than deny these
human rights violations, Contras used a "bad-egg" defense: they had not
been able to control every individual combatant during the war.

The just-war, relative-weight, and bad-egg defenses provided important
explanations during the war era. But they proved less convincing when
Recontras rearmed after the war against a democratically elected government relatively favorable to their cause. The Contras had difficulty balanc-
ing the two competing moods that prevailed in postwar Nicaragua. On one
hand, war fatigue had created a feeling of revulsion for any type of violence.

On the other, ex-combatants' pent-up frustrations with the peace accords had generated support for Recontra activity. The Contras addressed these conflicting sentiments by spinning contradictory views of the Recontras. They simultaneously rejected and supported the Recontra movement.

The Contras justified the Recontras' violence by claiming that the Chamorro government could not understand any other kind of pressure. In failing to keep its promises to the ex-combatants, Chamorro had forced the rearming. No one wanted to rearm, but the situation demanded it. In other words, the Contras formulated a just-war defense. But the Contras also denied certain charges against the Recontras disseminated by the Chamorro government's propaganda apparatus. Recontras did not prey on the peasantry, as the government claimed. Instead, the Contras blamed ex-combatants in the EPS, called *recompas* (after rearmed *compañeros,* or comrades) for rural crimes. Contras argued that a commitment to social change distinguished Recontras from *recompas:*

> The rearmed are not all bad. There are some good ones in 3-80. The EPS is out to kill them all. There were some tractors burned. It was either the *recompas* or the thieves—not the 3-80 people. The people of Charro's [3-80] group don't rob; they kill the [thieves] and rapists. The majority think that they do, but they really don't rob. [interview 52]

But while the Contras I interviewed forcefully distinguished between the two groups, they could not explain how they knew whether those who attacked were Recontras or *recompas.* This is the type of answer I received: "The rearmed groups are from the FSLN, the *recompas.* These are delinquent bands. They have no political struggle. They are criminals. Charro is with us. The government didn't fulfill the agreements, and he is pressuring for that end. . . . The cause is the same. His is a different way to apply pressure" [interview 58].

Contras, however, did not consistently defend the Recontras. They spun an alternative interpretation casting them as a product of war and a symptom of the failed peace agreements. Without physical protection, employment, arable land, useful skills, or psychological counseling for posttraumatic stress syndrome, ex-combatants could not adapt to civilian life. They had spent a decade of their lives fighting a guerrilla war in which they both witnessed and committed violent atrocities. And having served their country, they returned home expecting a heroes' welcome but were met with hostility and poverty instead. They did not have the psychological strength or the economic or physical security to live in peace. One member of an international nongovernmental organization involved in resettling Contras described the postwar culture in this way:

> In 1991—in January—the rearming began. There were two causes: human rights and social and material well-being. But there is also a third: the war culture, the psychology of the ex-combatants. They were not able to adapt. . . . Many of those who rearmed are crazy. This is the majority now. They are demented. You can tell by the way they kill, the way they treat others. They are unadaptable to normal life. [anonymous]

Contras shared this view of the war culture but showed more compassion for the afflicted ex-Recontras:

> All of these [Recontras] had the same motives. They were motivated by threats to their personal security. They felt that they had to defend themselves. The intoxication of the war still existed. Feelings were still strong. They felt naked without their guns. People would stand with their backs against the wall. The government had done nothing to bring about reconciliation. . . . Now we don't feel so insecure. We used to have to disconnect the telephone because we would get threats in the middle of the night. [interview 33]

> You can take away the weapon, but these people have been trained in war. Their weapon is their wife, mother, and child. The person has been trained to be a fighter and is still a *guerrillero,* a commando. . . . Even though they are now dressed in civilian clothes and broken shoes, they still stop and salute when their commanding officers walk by. They are still military people. The work of reintegration is double work. It involves changing the way one has been thinking about the world. First the person feels naked. The weapon gave him food, respect, and a companion. It was an integral part of his life. The social work we must do is to break this war mentality. [interview 46]

Opinions like these led the Contras to include in their list of demands psychological counseling for ex-combatants suffering from posttraumatic stress syndrome. But this, like many of their other demands for social services, was ignored by the Chamorro government—as much from ignorance about the psychological ramifications of war and the difficulties faced by soldiers returning to civilian life as from financial constraints:

We demobilized in April 1990. The process was very difficult. It was a dramatic change. We were not mentally armed for this experience. This was the first demobilization in Latin America. It was difficult to accept. AID [the Agency for International Development] and other institutions began a process of education—teaching trades. But no one dealt with the psychological dimension. Most of our combatants had a low level of education. And of the seven thousand combatants in total [in the Atlantic Coast], 50 percent, or thirty-five hundred, never handed in their arms. They went into hiding, or they repatriated and hid their guns. In any event, they remained armed. Of those who did hand in their arms, many cried. They didn't know how to do anything else but war. This was an emotional experience. It was a new experience. People felt very insecure about their physical safety. In the Atlantic Coast there were a lot of people who remained armed. This gave them some sense of protection. But it was a tense situation. [interview 79]

While voicing compassion for, and justification of, Recontra activity, Contras simultaneously rejected the rearming and concurred with the Chamorro government that Recontras had become rural bandits. This view of Recontra activity began to emerge after the politically motivated Recontras had demobilized, accepting negotiations with Chamorro. Charro remained mobilized but refused to negotiate with the government. He had also lost control over his group; bands of rearmed combatants claiming to be allied with him roved the countryside, raping, robbing, and killing peasants. The Contras shifted the emphasis of their discourse from denials of criminal violence to invocations of the bad-egg defense. As one PRN leader commented, "We used to assume that Sandinistas would kill us, but now we just have Contras killing Contras" [interview 46]. The PRN rejected rearming of any kind: "Since Chacal, the rest [of the Recontras] don't listen. They won't disarm. We tell them, 'Disarm. Nicaragua is big, and you can find another way. There is no justification for arming. We need to learn to live together with the Sandinistas'" [interview 33].

The Contras' view of the Recontras converged with that of the government. After unsuccessfully negotiating with the politically oriented Recontras, the Chamorro government began using force to eliminate the non-political rural armed groups. The remaining Recontras had little chance of survival, as this PRN leader noted:

Peasants have helped [the Recontras] and sustained them. But the Recontras don't have enough equipment or war capacity to last. They are shrinking. They engage in delinquent acts to stay alive. It's like the story of the hungry dog: if you give it something to eat, it keeps following after you begging for more and threatening to bite you. There aren't any more negotiations. . . . [The Recontras] are like fleas on a dog: they bother it but don't kill it. [interview 33]

The Recontra controversy effectively ended in 1996 with the presidential elections and Charro's murder. The PRN, mobilizing for the elections, withdrew its support for the Recontras. Recontra violence had tarnished the Contras' image in a war-weary country. Some Sandinistas tried to evoke the specter of Contra violence with comments like this: "There is likely to be a social eruption. There are arms. There is ammunition. There are Contras" [interview 73]. But Contras countered that these new groups threatening to rearm had neither the capacity nor the support to do so. One such Atlantic Coast leader was described in this way: "He wants land, that's all. And there aren't arms here. If there are, they aren't in good condition. And there isn't ammunition" [interview 64]. Discussing another potential Recontra leader on the Atlantic Coast, a Sandinista leader expressed his doubts that such a mobilization would attract followers: "He is irrelevant. He needs to get better prepared with a program and a message" [interview 79].

To further distance themselves from their warrior image, the Contras called for an end to ideological polarization. They claimed to embody the spirit of unity necessary to resolve the national crisis. After all, they argued, the guardsmen and the revolutionaries had put aside their differences to fight a common anti-Sandinista cause. Universal and nonsectarian language permeated their public statements, like the PRN's Declaration of Principles. The PRN president presented the party as a kind of "all things to all people" party: "The philosophy of the party can be found in its ideological principles: democracy, nationalism, evolutionism, civility, humanism, God, motherhood, the peasantry, the fight against arms, liberty, humanity, the universal declaration of human rights. The philosophy is consistent with all of the U.N.'s 1948 declarations" [Gadea, 10 March 1995].

The experience of war, the Contras argued, further qualified them to forge unity in Nicaragua. After ten years of combat, they embraced peace. They could not imagine leaving their country, friends, and families in order to take up arms again. One ex-combatant, for example, stated, "We had learned that war doesn't bring any advantage. It doesn't bring development. Instead it brings sadness, backwardness, widows, orphans, destruction" [interview 40]. A leader of the PRN claimed, "We're not a militaristic party. We formed in order to avoid having to take up arms again to fight for our cause" [interview 46]. The PRN, in other words, used the war to promote peace and unity:

> We don't want to keep killing each other. Those who fought want peace and tranquility—to forget the differences and to look for things that we share in common. No one wants more war. We have to defend what we fought for in the mountains, but now by civic means. We have to work for dialogue and tolerance. Violence only breeds more violence. We have to put down our guns and work for peace. [interview 32]

Some PRN leaders even suggested that they could put their own animosities behind them and join forces with Sandinistas. An FSLN congresswoman who was kidnapped and taken hostage by Recontras admitted that the two sides had a lot more in common than their ideological polarization would suggest. She stated that during her captivity she got to know some of her captors and wondered why it had been so difficult to get along with Contras. She felt that a basis of mutual respect, trust, and friendship was established that has since allowed them to work together [Doris Tijerino, 24 March 1995]. An MRS leader shared this view, portraying the Contras as pragmatists determined to resolve rural problems, rather than opportunists driven by partisanship:

> The Resistance is not a group on the extreme right. It is a mistake to put them all in one package. There were people on the extreme right in the leadership and even among some of the troops. But most of the right-wing forces came from the politicians. . . . [Most of the Resistance] mobilized against the errors, the style, the methods [of the FSLN]. The political project was imposed on them. This leads to the fact that they have a different way of organizing and acting in the democratic period. They are likely to ally with any party—whether it is right, center (or at least appears to them to be center), or left. They will go with whatever party seems to offer a solution to their problems. Just like in the past. They wanted a solution to the land problem, but not agrarian reform. They wanted economic development, but not in the way it was implemented. They have concrete demands. If they think a party will resolve the land and property issue, they'll go with it. If they think it will resolve employment problems, they'll go with it. [anonymous]

This comment suggests political expediency. But while alliances provided some long-term viability for the party, not all Contras accepted this approach.

Some hoped to build a grassroots movement that would represent peasants at every level of government. One PRN leader stated, "We don't expect to win the presidency. We want mayoral positions and deputies . . . in the regions of the North, the Atlantic Coast, and where we have been the strongest traditionally" [interview 46]. These Contras defended a rural development program that surged from local and regional bases:

> We have to offer the people a program of municipal government. We need to defend the interests of the most marginalized class, the poorly paid, those in the health professions, teachers, peasants, laborers. We need to defend the interests of our class—the poor—who know about hunger, isolation, the lack of clothing. The Sandinistas also defend this class. The PLC [Liberals] and the Conservatives have never listened to us. They are never going to defend the marginalized classes. The PLC promises employment, that there won't be any shortages; [they promise] medicine, justice. . . . The Conservatives . . . say that they are going to work [hard] and put Nicaragua ahead. We don't believe these messages anymore. The PRN is probably the party that is least talked about. But it can resolve problems here in the village, in the municipalities, in the department. They see things. We need a government that comes from the poor class, a mayor who is from the poor class. [interview 10]

> Our objective is to be united. We want to be the spokespeople for the peasants—to defend their legitimate interests. [The PRN] is an agrarian party for the poor. And we want to carry forward socioeconomic development: schools; health centers—and not just a clinic building, but one that is actually stocked with medicines; redistribution of lands and the construction of new roads so that vehicles can enter the communities and buy the products produced, creating small-business people; a rural bank that can help the peasant and small landholder finance production. . . . We want a higher standard of living—not land in the hands of a few, but a much more just division of land. I believe in a limit to the amount of land one person can hold. And this may mean that we have to prevent the selling of land that is distributed by land reform. [interview 13]

But pragmatism and ideological eclecticism sometimes worked at cross-purposes with the Contras' modern and democratic image. The Contras' objectives—to control the Sandinistas and the left, to respect private property, to increase employment opportunities, and to defend the free-enterprise system—could be fulfilled by either an authoritarian or a democratic regime. And some Contras even expressed ambivalence about democracy as an efficient means of resolving development concerns: "The struggle for democracy, for liberty, wasn't really our priority. That there is democracy and liberty, fine, but this is not going to solve our problems. We wanted our historical rights to be recognized, our lives, our history. These were the reasons why we joined the Resistance" [interview 8].

Moreover, the Contras' willingness to ally with parties on the left is greatly exaggerated. Their anti-Sandinista history prohibited such alliances, since an association with the MRS, or any other Sandinista spin-off group, would have alienated their firm right-wing backing. Any flirtation with leftist ideas must be read as "coding," since an actual alliance with the left would have eroded the Contras' fragile support structure. Above all else, the Contras had to be anti-Sandinista, as the president of the PRN made clear: "They call us extreme right. I don't know if we are. We certainly aren't left, so I suppose they can call us extreme right. We certainly know who is left: the Frente" [Gadea, 24 April 1996].

But alliances with the right also proved potentially explosive, albeit less so. The PRN faced serious problems during the 1996 presidential elections over its alliance with candidate Arnaldo Alemán. PRN leaders argued that the alliance was tactical rather than ideological. Only by allying with Alemán could they defeat the FSLN in the 1996 elections. Arnaldo Alemán, former mayor of Managua from the PLC (Liberal Constitution Party) is described by individuals at various points on the ideological spectrum as "Somocista." His campaign platform was mostly anti-Sandinismo. While he touted a commitment to reconciliation, his conciliatory message was contradicted by the rhetoric of his speeches—for example, by references to the "dark nights" of Sandinista rule. And he continually cast blame on the Sandinistas for having created the current problems. He even blamed them for the fact that people had to stand in long lines to buy basic goods—an ironic accusation, since those lines were the result of the U.S. embargo on Nicaragua, not Sandinista policy.

For ex-revolutionary Contras, an alliance with Somocismo was as incomprehensible as an alliance with the FSLN. One leader described himself as 100 percent anti–Liberal Party. He had participated in the anti-Somoza guerrilla movement in the 1950s, and the Somoza regime had imprisoned him eighteen times. He had supported the victorious Sandinistas but joined the forces against the FSLN when he felt that it had begun imitating Somocismo.

Similarly, he felt betrayed when the PRN allied with the PLC. In his own words, "I have torture marks that will keep me from ever voting for the Liberals. I am adamant about this. If the vote comes down between Ortega and Alemán, I won't vote. Alemán is surrounded by the criminals of the Somoza era" [interview 2].

The eclectic forces within the Contra movement not only prevented strategic alliances, they also generated problems of leadership. Paradoxically, while a strong leader might have unified the Contras, the disunity within the movement prevented consensus around such a leader.

Enrique Bermúdez (Comandante 3-80), a former National Guard officer, became the single most powerful leader of the Contras. The United States put Bermúdez in charge of not only the Northern Command dominated by his own National Guardsmen but also the Southern and Atlantic Coast Commands. Not surprisingly, the ex-revolutionary and indigenous Contras initially felt uneasy about a National Guard commander. One Southern Command leader described the skepticism in this way: "In the South, people knew why they were fighting. They had good political leadership. The North was primarily military leadership. They didn't know why they were fighting. They were forbidden to speak of politics. I had fought against the guard and now was fighting with them" [interview 22]. The indigenous peoples of the Atlantic Coast Command also struggled with the Northern Command and former guardsmen but accepted the command structure for pragmatic reasons:

> We had a history of struggle inherited from our ancestors, and a belief in our rights as Indians. The FSLN didn't bring anything but slavery.... This is what provoked the war.... We had to defend our rights. And for this reason we were in the war for ten years. This is what made us different from the FDN. We were in the war because we had lost our rights. They didn't have a common cause with us. We had our cause. They didn't have a cause. They were obligated to go. The only thing we shared was anticommunism. Our cause was different. So we worked together to overthrow communism, and we understood each other on that level. We also depended on them because they provided everything we needed for the war. We were united but not mixed up.... Some of them had a cause, but most of them were lost. They had been defeated. The Miskito was different. We had been massacred. The FSLN was worse than what had been there before. [interview 1]

But after Bermúdez had won respect from the various Contra divisions and consolidated power, the United States decided that the Contras required a public-relations makeover. Given the waning of support for the Contra war among the U.S. electorate and international allies, Washington determined that the Contras needed a leader who was not a former guardsman and Somocista. The United States pressured Bermúdez to leave and replaced him with less politically charged personalities in top leadership positions.

Even though Bermúdez was officially out of power, Contras still considered him the commander-in-chief. Once the war ended, the political activists within the PRN (i.e., the entrepreneurs) sought out Bermúdez to discuss the Contras' political future. During one of these meetings at the exclusive Hotel Intercontinental, Bermúdez received an urgent call, left the restaurant, and was murdered in his truck in the parking lot by a bullet to his head. Had he lived, he might have united the Contras behind a single leader. Even the ex-revolutionary Talavera brothers seemed to admire him, since they took Bermúdez's nom de guerre for the name of their Recontra group 3-80.

Bermúdez, however, probably could not have developed the kind of charisma that brought success to other uncivil movements. He was neither young nor handsome, modern nor democratic. He could not deny his military background or his association with the Somoza dictatorship. And his close association with war and right-wing authoritarianism gave him limited appeal in a country tired of dictatorship, ideological polarization, and warfare. And no charismatic leaders stepped forward to fill Bermúdez's shoes after he left the High Command or after his death. Movement entrepreneurs might have transformed one of Bermúdez's successors into a charismatic leader. These leaders came from peasant and indigenous backgrounds. Although they had fought in the Contra war, they could plausibly deny their association with Somoza's right-wing authoritarianism. They were young and heroic, and their own war fatigue would resonate with a war-weary society. But no movement entrepreneurs emerged to transform Bermúdez's successors into political leaders. Moreover, most Contras did not respect his successors. On the contrary, they blamed them for signing away the Contras' leverage in a unilateral cease-fire agreement. Contras relinquished their arms in exchange for the mere promise of jobs, land, and reintegration programs. When these promises were broken, they had no means of forcing the government to fulfill its commitments. Respect for these leaders further waned when Contras began to suspect them of having negotiated private deals with the Chamorro government. For Contra ex-combatants, such deals explained why the leaders lived well, turned their backs on ex-combatants, and joined the government party instead of the PRN.

With neither Bermúdez nor his successors in charge of the Contras in the postwar era, the PRN was forced to invent a new leader who could symbolize the Contra struggle and appeal to a broad cross-section of Nicaraguan society. Luis Angel "Leonel" López of the Southern Command became the first of several disputed PRN presidents. Some Contras opposed the notion of having a military commander as the PRN president because he would evoke images of war and violence. But others were equally adamant about the need for a military leader. They argued that at least during the early years, the party would be able to earn the trust of combatants and their families only if it had a military commander at the helm; only a military commander could unite the demoralized and divided Contras.

Even those who favored having a military commander at the party's helm, however, rejected Leonel's leadership. They associated him with Eden Pastora—whom many Contras in the North distrusted—because he had fought with the Southern Command and assumed control after Pastora stepped down. Pastora's heroism in the revolution and his former association with the FSLN led them to suspect him of being a spy or a double agent. Because of his inconsistent attitude toward the United States—he alternated between demanding more support and denouncing U.S. intervention in Nicaragua—Contras also considered him mentally unstable at best, insane at worst, and egocentric in any case. Although Leonel had personally delivered to Pastora the message that stripped him of his Southern Command, Contras still distrusted his earlier loyalty to Pastora. Leonel served as the party's president for only a short time before members voted him out in 1995.

Fabio Gadea replaced Leonel as president of the PRN. A civilian, Gadea owned one of the best-known radio stations in Nicaragua, Radio Corporación. His political broadcasts had antagonized first the Somoza regime and then the FSLN. While in exile in Costa Rica during the 1980s, he continued to broadcast to Nicaragua. These broadcasts included "Love Letters" to Nicaragua in which Gadea discussed the struggle of the common person against Sandinista oppression. His program also included a stereotypical "Nica" personality who explained Nicaraguan politics in common country dialect; during the war this personality extolled the values of the Resistance. Fabio Gadea and Radio Corporación allegedly received grants from the National Endowment for Democracy to continue their political work, although Gadea denied that he personally received any money.

Gadea seemed to embody all the necessary attributes of a charismatic leader. As a radio personality in a poor country with isolated regions—the kind of country whose people depend primarily on the radio for news—he enjoyed wide recognition. Moreover, he lacked the stigma of association with Somoza. Indeed, his broadcasts had antagonized the Somoza regime as well as the Sandinistas, both of which had retaliated by bombing and burning his radio station; he had the photographs to prove it. Gadea also personified the civilian Resistance. With such a leader at the helm, the party could distance itself from war, violence, and devastation while still projecting an image of heroism. Gadea would show that the Contras had joined the civic and democratic struggle. And he would unite Contra combatants and the civilian Resistance, who had both received inspiration from his radio programs during the war. In short, his leadership linked the Resistance to both historic struggles: those against the FSLN *and* against Somoza. And he could effectively portray the struggle as being both armed and civilian, fought both in Nicaragua and in exile. As one of Gadea's supporters put it, "We needed to balance two things. A commander would have united the party, but this would have given the party a militaristic image. We want people to understand that we are not professional soldiers. We were involved in a war for historic reasons. We did it to protect rights" [interview 66].

Gadea, unlike most Contra combatants who might have assumed leadership of the PRN, also possessed resources useful to the party. He had a thriving business and a middle-class lifestyle that afforded him the luxury of devoting his free time to leading a political party. Most Contra commanders, given their peasant backgrounds, spent any "free time" they had trying to keep their families out of poverty. Living in a time of 60 percent unemployment and having few skills other than military leadership, they were hard-pressed to make ends meet. And Gadea's business—a radio station—provided the extra bonus of free publicity and a team of skilled communicators to design effective messages.

Gadea did not appeal to all combatants, however. For those who wanted a military leader at the helm, he personified the cowardly civilian Resistance, for which they had little respect. In their view he was just another member of the wealthy class who had gone into exile and played it safe until the war was over. They deplored his lack of combat experience. But they had to admit that Gadea did not resemble the politicians who had backed the Contras during the war and turned their backs on them later. Although he had the same political and social profile as those politicians, he had remained close to the ex-combatants.

Gadea, like Leonel before him, faced competition within the party. A new leader, Enrique Quiñonez, won the party presidency in 1996 in a highly contested election. The existing PRN leadership would not concede the vote. Accusations against Quiñonez proliferated: he lacked combat experience, contrary to his own claim; his wealth originated from drug deals; the Sandinistas had financed his campaign in order to divide the party. Quiñonez countered these accusations with an offensive attack on Gadea for compromising Resistance values through an alliance with the authoritarian presidential candidate Arnaldo Alemán, Gadea's Achilles heel.

The party split in two. Gadea and Quiñonez held separate party meetings. They each had supporters that included both ex-combatants and members of the civilian Resistance. Each claimed to represent Contras, and each considered himself to be the head of the PRN. The division effectively dissolved the party, since no one knew who was ultimately in charge.

In the end, neither Leonel, Gadea, nor Quiñonez could unite the Contra movement. None offered a new direction or a vision for the future. None had a background that evoked a Sandino image. None had the capacity to bridge past and modern movements. None could overcome the factions within the movement.

Could anyone have succeeded where these three failed? One of the Talavera brothers, either José Angel (Chacal) or Salvador (Esteban) might have provided the PRN with the type of charismatic leadership exemplified by the Carapintada's Aldo Rico or the UDR's Ronaldo Caiado. They are from a revolutionary family; José Angel even fought in the revolution. They are from peasant stock, which links them to Sandino. And they have used their disputes over the Sandinistas' rural policies to deepen their connection with Sandino's struggle for peasants. Moreover, although they joined the Contras, they later broke with Bermúdez. Following in Sandino's footsteps, they rejected the North American control over the war, particularly the U.S. strategy to negotiate the end of the war rather than militarily defeat the Sandinistas. They did not accept the cease-fire agreements and retained their arms. When they went into exile, they went to Canada rather than the United States. After returning to Nicaragua at the end of the war, they faced death threats and assassination attempts. They called on the Chamorro government to uphold the peacekeeping agreements. When the government failed to do so, they took up arms again and directed one of the most powerful Recontra forces.

The Talaveras were formidable in their negotiations with the government, gaining control over a large section of the country and even securing a position within the government for Salvador. And these brothers are charismatic: young, passionate, handsome. They represent the revolutionary and social-change faction within the Contras. The Talaveras, however, have expressed no interest in assuming control of the PRN. They have dedicated themselves instead to local politics: they ran for local office under the PRN and are seeking to stabilize the part of the country they obtained in their negotiations with Chamorro.

Limitations on the Contras' Power

The Contras did not prove as effective in framing, cuing, and mythmaking as the other uncivil movements examined in this book, which weakened their influence over the democratic process. Analyzing this weakness will help us identify the factors that contribute to successful framing, cuing, and mythmaking, as well as the factors that detract from it.

The type of threat the Contras faced in the early stages of the redemocratization process proved more challenging for mobilization than other political transitions. Although violence and insecurity, unemployment, and insufficient social services affected nearly all Contras, movement leaders could not transform those threats into political mobilization. And while the Contras faced the same kinds of limitations as other uncivil movements—burnout, factionalism, and political competition—these factors were hindering them before they even got their movement off the ground.

The debilitating burnout suffered in the wake of the protracted Contra war defies comparison with the burnout from high-energy, high-risk political action discussed in the other uncivil movement cases. The desire among Contras to return to "normal life" after the war was so strong that it eroded much of the movement's mobilizing capacity. Ex-combatants tolerated the postwar situation, despite the unfulfilled peace accords, because of their overwhelming desire to end the war. Memories of war drove many to try to forget their past. Some did not even want to be identified as Contras anymore:

> I don't want to have any part of the war anymore. I am dedicating myself to my family: my wife, my girls, a future. This is why I'm studying. [interview 44]

> There's still danger, but for your own mental health you can't think about it. I have to have a normal life. And I feel tranquil. I won't get into politics for that reason—not one political party. I'll vote, but not do politics. Maybe I'm wrong, but the political parties just don't seem to be very well oriented. I like to work in this office from Monday to Friday

and take off on Saturday and Sunday to work my land. People have asked me to be mayor of the town where I have my land. But I don't want to. I like my tranquility. [interview 18]

Nicaraguan kinship structures explain in part the underlying need to leave the war behind. Numerous families, like the Chamorros, were divided during the war. Brothers, sisters, and cousins fought on different sides. The goal of reuniting families and communities after a decade of war compelled Contras and Sandinistas alike to seek reconciliation: "Sixty percent of us in the Resistance had family members who were Sandinistas. This helped us forgive and forget [*borrar la cuenta*]. I'm not going to go against my brother again" [interview 46].

The goal of unity in postwar Nicaragua seemed highly unrealistic after President Alemán's election in 1996. He was the only presidential candidate who exploited ideological polarization. Political analysts attribute his appeal to the perception that he would provide jobs, a perception cultivated by his success as Managua's mayor. But even his colleagues on the right fear that he could end the process of reconciliation and heighten polarization, a fear they say is based on his way of controlling the Contras:

The Sandinistas have punished the victors. Instead there should be an appreciation for all that they have done. They did, after all, open the way for negotiations. Alemán isn't going to fulfill this role. He has used [the Contras], and he will continue to use them. I think of him as keeping them like Doberman pinschers, ready to attack the moment he tells them to. He can organize the Resistance, arm them, give them a certain amount of power, and use them like his personal ad hoc army. I hope I'm wrong about that. [interview 12]

On the other hand, two significant factors mitigated this trend toward polarization: the national economic crisis and war-weariness. As for the first, poverty is an equalizer. The demobilized EPS, the demobilized Contras, and most other Nicaraguans are struggling for survival. While ideological conflict is fought out among political leaders, voters are battling economic hardship and failed government policies. Everyone is seeking practical solutions to the country's emergency survival needs. As one Sandinista stated, "Conflicts [today] are not partisan; they are about being poor. Seventy-five percent of the population lives below the poverty level, many in extreme poverty. In Jalapa there are ex-Resistance and ex-Sandinistas who are all trying to get their land legalized" [interview 11]. This view is shared by Contras:

"Those who fought in the war [on either side] are less polarized than non-combatants. We face the same problems: hunger, calamity. We don't want any more war. The divisions are with the politicians. They live off this. There are some settlements in which half the settlers are Resistance and half are EPS, but they live together [in peace] because of their common needs" [interview 75].

Contras and Sandinistas alike point to examples of unity across partisan lines. In the Atlantic Coast region, ex-Contras and ex-Sandinistas work together to promote regional autonomy and development. Foundations unite Sandinistas and Contras behind solutions for the alleviation of poverty and unemployment affecting demobilized Contras and EPS soldiers. Groups of mothers of the Resistance and Sandinista "heroes and martyrs" have joined together in carrying out housing and community projects and staging rallies. They described their unity in terms like these:

> We work together with the Mothers of the Resistance. We have some projects together, and we support each other. We have a housing project with 150 houses that will be distributed to mothers and the wounded from both the EPS and the Resistance. We don't want any more war. We want to help work things out. It is a very slow process, and it is psychologically difficult for both sides. . . . We get along with [mothers] from the Resistance. We all want peace. We have all suffered. And if we're going to be truly Christian, we have to forgive. [interview 28]

> We are the mothers and widows of Resistance soldiers, although we do have a project in Waslala where we work together [with the mothers of deceased Sandinistas]. In 1992–93 we began this project together. We realized that alone we wouldn't be able to do much. And we had the same needs. So we have a farm where there are six women from the Frente and six from the Resistance. We worked for it together. [interview 52]

The fear of another war and the common struggle for postwar recovery have together created a strong impetus toward peace.[18] This does not mean that hatred has disappeared, but it does mean that pragmatism has provided the means to put differences aside:

> There is bitterness [*rencores*]. We fought a war for ten years, after all. There is hate. But we can live in peace. [interview 32]

> This has been hard for us. It isn't easy to sit at the table with your
> enemy. When I see their uniforms it brings back this feeling. But you
> have to get over it. That's the good thing the government did: it brought
> the two sides together. [interview 37]

One personal story illustrates how warlike feelings have persisted without
escalating into actual war. I had interviewed a Contra leader at my hotel,
and afterward the young hotel guard asked me to identify him. When I referred to him by his nom de guerre, the young guard nodded and told me
that he had spent two years of his military service in the mountains looking
for that particular Contra, carrying a photocopied picture of him in his
pocket. Upon coming face to face with him in the hotel, the guard said, a
war impulse overcame him, and he reached for his gun to kill him. But then
he remembered that it was peacetime and that this Contra was just another
guest at the hotel where he was working as a security guard. Feelings of polarization and conflict remain strong in postwar Nicaragua, but they are
usually overcome by the desire to live in peace.

Absent polarization, however, the Contras had no identity or sense of
unity. They existed only to defeat the Sandinistas. Once they succeeded in
that goal, they lost their sense of purpose. At that point all the differences
within the movement surfaced, demonstrating that the Contras were, after
all, little more than a tactical alliance. Like the other uncivil movements examined here, the Contras fragmented over the future direction of their movement: armed struggle or institutional politics. But the movement also fragmented along its original political and cultural fault lines: revolutionary and
counterrevolutionary, peasant and nonpeasant, indigenous and nonindige-
nous. The fundamental lack of unity that had characterized the movement
from its inception ultimately undermined it.

The clearest faction within the movement was the Atlantic Coast constituency. The 1994 regional elections on the Atlantic Coast marked an important shift away from a Contra political identity. Although the PRN finished fourth, receiving more votes than several longstanding parties, it did
not win a single political office. Given that the Atlantic Coast is dominated
by former Contras, this was a serious blow to the party. It also reflected the
weakness of the Contra identity. After the war the Atlantic Coast Contras
organized Yátama, a political movement that would have more salience than
the Contra party. Yátama sought to defend the Atlantic Coast Contras' autonomy and indigenous identity.[19] It was intended to overcome partisan di-

visions within the indigenous community: "We are bombarded by political parties. They are trying to destroy us, destroy Yátama. We do not agree with the partisan efforts. They have divided us. . . . They take advantage of our misery. We are divided politically because of the political parties. They provide lots of incentives for people to go with them" [interview 8].

The issue of autonomy is so salient along the Atlantic Coast that it has nearly trivialized the question of Resistance. The PRN has some leaders on the Atlantic Coast, but they recognize the party's limited appeal. Indeed, they believe that the most strategic action the PRN can take in the region is to identify powerful leaders—PRN or not—and endorse them. In this way the PRN can associate itself with leaders possessing significant cultural capital and discourage sectarianism and partisanship. The Contra identity is not, and never was, as salient as ethnic identity, as expressed in this remark: "I am not Resistance; I am a combatant for Yátama" [interview 8].

Partisan factions also surfaced after the war. The politicians in the civilian Resistance who had proved so instrumental in defending the Contras in Washington during the war returned to their own political parties afterward. And they invited the Contras to join them. The ruling party, renamed PRONAL during the 1996 elections, attracted many Contras. The chief in command of the Contras at the time of the disarmament, for example, joined the government party. He described his choice in this way:

> We are with PRONAL. All of us. We're not with Antonio Lacayo [the head of the party]. We are with the principles of the party. The other traditional parties don't satisfy those principles: new leaders, new politics, without a prior history that has harmed Nicaragua. We [Contra leaders] have worked hard in PRONAL from the beginning: Zelaya Cruz, Pepe Matos, Mack, Dany, Emiliano, me. We don't work just for the Resistance but for any peasant who was affected by the war. We're working to create new candidates for mayor—new people who come from peasant extraction, or students, or women. We think differently. We want to continue the struggle. [interview 72]

Various political parties from the right to the center have attracted Contra leaders. Even Eden Pastora formed a party called MAD, and later PAD (Democratic Alliance Movement, or Party). All of these parties claim to be Resistance. This could lead one to believe that Contras constitute a significant voting bloc, as the following comment suggests: "Every party is going after the Resistance, because almost everyone is Resistance. And everyone is afraid of the Resistance. The Resistance is a live expression of the Nicaraguans' rebellious spirit and heroism. It is a political-military project with lots of potential. There is a close identification with the people.... It is in all sectors of society, even in the United States embassy and in the Frente Sandinista" [interview 68].[20]

In truth, however, the Contras are so fragmented into various parties that their overall electoral power is diluted. Moreover, Contra leaders enjoy only a limited role within these parties. PRN leaders accuse the Contra leaders who joined these parties of receiving payoffs from the government. They are seen as "sellouts," willing to lend their Contra name to the highest bidder. In addition, these parties have done little for the Resistance, despite their claims to the contrary. They have not proposed any policies that specifically focus on the needs of ex-combatants. Instead the parties are accused of using the term *Contra* simply as a rallying cry: "There is some recognition of the potential power of the Resistance, but very little. They are used. People who used to be afraid to say the word *Contra* in the 1980s are with them in the 1990s. There is a great amount of corruption of the term. Now anyone is a Contra; anyone is a commander; any idiot can become a congressman for the Resistance. There is a total lack of respect for the Resistance" [interview 12].

In other words, the parties do not have to court, negotiate with, or even represent the Contras to use their moniker. Political parties manipulate the symbolic appeal of the Contras to attract Contra votes and allegiances:

> Alemán can get these votes without an alliance with the PRN. The zones of conflict will vote for him. He doesn't need to negotiate to get his vote. Why should he give away something when he doesn't have to? In 1994 he won the Atlantic Coast because of Stedman Fagot. He delivered the votes along the Rio Coco. The PRN is without any importance. And now [with Quiñonez as the presidential candidate] it is associated with corruption. [interview 21]

The Contras, in other words, have only symbolic power, which has not translated into electoral or political power. The PRN tried to become a Contra voice, but the dispersion of Contras into a plethora of political parties left few available for the PRN to mobilize. One anonymous analyst of the PRN told me that the PRN represents only about 15 percent of the Contras. The following remarks capture the PRN's frustrations over its mobilizing efforts:

This is a polarized country, polarized between Liberals and Sandinistas. The Resistance doesn't have any role. . . . In this election you need to get 5 percent of the vote to stay alive as a political party. The only parties with 5 percent right now are the FSLN and the Liberal Alliance. The rest are dead after these elections, even the Resistance. [interview 76]

I had not imagined that it would become so factionalized. The Liberals are factionalized. The Conservatives are, too. But the Resistance is even more so and confused. No one is capable of resolving the situation. They were tricked in the past, and they continue being tricked. [interview 72]

Certainly competition from other political parties for the Contras' support and symbols contributed to the weakness of the Contras' political party, but so too did the Contras' internal competition for leadership. Leaders sniped at each other and undermined the party's dignity, eventually eroding its support. One observer described the situation in this way: "The PRN leaves one wondering what the party of the Resistance is. It is needed. But there is so much division that it has become a disgrace" [interview 78]. Even one of the PRN's founders lamented the current situation: "The party is a mess right now." The timing of the "mess" issued a death knoll to the PRN. It is unlikely to attract any support in its current form.

Some PRN leaders believe that their party can overcome burnout, competition, and infighting. They suggest that the party's current problems are merely the result of inexperience: "We have been acting like children, but we will grow up. This crisis is also an experience" [interview 38]. But it is not clear that the Resistance will have the opportunity to develop further. First, it is not clear whether the party continues to win enough electoral support to survive.[21] If it does, its medium-term goal is to develop a cause sufficient to warrant a separate Resistance party. When I asked the Contras I interviewed when they would stop being Contras, most of them answered that they would always feel Contra. But one described the following scenario:

The PRN is an attitude. We are not being represented. The solution is that our people will no longer be in second or third place. That the best land won't be in the hands of Sandinistas. That the loans won't be in the hands of the elites. That we will have legal authority. That we won't be persecuted. And that we will be represented in the authorities, like the police. Until that happens we will always feel Resistance. We will be the Resistance until we have real representation, have our own voice in the parliament, in the national assembly, and don't have to go asking someone to represent us. We need to have a congressman who is ours, who speaks for us. [interview 68]

Another stated, "We need to have the party for a hundred years, to immortalize the Resistance" [interview 22].

The PRN implicitly assumed that its very existence would immortalize the Resistance. But the party also developed an explicit project to rewrite history from a Resistance perspective. The Resistance could clear its name and form part of the cultural stock of heroism through this project. Consider, for example, this excerpt from an interview:

The objective is to get people through the electoral process and defend the right to vote. Also [to ensure] that people know our story—that we were not created by the United States. We are not mercenaries or assassins. We are the people: workers and professionals. We have made great sacrifices throughout our history. The Resistance fought to consolidate democracy, and we want future generations to know that. We need to oppose the other version. We want the youths, all Nicaraguans, our children, to know the great effort that we made—that peasants made—so that everyone could vote today. [interview 42]

The chances of immortalizing the Resistance seem very slim. Aside from the obvious problems of maintaining party unity, there are generational difficulties. The Resistance party lacks any youth group. Indeed, party leaders told me that while their wives and children support their party activity, family members do not usually participate in, or join, the party. The women and youths who participate in the movement are combatants themselves. The Contras included a small number of women combatants, but most Contra women served as nonfighting forces in communications and delivery of basic services. Women combatants and women noncombatants also play a negligible role in the party. But PRN leaders seem unconcerned with the gender gap. Indeed, they appear visibly uncomfortable with the prospect of an expanded role for women in the movement. One commander smugly described this discomfort as a fundamental difference between Contra men, who want to protect their women, and their Sandinista counterparts, who exploit them [interview 68]. Women explained the situation differently. A feminist Sandinista leader attributed the difference to access to education and power. Contra women had less education and power to draw on than their Sandinista counterparts, which limited their capacity to demand equality in the Contra movement. I observed one confrontation involving a woman Contra combatant who demanded, to deaf male ears, women's inclusion in the party. In my follow-up conversations with women in the party, most concurred with this combatant's assessment but expressed resigned acceptance of their limited role in the party.

The Chamorro government's tactics were critical in further limiting the Contras' political power, while the Contras' existing weakness certainly increased the government's range of strategies for controlling them. One strategy involved negotiations with key actors. The government negotiated political appointments in low-level bureaucracies with top Contra leaders. In this way the government purchased loyalty while simultaneously limiting Contra influence over policy implementation.

The settlement with Chacal (José Angel Talavera) and his Frente Norte 3-80 provides the best example of the result of key negotiations with Contras. After having violated the cease-fire agreements, carried out assaults on the army and peasant populations, and kidnapped members of Congress, Chacal and his group were rewarded by the Chamorro government with land, a police force, and a ministerial position for Chacal's brother, Salvador, enabling him to oversee the government's compliance with the negotiated agreements. The negotiations with Chacal and others before him, while costly for the government, effectively defused the rural violence. But if the negotiations provided the carrot to disarm, the EPS rural patrols provided the stick. The security apparatus used force to eliminate those Recontras unwilling to negotiate. Rather than continue to take up arms, the Recontras have demobilized.

Unless one subscribes to an ends-justifies-the-means rationale, the Chamorro government's strategies are hardly laudable. Not surprisingly, the government received severe criticism for its use of payoffs and violence in ending the Recontra mobilization, as in the following indictment:

> Political violence has dropped off to a minimum. Common crime still
> exists, though, and this often involves the demobilized on both sides
> acting together. Nobody wants war. There are some delinquents in the
> mountains involved in frequent assaults. They learned how to use a
> weapon during the war, and they keep using it. But the government
> hasn't used its strong arm to end the violence. We oppose the amnesties
> [the government grants]. There has to be a state of law. No buy-offs—
> that money creates incentives to rearm and to continue the violence.
> The Nicaraguan people are at war . . . a people who wanted to end the

war. But the combatants aren't capable of shifting from using their guns to using a machete. They use that gun to rob instead of working. It occurs less and less, but I still hear incidents like the case of the Coffee Plan [wherein the EPS patrolled rural areas to "protect" against violence that might have threatened the coffee harvest] and abuses by the army and the police. The police and the army need to find political solutions. We don't want any more of these "accidents" to occur. [interview 7]

The uncivil movements approach does not advocate government payoffs and violence as ideal remedies for uncivil movement violence. Nonetheless, the lack of an effective judiciary in Nicaragua left little possibility for prosecution of violence. Chamorro's strategy might be viewed as one of artful negotiations and prosecutions. In an interesting twist compared with the other cases of uncivil movements examined here, it was the Contras who felt victimized by the culture of impunity:

I had to investigate the Bermúdez murder on 6 February 1991. It was obviously a political murder, very well planned—the work of Sandinistas. Otherwise the Sandinistas would have been trying to find someone else to take the blame and keep their hands clean. They didn't care about the cost of the murder. The government really didn't have any will to investigate or protect human rights. There is total impunity. International institutions don't do anything, either. There really isn't any interest in investigating. [interview 33]

Of course, Sandinistas made the same accusation, claiming that the government turned a blind eye toward Contra violence.

The Nicaragua case confirms the inability of weak judiciaries to reduce uncivil movements' power and strengthen democracy. At the same time, it suggests some creative, if not always ethical, ways in which democratic governments can compensate for weak judiciaries.

The Chamorro government was able to take advantage of the weak domestic and international support for the Contras. As discussed earlier, fragmentation, competition, leadership, and identity factors eroded the movement's domestic support. The Contras' international appeal also fell dramatically after the war. The Contras made alliances in Miami with Nicaraguan and Cuban counterrevolutionaries, but they could not rely on these allies for anything beyond moral support. They even faced some conflict with the *confiscados*, since the latter had claims on land that had been distributed to Contras. The Contras tried unsuccessfully to generate support from the individuals, foundations, and government officials in the United States and elsewhere who had helped them during the war. Indeed, many of the Contras I interviewed indicated that the party was counting on assistance from its old allies: "We'll need help from our friends. Party militants can put in 100 córdobas [about $16] a month. We'll also need radio announcements and programs. We'll have to get help from Miami and Washington, from the National Endowment for Democracy. They can donate something, maybe a computer. We'll paint the house we have. And we'll get 250,000 votes" [interview 16]. The party has discovered, however, that its politician allies in Nicaragua have returned to their own parties and party politics, and that Washington is no longer interested in assisting the Contras. For the Contras' political allies, both domestic, and international, the Contra cause ended when Daniel Ortega stepped down in 1990.

Perhaps because of their weakness, the Chamorro government did not need the Contras. Indeed, by demanding housing, jobs, and health care, they only created problems for the regime. The government addressed their needs only because they rearmed. While the Chamorro government hardly exemplifies the kind of effective government that democratic scholars advocate, it cobbled together a compromise between two warring factions, as the following excerpt contends: "This government has been painful—a wheelchair government. But with an ultra-right government we would have had more polarization. We have had to bear everything. But it helped undermine the Sandinistas. They don't have the same force. And there isn't that terrible polarization. [The FSLN] isn't as strong as it was in 1980. There might have been war in the street. And so it has been positive" [interview 22]. The Contra case suggests, therefore, that even less-than-ideal governments can negotiate with uncivil movements to reduce the latter's political power. The Chamorro government's willingness to negotiate, and its understanding of the Contras' inherent weaknesses, proved essential to its success in dividing and conquering them.

Conclusion

"This country should come with a warning label: Caution! Extremely Fragile Democratic Country" [interview 46].

The Nicaraguan case hardly provides a model for democratic stability. Nonetheless, it sheds light on (1) the variety of domestic and international factors that lead to an uncivil movement's emergence, (2) the circumstances under which uncivil movements threaten democracy, and (3) government strategies that effectively reduce the power of uncivil movements over democracies.

The Contra case demonstrates that international factors and actors can play a central role in the emergence of uncivil movements. The institutions approach focuses almost exclusively on government policy, but not the broader international arena. While I do not wish to argue that the United States invented the Contras, they would not, without U.S. support, have become a competent force capable of defeating the Sandinistas. The movement's profound impact on Nicaraguan politics resulted from U.S. backing.

Just as the United States created a powerful movement, however, its withdrawal of that support helped undermine the movement. The Contras had no function, from the U.S. perspective, once Ortega stepped down. Without a purpose or outside support, the Contras could not sustain their movement. They went through the motions of framing a new threat after the war, cuing up the movement with past heroes, villains, and repertoires of collective action, and spinning myths. But the lack of a core identity and sense of purpose eroded the movement's meaning and resonance within Nicaraguan society.

Why did the Contras fail to establish an identity around which to mobilize? Once the FSLN left government, neither the "Contra" label nor the "Resistance" label made sense for contemporary struggles. Certainly it had meaning in Nicaragua's past, and the Contra movement will no doubt form part of the cultural cues of heroism and repertoires of collective action upon which future uncivil movements will build. But in its efforts to remake itself as a movement with political salience in the immediate postwar era, it fell short. Indeed, even future Nicaraguan uncivil movements may have difficulty spinning heroic myths out of the Contras and the Contra war.

The Contras united for a specific purpose crafted by the U.S. government. But that unity dissolved, as in the cases of the other uncivil movements analyzed in this book, over the struggle between institutional and uncivil politics—that is, the PRN versus the Recontras. But the Contras also faced an existential struggle over what it meant to be a Contra after the war. Competition among political parties for the mantle of Sandino and Resistance eroded the uniqueness of the movement. Each conservative party incorporated Contra discourse, symbols, and leaders. With so many parties claiming a Contra origin, even the "pure" Contra party lost its marketing value. Moreover, Nicaragua's high unemployment and inflation equally afflicted peasants and the urban poor of both ideological perspectives—Contra and Sandinista. By creating a Resistance party to defend the poor, the Contras divided the movement for social change. And by tying itself so narrowly to a specific historical moment, the movement lost a more generic, enduring resonance. In addition, the formation of Yátama, and the defection of most of the Atlantic Coast leadership from the Contras graphically illustrated the shallow and ephemeral nature of the Contra identity, and how more meaningful political and cultural struggles supplanted Contra mobilization.

Good political leadership might have overcome some of these problems. A leader like one of the Talavera brothers might have crafted a new identity sufficiently complex to attract broad support. The Talaveras, for example, possessed charisma in their embodiment of legitimating myths. As peasants, revolutionaries, anti-imperialists, anti-Sandinistas, Contras, and Recontras, they embodied the Contras' contemporary image. But they did not become party leaders. Perhaps the Talaveras, and others like them, doubt the long-term significance of such a movement in the postwar era and prefer to focus on more immediate, local and/or cultural issues.

But U.S. withdrawal, political competition, and ineffective movement crafting alone cannot explain the weakness of the Contra movement. The Chamorro government's exploitation of these weaknesses further reduced the Contras' political power. Chamorro diverged from the practice of other transitional governments by refusing to capitulate to Contra demands. She recognized that the Contras did not constitute a threat to her government or to democracy in general. Even though the Contras had a history of violence and rearmed as Recontras, she did not accommodate them. On the other hand, she did not completely ignore the Contra threat. She negotiated directly with key individuals. In the case of disarmament, she negotiated with Contra commanders. In the case of the Recontras, she negotiated with the group's leader, not with the PRN or other Contras distant from the violence. She did not reify the movement's power but rather divided it by buying off key leaders with low-level government positions, limited security protections, and land resources. Against the violent leaders who would not negotiate she directed the full force of the public security apparatus, eliminating them. Such a response might have prompted a strong outcry, martyrdom, and increased support for Recontra mobilizing if it had occurred earlier, before negotiation attempts, or if it had been directed against well-respected Recontra leaders. But by reserving the use of force for employment against the few remaining Recontras who were acknowledged by Contras as delinquents detrimental to their cause and to peasants, Chamorro won political points.

The uncivil movements approach advocates investigation and prosecution over force as a means of reducing the power of uncivil movements. But Nicaragua lacked an independent and powerful judiciary after its long history of dictatorship and civil war. Transitional settings usually involve weak judiciaries. By negotiating with the Contras and eliminating the criminal and extremist elements, Chamorro, albeit unwittingly, spun countermyths about the Recontras. She separated those with broad appeal from those without, thus conquering the latter.

What does the Contra case tell us about the institutions approach? With regard to moderation, Chamorro probably fits. Contras experienced difficulty uniting against her, since they perceived her as the only alternative between the extreme-right Somocistas, which some Contras rejected, and the extreme-left FSLN, which all Contras opposed. Nonetheless, they criticized her endlessly for capitulating to the FSLN, suggesting that moderates are rarely perceived as such by uncivil movements. Chamorro also lacked the governmental expertise that institutions scholars advocate. And yet she proved successful in dealing with the Contras on their terms.

Certainly the creation of the PRN provided the Contras' democratic faction a channel for expressing its demands within the political system. But the Recontras mobilized at the same time. Thus, as with the other uncivil movements examined here, institutions did not eliminate the use of violence; they simply became another weapon in uncivil movements' political arsenal. The political party option reduced some of the Contras' power, but not in the way institutions scholars would have anticipated. The PRN simply could not compete with other political institutions. The Contras dispersed into a variety of political parties, leaving the movement without a single voice. "Contra" thus became merely a symbol around which future uncivil movements might spin myths of heroism. The erosion of power had less to do with institution-building than with ineffective identity formation through political framing, cultural cues, and movement myths.

The warning cited at the beginning of this conclusion is not, therefore, about the specter of Contras overthrowing democracy; it concerns ungovernability. While the polarization between Contras and Sandinistas has abated over time because of a practical need to bury the war, the inability of political institutions—the executive, the legislature, and the judiciary—to resolve crises remains. In this sense the institutions approach accurately identifies a problem of democratic vulnerability. Political parties in Nicaragua represent not political ideas but only the whims of political party brokers, without any accountability. In the Contra case, interestingly enough, the party never developed a broker. Its greatest strength—a peasant base—limited its ability to do so. Unlike the other uncivil movements analyzed in this book, the postwar Contras lacked traditional bases of political power; they did not represent an established military faction or prominent landlords or politicians. Their strongest brokers were the United States and wealthy individuals abroad, at least for a time. But once they lost this support, the government could ignore them and minimize concessions to them.

In sum, the Contras lacked a traditional base of power. Moreover, they failed to develop the political framing, cultural cuing, and movement myths they needed to form a powerful uncivil movement. As a result, they posed little threat to democracy in the postauthoritarian era.

6 Uncivil Movements in Comparative Perspective

The analytical threads woven into the fabric of this book from its theoretical introduction through the empirical case studies have drawn implicitly from comparisons with other uncivil movements. This conclusion
revisits the book's four main theoretical contributions and develops them
by drawing explicitly on comparative cases.

One of the book's central claims is that uncivil movements constitute not
a new political actor but rather an unexamined one. Uncivil movements are
defined by their unique blending of civil-institutional and uncivil-mobili-
zational politics. The right-wing uncivil movements examined in this book
employed the mobilizational style of social movements in democratic civil
society, the violent political action of authoritarian movements, and institutional politics. Indeed, uncivil movements overlap with, and transform
into or out of, recognized political actors, such as authoritarian movements,
antiestablishment political parties, populist movements, and terrorist organizations.

Not only are uncivil movements a distinct political actor, they also emerge
and evolve in a variety of contexts. The comparative analysis conducted for
this project involved study of uncivil movements in other Latin American
countries with distinct political histories (e.g., paramilitaries in Colombia,
ARENA in El Salvador, FRAPH in Haiti, and MBR-200 in Venezuela), in
transitional democracies outside Latin America (the AWB in South Africa),
and in consolidated democracies (the militia movement in the United States,
Jean-Marie Le Pen's National Front in France, and Meir Kahane's movements in Israel). Uncivil movements, in other words, develop in various regional and political contexts. No democracy, in other words, is immune to
uncivil movements.

The book's second claim is that successful uncivil movements gain power through political threats, cultural cues, and legitimating myths. Uncivil movements face no shortage of political threats around which to mobilize. It is not a particular transitional context that gives rise to an uncivil movement, but rather its crafting strategy. The success of that crafting depends on the way in which movements frame the threat, its source, and its solution. But it also depends on cuing up the movement with past heroes and their repertoires of collective action, as well as mobilizing against cultural villains. Furthermore, successful uncivil movements distance themselves from negative associations, both past and present, by creating legitimating myths to sustain support from the militant hardline while spinning contradictory images and discourse around the movement, its leaders, and its political action to appeal to more pragmatic members. And comparative analysis demonstrates that successful crafting of movements around cultural cues and legitimating myths takes place in a variety of regional and political contexts.

The third central argument of this book is that uncivil movements—even successful ones—face inherent tensions that weaken them over time, albeit frequently after they have profoundly impacted democracy. Comparative analysis confirms this conclusion and provides nuance lacking in a three-country study. For example, institutionalization, charismatic leadership, and political competition do not have a uniform impact on uncivil movements' political power. Comparative analysis, in other words, further and more accurately specifies the relationship between uncivil movements and democracy.

The book's fourth claim is that democratic governments can exacerbate such internal tensions and erode uncivil movements before they have a chance to influence democracy. Comparative analysis reveals an array of strategies states might undertake and suggests that a government's perception of uncivil movements' threat shapes that government's will and capacity to reduce such movements' power. The perception of threat is often, though by no means always, higher in transitional contexts than in stable ones. Transitional governments and stable ones alike have demonstrated will and capacity in relation to uncivil movements.

Defining Uncivil Movements Comparatively

Uncivil movements are defined by their dual political strategy. They participate, on one hand, in some form of institutional politics, whether through political parties, representation in government, or interest group lobbying. At the same time, they operate outside the institutional apparatus, employing both the mobilizational strategies of social movements and violent political action against their government or civil society adversaries. They adopt the language of democracy, the superficial characteristics of social movement activism, and the facade of democratic institutions, but their goals are antidemocratic. They strive to eliminate competition and perpetuate and expand their exclusive political power and privileges. Thus, the Argentine Carapintada engaged in military coup attempts while simultaneously developing a political party oriented toward representing the economically disenfranchised. The Brazilian UDR formed a powerful political lobby while its members murdered rural environmentalists, labor union activists, and supporters of the landless peasant movement. The Nicaraguan Contras mobilized after the war into a peasants' political party linked to a paramilitary movement.

These three cases provide insight into the types of uncivil movements that commonly emerge in democracies. But comparative analysis illustrates that such movements are not unique to a particular phase of democracy or geographical location. For example, while the Carapintada exemplify the military roots of uncivil movements, a similar type of movement emerged in Venezuela's longstanding democracy. Hugo Chavez, mentioned in the introduction to this book, won the 1998 presidential elections, just two years after serving a prison sentence for an unsuccessful military coup.[1] Argentina, given its history of military intervention in politics, is not a surprising context in which to find a military-oriented uncivil movement. But Venezuela's military movement emerged in a stable two-party system that had experienced only a short-lived and historically distant military intervention.[2]

While the Contras also had a military origin, they evolved into a peasant paramilitary force. The influential role of the U.S. government in the formation and evolution of the Contra movement, and its separation from the formal military apparatus, distinguishes it from the military movements described above. But the Contras are not unique, either. Haiti's FRAPH (Revolutionary Front for the Advancement and Progress of Haiti) also developed into a political party from paramilitary (death-squad) origins and received U.S. support.[3] There are other similarities between Nicaragua and Haiti: both experienced long-term dictatorial control by a single family, the Somozas and the Duvaliers; both dictatorships depended on personal armies for their control, the National Guard and the *tonton macoutes;* and uncivil movements in both countries arose from these personal armies, in reaction to the mobilization of progressive political struggles for democracy under the FSLN and Jean-Bertrand Aristide's Lavalas movement.

On the other hand, paramilitary-style uncivil movements with U.S. support have emerged in entirely distinct political contexts. Paramilitary units in Colombia, partially supported by the United States, defy simplistic interpretations of the causal effect of political transitions. Colombia, in contrast to Haiti and Nicaragua, went through a transition from authoritarian rule in the late 1950s. After a relatively brief dictatorship under Gustavo Rojas Pinilla (1953–57), the two main political parties crafted a National Front (1958–74) to avoid political ruptures. Colombia has enjoyed relatively stable longstanding democratic institutions rather than the institutional instability of democratic transitions. Nevertheless, it has also seen the emergence of similar uncivil movements.[4]

Not all uncivil movements involve militaries or paramilitaries, as the Brazilian UDR illustrates. The UDR was a political or sectoral movement that used hired guns and violent "operatives" to reinforce its political power. It emerged during the uncertainty of the political transition in Brazil, not unlike a similar movement in South Africa. The South African AWB (Afrikaner Resistance Movement) is a cultural movement of Afrikaners that has employed both violent and legislative strategies to resist changes to apartheid.[5] The AWB shares not only the political-transition moment with the UDR; most of its members have agricultural backgrounds and sought to protect their political rights and privileges. But the AWB, unlike the UDR, involves mostly small farmers with a cultural history distinct from other South Africans.

Movements similar to the UDR also emerged in nontransitional contexts. Consider, for example, Rabbi Meir Kahane's Zionist movement in Israel, a so-called consolidated democracy. Kahane's movement pursues its agenda by means of a political party, Kach (Thus), yet it also encourages its members to carry out violent attacks on Arabs living in Israel.[6] The religious, or cultural, identity of the movement merged with its nationalist and political struggle. This same kind of uncivil movement has also emerged in democratic France. Jean-Marie Le Pen's far-right National Front employs both civil and uncivil strategies—the activities of an institutionalized political party as well as violence perpetrated by members against foreigners—to promote a nationalist agenda and to protect the rights and privileges of a distinct group.

El Salvador's ARENA (Nationalist Republican Alliance) party and the U.S. militia movement provide examples of blended uncivil movements. Soldiers, ex-soldiers, and paramilitaries are central to both, but they also depend on nonmilitary sectors. ARENA comprises the business and landed elite who mobilized within the political system to defend their interests while death squads and hit men eliminated their adversaries. The U.S. militia movement is a loose coalition of military, paramilitary, and nonmilitary groups, ranging from Green Beret veterans of the Vietnam War to survivalists and "gun-rights" activists to violent skinheads, white supremacists, and neo-Nazis.[7]

In short, uncivil movements emerge and evolve in a variety of democratic settings. They are not confined to a specific geographical region or political history. They have emerged in the Third World and the First World, at the end of civil wars (e.g., in Nicaragua and El Salvador), in countries making the transition from authoritarian regimes (e.g., Argentina, Brazil, South Africa, and Haiti), and in countries with longstanding procedural democracies (e.g., Colombia, France, Israel, the United States, and Venezuela). Regardless of their historical underpinnings and political contexts, uncivil movements share goals and strategies. They also share a political recipe for success.

Crafting Successful Uncivil Movements

I have argued here that when uncivil movements effectively employ three different devices—political framing, cultural cues, and legitimating myths—they achieve political power and influence over democratic governments. Threats exist regardless of the stability or instability of the political context because effective framing transforms even minor problems into universal and urgent threats that require mobilization. Cultural cues play a key role in mobilizing in that they provide reference points: they identify current threats with past cultural villains, and current solutions with past heroes and heroic acts. Movements expand through legitimating myths and consistently articulated messages. These myths attract a militant hard core who carry out the violence while simultaneously appealing to the pragmatists who legitimate the movement.

The uncivil movements examined in this book utilized political framing, cultural cues, and legitimating myths directly or indirectly related to the overarching transition from authoritarian rule. Broadening our investigation beyond these three cases provides insights into how the threats, cues, and myths available to uncivil movements evolved in other political and regional contexts.

POLITICAL FRAMING

Transitional moments generate catalyst threats around which uncivil movements mobilize. The Argentine Carapintada, for example, initially mobilized to end the human rights trials. They blamed the democratic government and the military High Command loyal to that government for trials that undermined the military's dignity and, by extension, national security. The Brazilian UDR mobilized against the democratic government's agrarian reform. Although Brazil's military regime had carried out its own reform, the struggle took on a distinctively postauthoritarian flavor; landlords confronted reactivated rural social movements in Brasília's legislative halls and in the open field. In Nicaragua, the Contras mobilized for what they considered to be justice in the postwar era: having fought for ten years to guarantee democracy, they expected compliance with the peace accords. Yet they faced poverty, unemployment, a lack of social services, and deaf ears in the government.

Other transitional cases exhibited similar threats directly attributable to political change. ARENA, FRAPH, and the AWB all mobilized to check the reemergence of the political left at the end of the authoritarian era. ARENA mobilized primarily against the FMLN (Farabundo Martí National Liberation Front). FRAPH mobilized against President Aristide's social reforms to distribute wealth and services to the poor. The AWB mobilized to prevent changes in the apartheid system generally, and the presidential election of African National Congress leader Nelson Mandela specifically. In each case the uncivil movement gained strength via a four-step process: naming the threat, blaming individuals within the government and civil society, aiming violence at them, and claiming victories.

Uncivil movements do not require the uncertainty of transitions to mobilize, since democracies generate uncertainty even when they are entrenched.[8] Even in longstanding democracies, uncivil movements find threats around which to mobilize. Hugo Chavez's movement mobilized around corruption in the Carlos Andrés Pérez government. After Pérez left office, Chavez and his followers mobilized around the antiquated, undemocratic, and self-interested Venezuelan party system. Kahane exploited disillusionment with Prime Minister Menachem Begin's Camp David agreements, which ceded control over Sinai and the West Bank to the Arab enemy. The Yom Kippur War and the 1982 Lebanon war further fueled disillusionment and won Kahane support. Kahane even admitted, "The worse it gets for Israel, the better it gets for me."[9] Le Pen mobilized in defense of a quality of life, and

against the destruction of French culture and the loss of jobs to foreign workers. The U.S. militia movement organized around the threat of an excessive,
out-of-touch, and unrepresentative centralized government that encroached
on citizens' and states' rights. Gun control, particularly the Brady Bill, provided the catalyst to frame the threat in terms of an erosion of individual
rights, specifically the right to bear arms.[10]

In other words, regardless of the political context, uncivil movements find
catalyst threats around which to mobilize. They frame these threats as universal, transforming them from sectoral complaints, or "invented" threats,
to urgent universal threats to the nation. The threats are framed not in ab-
stract structural terms but rather as concrete events with real political actors
to blame, as well as real solutions. Uncivil movements enhance their appeal
by pointing to their success in overcoming such threats.

CULTURAL CUES

To increase the public perception of the threat's intensity and the
movement's claim to overcome it, uncivil movements draw on a cultural
stock of symbols. They cue up their movement to past forms of heroism,
historical enemies, and political practices. These cultural cues do not depend on particular regions or cultural contexts. Like threats, they are readily
available for uncivil movements' exploitation. Nonetheless, particular histories and movements' links to them can facilitate or constrain the mobilizational potential of cultural cues.

Uncivil movements tend to draw on foundational symbols and myths to
cue up their movement with heroism. In Argentina, for example, the
Carapintada drew on founding fathers from their Independence era, like
General Rosas, as well as the founders of contemporary Argentine national
identity, like General Perón. Both symbolized military intervention as a form
of political action necessary to save the nation from a perceived threat. But
the symbols seized upon by the Carapintada were not exclusively military;
the movement associated itself with civilian repertoires of political action
like the Peronist Party and markers of national identity like the *mate* bowl
and straw, the tango, and populist discourse on national economic development.

Not surprisingly, Hugo Chavez's movement took its name from Simón
Bolivar, the Venezuelan-born "liberator" of Latin America during the Independence era. With this symbol Chavez not only cued up his movement
with heroism and military repertoires of political action; he also associated
it with national historic struggles for sovereignty, development, and iden-

tity. He identified the historic enemies as foreign business interests that control national politics and the economy, and national governments that act as the handmaidens to those foreign interests.

Civilian uncivil movements generally eschew militaristic symbols but still build on national and foundational moments. The AWB, for example, cues up the 1838 Great Trek and the Boer War to identify itself with the heroic struggle against elimination by cultural enemies.[11] The U.S. militia movement draws on culturally embedded images of heroism and manhood: the frontiersman, the pioneer, the rugged individual who resists domination. But it also makes specific references to the War of Independence; it equates contemporary militias with the citizen militias formed in the colonies to check a tyrannical King George.[12] Meir Kahane cued up his movement with the Zionist heroes who against all odds achieved Israel's nationhood.[13]

Not all uncivil movements have successfully associated their struggle with cultural heroes, villains, and repertoires of political action. As we have seen, the Contras failed in their effort to appropriate the symbol of Sandino as their heroic icon. Their enemy—the FSLN—had already adopted that image, and the Contras represented everything Sandino rejected: the National Guard and the United States. Comparative analysis reveals that the other movements, with the exception of the U.S. militia movement, faced difficulties in developing cultural cues. Neither FRAPH, ARENA, nor the Colombian paramilitaries successfully adopted cultural cues. Where uncivil movements have developed to serve particularly powerful groups in society, they have become stigmatized by their violence and exclusivity, posing particular problems for their use of cultural cues of heroism, villains, and repertoires of collective action. Just as the Contras could not shed the association with Somocismo and the United States, FRAPH could not disassociate from Duvalierisme, ARENA from the "fourteen families," or the Colombian paramilitaries from death squads. When uncivil movements overcame these negative associations, they did so by means of legitimating myths.

LEGITIMATING MYTHS

Uncivil movements are caught in a double bind. They depend on violence and antidemocratic political action for their power. Their strongest support comes from militants who desire this kind of unconventional political action. Their violence forces the government and civil society to take them seriously despite their small numbers. Violence also procures the media coverage they need to spread their message. Yet violence alone is political suicide for these movements. To achieve any legitimacy within the democratic system, they must deny their violence and conceal it behind a facade of democratic discourse and action. Yet uncivil movements do not want to lose their militant hard core. Therefore, they must also admit to their violence and justify it using relative-weight, bad-egg, and just-war arguments. These contradictory accounts of itself are the legitimating myths that protect the movement from government retribution, enable its pragmatic members to justify their membership in it, and expand its power within the political system.

Gendered discourse and images, charismatic leadership, cultural cues, ideological confusion, and outright contradictions are the elements that comprise the legitimating myths created by uncivil movements. The Carapintada, for example, denied the coups that it fomented, evidence notwithstanding. They spun an alternative image of themselves as soldiers seeking to protect the nation from the problems of the military regime: corruption, mismanagement, and foreign control. This alternative image included a central role for women, a courting of the left, a charismatic leader difficult to identify as either anti- or prodemocratic, and both anti- and prodemocratic action and discourse.

The UDR usually denied any involvement in violence, portraying itself instead as a civic-minded modern lobby. To counter their *coronel* image, its members referred to themselves as "producers." The handsome and charismatic doctor-leader at the helm and the participation of women in the movement's civic activities dispelled the UDR's traditional redneck image. But the movement did not abandon its violent image completely; it balanced denials of violence with admissions and justifications.

The Contras attempted the same strategy. They denied their Somocista and National Guard background in favor of an image of themselves as a disenfranchised peasantry and indigenous people mobilizing within the political system to extend the rights of citizenship. Although the image the Contras cultivated was perhaps closer to reality than the Carapintada or UDR image was, they had a harder time mobilizing around it and distancing themselves from authoritarian associations. No leader emerged from the movement with anything approximating the charisma of Aldo Rico or Ronaldo Caiado. The Contras could not spin powerful legitimating myths about themselves. They also could not distance themselves from violence and never gained sufficient power within the political system to demonstrate their involvement in other, more legitimate types of action. And they did not have the resources that they had enjoyed during wartime to develop a political party.

Successful cases follow the Carapintada and UDR model. Hugo Chavez, for example, ostensibly takes a left-wing line against the corruption and accommodation of the mainstream political parties. Very similar to Rico in his heyday, Chavez assumes a caudillo role to resolve national crises. His populist discourse sounds democratic and masks the antidemocratic character of his acts. After the war ARENA disguised its death-squad origins by replacing its authoritarian figurehead, Roberto D'Aubuisson, with Alfredo "Fredy" Cristiani, a leader whose young, modern, democratic image belied the movement's uncivil past.

One might attribute these successes to regional stereotypes, cultural politics, or authoritarian nostalgia, except that comparative cases outside Latin America, in countries without an authoritarian past, tell the same story. In democratic Israel, for example, Kahane played a role similar to that of leaders of uncivil movements elsewhere. There is little doubt about his militant charisma.[14] One scholar described him as "a bundle of unrestrained emotions, violent eruptions, and an insatiable thirst for publicity."[15] In his mobilizational style, Kahane balanced militancy with religious legitimating myths. Biblical scripture provided him with justifications for the use of violence against Arabs.[16] Kahane likened himself to King David, who in his words "studied every night, and in the morning . . . would wake up and make war."[17] But he simultaneously claimed to reject the use of violence.[18] He formed a political party, competed in democratic elections, and used the Knesset to advance his causes, but he simultaneously referred to democracy as an alien, Gentile, idea.[19] He used democratic language toward undemocratic ends, as when he claimed that Jews have an "inalienable right" to all of Israel's territory.[20]

The U.S. militia movement's legitimating myths also overcome the negative images associated with the groups that comprise it: white supremacist movements like the Ku Klux Klan and skinheads, anti-Semitic and neo-Nazi movements, and cold warriors from anticommunist movements. At every militia meeting or rally, these groups sell their literature and paraphernalia. Yet the militia movement's link to these groups is often coded. Militias support "states' rights" and "county supremacy," drawing on the strategy white supremacists use to shield discriminatory acts from federal government oversight. They warn about conspiracies of "international bankers," the "Federal Reserve," the "Trilateral Commission," or "eastern elites" in thinly disguised shows of anti-Semitism. Militias also openly justify violence, often in religious terms. One movement spokesperson, for example, rhetorically asked, "Do you know why Jesus was killed? There was no militia. Think of that for a moment. There was no one there to respond, to say, 'You can't do that.'"[21] A leader of Gun Owners of America provided a similar religious defense of armed violence: "This is not a political issue. This is something that comes first and foremost from the Scripture. What I see in Scripture is not that we have a right to keep and bear arms, but that we have a responsibility to do so. For a man to refuse to provide adequately for his and his family's defense would be to defy God."[22] But like other uncivil movements, militias also publicly deny their use of violence and hide their uncivil acts behind a veneer of civil politics. Consider this militia leader's comment: "We don't want bloodshed. We want to use the ballot box and the jury box. We don't want to go to the cartridge box. But we will if we have to."[23]

Some uncivil movements, like the Contras, failed to create legitimating myths. The AWB provides an example. Its leader, Eugene Terre'Blanche,[24] typifies an unreconstructed authoritarian leader, like Seineldín in Argentina. He drew passionate support, but only from Afrikaner extremists. The media covered him as much for his entertainment value as for anything else. One journalist admitted that "reporters loved interviewing grizzled Afrikaners, who breathed fire and slaughter and wore neo-Nazi garb."[25] Terre'-Blanche became a particular media favorite because he "knew how to move his people at the hustings" with histrionics, tears, poems, and folk tales.[26] And he certainly performed for the media. A 1991 British television documentary, for example, showed him preparing tear gas in his kitchen while urging followers to protect their weapons from government seizure and admitting that the AWB might use political assassinations to defend itself from government threats.[27] Terre'Blanche's AWB showed little interest in disguising its violence but did try to deny associations with Nazism.[28]

As these cases illustrate, crafting plays an important role in determining an uncivil movement's political success. However, it is not the only important factor. Domestic political and cultural factors also play a crucial role. Hugo Chavez and ARENA's Fredy Cristiani assumed presidential office under extremely different political conditions. While Chavez rose to power in a relatively stable democracy, Cristiani took office after a civil war. The lack of an authoritarian regime may have helped Chavez distance himself from the stigma of violence and authoritarianism. Similarly, Cristiani put a civil face on the uncivil movement formerly dominated by D'Aubuisson. Each seemed to benefit from legitimating myths as well as political framing. The distinction between them lies in their use of cultural cues. While both had access to cultural villains, Chavez consciously modeled his movement on the national hero Simón Bolívar. Cristiani, however, did not build on the foundational myth. Chavez also used a military repertoire of political action—intervention to save the nation—to cue up his movement, while Cristiani followed a conventional party route. Crafting alone, therefore, does not determine the success of uncivil movements.

On a lesser scale, both Le Pen and Kahane won seats in national congresses. Judging from their electoral support, these individuals successfully crafted their movement to appeal beyond an extremist fringe. For example, Kahane's natural constituency—religious fundamentalists—provided only a minor base of support. His message resonated most strongly with religious and secular West Bankers facing economic and physical insecurity.[29] Kahane also appealed to security forces: in the 1984 elections, 2.5 percent of soldiers voted for him. Perhaps illustrating the power of legitimating myths, Kahane's constituency included the poor and the working class as well.[30] His antimainstream politics and political-action orientation also seemed to appeal to young people. In one poll of high school students, for example, 40 percent said they agreed with him and 11 percent said they would vote for him if they could.

The movements that most resemble the Contras in the limited extent to which they achieved political power are the AWB, the U.S. militias, FRAPH, and Colombia's paramilitary. These groups neither infiltrated the political system nor achieved their political goals outside of it. None of these groups had any difficulty framing the threat. In addition, the U.S. militias and the AWB successfully linked their projects to foundational myths. Where all the groups fell short, it appears, is in the generating of legitimating myths. Because these movements defined themselves in terms of weapons, they had little success in winning support among pragmatists. The AWB's appeal remained limited to the most militant Afrikaners.[31] "A natural haven for fanatics," as one journalist called it, the AWB attracted primarily former policemen, volunteers in the war against Namibian guerrillas, and lone violent racists.[32] The description of its members as "rockspiders, crunchies, [and] hairybacks" sums up the narrowness of the movement's appeal even among Afrikaners.[33] An inability to spin myths about the movement that might distance it from an authoritarian past and provide an alternative modern image meant that the AWB could not extend its appeal to a new generation of Afrikaners. As one scholar put it, "Stories about the Great Trek, the Boer War, and the heyday of Nationalism no longer hold a fascination."[34]

The U.S. militia movement probably enjoys broader support than the AWB among individuals who do not openly endorse anti-Semitic or other racist attitudes, although it certainly includes people falling into those categories.

Its message attracts a broad spectrum: law-abiding citizens as well as criminals; youths and middle-aged supporters; mostly men, but also some women; the wide range of individuals opposed to government intervention:

> People who have never given a thought to blacks or Jews were attracted to these groups because they cared about other things—guns, the environment, abortion. People were not joining militias as they would the Ku Klux Klan, to beat up on minorities or give vent to racist ideas. The organizing principle of the militias was that the government had been taken over by evil forces and could not be reformed, that it had to be combated—with arms.[35]

The movement conceals its use of violence behind a screen of civic engagement on political issues, allowing its members to view the militias' political acts as acts of civil disobedience. For example, the refusal to register one's cars or guns, carry a driver's license, pay taxes, or send one's children to public school are presented as a way in which citizens can resist government control. Similarly, militia groups' "wise-use" land policies are presented as a means of replacing federal government control over land and the environment with local community, or citizen, control. The militia movement's orientation toward local rather than national politics may ultimately limit the role it can play in defining the national political agenda. On the other hand, that local orientation may simply obscure the extent of the movement's political success. It may be too early to discern the movement's true impact.

These comparative cases permit us to draw tentative conclusions about the crafting of uncivil movements and their political success. Political threats provide uncivil movements with ample opportunities to mobilize. All of the comparative cases demonstrate that uncivil movements can take advantage of uncertainties and insecurities in either transitional or consolidated democratic contexts and transform them into mobilization. The difficulty that uncivil movements face is in building support for their movement. Even when the threat is credible, uncivil movements are stigmatized by their association with violent and antidemocratic political action. Where they are capable of developing cultural cues, discourse, action, or charismatic leaders that distance them from illegal, violent, and antidemocratic action, they may be able to overcome the stigma and even achieve presidential or legislative office. This ability depends in part on crafting, but political context may also constrain or facilitate it.

Tensions in the Evolution of Uncivil Movements

The cases examined in this book illustrate uncivil movements' inherent weaknesses. Paradoxically, the same factors that enhance their power also undermine them. This is particularly true of the movements' leadership, success, and opposition. For example, the charismatic leaders who brought about the Carapintada's and UDR's success eventually eroded their power. These leaders began to amass personal power, which drove them to seek their own personal political goals. For Rico, this involved purging the movement of competitors and running the movement as his own personal whim. Caiado left the UDR to pursue political self-aggrandizement in electoral politics. Neither strategy enhanced the individual's political power. Moreover, the movements eroded as a result of their leaders' betrayal and abandonment.

Other uncivil movements exhibited the same weakness around the cult of personality. The AWB was undermined in part by Terre'Blanche's indiscretions. In one of his notorious drunken and womanizing pranks, he broke into a sacred Afrikaner shrine (Paadekraal monument) accompanied by an alleged mistress, a journalist for an English-language newspaper. The sacrilege of breaking into an Afrikaner shrine, with "the enemy," proved too much for most AWB leaders. To make matters worse, Terre'Blanche's reporter girlfriend later referred to him in print as "a pig in a Safari suit."[36] Having become a laughingstock, Terre'Blanche was abandoned by most AWB leaders, his political power waned, and no charismatic leader replaced him to rebuild the movement.[37] One observer captured the difficulties the Afrikaner right wing faced in forging unity: "Like most splinter movements that collect around charismatic leaders, these were forever declaring alliances, quarreling, dividing, or disappearing altogether."[38]

An absence of leadership can weaken uncivil movements as much as overbearing leadership can. The murders of Enrique Bermúdez and Meir Kahane provide two examples. Bermúdez had provided the Contras with consensus leadership, however flawed. His death sealed the movement's fate, since no other leader—charismatic or otherwise—could unite the various Contra factions. Fragmentation also plagued Kahane's movement after his death in 1990.[39] His legacy lived on among right-wing loners and in secret organizations and splinter movements that lacked coordination.[40] No one could fill the void he left. He had been the "sole ideologue, the only decision-maker, the key speaker, and the fund-raiser," and he had purged "any talented member who rose to prominence" within the movement.[41] Kahane himself acknowledged the personal power he wielded: "It's a good thing Kach isn't a democracy. I'm the only one to decide what will and will not be."[42] Because of his totalitarian control over the movement, local organization remained weak.[43]

In the case of the U.S. militia movement, no single leader has emerged. Indeed, the movement even calls on "single cells" (one individual acting on his or her own) to organize political action. This type of organizational structure lacks the coordination that might bring political power and influence.

Uncivil movements sometimes overcome these leadership problems. After its defeat in the 1985 assembly elections, ARENA attempted to shed its death-squad image. ARENA's entrepreneurial leader, Roberto D'Aubuisson, a former military intelligence officer with a long history of death-squad activity, recognized the importance of legitimating myths and began grooming Fredy Cristiani to become the civilian face of the movement. Cristiani won the presidency, and ARENA survived D'Aubuisson's death. Indeed, his death may have assisted the party in making the transition from death squad to uncivil movement.

A common problem for uncivil movements is survival after success. Paradoxically, success over the threat hastens their demise. Having eliminated the catalyst threat, they have little reason to remain mobilized. Moreover, the high-risk, high-intensity political action leads to burnout, particularly among the pragmatists. The militants, on the other hand, consider moderation or institutionalization a betrayal and a sellout. Institutionalization heightens fragmentation within uncivil movements, especially among militants and pragmatists, but along other fault lines as well.

The UDR provides the best example of an uncivil movement's success leading to its demise. Having defeated agrarian reform, the movement lacked a common cause. It began to fragment along regional, sectoral, ideological, and strategic lines. Caiado's withdrawal from the movement exacerbated these tensions and left the movement without a leader to reunite the disparate factions. MODIN's success in ending the human rights trials also led to fragmentation. Normal politics gave way to differences in political strategies and ruptured the Carapintada unity. Rico's departure from MODIN rendered the party unviable. It is too early to judge what will happen with Hugo Chavez's victory, but given its unlikely alliances, fragmentation seems a certainty.

Failure, of course, can also bring about an uncivil movement's demise, as the case of the AWB demonstrates. The AWB's fragmentation did not result from Terre'Blanche's leadership alone. The movement's adaptation to the postapartheid system exacerbated internal tensions. Along with the Conservative Party and other extremist Afrikaner groups, the AWB shifted from endorsing partition (apartheid) to endorsing separatism (a white homeland). But this position led to internal division over which regions to establish as homelands and who would be allowed into them.[44]

Competition also threatens uncivil movements' longevity. These movements generally define themselves in opposition to a particular government, policy, or change. While they remain the only opposition, they are likely to win support, especially if they successfully craft the threat, cultural cues, and legitimating myths. Once they lose their monopoly over the opposition, however, uncivil movements lose their unique role. MODIN, for example, initially provided the opposition that disgruntled Peronists sought. But when a more experienced and programmatic party joined the opposition to Menem (FREPASO and then Alianza), MODIN lost its unique role. The competition had more experience and carried less stigma than MODIN. Competition also poses problems for uncivil movements' image among the militants. Militants lose interest in political candidates who begin to look mainstream. Thus, Caiado did not even win a majority of UDR members' votes when he ran for office. The Contras faced similar problems in electoral competition. They did not represent the Resistance, since every party against the Sandinistas claimed to be Resistance. The Contras had neither the resources nor the experience to compete with these well-established parties.

Over time, in other words, uncivil movements tend to lose their political power or to become less uncivil, or both. However, this book does not recommend that governments wait until that happens to deal with such movements, because they shape political outcomes in profound ways before their demise. Instead, it advocates an interventionary role for governments so as to exacerbate uncivil movements' internal tensions and reduce their appeal.

Government Responses to Uncivil Movements

Comparative research suggests that institutionalization can reduce uncivil movements' political power, but often too late, after they have already had a profound impact on the shape of democracy. In Brazil, for example, the UDR closed its doors only after achieving its legislative victory over agrarian reform. So too the Carapintada began to pursue an institutional and civil route only after they had effectively eliminated the threat of human rights trials. The UDR and the Carapintada cases demonstrate additional weaknesses in an institutional model for reducing the power of uncivil movements.

Moreover, the MODIN example suggests that institutionalization, at least in its early phase, enhances uncivil movements' political power. MODIN, after all, became the third most powerful political party in Argentina during its early years. The Cristiani, Chavez, and Le Pen cases also illustrate that institutionalization heightens uncivil movements' power. Cristiani and Chavez both won the presidency. Le Pen won 15 percent of the vote in his 1995 presidential bid. Caiado, Rico, D'Aubuisson, Le Pen, and Kahane all won seats in legislatures that shape policies. In other words, it is only after some time that the internal tensions involved in institutionalization surface and undermine the movement.

The UDR case illustrates another limitation of the institutional model for reducing uncivil movements' political power. Although the UDR closed its doors after it defeated agrarian reform, it later resurfaced to address another threat to landed elites' interests. In other words, uncivil movements do not permanently disappear after their success or institutional demise; they may resurrect themselves or transmogrify into a new uncivil movement. Indeed, past successful uncivil movements may even comprise the new set of heroic symbols and repertoires of collective action upon which subsequent uncivil movements build.

Given the limitations of the institutional model, this book advocates alternative government strategies for reducing uncivil movements' power. Drawing on comparative cases, it endorses parallel processes of negotiations with pragmatists, investigations and prosecutions of militants, and the creation of delegitimating myths. In concert these strategies make it more difficult for uncivil movements to deny their involvement in violence, weakening their appeal. Investigations and prosecutions of the militants provide evidence of violence and become part of the delegitimating myths. Simultaneous negotiations with the pragmatists can create an exit option for leaders and members to separate from the hardline violent faction without necessarily surrendering political power.

The Chamorro government provides the best example of negotiations with pragmatists. Perhaps recognizing the Contra and Recontra leaders' prestige at the end of the war, Chamorro negotiated solutions to the armed conflict, providing Contra and Recontra leaders with political positions and land for development in exchange for loyalty. Having negotiated solutions with these "legitimate" leaders, Chamorro took a "no-tolerance" stance and used force against subsequent rebels. Had she used such a strategy earlier against the legitimate leaders, she might have provoked a martyr syndrome, heightening the power of these leaders and creating a threat around which Contras could remobilize.

The U.S. militia movements provide an example of how the use of excessive force by the democratic government can stimulate uncivil movements. The militia exploited the "murder of innocents" by U.S. public authorities at Ruby Ridge and Waco to portray a government out of control. Militia leaders used the government's excessive show of force to defend their own movement against accusations of violence. One militia leader, for example, pointed to Ruby Ridge and Waco and asked, "Who's got the track record of killing children?"[45] Another stated that "it was, after all, the taking of lives by the government at Ruby Ridge and Waco that provided the innocent blood that gave birth to the militia and the associated anti-government feeling currently sweeping the nation."[46]

The example of the Menem government hints at the success of a combined negotiations and prosecutions model. Although Menem did not negotiate directly with the military, he made concessions to it (e.g., pardons, public acknowledgment of military heroism in the Malvinas, and establishment of a military role in the postauthoritarian era) in exchange for loyalty. Most military officers understood this exchange agreement, but not Seineldín. His 1990 coup violated the implicit agreement, and the Menem government reacted with force, investigation, prosecution, and life sentences. The use of force at an earlier stage might have created martyrs and stimulated a stronger movement, as happened in the case of the U.S. militia movement. Because Menem's concessions had already provided the military with civil options, the coup repertoire lacked legitimacy at that moment. The legal process, in other words, constituted a delegitimating myth: it exposed the violence behind the militant faction of the movement and contrasted it with the loyalty to civilian rule among the majority of the armed forces and the pragmatist (MODIN) faction of the Carapintada.

Transitional governments may face more difficulties than stable ones in using judicial remedies to reduce uncivil movements' power. Postauthoritarian judiciaries often lack the political will to investigate and prosecute crimes committed by supporters of the old authoritarian order, especially when those crimes target the old order's adversaries. Where new judicial systems, judges, and lawyers have emerged, they may lack the experience and manpower to investigate and prosecute. It is not surprising, therefore, that stable democracies show a higher incidence of judicial actions against uncivil movements. While almost no landholders in Brazil faced prosecution, Chavez, Le Pen, Kahane, and U.S. militia leaders have faced punishment for their uncivil acts.

Le Pen was convicted in 1997 for assaulting a Socialist Party candidate during the French legislative elections.[47] He faced a $4,000 fine and a three-month jail term, although the judge suspended the latter. More important, however, the conviction bars Le Pen from running for political office for two years. Given that the European Parliament elections occur in June 1999, this sentence severely constrains the party. While Le Pen insists that his wife, Jeanne-Marie, who has remained outside of politics, will take his place, some party leaders have backed Le Pen's deputy, Bruno Mégret. The sentence, in other words, serves several functions. Not only does it highlight Le Pen's uncivil behavior, debunking the movement's legitimating myths, it also heightens tensions between the militant and pragmatist factions of the movement. Tensions regarding the personalistic control of the charismatic leader emerge or increase. And troubles of this nature for the National Front will no doubt continue, since the European Parliament lifted Le Pen's immunity to begin a criminal investigation against him for belittling the Holocaust. In June 1999 a Munich court convicted Le Pen of inciting racial hatred because of his reference during a 1997 news conference to the Holocaust as a "detail in the history of World War II."[48]

Kahane also faced investigation and prosecution. In 1974 the Israeli government banned Kach and in 1984 tried to prevent Kahane's election to the Knesset.[49] Kach was outlawed under a 1985 law that banned any party that "incites racism" or rejects "the democratic nature of the state."[50] The Knesset barred Kach from Parliament in 1988, and the Israeli Supreme Court upheld the decision. In 1994, following the Hebron massacre, the Knesset outlawed Kach as a terrorist organization. The Israeli government also accused Kahane of sedition. The 1995 Omnibus Antiterrorist Act prohibited U.S. contributions to the group, eliminating an important source of its revenues.[51] Israel's Broadcasting Authority also resolved not to cover Kahane's activities, which greatly reduced his primary source of publicity, and hence his appeal. Moreover, Kahane and his followers faced legal investigations, convictions, and prison sentences for their violent acts.[52]

These legal measures only partially limited Kahane's movement, however. With certain political avenues closed off, the movement diversified its tactics. It continued to engage in confrontational political action to obtain press coverage, and it used newsletters, Web sites, and advertisements to communicate with its constituents in Israel and the United States. Nonetheless, the loss of Kahane's legislative seat at the height of his political career eroded his legitimacy. Even Kahane's right-wing supporters began to edge him out of leadership positions because of the stigma he carried.[53] Indeed, right-wing parties deliberately distanced themselves from the extreme and antidemocratic Kach, while left-wing parties tried to weaken Likud by referring to it as "Kahanism."[54]

Similarly, legal remedies have only partially succeeded in reducing the power of the U.S. militia movement. The trial of those accused of carrying out the 1995 Oklahoma City bombing that killed over 150 innocent people appears to have reduced the militia movement's power slightly. Some militias distanced themselves from violence by taking the term *militia* out of their name, closing down, or purging the radical elements from their group. But others went underground to avoid investigation and prosecution. A few militias even took the offensive and spun the conspiracy theory that the U.S. government had staged the bombing to undermine the militia movement.[55] Some evidence suggests that these strategies have worked; the bombing and subsequent trials may have even stimulated militia movements by providing them with free advertising. One government source documented 224 militias in thirty-nine states after the Oklahoma bombing.[56] The free publicity provided militias with an opportunity to spin legitimating myths. They denied that Timothy McVeigh had links to the militia movement, despite evidence to the contrary.

The trial also provided militias with an opportunity to create a new image for their movement. "Clean-shaven, business-attired, middle-aged" militia leaders appeared on television talk shows, on radio, in Congress, in magazines, and in newspapers presenting an alternative image of the movement and its activities.[57] These individuals did not look like murderers. Indeed, in a Senate hearing one militia leader argued against the government's image of the militias: "You're trying to make us out to be something we're not. . . . We stand against corruption and tyranny. . . . There is intelligent life west of the Alleghenies. . . . You're wasting precious time."[58]

The Kahane and U.S. militia cases point to some of the limitations of judicial remedies. Investigations and prosecutions of individual members are not enough to delegitimize uncivil movements, which can use these prosecutions to spin legitimating myths that heighten their power. Only by directly linking the movement itself, or its top leaders, with violence can democratic governments begin the process of generating delegitimating myths. Another limitation in the militia case, however, is complicity among local authorities. This is not, in other words, an issue unique to transitional political situations. Even in the United States, uncivil movements recruit from within the local and federal authorities, thereby receiving some protection. U.S. militias include local police, sheriffs, and members of the military. Moreover, militias have used intimidation, particularly the threat of physical harm, to reduce the will and capacity of public officials to investigate and prosecute them.

Stable democracies like Israel and the United States typically show greater will and capacity than transitional ones to convict the leaders of uncivil movements, but the South African case challenges this rule. The AWB provides an example of how transitional governments can investigate and prosecute uncivil movements and contribute to their demise. The government of P. W. Botha, perhaps fearing a new Boer war, followed a pattern typical of transitional governments; it tolerated the AWB, fueling its growth.[59] But the subsequent democratic presidents acted more like governments in stable democracies. F. W. De Klerk, for example, quickly and decisively arrested and tried right-wing militants under the Internal Securities Act.[60] Nelson Mandela, although more vulnerable to a right-wing putsch, balanced negotiation and prosecution. A significant example of this strategy is Mandela's response to the murder of the black activist leader Chris Hani. The courts sentenced a radical right-wing leader to life imprisonment for the murder, but Mandela publicly acknowledged the help of the Afrikaner woman who had risked her life by reporting Hani's killer to the authorities. In June 1997 Terre'Blanche was sentenced to six years in jail for the attempted murder of a black man. He is also charged with ordering a 1994 bombing that killed twenty civilians—a case still under investigation by South Africa's Truth and Reconciliation Commission. The Mandela government accepts the institutional, or parliamentary, intervention of radical Afrikaners through the Conservative Party, but not their violent acts.

The degree of threat from the AWB does not explain the South African difference. Although some observers have referred to the AWB as a "brandy and Coke" group (i.e., one of all talk and no action), it does not always bluff.[61] Security forces have responded to the AWB's violence as it might treat any criminal group, thereby denying the AWB any political leverage. When security forces summarily arrested right-wing bombers before and after the 1994 elections, they demonstrated that they "retain the capacity and, more importantly, the will to curb violence on the right."[62] The result was that the AWB began to reduce its level of violence, which eroded some of its hard-core support. Those who believed that the AWB would wage war to prevent Mandela from governing felt betrayed by the movement: Mandela assumed the presidency without an AWB revolt.[63] The pragmatic consistency also abandoned the movement as delegitimating myths began to surface. Legal investigations and prosecutions of violent and criminal acts challenged the myth that the group respected laws and civility.

Conclusion

While discussing the neo-Nazi movement in Europe, Ted Koppel remarked, "I don't know, when I listen to this kind of trash, whether to think it's frightening or just to think it's silly."[64] Such is the enigma of uncivil movements. Each movement has some aspect that makes it difficult to take seriously as a political player: commando games, conspiracy theories, uniforms and slogans and discourse that distort reality. And yet these groups are dangerous; they don't just talk about violence, they kill their enemies.

So what should democratic governments do? While I have argued that uncivil movements plant the seeds of their own destruction, strategies that do not take uncivil movements seriously and passively await their demise within the institutional system may backfire. As we have seen in these case studies, uncivil movements have proven politically adroit, capturing legislative and executive elections. We have also observed that successful uncivil movements collapse *after* they have shaped democratic politics, not before. Moreover, uncivil movements succeed both in transitional democracies, like Argentina, Brazil, and El Salvador, and in relatively stable democracies, like France, Israel, and Venezuela. No political system, in other words, is immune to uncivil movement mobilization.

At the same time, however, democratic governments may empower uncivil movements by taking them too seriously. When democratic governments believe uncivil movements' threats, they often capitulate to them to avoid destabilizing outcomes. This strategy also backfires by heightening uncivil movements' influence over the political system.

This second strategy points to the importance of democratic governments' perception of uncivil movements. While uncivil movements emerge in so-called consolidated and transitional governments alike, it is the transitional democracies, and not the consolidated ones, that have tended to capitulate to them. Without exception among the cases examined here, stable democratic governments have investigated and prosecuted uncivil movements: France, Israel, United States, and Venezuela. Investigations and prosecutions have posed problems for uncivil movements. Legitimating myths cannot sustain support from the pragmatists with incontrovertible evidence linking the movements to violence. Pragmatists responding to investigations generally moderate and institutionalize the movements to protect them, driving out their militant supporters. Of course, uncivil movements can exploit the exercise of excessive governmental force against them, as in the case of the United States at Ruby Ridge and Waco. Similarly, amnesties and pardons can erase the tempering effect of prosecutions, as in Hugo Chavez's presidential bid in Venezuela. Finally, investigations and prosecutions may not always succeed. Uncivil movements may prove immune to these strategies; these strategies may neither eliminate them nor reduce their political power. But whether or not these strategies work in all cases, consolidated democracies enjoy greater freedom to use the law and informational strategies against uncivil movements. Unafraid that such movements could topple the government, such regimes are less hesitant to treat uncivil movements as criminals rather than as threatening political players.

Transitional democracies do not often have that liberty. They may lack the infrastructure to investigate or prosecute uncivil movements. They may lack the political will to investigate, much less prosecute, them for fear of an overthrow or because of uncivil movements' utility during transitional moments. Democratic governments may not want to risk a coup by confronting uncivil movements; thus, they opt for a safer, conciliatory route. Democratic governments may rely on alliances, loyalty, or the order uncivil movements provide, limiting their range of acceptable policy options.

The South African and Nicaraguan cases demonstrate, however, that not all transitional governments capitulate to uncivil movements. The South African courts investigated and tried AWB leaders for violent acts. Nicaragua's weak judiciary did not prevent the Chamorro government from reducing the power of the Contras and Recontras; the government used a combination of negotiation and force to eventually eliminate the movement. Were the AWB and Contra movements weaker than other uncivil movements in transitional contexts? Not perceptibly, but the democratic governments' political will was stronger.

In sum, uncivil movements emerge in democratic and democratizing countries alike. They have more power in the latter not because of a greater degree of uncertainty or political opportunity, but because they can capitalize on political fears and the undeveloped state of government infrastructures for investigation and prosecution. Democratizing governments can overcome these weaknesses, however. Through investigation and delegitimating myths, democratic governments can dilute uncivil movements' legitimating myths, weakening support among pragmatists. Negotiation with pragmatic leaders can also fragment the movement, reducing its power and the threat it poses to democracy. In either case, however, the governments' perceptions of uncivil movements and their political will dictate acceptable policy options.

Notes

INTRODUCTION

1. George and McKeown, "Case Studies"; George, "Case Studies."

2. Young, "Dialectics."

3. Geertz contends that primordial identities may result from defining oneself in opposition to "the other." That is, even in the absence of a conscious attachment to a specific identity, identity can emerge with the arrival of a competing group or identity. Furthermore, identity not only is a product of self-perception but also depends on external perceptions: how one is seen by others. Primordial identities are transmitted through socialization in the family, community, or nation and sustained through customs, symbols, language, rites, and myths. Geertz, "Integrative Revolution," 128.

4. Some scholars using the primordial approach have raised questions about the essentialism generally attached to primordial identities. They allow for some fluidity even in primordial identities. Epstein, for example, states, "None of us has a single identity, as members of society each of us carries simultaneously a range of identities just as each of us occupies a number of statuses and plays a variety of roles." Epstein, *Ethos*, 100. Epstein adds that primordial identity cannot be distinguished from situational analysis because they are intertwined in a complex interaction. Identity becomes an "interplay of the external and internal, the objective and the subjective, and the sociological and psychological elements" (112). Social context determines the identity that will be stressed in a given situation (113). Isaacs shares this perception. He states that primordial identity "is not a fixed, sculpted object but a live thing, changing in shape and size under varying conditions." Isaacs, *Idols*, 41. And Barth, while establishing the existence of "ethnic boundaries," suggests that even those boundaries are not fixed but allow for shifting identities. Barth, *Ethnic Groups*, 17–24. Barth and Epstein share the idea that individuals have some, albeit limited, choice about their identity. Choice is bounded by features within the social system, particularly the availability of opportunities to shed ethnic identities and of alternative identities, and internal needs for identity. Epstein, *Ethos*, xiv–xv. Individuals also

see themselves in different ways, and are seen by others in different ways, that make them fall between categories of identification. Barth, *Ethnic Groups,* 29. Even Geertz admits, grudgingly, that identities, even though primordial, can change: "The patterns of primordial identification and cleavage within the existing new states are not fluid, shapeless and infinitely various, but are definitely demarcated and vary in systematic ways." Geertz, "Integrative Revolution," 118.

5. I am not alone in becoming confused about the "friendly" relationship I developed with my informants despite my abhorrence for what they represent and do. In discussing her relationship with "defense intellectuals," Carol Cohn writes, "What is striking about the men themselves is not, as the content of their conversation might suggest, their coldbloodedness. Rather it is that they are a group of men unusually endowed with charm, humor, intelligence, concern, and decency. Reader, I liked them. At least, I liked many of them. The attempt to understand how such men could contribute to an endeavor that I see as so fundamentally destructive became a continuing obsession for me, a lens through which I came to examine all of my experiences in their world." Cohn, "Sex," 690. Tina Rosenberg, reporting on violent groups in Latin America, shares this confusion: "Friends have asked me what it's like to spend time with torturers, guerrillas, and hit men. In truth, I found many of them likable. . . . I would have preferred them to be monsters. Coming to understand that this is not the case was disturbing—for what it taught me about these people, and ultimately, about myself. I did not want to think that many of the violent are 'people like us': so civilized, so educated, so cultured, and because of that so terrifying." Rosenberg, *Children,* 18.

6. George and McKeown, "Case Studies," 35.

1   DEFINING UNCIVIL MOVEMENTS

1. One definition of civil disobedience is "the refusal to obey certain laws or governmental demands for the purpose of influencing legislation or governmental policy, characterized by the employment of such *nonviolent* [my emphasis] techniques as boycotting, picketing, nonpayment of taxes." *The Random House Dictionary of the English Language,* 2d ed., unabridged (New York: Random House, 1987). Other conceptualizations of civil disobedience allow for the use of violence—for example, violent and illegal strikes as a way of extending the democratic rights of the working class. Cohen and Arato, *Civil Society,* 566–98, draw on writings by Hannah Arendt, John Rawls, and Jürgen Habermas to make these claims.

2. For a very concise description of new social movements' political action, see Klandermans and Tarrow, "Mobilization."

3. Alvarez, *Engendering Democracy.*

4. This idea is promoted in Payne, *Brazilian Industrialists,* 39–55, and Stepan, "New Professionalism," 47–65.

5. See Diamond and Linz, "Introduction"; DiPalma, *To Craft;* and O'Donnell and Schmitter, *Transitions.* These analyses tend to draw heavily on Rustow, "Transitions."

6. Diamond and Linz, "Introduction," 23. DiPalma also states that "the more re-calcitrant the players, the more the transition will need to seek democratic rules that stress coexistence above everything else." DiPalma, *To Craft*, 46. O'Donnell and Schmitter claim that, "chaotic as it may seem to have several players attacking and retreating on various levels at once, it is better to have them in the game, and per-haps committed to its emergent rules, than outside it, threatening to kick over the board." O'Donnell and Schmitter, *Transitions*, 67. For examples of specific institu-tional arrangements, see Coppedge, *Classification*; Lijphart and Waisman, *Institu-tional Design*; Linz and Valenzuela, *Failure*; Mainwaring and Scully, *Building*; and Shugart and Carey, *Presidents*.

7. Dahl, *Preface*, 97–99, 102–5.

8. O'Donnell and Schmitter, *Transitions*, 23–24, 28–32; Diamond and Linz, "In-troduction."

9. Linz, *Crisis*, 18–23.

10. Diamond and Linz claim that "enduring democratic value commitments make it more difficult to consolidate and perpetuate authoritarian rule." Diamond and Linz, "Introduction," 13. This issue of habituation is also developed in Rustow, "Tran-sitions."

11. O'Donnell's work on the bureaucratic-authoritarian state depends explicitly on rising social unrest as a cue to the military to intervene and establish order. O'Donnell, *Modernization*. Linz's work on the breakdown emphasizes government incompetence, specifically its inability to satisfy demands and provide physical pro-tection, as a key ingredient behind the coups. Linz, *Crisis*.

12. O'Donnell and Schmitter accept, only with resignation, the inevitability of conservative democracies. O'Donnell and Schmitter, *Transitions*, 27–28. They la-ment that this cautious and conservative path is the only safe route to democratic consolidation (62). They charge that "an active militant and highly mobilized popu-lar upsurge may be an efficacious instrument for bringing down a dictatorship but may make subsequent democratic consolidation difficult, and under some circum-stances may provide an important motive for regression to an even more brutal form of authoritarian rule" (66). They add that "only once the transition has passed and citizens have learned to tolerate its contingent compromises can one expect political development to induce a more reliable awareness of convergent interests and to create a less suspicious attitude toward each other's purposes, ideas, and ideals" (72).

Institutions scholars recognize that popular sector disenchantment can weaken democratic systems. DiPalma, for example, states that "if the regime is interested only in limited reforms, civil society may not put much trust in those reforms and may lack the capacity (and possibly the interest) to obtain more." DiPalma, *To Craft*, 162. O'Donnell and Schmitter charge that "the disenchantment it leaves behind is a persistent problem for the ensuing consolidation of political democracy." O'Donnell and Schmitter, *Transitions*, 56. These scholars assume, however, that at least in the foreseeable future democracy's protection against the "oppression of arbitrary and undivided rule" (DiPalma, *To Craft*, 19) and its emphasis on "civil and political liberties" (Diamond and Linz, "Introduction," 3) will override popular sector disappointment with the particular policies of democratic governments. Diamond and Linz summarize this view as follows: "Democracy—with its relativism and tolerance (so disturbing to those certain of the truth), and its 'faith' in the reasonableness and intelligence of the common people, deciding freely (and with a chance to change their minds every four or five years) and without the use of force—seems a better option" (3). The memory of authoritarian rule and the legitimacy of democratic rule in the contemporary period guarantee democratic stability. Diamond and Linz even state, "Democracy is the only model of government with any broad ideological legitimacy and appeal today," although they do make an exception for the Islamic world (2).

13. Cohen and Arato, *Civil Society*, 592; Friedman, "Introduction," 12.

14. Some new scholarship is moving away from the dichotomized notions of democracy containing all that is good and authoritarian rule containing all that is evil. For one example, see Collier, "Democracy."

15. For some examples of the social movement approach, see Alvarez, *Engendering Democracy*; Alvarez et al., *Cultures*; Eckstein, *Power*; Escobar and Alvarez, *Making*; Foweraker, *Theorizing*; Levine, *Constructing*; Schneider, *Shantytown*; Slater, *New Social Movements*; and Stokes, *Cultures*.

16. Schneider, "Chile Shantytowns."

17. Keck, *Workers' Party*, 64, 75–76.

18. Alvarez, *Engendering Democracy*.

19. Klandermans and Tarrow, "Mobilization," 23–29.

20. Stepan, "Paths."

21. Linz, *Crisis*, 18–23.

22. For some empirically based studies, however, see Walton, "Debt"; Hochstetler, "Democratizing Pressures"; and Jelin and Hershberg, *Constructing Democracy*.

23. Weber, *From Max Weber*, 78.

24. Gellner, "Importance," 32–34.

25. Hall, "In Search," 3–4.

26. Bryant, "Civic Nation," 143.

27. Cohen and Arato, *Civil Society*, 507.

28. Dahl, *Polyarchy*. For some recent examples of efforts to problematize democracy, see Collier, "Democracy," and Alexander, "Aspectos."

2   A THEORETICAL APPROACH TO UNCIVIL MOVEMENTS

1. Advocates of the relationship between mechanics and meaning include Conover and Gray, *Feminism*, and McAdam et al., *Comparative Perspectives*.

2. The explosion of social movement scholarship began with an emphasis on grievances as an explanation for political mobilization—for example, Gurr's *Why Men Rebel*. But scholars recognized that even very serious grievances can exist without necessarily producing successful social movement mobilization. Grievances might

provide a necessary, but certainly not a sufficient, explanation for social movement power. Scholars have moved away from explaining "why" movements emerge to focusing on "how" grievances are transformed into successful political action. This shift in orientation began the resource mobilization school. For some examples, see Jenkins, "Resource Mobilization"; and McCarthy and Zald's "Resource Mobilization" and *Trend*. The political process model followed on the heels of resource mobilization. McAdam's political process model contends that social movements emerge when cataclysmic events shift power balances in their favor. The power shift provides them with new opportunities and resources for mobilizing. Among these cataclysmic events, McAdam includes industrialization, war, international and political realignments, prolonged unemployment, and demographic changes. McAdam, *Political Process*.

3. This has been called "empirical credibility," or "the fit between framing and events in the world." Snow and Benford, "Ideology," 208.

4. O'Donnell and Schmitter, *Transitions*, 3–5, 66–67; Przeworski, "Some Problems."

5. The "framing" literature calls this process of uniting a diverse constituency around a common goal or threat the "unifying frame." One stage of the process is "frame alignment" in which movements capture various grievances that exist in society, incorporate them into coherent movements, and create out of those grievances a common struggle. Snow et al., "Frame Alignment."

6. Smith-Rosenberg, *Disorderly Conduct*, 90.

7. For a discussion of these cuing techniques, such as "experiential commensurability" and "narrative fidelity," see Snow and Benford, "Ideology," 197–217.

8. Geertz, "Integrative Revolution," 128.

9. The framing literature describes this process of creating a cultural villain. Movement entrepreneurs create a sense of a grave injustice ("injustice frame") but also identify the perpetrator of that injustice against whom the movements will mobilize ("attributional orientation"). Snow et al., "Frame Alignment."

10. Snow and Benford refer to this process as "diagnostic framing," identifying a problem and attributing blame or causality. Snow and Benford, "Ideology," 200.

11. Rogin, *Ronald Reagan*, 12.

12. This has been called "prognostic framing," whereby the movement establishes not only solutions but also strategies, tactics, and targets to specify what is to be done, and also "motivational framing," which constitutes a rationale for action, a call to arms. Snow and Benford, "Ideology," 201. The concept of repertoires of collective action is found in Tilly, *From Mobilization*.

13. Wagner-Pacifici, *Moro Morality*, 7.

14. Anderson, *Imagined Communities*.

15. Norval, *Deconstructing*, 97–98.

16. Zald and Useem, "Movement," 271.

17. Tilly, *From Mobilization*, 154–55.

18. Ibid., 155. In a quite effective analogy, Tilly relates repertoires of collective

action to elementary language: "A population's repertoire of collective action generally includes only a handful of alternatives. It generally changes slowly, seems obvious and natural to the people involved. It resembles an elementary language: familiar as the day to its users, for all its possible quaintness or incomprehensibility to an outsider" (156).

19. Goffman describes a similar process with his "keying" concept: "a set of conventions by which a given activity, one already meaningful in terms of some primary framework, is transformed into something patterned on this activity, but seen by the participants to be something quite else." Goffman, *Frame Analysis*, 43–44.

20. This is how Roger Lancaster refers to custom or tradition in Lancaster, *Life Is Hard*, 90.

21. See Adorno et al., *Authoritarian Personality*.

22. Individuals who scored high on the F-scale, a scale designed to measure potential fascism, shared this authoritarian personality syndrome. Ibid., 224–79.

23. See, for example, the study in which high TAP scores were found in individuals who did not share a restrictive upbringing. Altemeyer, *Enemies*.

24. See Milgram, *Obedience*. In the Milgram experiments, however, about 35 percent of the subjects seemed unaffected by "context" and refused to apply electrical shocks. TAP scholars even recognize the importance of context. Authoritarian personalities do not necessarily produce authoritarian actions. Sanford, for example, argues that because of their authoritarian personality, certain people will submit without coercion to authority and harm other individuals without provocation from those individuals. But he states that TAP study explains only "the varying degrees of susceptibility in individuals to the kinds of [economic and social] situational pressures" that may lead to their activation in authoritarian groups. Sanford, "Authoritarian Personality," 156–57.

25. See Finkel et al., "Personal Influence"; Hardin, *One for All*; Hechter, "Rational Choice"; Klosko et al., "Rebellious"; and Muller and Opp, "Rational Choice."

26. Klosko et al., "Rebellious," 557.

27. Finkel et al., "Personal Influence," 855–903; Muller and Opp, "Rational Choice," 471–87.

28. Acting altruistically, called "the martyr syndrome," is in individuals' self-interest because of the psychic rewards they achieve. This psychic reward will lead individuals to participate in rebellious collective action even when they perceive that participation to be costly in terms of physical danger. In other words, individuals' choice to engage in rebellious collective action results from a "public-goods" preference; they will make sacrifices for public welfare when they identify deeply with that particular collectivity. Scholars further contend that rational individuals act collectively if they believe that such action will be efficacious. These scholars refer to this challenge to the free-rider problem as "the unity principle." The public-goods preference and the unity principle together form "collective rationality" and explain individuals' mobilization behind political actions that involve high individual risk and low individual reward. For a more developed argument along these lines, see Finkel et al., "Personal

Influence," 900; Klosko et al., "Rebellious," 557; and Muller and Opp, "Rational Choice."

29. Bell, *Radical Right*. The articles included in this volume make a number of claims regarding the structural roots of radical-right mobilization. One scholar contends that the more privileged classes sense that their traditional bases of status and power have eroded, stripping them of their dignity. Hofstadter, "The Pseudo-Conservative." Another argues that the classes rising within the traditional social hierarchy feel that their status claims are vulnerable to changes in the rules and norms of social advancement, generating "status anxiety." Lipset, "Sources." A third describes the "dispossessed," those who mobilize in a radical direction because they find themselves without a role in a world that has become highly complex and technical. Bell, "Dispossessed." Right-wing movements offer simple explanations and scapegoats that draw multiclass coalitions together around a "politics of frustration." Hofstadter, "Pseudo-Conservative," 68–69. A structural approach to the rise of right-wing extremists from a Marxist perspective can be found in Fishman, "Right-Wing Reaction."

30. Hofstadter refers to them as "pseudo-conservatives." Hofstadter, "Pseudo-Conservative" and "Pseudo-Conservatism."

31. Most recent studies reject the purely biological determinant of male aggression—the so-called aggression hormone—and instead view masculine roles as growing out of a biological need. In other words, biological difference drives social construction of masculinities. For some examples of this literature, see Badinter, *XY*; Bly, *Iron John*; Daly, *Pure Lust*; Keen, *Fire*; and Thompson, *To Be*.

32. Instead of viewing biology as driving social constructions, an alternative perspective examines how social constructions "biologize," and in that sense justify, gender differences. This literature speaks to the masculine myths that "essentialize" male aggression. Some examples include Brittan, *Masculinity*; Brod and Kaufman, *Theorizing Masculinities*; Connell, *Gender*; Enloe, *Morning After*; Gerzon, *Choice of Heroes*; Mosse, *Image of Man*; and Smith-Rosenberg, *Disorderly Conduct*, particularly the essay entitled, "Davy Crockett as Trickster: Pornography, Liminality, and Symbolic Inversion in Victorian America," 90–108.

33. This definition is taken from Smith-Rosenberg, who draws from Barthes, *Mythologies*. See Smith-Rosenberg, *Disorderly Conduct*, 102.

34. Cohen, *Symbolic Construction*, 18.

35. Ibid., 18.

36. Cohn speaks about the capacity of language to censor thought. Of her own experience trying to counter the nuclear defense establishment on its own terms, she makes the following observation: "I found . . . that the better I got at engaging in this discourse, the more impossible it became for me to express my own ideas, my own values." Cohn, "Sex," 708.

37. For more on the use of "coding," see Omi and Winant, *Racial Formation*, 113–14, 118–22.

38. For a good discussion of the debate over professional and nonprofessional leaders, see Stagenborg, "Consequences."

39. Stagenborg describes movement entrepreneurs as leaders who "found movement organizations and initiate tactics for the same reasons that other constituents join them. That is, they have personal experiences and ideological commitments which make them interested in the particular issue(s) of the movement." Ibid., 593–94.

40. Madsen and Snow advocate an end to "context-free" charisma and advocate instead a bond between leaders and followers that is based on the political environment and cultural context. The charismatic bond is developed around a "psychological crisis writ large." Madsen and Snow, *Charismatic Bond.*

41. For a discussion of right-wing antipolitics, see Krejcí, "Introduction"; Lipset, "Sources"; and McClosky and Chong, "Similarities."

42. Interestingly enough, studies conclude that the violent groups that are most successful are, like uncivil movements, those that are *not* attempting to replace their targets. Gamson, *Strategy,* 79–80.

43. Ibid., 141.

44. Ibid., 82.

45. Gilbert, *Terrorism,* 5–12.

46. See, in particular, Bunster, "Watch Out"; Durham, "Gender"; and Koontz, *Mothers.*

47. Cohen, *Symbolic Construction,* 17.

48. This partially fits with McAdam's political process model. He explains that movements often borrow leadership, membership, communication networks, and organizational structures from precursor movements. McAdam, *Political Process,* 43–48.

49. Shupe, "Accommodation."

50. Schedler, "Anti-Political-Establishment Parties."

51. Tarrow refers to these types of members as "conscience constituents." Tarrow, *Struggling,* 32–34.

52. Duch and Gibson, "Putting Up."

53. The institutions approach to redemocratization would fall within this framework, contending that democratic reformist governments *are* vulnerable to right-wing authoritarians and *should* accommodate them.

54. Tarrow, *Struggling,* 32.

55. Gamson, *Strategy,* 80.

56. Sullivan et al., "Education"; Wood et al., "Tolerance."

57. These scholars argue that previous research has failed to identify widespread intolerance because it did not provide a large enough selection of groups toward which one would feel intolerant. Once individuals selected the group that they disliked the most, they proved highly intolerant toward that specific group. Sullivan et al., "Alternative."

58. Marcus et al. argue that it is "responsible of political elites to provide cues to

the general public based on democratic principles and realistic information about any threats to political freedom." Marcus et al., *With Malice*, 226.

59. Zald and Useem, "Movement."

60. For a political psychology discussion of the role past beliefs play in contemporary settings, see Marcus et al., *With Malice*.

3 THE ARGENTINE CARAPINTADA

1. A pseudonym is used to shield the identity of this informant.

2. The actual numbers of murdered and disappeared are still unknown. CONADEP documented 8,960 cases of disappeared but believed that the actual number exceeded 9,000. Comisión, *Nunca más*. Amnesty International established over 15,000 cases. Amnesty, *Argentina*. In addition to these documented cases, the director of the Mar del Plata branch of CONADEP stated, "It is not an exaggeration to speak of 30,000 disappeared persons"—the number used most consistently by the Madres de Plaza de Mayo, although they sometimes speak about 45,000 disappeared. See, for example, Guzman, *Revolutionizing Motherhood*, 31.

3. File on "Major Martinez" located at Centro de Estudios Legales y Sociales (CELS), Buenos Aires, 1994. Martinez's superiors, Generals Luciano Benjamín Menéndez and Juan Bautista Sassiaín, also faced charges for human rights abuses at La Perla.

4. In Spanish, this informant said that Martinez "remató la gente" [1 August 1994].

5. This was General Héctor Ríos Ereñú.

6. Sain, *Los Levantamientos*, 1:101.

7. According to Ríos Ereñú, only four hundred military officers faced charges before the Due Obedience Law—contrary to the two thousand mentioned in the Martinez quotation above—and most of those cases would have been dismissed under the statute of limitations. He concludes that only twenty or thirty cases would have been heard, and the Due Obedience Law reduced those to ten or twelve. Sergio Ciancaglini, "Cien horas que hicieron historia," *Clarín*, 30 March 1997, 3–5. The four hundred cases mentioned by Ríos Ereñú are confirmed by Americas Watch, *Verdad*, 66–67.

8. In April 1986 Alfonsín had issued "instructions" to the military High Command's prosecuting officer limiting prosecutions to those who had ordered abuses, and excluding those who had been following orders. Congress later rejected these instructions. See Acuña and Smulovitz, "Guarding the Guardians," 111–13.

9. General Isidro Cáceres, the army chief of staff, had been a witness at the meeting of the two military men, upon the request of Seineldín. Cáceres confirmed Seineldín's version until he became army chief of staff, when he categorically denied the agreement.

10. Seineldín was in prison at the time for writing a letter to President Menem wherein he stated his dissatisfaction with the internal sanctions being placed by the army chief of staff, General Martin Bonnet, on Carapintada sympathizers. In the letter Seineldín warned Menem of the unsustainable nature of this situation.

11. Apparently this was provoked during the takeover of the infantry regiment in

Patricios when rebels killed Lieutenant Colonel Hernán Pita, Major Federico Pedernera, and junior officer Daniel Orlando Morales, breaking the unspoken agreement about never opening fire on fellow army officers. J. Samuel Fitch in a private communication on 4 June 1993 also argued that Seineldín's power among officers proved so limited by December 1990 that he had to rely on subofficials, facilitating the officers' willingness to suppress the rebellion.

12. Law 23.077 (Law for the Defense of Democracy) states that "any person taking up arms to change the constitution, oust any of the powers of the national government, demand from them any concessions, or impede, even temporarily, the free exercise of their constitutional faculties" would face a sentence of eight to twenty-five years (in the case of a military leader of such action, the minimum sentence would be eleven years). The law received final congressional approval on 9 August 1984. The military code of justice specifies execution for a leader of a rebellion that results, as in this case, in bloodshed.

13. Seineldín's allies also faced sentences, including Colonel Luís Enrique Baraldini, Lieutenant Colonel Osvaldo Raúl Tevere, Majors Hugo Reynaldo Abete and Pedro Edgardo Mercado, and Captain Gustavo Luís Breide Obeid. Many of these recently left prison after having served five years of their ten-year sentences. Seineldín remains in jail, although he works half-time outside the jail.

14. The only unusual aspect of this interview, indeed, was the process of arranging it. Although Martinez has remade himself, he is not exactly accessible. For reasons I still do not entirely understand, his political associates were unwilling to provide me with information regarding his whereabouts. A staff assistant of a politician I interviewed secretly provided me with an address, and only after I mentioned to Martinez's associates that I had an address did they provide me with a telephone number. The address and phone number connected me to Martinez's lawyer, whom I had to interview (or who had to interview me) before I could gain access to Martinez himself. The lawyer claimed to have prepared Martinez's legal defense when he refused to appear for trial. (His defense, according to the lawyer, consisted of a conscientious-objector claim.) The lawyer had also helped form MODIN and had run for political office on the MODIN ticket.

15. Arendt, *Eichmann*, 228–31, 253–56.

16. So confident is he of his role in the past that he suggested that he use his own money to come to Madison and discuss the Dirty War. I delicately suggested that he would face hostility from a highly politicized student body. He responded that he could deal with confrontation but not with rudeness. I told him that he would probably have to expect rudeness, since the students were unlikely to be polite in view of his actions. He seemed surprised. Indeed, his own experiences in the United States had given him the opposite impression of how his actions would be perceived. He had traveled to the United States when he sensed that the military regime was nearly over and that the military officers needed to guarantee that they would not be held accountable for human rights violations. He formed a group called the Fundación Argentina and in 1979 traveled to the United States to talk about the situation with

Reagan administration staff. He sensed that all the individuals he had spoken with had understood the situation in Argentina and were willing to help. The Argentine military High Command, he believes, was oblivious to the problem and failed to implement the necessary institutional guarantees.

17. For examples of these efforts, see Feitlowitz, *Lexicon;* Jelin and Kaufman, "Layers"; Taylor, *Disappearing Acts;* and Valenzuela, *Cambio* and *Realidad.*

18. For public admission of the widespread responsibility for torture within the navy, see confessions by Adolfo Scilingo, Antonio Pernías, and Juan Carlos Rolón in Verbitsky, *El Vuelo.*

19. Martinez's "closest associate" also appears in the CELS list that is compiled primarily from the CONADEP files. I reached him by telephone, but he was unavailable for an interview. He stated during that conversation, however, that he endorsed everything Martinez had said in my interview with him. I found only one other Carapintada on the list of repressors, but because of the Due Obedience Law, he did not stand trial. The Madres de Plaza de Mayo include on the back page of their newsletters a list called the "Gallery of Repressors," which exposes the repression and the individuals involved in it.

20. For more information on this subject, see Frontalini and Caiati, *El mito,* 55, and Norden, *Military,* 56–57.

21. Seineldín recently denied both the existence of the Triple A and the kidnapping of political prisoners' children during the Dirty War. On the first, he simply pleaded ignorance. On the second, he claimed that because subversives used their noms de guerre and not their real names, military officers could not find the children's families. These officers took the children in and cared for them as if they were their own. Dario Pirogovsky, "Videla era un hombre bueno," *Página 12,* 28 June 1998.

22. These include Monsignor Emilio Grasselli, one of the clergy directly involved in the military's Dirty War, and the French bishop Marcelo Lefevbre, described as a right-wing nationalist of the *integrismo* orientation. See Mignone, *Iglesia,* 33–37, and Feitlowitz, *Lexicon,* 217–19.

23. Seineldín formed Orden as an intergenerational lodge or club within the military. Members of this secret society saw themselves as a group of bright military leaders, primarily from the infantry division, who shared a vision of reality that they believed to be crucial to the military. Although Seineldín and a few of his followers pushed a Catholic fundamentalist perspective, this view was apparently not shared by all of the seventy or eighty officers in the group.

24. Norden, "Rise."

25. See Timerman, *Preso sin nombre.* See also Graziano, *Divine Violence.*

26. Rico's cultural adviser continued to believe that Rico should ally with Francisco "Pino" Solanas of the Communist Party.

27. Many of these comments surfaced with regard to immigration and stand in sharp contrast to attitudes about immigration held by other right-wing nationalist parties like the Partido Nacionalista Constitucional and the Fuerza Republicana. In my interviews with them, leaders from those parties said that they favored immigra-

tion—even Asian immigration—to increase production and compensate for Argentina's negative birth rate.

28. "Fueron detenidos tres jóvenes del MODIN por pintar cruces esvásticas en Balvanera," *Diario Popular,* 12 May 1994.

29. This bombing killed eighty-six individuals and wounded three hundred. Lanata and Goldman, *Cortinas de humo.* For specific references to Carapintada involvement, see pp. 42–49, 175–76, and 202. On Morello's involvement, see "El MODIN pinta la cara y ataca a Galeano," *Página 12,* 9 December 1995, 14.

30. Only the Madres de Plaza de Mayo protested the presence of MODIN, charging that MODIN is an illegitimate voice in democracy.

31. MODIN also disassociated itself from the PRN by condemning its corruption, thereby building on widespread anti-PRN feeling within the military. The following remark captures the military view of the PRN's corruption: "The PRN wanted to end corruption and produced corruption. They never recognized their errors. They see themselves as martyrs. The majority of the armed forces—at least those who are active duty—are against the PRN" [interview 21].

32. The Seineldín group does not deny that they were staging a coup, but they do try to deny any responsibility for the violence. One of Seineldín's co-conspirators claimed that "people died, but we did not kill them. It was snipers [*francotiradores*] from intelligence who created all of the violence. We were framed" [interview 34].

33. Andersen, *Dossier Secreto,* 120–23. One nationalist leader I interviewed stated, "If you have any doubt that the Montoneros were employees of the army intelligence, forget it. It is proven" [interview 36].

34. The Ley de Cupo Feminino, embodied in law 24.012, article 60, passed in March 1993, required 30 percent women in all electoral slates.

35. In 1996 Seineldín and twenty-two other officials were moved from the Magdalena military penitentiary in La Plata to Campo de Mayo. Seineldín reportedly teaches classes on military strategy while interned and also spends half of his day working outside the prison in a factory.

36. Frondizi's intervention occurred in September 1994. Just weeks later Menem took the opportunity to praise Argentine soldiers' heroism in the Malvinas War and the War against Subversion but simultaneously announced that he did not intend to pardon Seineldín.

37. In November 1998 I passed a Buenos Aires storefront displaying a poster for Seineldín's 1999 presidential bid. It was the party headquarters of the FNP (Frente Nacional y Popular, or National and Popular Front). I asked the person manning the front desk what the party would do if their candidate remained in jail. He responded that he was sure that the pardon would come through soon, and if not, they would go in and get him out of jail themselves. I asked him why Seineldín would go with them instead of with his adviser, a co-conspirator who had recently been released from jail and formed the PPR (Partido Popular de la Reconstrucción, or Popular Reconstruction Party). The person did not immediately recognize the name of that party or its leader, but he assumed that it formed part of the FNP.

38. Olga Wornat, "Memorias tras las rejas," *Página 12,* 7 February 1998.

39. Martinez took with him the party label, which Rico only later won back in court. Martinez, without MODIN, attempted to ally with other parties but without ever finding an acceptable political home. He has dropped out of politics temporarily but seems interested in keeping political options open for the future.

40. The specific issue in this altercation was Rico's agreement with the Peronist governor of the province of Buenos Aires, Eduardo Duhalde, to hold a plebiscite on whether to allow a second term for the governor. Rico and MODIN have consistently fought against pact-making as corrupt and antidemocratic. He advocates, instead, open politics, confrontation, and popular vote. But, apparently furious over his exclusion from Carlos "Chacho" Alvarez's front against Menem, Rico retaliated by forming his own pact with his enemy. In his defense, he claimed to continue to oppose Duhalde and to mobilize the masses to vote against a second term in a plebiscite. Polo had vocally opposed this position prior to Rico's decision. It was only a matter of days before he and his followers left the party. Trouble had already been brewing in Buenos Aires Province, however. Criticisms of Rico's habit of hand-picking successors, rather than using the political party process, generated complaints and presaged the fragmentation of the party. Polo and Carreto formed a political party called Movimiento Azul y Blanco (Blue and White Movement), often referred to as MODIN Azul y Blanco.

41. These critics argue that Rico and his family are tired of just scraping by, and the political victories have brought them the means to buy property and invest in business so as to establish a nest egg. Neither Rico nor his wife comes from a family with money. Their adult daughters have married military officers, limiting their own financial security, and they still have a young son at home. As one of Rico's associates commented, "They love money. They've made money. My sense is that Rico and his wife got tired of being poor. They put together a construction company. Rico has moral problems. He has no loyalty" [interview 6].

42. In May 1996, MODIN leaders in Buenos Aires Province and Congressman Fernando Gill left the party and joined the Peronist Party. During this time Rico had explored options to join Fuerza Republicana, but longstanding animosities between Rico and Bussi apparently prevented that alliance and led to Rico's alliance with PJ. In the 1997 elections, Rico ran both for Congress on the MODIN slate and for mayor of San Miguel on the PJ slate. He lost his congressional seat but had the mayoral position as a fallback. Rumors have circulated that Rico's political shift might be the result of a terminal illness that has led to three back operations.

43. "El Grupo de choque de Duhalde," *Página 12,* 16 September 1997.

44. "Aldo Rico en una campaña dura," *Clarín,* 14 September 1997.

45. For an examination of the lessons from Argentina and the probabilities of a coup, see Przeworski, *Democracy,* 26–34, and Stepan, *Rethinking,* 121–27, 136–40.

46. Thalhammer et al., "Adolescents"; Karen Bird et al., "Not Just Lip-Syncing."

4 THE BRAZILIAN RURAL DEMOCRATIC UNION

1. For more information on the Chico Mendes case, see Mendes, *Fight for the Forest*, and Revkin, *Burning Season*.

2. For a fictional representation of the rural *coroneis*, see Amado, *Terras do sem fim*, or its English translation, *The Violent Land*.

3. "A Guerra na selva," *Veja*, 4 January 1989, 24.

4. "Nordestinos resistem a Caiado," *Folha de São Paulo*, 30 December 1988.

5. For more information on these movements, see Hammond, "Retaliatory Violence"; Maybury-Lewis, *Politics;* Paiero and Damatto, *Foices;* Pereira, *End of the Peasantry;* and Stédile, *Questão*.

6. This representative was a successful São Paulo farmer who claims he never joined the UDR, but who UDR leaders say was active in the movement. Perhaps because of this historic relationship between the Ministry of Agriculture and the UDR, landholders felt betrayed by Fernando Henrique Cardoso's selection of a banker as minister of agriculture.

7. Presidents in the past selected individuals for INCRA or MIRAD who had endorsements from the MST or CONTAG and who clashed with the UDR. The president of INCRA, José Eduardo Viera Raduan, for example, brought a suit against Caiado in 1987 for defamation of character. The ministers of the now defunct MIRAD also tended to favor the rural social movements. Minister Nelson Ribeiro, under President Sarney, is particularly noteworthy. He had strong support from the progressive wing of the Catholic Church and was eventually forced to resign under extreme pressure from the UDR because of his promotion of the PNRA. Dante de Oliveira, an ex-militant on the left, replaced Ribeiro and harshly criticized the UDR. His successor, Marcos Freire, continued the harsh criticism. So bitter were these exchanges between the minister and the UDR that many believe that the UDR was involved in the mysterious airplane crash that killed Freire.

8. Araujo was replaced by an INCRA president more sympathetic to rural social movements' interests, Francisco Graziano. Graziano claims that he was forced to resign under pressure from landholders. If this is true, then the setup was extremely elaborate. Graziano was forced to retire because of having ordered the illegal wiretap of the ambassador to Mexico while Graziano was President Cardoso's chief of staff.

9. The case began in August 1988 when the PT (Workers Party) candidate for São Paulo town council, Eduardo Suplicy, complained to the minister of justice, Paulo Brossard, that the UDR was committing acts of corruption and abusing economic power by financing political campaigns. Antonio Carlos Mendes, representative of the regional electorate in the Attorney General's Office in São Paulo, filed two actions in the Regional Electoral Tribunal against the UDR. The first called for the dissolution of the entity and the seizing of its funds. The second demanded a temporary restraining order on UDR activities until the investigation ended and a decision was taken. The UDR, Mendes claimed, had illegal objectives since it was in-

volved in political activities allowed by law only for parties. "Procurador pede fim da UDR e incorporação de patrimonio a União," *Jornal do Brasil*, 19 January 1989.

10. Dante de Oliveira cited in "Dante acusa UDR de promover boicote de carne e leite," *Folha de São Paulo*, 12 July 1986.

11. "UDR da apoio a constituintes contrarios a reforma agrária," *Folha de São Paulo*, 7 September 1988.

12. This "ordinary" law regulates articles 184, 185, and 186 of the Federal Constitution (or the agrarian law). It establishes percentages of land that can be left idle in each geographical region.

13. "O Campo mostra os dentes para o governo," *Veja*, 18 February 1987, 20–23.

14. "UDR si, as ruas pela propiedade," *Visão*, 22 July 1987, 18.

15. Scott Studebaker, "Brazil's Judicial System," *Brasilinform* (C.V. Brasil Comercio Informativos Ltda, Rio de Janeiro), 9 June 1993.

16. Lindblom, *Politics and Markets*.

17. Amado, *Violent Land*, 178.

18. There is a cruel irony in the Expedito case. Like the Chico Mendes case, the case is noteworthy for finally breaking the pattern of absolving landholders of any involvement in these rural crimes. And yet the investigation was extremely poorly conducted. The possibility that torture was used to coerce a confession has been raised on a number of occasions. The first suspect escaped from detention, leaving the police with no capacity to close the case. Miraculously, the police latched on to a different suspect and implicated a different landlord. Their only evidence seems to be the name of the hired gun and the victim on a check made out to the landlord's farm manager. As one of the attorneys for landholders stated, "[Landlords] don't pay [for a hired gun] with a check. They don't use their own employees to make the contact with a hired gun. That could be traced back to them. In this case [of the murder of Expedito], there was a lot of national and international pressure, so they had to get someone. They got the wrong people" [interview 31].

19. One informant complained that prosecutors often have over three thousand cases to litigate at a time. Since trying all of these cases would prove impossible, these prosecutors are inclined to make decisions about which ones to pursue based on the strength of the investigation and the prosecutor's own feelings about the strength of the case (e.g., who he or she could successfully argue against) [interview 38].

20. Only one of the charged individuals—the father—was recaptured and is serving time. The son, who shot Mendes, remains at large.

21. For more information on the democratic opposition in Brazil, see Alvarez, *Engendering Democracy*; Alves, *State and Opposition*; Keck, *Workers' Party*; and Stepan, *Democratizing Brazil*.

22. For more information on the Pontal, see Mançano Fernandes, *MST*.

23. The term used in Portuguese for individuals who falsified their documents is *grileiros*. This comes from the term *grilo*, or cricket. To make falsified documents look legitimate, *grileiros* took new documents and put them in a bag containing

crickets. When the documents were later removed, they had been "aged" by the stains and nibbles of these crickets.

24. Keck, *Workers' Party,* 49–51.

25. *Pelego* literally means the blanket between the saddle and the horse, a way to cushion pressure from above. The *pelego* labor unions were those whose presidents did not confront but rather cooperated with the military regime.

26. Amado, "Blood Fertilized These Lands," foreword to *Violent Land,* vii.

27. *Brasil: Nunca mais;* Page, *Revolution That Never Was.*

28. Roque dos Santos hastened to add that he played an instrumental role in transforming the movement from a militia into a legal lobbying entity. As a lawyer himself, he claimed that he would never participate in a rural militia.

29. "Tiroteio no campo," *Istoé,* 14 May 1986, 38–39.

30. Dassin, *Torture,* 106–11.

31. The view is summed up in this remark: "They [in the PT wing] always wanted conflict. They wanted to create conflict. They do this because it is easy to promise things to end poverty: just distribute other people's lands. That's the way to get followers: promise them that they'll never be hungry again" [interview 90].

32. The Nobistor scandal involved a shipment of pharmaceuticals under which heavy artillery was found. The link to the UDR was made by federal agents. There were also reports that the UDR was buying heavy machinery in Miami and Paraguay, and even from the Brazilian army. See *Este—Revista mensal de informação,* R. nō. 21, and articles in the *Jornal do Brasil* and *Estado de São Paulo* on 10–12 October 1986. See also "Mais armas na rota da UDR," *Istoé,* 6 August 1986.

33. As one left-wing activist asked, "Were they unaware or conscious of Hitler's final solution when they gave the firm [Solução] that name?" [anonymous].

34. "Fazendeiro conta como vingou morte do filho," *Estado de São Paulo,* 5 November 1994.

35. Salvador Farina, quoted in *O Germinal,* April 1987. In my interview with him Farina claimed that the reporter had not understood his reference to arms: "I talked about how the landholders had to arm themselves to defend what is theirs, and how the weapon of the rural producer was his brains. In the same discourse I talked about the cattle auctions and putting together sixteen hundred head of cattle. Well, when the article came out everything was taken out of context and reorganized, and it came out saying that we had used the cattle auctions to buy arms to defend ourselves against invasions. I never said that" [Salvador Farina, 16 August 1995].

36. This landholder seemed to have some reservations about this comment after the interview was complete and he had a chance to talk it over with his daughter, who had been present during the interview. He never made clear to me what his concern was, but he seemed uncomfortable about having referred in the interview to destroying "the anthill."

37. See "Fazendeiros procuram oficiais para milicias," *Estado de São Paulo,* 21 February 1986, and Nelson Letaif, "O Lobby do latifundio," *Senhor,* 3 June 1986, 26–31.

38. Landholders, like the industrialists I interviewed for my earlier work, were divided. About half considered General Médici the best president for Brazil, while the rest considered the democratically elected and populist Juscelino Kubitschek (1956–61) the best (despite their own admission that he had done nothing for agriculture). A very strong proportion of those interviewed provided unsolicited comments to the effect that the last two military presidents, and the ones who had initiated the transition from military rule—Generals Ernesto Geisel (1974–79) and João Batista Figueiredo (1979–85)—were the worst presidents in the history of Brazil.

39. This was consistent with an analysis of the 1987 Brazilian Constituent Assembly, which found a majority self-identified as center-left. Martins Rodrigues, *Quem é quem*, 97. In contrast, a business lobbying group, Semprel, placed about 35 percent in the center and 26 percent on the right, and the *Folha de São Paulo* placed only 32 percent in the center, with 24 percent on the center-right and 12 percent on the right. For these figures, see Fleischer, "O Congresso Constituinte." Even those members of Congress who had a clear right-wing agenda and solid right-wing support referred to themselves as centrists. Brazilian legislators, like the UDR, eschewed the right-wing label because of its association with the military regime, torture, and authoritarian rule.

40. In my interviews, only an organizer of the UDR-Youth movement positioned himself on the right. Comments like this one, however, indirectly linked leaders to the right wing: "With facts there are always three versions: the left's, ours, and the center's" [interview 10].

41. The critics considered that vote "highly irregular." One top leader even claimed that when Caiado saw that the discussion was turning against him, he called in the press and ordered the vote. Few leaders were willing to vote against Caiado while the press was watching, so he got approval without having majority support [interview 4].

42. UDR leaders around the country did have telephone conversations to discuss the possibility of reorganizing the movement to help defend the producers in the Pontal de Paranapanema. They concluded, however, that the lack of leadership, of collective spirit, and of a sense of threat among Brazilian landholders made such a reorganization highly unlikely. Instead, the traditional representative entity—the Rural Producers Union—organized to defend landholders in the Pontal. Neither the president of the entity nor his directorate claimed an association with the UDR. They used negotiation with government representatives, rather than aggressive mobilization, to defend their land. The remobilization of the UDR, however, began only a year later.

43. The press identified an association of cattle ranchers, formed to defend price and credit policies, as a new UDR. The head of the new organization even filed a complaint with the newspaper because of this false association. He told me that he was a man on the left and would never consider any association with the UDR [interview 13].

5   THE NICARAGUAN CONTRAS

1. For a discussion of FSLN errors that led to peasant-Contra support, see Bendaña, *Una Tragedia*. The following statement by a politician-cum-Contra reflects the view that the FSLN had abandoned the 1979 revolution's goals: "I was in the [Sandinista's] governing junta [but] I began to find my position untenable. I didn't fight against Somoza to impose a Marxist revolution in Nicaragua. I fought for democracy and social justice.... They invited me to join the Resistance. I wasn't convinced by armed action. I believed in political action. I was friends with the Resistance, but not part of it.... But after the 1984 elections I was very disillusioned, so I joined the Resistance. I entered into the Resistance without believing in a military solution. But it was the only way to force a negotiation of the conflict" [interview 3].

2. The Sandinistas may not have been completely off-base in their accusations against certain Miskito leaders, however. One of the top leaders of Misurasata is rumored to have been part of Somoza's intelligence apparatus. These suspicions haunt him to this day and may explain why he has been passed over for top leadership positions on the Atlantic Coast.

3. Bendaña, *Una Tragedia*.

4. Politically conservative scholars and observers of Nicaraguan politics consider the entire duration of the Sandinista government a totalitarian era. Those on the left, in contrast, applaud the efforts the Sandinistas made in opening up some aspects of the political system to representation despite the constraints of war and political inexperience. So while the left marks the democratic transition with the 1984 democratic elections, the right recognizes democratic change only after the 1990 electoral defeat of the Sandinistas.

5. INRA records report distribution of land to 27,510 ex-combatants: 5,309 (19.3%) has gone to ex-members of the Resistance and 1,065 (3.9%) to ex-members of the EPS. In addition to the ex-Contras and the ex-EPS recipients, INRA also provided land to repatriated Nicaraguans (4.8%), ex-ministry of government officials (1.5%), *colonos* (67.7%), and others (0.5%). Instituto Nicaragüense de Reforma Agraria, "Consolidado de titulación del sector agrario reformado por beneficiario y sector," compiled in March 1996.

6. I visited one relatively successful coffee cooperative in which former Contras had finally begun to produce market crops. This cooperative confronted problems in health, sanitation, and agricultural techniques. But the greatest threat, its members noted, was expropriation by Nicaraguan exiles in Miami who demanded that the land be returned to them or that they receive full compensation at market value. The cooperative's members felt that they might lose all of the labor and money they had invested over the five years since they had begun working the land.

7. One of the Contras I interviewed vehemently rejected this idea, which was widespread among the ex-combatants. He argued that rural production being what it was, even peasant boys who joined the Contras at age ten or twelve would have already been involved in farm life and would not have had problems figuring out how to work the land after they returned from the war.

8. Most suspect that the EPS was involved in this highly professional murder. "If the Sandinistas were not involved," one investigator claimed, "they would have found the culprit to clear themselves" [interview 33]. Several Contra leaders, who asked to remain anonymous, hinted that the CIA might have been involved. One of them made this comment: "There were many people who were potentially involved. We immediately accuse the Sandinistas, our historical enemy. But it might have been the government or the CIA. They would have wanted to do away with the unity of the Resistance."

9. As one of the spokesmen from the Tripartite Commission sarcastically stated, "By some coincidence, those who have been killed include primarily the top leaders" [anonymous].

10. Sandinista human rights abuses have been documented by CPDH (the Permanent Commission on Human Rights) and ANPDH (the Nicaraguan Human Rights Association). The Contras' human rights abuses have been documented by CNPPDH (the National Commission for the Promotion and Protection of Human Rights), which found 863 cases of Contra kidnappings during the war, and CENIDH (the Nicaraguan Human Rights Center).

11. In the Atlantic Coast town of Waspam in 1992, for example, a group of Recontras led by Manuel "Tigre 17" Cunningham killed a member of the police in order to force the government to attend to their demands for getting some of the former Contras onto the police force. In Puerto Cabezas, Felipe Mitchell took hostages to force the government to fulfill its agreements regarding land and social conditions. In this uprising the Recontras beat at least one of their hostages when she pointed out to them that they had killed a baby whose mother could not make it to the hospital in time for a Cesarian delivery because they had seized the ambulance. That same year a group of fourteen hundred ex-Contras took over the highways in the Fifth Region of the country, blocking access to and from the city. In 1993 a group of ex-Contras seized the Colombian embassy and the CIAV-OEA offices. In 1993 the Recontra group FN3-80 kidnapped a commission sent by the government to negotiate a cease-fire with them.

12. The municipalities of Chontales, Rio San Juan, Zelaya, Quilalí, and Nueva Segovia all have had a sizable representation of ex-Contras on their police forces.

13. This occurred in the Atlantic Coast region, where Recontras mobilized in Waspam to put Contras on the police force. In the end, most of them were fired because of their poor training [interview 1].

14. A top leader in Frente Norte 3-80 claimed that the group achieved 50 percent of their demands. This included control over a section of the country, training for top police chiefs in their region, and social benefits for the population in the region (e.g., infrastructure development, improved health conditions, job training, and economic development). For the ex-combatants, in particular, they won preferential conditions for buying land and housing, acquiring title to land, receiving loans, and reincorporating into civil life.

15. According to one of the professed founders of the party, the idea behind the

party began in 1986 and 1987. At that time the party was to be called the Nicaraguan Agrarian Party (PAN). It was originally designed as a political arm of the Contras. There was opposition within the political leadership of the Contras, because they viewed the party as legitimizing the FSLN's government. Once the Contras were back in Nicaragua after the elections, the idea of a political party resurfaced. In 1991 they called themselves the Nicaraguan Democratic Alliance (AND) made up of the three different civilian groups of Contras that had been formed: YAAD, the Civic Association of the Nicaraguan Resistance, and the Peasant Front of Wenceslau Abilesco. After overcoming a series of obstacles, the PRN was established as a legal entity on 5 May 1993.

16. Sandinista leaders continue to use the Contra name and to reject the concept of Resistance. As one Sandinista leader stated, "Resistance? Why Resistance? It was a war. We were being attacked with money from the United States" [interview 65].

17. A number of cases of rape, torture, and murder have been documented, as well as cases of excessive force used by commanders against their troops [interview 29]. In addition, the Contras have been accused of kidnapping peasants and forcing them to fight the war. Some of these incidents involve lies told by Contras soldiers' parents to avoid retribution by the Sandinistas. But investigation revealed some clear cases of kidnapping [interview 48].

18. One puzzling aspect of the legacy of the Contra war is how people feel about it. People wanted to tell me remarkably little about it. On several occasions I asked people to explain what it had been like. I asked villagers what they used to do when they heard gunshots; I asked Contras and Sandinistas about their day-to-day lives. I rarely got a straightforward reply. Some people seemed to not understand the question and gave a completely unrelated answer. I wondered if war was such a commonplace thing in their lives that they couldn't even begin to answer—much as I might have been stumped for an answer if someone had asked me what it was like to go to elementary school in the United States. When I discussed this with a Nicaraguan member of an international peacekeeping mission, she said that she had seen the same type of evasion when accompanying a group of Japanese scholars on a tour through Nicaragua; the Japanese group had tried to share their war experiences with the Nicaraguans but found no common ground because the Nicaraguans would not talk about the war. She interpreted the reaction as a desire to forget past difficulties. What impact does selective amnesia have on individuals' attitudes toward democracy? The Nicaraguan experience suggests that if one can put the hatred behind one, it may be easier to get on with the process of reconciliation. The instruments that make that possible, however, are not always in place. In Nicaragua the importance of reuniting families divided by the war, the desire to live in peace, and the common struggle for economic survival seem to have overcome past animosities.

19. Ironically, one of the harshest criticisms launched at Yátama is that it is sectarian. It has tended to defend only one indigenous group (i.e., Miskitos). The Sumo or Rama peoples, not to mention the black creole or mestizo populations on the Atlantic Coast, have little voice within Yátama. Miskito domination has turned Yátama

into the kind of political broker that it condemns in conventional partisan politics. Yátama is also widely criticized on the Atlantic Coast for acting in the interests of its leaders, particularly their power and wealth, and failing to represent the people. It is criticized as well for being too closely tied to the government, and hence unwilling to confront or alienate it. Finally, Yátama is criticized for its incompetent leadership. Despite having held on to power for six years, the movement has not designed strategies for redefining autonomy in the region.

20. This speaker later clarified that he considers the Quiñonez people to be part of the Frente.

21. In the 1996 presidential elections the PRN won 5,900 votes, or 0.33 percent. In the National Assembly elections the same year it won 21,395 votes, or 1.23 percent.

6 UNCIVIL MOVEMENTS IN COMPARATIVE PERSPECTIVE

1. As a relatively new movement, not much has been written about it. For some information, see Norden, "Rise," and Kornblith, "Public Sector," 84–87.

2. Venezuela experienced a short but brutal authoritarian regime under Colonel Marcos Pérez Jiménez (1952–58).

3. See the following news sources on FRAPH: Joel Dreyfuss, "The Little Nation That Tests Our Loyalty to Democracy," *Los Angeles Times,* 23 October 1994; Stephen Engelberg, "A Haitian Leader of Paramilitaries Was Paid by CIA," *New York Times,* 8 October 1994; Jim Lobe, "U.S.-Haiti: Arrest of FRAPH Chief Poses Questions for U.S.," *International Press Service,* 12 May 1994; Allan Nairn, "Behind Haiti's Paramilitaries: Our Man in FRAPH," *The Nation,* 24 October 1994; Andrew Reding, *From Haiti: An Agenda for Democracy* (Washington, D.C.: World Policy Institute, 1996); Jeffrey Smith, "Haitian Paramilitary Chief Spied for CIA, Sources Say," *Washington Post,* 7 October 1994; and Tim Weiner, "Key Haiti Leaders Said to Have Been in the CIA's Pay," *New York Times,* 1 November 1993.

4. For more information on these paramilitary units and the United States' support for them, see Human Rights Watch, *Colombia's Killer Networks,* and Rosenberg, *Children,* 21–76.

5. The AWB is one of the oldest and largest of the estimated two hundred paramilitary groups in South Africa. Founded in 1973, it began to grow significantly only after the 1987–88 political reforms to the apartheid system that allowed Nelson Mandela's election to the presidency in 1994. AWB's uncivil actions include amassing weapons; creating paramilitary units, armies, and an air force; attempting to poison water supplies; violently disrupting adversaries' meetings; planting bombs; destroying adversaries' property; and physical harm to individuals, including murder. At the same time, the AWB has worked within the political system through an institutionalized political party. Van Rooyen, *Hard Right,* 45–46.

6. Kahane's movement is one of the oldest religious-right movements in Israel. Sprinzak, *Ascendance.*

7. The Rocky Mountain Rendezvous, held on 23–25 October 1992 in Estes Park, Colorado, identified the militia "movement" as a loose set of locally organized pri-

vate armies scattered throughout the United States, including independent groups, leaderless ones, and "single" cells (i.e., lone individuals). The movement united against centralized government control in the wake of the Federal Bureau of Investigation stakeout and murder of survivalists at Ruby Ridge, Idaho, in 1992. The movement gained momentum after the U.S. government siege of the Branch Davidian compound in Waco, Texas, in 1993, which ended in eighty deaths. "Waco revenge" is sometimes used to explain the 1995 bombing of government offices in Oklahoma City. Timothy McVeigh's bombing resembles the strategy advocated by James "Bo" Gritz at Estes Park, called SPIKE (Specially Prepared Individuals for Key Events), and the fictitious bombing described in the promilitia novel *The Turner Diaries.* Militia threats to public officials have become widespread, leading some to ask, "What could have led people to the point where a 'good American' no longer wanted to vote the bastards out but to shoot the bastards dead?" Stern, *Force,* 137. But militias also endorse electoral politics: "We must all arm ourselves with a voter registration slip and use it like a .308 sniper weapon to 'take out' the infectious bought whores of the new world government who are now proposing to rule us all with an Orwellian iron fist—forever beating us all into submission, while claiming to protect us." Louis Beam quoted in Dees and Corcoran, *Gathering Storm,* 61. In some cases militia leaders have run for office. Randy Weaver, a survivor of the events at Ruby Ridge, ran for sheriff in 1988, and "Bo" Gritz ran as vice-president on former Klansman David Duke's Populist Party bid for the presidency in 1992.

8. Przeworski, "Some Problems," 47–63.

9. *The Nation,* 29 October 1990.

10. The Brady Bill, which eventually formed part of the federal crime bill in 1994, required a "waiting period" to allow time for background checks on individuals desiring to purchase guns. The federal government, militias argued, attempted "to take guns away from true patriots, tax them into poverty, strip them of their constitutional rights, and place them under the boot of a one-world government." Dees and Corcoran, *Gathering Storm,* 81. The militia movement points to these threats as the rationale for assuming an armed response to defend citizens against a government takeover. These signs, spotted at the Waco stakeout, summarize that view: "Dictators Love Gun Control"; "Ban Guns. Make the Streets Safe for a Government Takeover"; "Your Gun Permit: The Second Amendment"; and "Remember Waco: You Are Next." Stern, *Force,* 61.

11. The AWB missed no opportunity to resurrect images of the 1838 Great Trek, in which Afrikaners had persevered against adversity to claim two independent republics. Packing up their families and belongings in ox-wagons to escape from British control in the Cape, which they had inhabited since the seventeenth century, the Afrikaners crossed mountains and rivers, risking their lives in battles with Zulus. Leach, *Afrikaners.* The Boer War (1899–1902) against the British, in which the Afrikaners lost their independent republics, plays less of a role as a source of heroic images, but it contributes to the development of cultural villains against which Afrikaners must remain vigilant.

12. Militia leaders frequently link their movement to the American Revolution, associating themselves with Minutemen and revolutionary leaders and referring to particular battles for freedom. See Dees and Corcoran, *Gathering Storm,* especially 1–2.

13. Kahane used Zionist heroes like Vladimir Jabotinsky and David Raziel to ground his violence in a cultural-historical context. Kahane seized on to Jabotinsky's idea of Barzel Yisrael, or Israel's Iron, to justify a strong Israeli army and violence as retribution for assaults on Jews. Sprinzak, *Ascendance,* 235.

14. Kahane's electoral power increased from 1977 and 1981, when he won only 0.2 percent and 0.3 percent of the vote, to 1984, when he won 1.3 percent and a seat in the Knesset. Although his party was banned from the 1988 elections, scholars speculate that it might have won 10 percent of the Knesset seats. Ibid., 305. This estimate is based on Kahane's rise in public-opinion polls between 1984 and 1988. The power his movement wields within Israel's political culture has led some scholars to refer to it as "the main threat to Israel's civic order" (179).

15. Ibid., 87.

16. Kahane, for example, justified his movement's violence against Arabs as "an act of sanctification of God's name," claiming that as God's chosen people, Jews had to match strength with strength, power with power, violence with violence, to protect themselves and serve God's will. Rabbi Meir Kahane, *The Story of the Jewish Defense League,* quoted in Cromer, *Debate,* 235.

17. Kahane quoted in Sprinzak, *Ascendance,* 214.

18. Kahane made this claim in the *Washington Post* (8 March 1984), but he has also argued the opposite: "Jewish violence to protect Jewish interests is never bad." Sprinzak, *Ascendance,* 53. Kahane's villains included not only Arabs but also Israeli leaders whose passivism allowed Arabs to commit atrocities against Jews.

19. He particularly attacked Israel's Declaration of Independence, which called for equal rights for all inhabitants of Israel regardless of race, religion, or national origin. Kahane considered the declaration a slippery slope leading to Arab domination of the Jewish state of Israel. Sprinzak, *Ascendance,* 83.

20. The antiassimilation bill that Kahane submitted to the Knesset has been likened to the Nazis' racist Nuremberg Laws and to apartheid. The bill called for separation of Jews and non-Jews in schools, camps, dormitories, beaches, neighborhoods, and apartment buildings. It barred dating or marriage between Jews and non-Jews and called for punishment of Gentiles who seduce Jewish women. Ibid., 239.

21. Samuel Sherwood, head of the United States Militia Association, quoted in Stern, *Force,* 165.

22. Larry Pratt quoted in Dees and Corcoran, *Gathering Storm,* 53–54. See a similar "Christian defense" by Louis Beam in the same volume, 56.

23. John Trochman, founder of the Militia of Montana, quoted in ibid., 5–6.

24. Rumors suggest that Terre'Blanche changed his name to signify his commitment to a "white land."

25. Mallaby, *After Apartheid,* 96.

26. Ibid. He enraged and mobilized Afrikaners with speeches like this one: "If the blacks start a revolution to destroy our property, rape our women, even our children, there will be a white force under the leadership of Afrikaaner Weerstandsbeweging that will fight back." Martin, *In the Name*, 212. Even some reporters claimed to find him mesmerizing: "Right now I've got to remind myself to breathe. I'm impaled on the blue flames of his blow-torch eyes." Jani Allen quoted in Mallaby, *After Apartheid*, 97.

27. It further showed an AWB training camp where "wild-eyed bully boys staring into the camera [swore] that they would fight De Klerk." Mallaby, *After Apartheid*, 97.

28. Despite the similarities between AWB and Nazi symbols and uniforms, the AWB denies any association with Nazism, arguing that Jews are welcome to join the movement as long as they convert to Christianity. A link to pro-Nazi movements exists through the Afrikaner Ossewabrandwag (Ox-Wagon Fire Guard), or OB, of the 1930s and 1940s. The OB sabotaged the Allied war effort, using *stormjaers* (storm troopers) to blow up railroads and other installations upon which Allied forces relied. The AWB resembles the OB in its use of violence, military orientation, emphasis on the primacy of the *volk*, cult of a strong leader, anti-Semitism, and use of flags and emblems. Van Rooyen, *Hard Right*, 45–47. The "Christian defense" used by the AWB to deflect criticism is based on the Dutch Reformed Church's "Christian" justification for racial segregation. Mallaby, *After Apartheid*, 95; Leach, *The Afrikaners*, 8.

29. Kahane's Kach and other radical-right movements have used the message of the indivisibility of Israel's land, the Arab threat, and religious fundamentalism to appeal to the approximately one hundred thousand individuals in the occupied territories.

30. Perhaps Kahane's scapegoating of Arabs for Israel's economic insecurity won over the poor and working class. Kahane blamed Israeli employers for hiring Arabs instead of Jews: "I talk to young Jews who are just out of the army and they do not have jobs. No jobs? There are jobs! The Arabs have jobs! . . . Why? Because the greedy Jewish employer keeps two Arabs for the price of one Jew." Sprinzak, *Ascendance*, 239.

31. One scholar estimates that the group has between 5,000 and 9,000 "signed-up" members, along with 150,000 supporters and 500,000 sympathizers. Van Rooyen, *Hard Right*, 173. Another indicator of the potential support for the AWB is that half of the Afrikaner voting population voted against National Party reforms in the 1992 referendum.

32. Leach, *Afrikaners*, 110.

33. Mallaby, *After Apartheid*, 83. The AWB's constituents have been described, variously, as downwardly mobile, insulated hillbillies; peasant stock; debt-ridden farmers; blue-collar workers; minor civil servants; policemen; and racist and fascist extremist Afrikaners. Descriptions of AWB rallies evoke images of a rural working class, dressed in neo-Nazi regalia, who gather with their families, picnic lunches, and beer to cheer on the impassioned Terre'Blanche with fists raised and shouts of "Ah—Vee—Bay."

34. Leach, *Afrikaners*, 214.

35. Stern, *Force*, 246.

36. *Sunday Times*, 9 August 1992, quoted in Van Rooyen, *Hard Right*, 94.

37. His hopes of being nominated by the Conservative Party to run for Parliament in the 1989 general elections were not realized. The AWB registered its own party, Blanke Volkstaat, only in 1988.

38. Mallaby, *After Apartheid*, 99.

39. A U.S. citizen of Egyptian descent, apparently acting on his own, gunned Kahane down in New York while he was delivering a speech. Twenty thousand mourners attended the burial ceremony.

40. Yigal Amir, a member of the offshoot group Eyal, murdered Yitzhak Rabin, justifying it as a religious mission.

41. Many of those who left or were purged complain about Kahane's brutal treatment of those who disagreed with him. They also cite his public conduct, combative style, constant pursuit of media attention, inability to delegate authority, and unwillingness to compromise as constraints on the movement. Sprinzak, *Ascendance*, 243–44, 275–76.

42. Ibid., 245.

43. All of the local organizations were run by working-class volunteers, out of private homes, during their highly limited spare time. The local movements therefore became active only for specific events: a Kahane visit, elections, or to follow Kahane's personal orders. Ibid., 213.

44. See Giliomee, "Growth"; Le May, *Afrikaners*; and Sparks, *Tomorrow*.

45. Linda Thompson, Indiana militia leader, quoted by Dees and Corcoran, *Gathering Storm*, 175. Militias have also spun conspiracy theories about computer chips implanted in citizen's heads to track and control them, numbers painted on the back of road signs to indicate which concentration camp neighborhood residents will be sent to, and black helicopters spying on citizens.

46. Louis Beam quoted in ibid., 174.

47. The assaulted Socialist Party candidate was running against Le Pen's daughter in these elections.

48. "Germany: Le Pen Convicted," *New York Times*, 4 June 1999. French courts had already fined him $217,000 in 1987 for referring to the concentration camps as a detail of history. In Germany, Le Pen was fined an undisclosed amount.

49. The effort was passed through the Central Elections Committee but was overruled by the Supreme Court because of the lack of proper legislation.

50. "Removal of a 'Racist,'" *Newsweek*, 17 October 1988, 41.

51. Tom Asland, "Exporting Extremism," *Newsweek*, 27 November 1995, 47.

52. One example is the 1974 TNT (Terror Neged Terror, or Jewish Terrorism in Reaction to Arab Terrorism) campaign, for which Kahane and his followers served prison sentences. Kahane was also arrested and detained for nine months for plotting to destroy the Dome of the Rock on the Temple Mount using a long-range missile. Sprinzak, *Ascendance*, 236.

53. For example, in 1989 a right-wing alliance formed to create a new "Independent State of Judea" but expressly prevented Kahane from playing a role in the effort because of the stigma attached to him.

54. Sprinzak claims that the government ban on Kahanism "greatly reduced its chances of gaining legitimacy and becoming an influential force in the nation's public life." Sprinzak, *Ascendance,* 245. See also Robert Friedman, "The Brooklyn Avengers," *New York Review of Books,* 23 June 1994, 41.

55. The head of the Ohio Militia even claimed that militias were "the ones who calm people down." James Johnson quoted in Dees and Corcoran, *Gathering Storm,* 188.

56. Senator Arlen Specter cited in Stern, *Force,* 245. Stern himself puts the number of active members at between ten thousand and forty thousand, and the sympathizers in the thousands or millions (16). Dees and Corcoran put the number of militias at 441, with at least one in each state. They also claim that 368 allied Patriot groups that promote the formation of militias also exist. Dees and Corcoran, *Gathering Storm,* 199. There are over one hundred Web sites that hard-core white supremacists and antigovernment "patriots" can access (207). Moreover, global communication, particularly as facilitated by the Internet, fax, and cable television, has expanded the sphere of influence of these movements beyond U.S. borders. Stern particularly notes Europe, Canada, and Australia as places where similar groups have emerged, modeled on and communicating with U.S. militias. Stern, *Force,* 239–44.

57. Dees and Corcoran, *Gathering Storm,* 185.

58. Norman Olson, founder of the Michigan Militia, quoted in ibid., 187.

59. Botha failed to squelch Terre'Blanche's occupation of various political meetings. He declared an AWB rally a "cultural event" rather than outlawing it as a political event. But Botha may have benefited from the AWB's violence; he could argue to the international community that the political situation was too dangerous for him to move too far or too quickly on reform. See Leach, *Afrikaners,* 97–100.

60. For example, when farmers took over Pretoria in 1991, police evicted them within twenty-four hours. The police also promptly quelled the AWB's protests of de Klerk's visit to Ventersdorp. Rather than using the AWB as an excuse to halt reforms, de Klerk used it to discredit the Conservative Party. The government pointed out Conservative Party members of Parliament who belonged to the AWB.

61. On bluffs, see Van Rooyen, *Hard Right,* 195. On AWB violence, see Leach, *Afrikaners,* 97.

62. Shaw, "Bloody Backdrop"; Friedman and Atkinson, *Small Miracle,* 207.

63. The AWB threatened, for example, to make De Klerk's job impossible, call a white strike, and declare a "Boer Holy War." But not even Nelson Mandela's assumption of the presidency mobilized the allied right-wing forces into collective action.

64. Quoted in Hasselbach, *Führer-Ex,* 271.

Bibliography

PUBLISHED SOURCES

Acuña, Carlos H., and Catalina Smulovitz. "Guarding the Guardians in Argentina: Some Lessons about the Risks and Benefits of Empowering the Courts." In *Transitional Justice and the Rule of Law in New Democracies,* edited by A. James McAdams, 93–122. Notre Dame, Ind.: University of Notre Dame Press, 1997.

Adorno, Theodor, Else Frenkel-Brunswik, Daniel Levinson, and Nevitt Sanford, eds. *The Authoritarian Personality.* New York: Harper, 1950.

Alexander, Jeffrey L. "Aspectos não-civis da sociedade: Espaço, tempo, e função." *Revista brasileira de ciências sociais* 33, no. 12 (1997): 169–79. Translated by Vera Pereira. (Last chapter of a forthcoming book provisionally titled *The Possibility of Justice: A Sociological Theory of Civil Society.*)

Altemeyer, Bob. *Enemies of Freedom: Understanding Right-Wing Authoritarianism.* San Francisco: Jossey-Bass, 1988.

Alvarez, Sonia. *Engendering Democracy in Brazil: Women's Movements in Transition Politics.* Princeton: Princeton University Press, 1990.

Alvarez, Sonia E., Evelina Dagnino, and Arturo Escobar, eds. *Cultures of Politics, Politics of Cultures: Re-visioning Latin American Social Movements.* Boulder, Colo.: Westview Press, 1998.

Alves, Maria Helena Moreira. *State and Opposition in Military Brazil.* Austin: University of Texas Press, 1985.

Amado, Jorge. *Terras do sem fim: Romance.* São Paulo: Martins, 1964. Later published by Rio de Janeiro: Editora Record, 1981. Translated by Samuel Putnam as *The Violent Land.* London: Collins Harvill, 1989.

Americas Watch. *Verdad y justicia en la Argentina: Actualización.* Buenos Aires: Americas Watch and CELS, 1991.

Amnesty International. *Argentina: The Military Juntas and Human Rights.* London: Amnesty International Publications, 1987.

Andersen, Martin Edwin. *Dossier Secreto: Argentina's Desaparecidos and the Myth of the "Dirty War."* Boulder, Colo.: Westview Press, 1993.

Anderson, Benedict. *Imagined Communities.* London: Verso, 1991.

Arendt, Hannah. *Eichmann in Jerusalem: A Report on the Banality of Evil.* New York: Viking Press, 1963.

Badinter, Elizabeth. *XY: On Masculine Identity.* Translated by Lydia Davis. New York: Columbia University Press, 1995.

Barth, Frederick. *Ethnic Groups and Boundaries.* Boston: Little, Brown, 1969.

Barthes, Roland. *Mythologies.* Translated by Annette Lavers. New York: Hill and Wang, 1972.

Bell, Daniel. "The Dispossessed (1962)." In *The Radical Right,* edited by Daniel Bell, 1–38. Garden City, N.Y.: Doubleday, 1964.

———, ed. *The Radical Right.* Garden City, N.Y.: Doubleday, 1964.

Bendaña, Alejandro. *Una tragedia campesina: Testimonios de la resistencia.* Managua: Editora de Arte and Centro de Estudios Internacionales, 1991.

Benford, David A., and Robert D. Snow. "Ideology, Frame Resonance, and Participant Mobilization." *International Social Movement Research* 1 (1988): 197–217.

Bird, Karen, John L. Sullivan, Patricia G. Avery, Kristina Thalhammer, and Sandra Wood. "Not Just Lip-Syncing Anymore: Education and Tolerance Revisited." *Review of Education, Pedagogy, and Cultural Studies* 16 (1994): 373–86.

Bly, Robert. *Iron John: A Book about Men.* New York: Vintage Books, 1992.

Brasil: Nunca mais. Petrópolis: Vozes, 1985.

Brittan, Arthur. *Masculinity and Power.* Oxford: Basil Blackwell, 1989.

Brod, Harry, and Michael Kaufman, eds. *Theorizing Masculinities.* Thousand Oaks, Calif.: Sage Publications, 1994.

Bruno, Regina Angela L. "UDR: Os 'sem terra' dos patrões." Paper presented at the Projeto de Intercâmbio de Pesquisa Social em Agricultura—PIPSA conference, Campinas, São Paulo, 6–9 April 1987.

Bryant, Christopher G. A. "Civic Nation, Civil Society, Civil Religion." In *Civil Society: Theory, History, and Comparison,* edited by John A. Hall, 136–57. Cambridge: Polity Press, 1995.

Bunster, Ximena. "Watch out for the Little Nazi Man that All of Us Have Inside: The Mobilization and Demobilization of Women in Militarized Chile." *Women's Studies International Forum* 2, no. 5 (1988): 485–91.

Cohen, Anthony P. *The Symbolic Construction of Community.* London: Routledge, 1985.

Cohen, Jean, and Andrew Arato. *Civil Society and Political Theory.* Cambridge, Mass.: MIT Press, 1992.

Cohn, Carol. "Sex and Death in the Rational World of Defense Intellectuals." *Signs: Journal of Women in Culture and Society* 12, no. 4 (1987): 687–718.

Collier, David. "Democracy and Dichotomies: Is Concept Formation Inherently Based on Qualitative Reasoning?" Paper presented at the Annual Meeting of the American Political Science Association, Washington, D.C., 28–31 August 1997.

Comisión Nacional sobre la Desaparición de Personas (CONADEP). *Nunca más.* Buenos Aires: Editorial Universitaria de Buenos Aires, 1984.

Connell, R. W. *Gender and Power.* Stanford: Stanford University Press, 1987.

Conover, Pamela Johnston, and Virginia Gray. *Feminism and the New Right: Conflict over the American Family.* New York: Praeger, 1983.

Coppedge, Michael. *A Classification of Latin American Political Parties.* Notre Dame, Ind.: Helen Kellogg Institute for International Studies, 1997.

Cromer, Gerald. *The Debate about Kahanism in Israeli Society, 1984–1988.* New York: Harry Frank Guggenheim Foundation, 1988.

Dahl, Robert A. *Polyarchy: Participation and Opposition.* New Haven: Yale University Press, 1971.

————. *A Preface to Democratic Theory.* Chicago: University of Chicago Press, 1959.

Daly, Mary. *Pure Lust: Elemental Feminist Philosophy.* Boston: Beacon Press, 1984.

Dassin, Joan, ed. *Torture in Brazil.* Translated by Jaime Wright. New York: Vintage Books, 1986.

Dees, Morris, and James Corcoran. *Gathering Storm: America's Militia Threat.* New York: Hill and Wang, 1994.

Diamond, Larry, and Juan J. Linz. "Introduction: Politics, Society, and Democracy in Latin America." In *Democracy in Developing Countries: Latin America,* edited by Larry Diamond, Juan J. Linz, and Seymour Martin Lipset, 1–58. Boulder, Colo.: Lynne Rienner, 1988.

DiPalma, Guiseppe. *To Craft Democracies.* Berkeley: University of California Press, 1990.

Duch, Raymond M., and James L. Gibson. "Putting up with Fascists in Western Europe: A Comparative, Cross-Level Analysis of Political Tolerance." *Western Political Quarterly* 45 (1992): 237–73.

Durham, Martin. "Gender and the British Union of Fascists." *Journal of Contemporary History* 27 (July 1992): 513–29.

Eckstein, Susan, ed. *Power and Popular Protest: Latin American Social Movements.* Berkeley: University of California Press, 1988.

Enloe, Cynthia. *The Morning After: Sexual Politics at the End of the Cold War.* Berkeley: University of California Press, 1993.

Epstein, A. L. *Ethos and Identity.* London: Tavistock Publications, 1978.

Escobar, Arturo, and Sonia Alvarez, eds. *The Making of Social Movements in Latin America: Identity, Strategy, and Democracy.* Boulder, Colo.: Westview Press, 1992.

Feitlowitz, Marguerite. *A Lexicon of Terror: Argentina and the Legacies of Torture.* New York: Oxford University Press, 1998.

Finkel, Steven E., Edward N. Muller, and Karl-Dieter Opp. "Personal Influence, Collective Rationality, and Mass Political Action." *American Political Science Review* 83 (September 1989): 885–903.

Fishman, Walda Katz. "Right-Wing Reaction and Violence: A Response to Capitalism's Crises." *Social Research* 48 (Spring 1981): 157–82.

Fleischer, David. "O Congresso Constituinte de 1987: Um perfil sócio-econômico e político." Brasília: Departamento de Ciências Políticas e Relações Internacionais, Universidade de Brasília, 1987. Mimeo.

Foweraker, Joe. *Theorizing Social Movements*. Boulder, Colo.: Pluto Press, 1995.

Friedman, Edward. "Introduction." In *The Politics of Democratization: Generalizing East Asian Experiences,* edited by Edward Friedman, 1–15. Boulder, Colo.: Westview Press, 1994.

Friedman, Steve, and Doreen Atkinson, eds. *The Small Miracle: South Africa's Negotiated Settlement.* Johannesburg: Raven Press, 1994.

Frontalini, Daniel, and Maria Cristina Caiati. *El mito de la Guerra Sucia.* Buenos Aries: CELS, 1984.

Gamson, William A. *The Strategy of Social Protest,* Homewood, Ill.: Dorsey Press, 1975.

Geertz, Clifford. "The Integrative Revolution: Primordial Sentiments and Civil Politics in the New States." In *Old Societies and New States,* edited by Clifford Geertz, 105–57. New York: Free Press, 1963.

Gellner, Ernest. "The Importance of Being Modular." In *Civil Society: Theory, History, and Comparison,* edited by John A. Hall, 32–55. Cambridge: Polity Press, 1995.

George, Alexander L. "Case Studies and Theory Development: The Method of Structured, Focused Comparison." In *Diplomacy: New Approaches in History, Theory, and Policy,* edited by Paul Gordon Lauren, 43–68. New York: Free Press, 1979.

George, Alexander L., and Timothy J. McKeown. "Case Studies and Theories of Organizational Decision Making." *Advances in Information Processing in Organizations* 2 (1985): 21–58.

Gerzon, Mark. *A Choice of Heroes: The Changing Faces of American Manhood.* Boston: Houghton Mifflin, 1982.

Gilbert, Paul. *Terrorism, Security, and Nationality.* London: Routledge, 1994.

Giliomee, Hermann. "The Growth of Afrikaner Identity." In *Segregation and Apartheid in Twentieth-Century South Africa,* edited by William Beinart and Sal Dubow, 189–205. New York: Routledge, 1955.

Goertzel, Ted E. "Authoritarianism of Personality and Political Attitudes." *Journal of Social Psychology* 127 (February 1987): 7–18.

Goffman, Erving. *Frame Analysis: An Essay on the Organization of Experience.* New York: Harper and Row, 1974.

Graziano, Frank. *Divine Violence: Spectacle, Psychosexuality, and Racial Christianity in the Argentine "Dirty War."* Boulder, Colo.: Westview Press, 1992.

Gurr, Ted. *Why Men Rebel.* Princeton: Princeton University Press, 1971.

Guzmán Bouvard, Marguerite. *Revolutionizing Motherhood: The Mothers of the Plaza de Mayo.* Wilmington, Del.: Scholarly Resources, 1994.

Hagtvet, Bernt, and Reinhard Kuhnl. "Contemporary Approaches to Fascism: A Survey of Paradigms." In *Who Were the Fascists: Social Roots of European Fascism,* edited by Stein Ugelvik Larsen, Bernt Hagtvet, and Jan Petter Myklebust, 26–51. New York: Columbia University Press, 1980.

Hall, John A. "In Search of Civil Society." In *Civil Society: Theory, History, and Comparison,* edited by John A. Hall, 1–31. Cambridge: Polity Press, 1995.

Hammond, John L. "Retaliatory Violence against Agrarian Reform in Brazil." Paper presented at the conference on Coercion, Violence, and Rights in the Americas, New School for Social Research, 17 April 1998.

Hardin, Russell. *One for All: The Logic of Group Conflict.* Princeton: Princeton University Press, 1995.

Hasselbach, Ingo. *Führer-Ex: Memoirs of a Former Neo-Nazi.* New York: Random House, 1996.

Hechter, Michael. "Rational Choice Theory and the Study of Race and Ethnic Relations." In *Theories of Ethnic and Race Relations,* edited by John Rex and David Mason, 264–79. Cambridge: Cambridge University Press, 1986.

Hochstetler, Kathryn. "Democratizing Pressures from Below? Social Movements in New Brazilian Democracy." Paper delivered at the Latin American Studies Association's Twentieth International Congress, Guadalajara, Mexico, 17–19 April 1997.

Hofstadter, Richard. "Pseudo-Conservatism Revisited: A Postscript (1962)." In *The Radical Right,* edited by Daniel Bell, 97–103. Garden City, N.Y.: Doubleday, 1964.

———. "The Pseudo-Conservative Revolt (1955)." In *The Radical Right,* edited by Daniel Bell, 75–95. Garden City, N.Y.: Doubleday, 1964.

Human Rights Watch. *Colombia's Killer Networks: The Military-Paramilitary Partnership and the United States.* New York: Human Rights Watch, 1996.

Isaacs, Harold. *Idols of the Tribe: Group Identity and Political Change.* New York: Harper Colophon Books, 1977.

Jelin, Elizabeth, and Eric Hershberg, eds. *Constructing Democracy: Human Rights, Citizenship, and Society in Latin America.* Boulder, Colo.: Westview Press, 1996.

Jelin, Elizabeth, and Susana G. Kaufman. "Layers of Memories: Twenty Years after in Argentina." Paper presented for the conference on Legacies of Authoritarianism: Cultural Production, Collective Trauma, and Global Justice, University of Wisconsin–Madison, 3–5 April 1998.

Jenkins, Craig J. "Resource Mobilization Theory and the Study of Social Movements." *Annual Review of Sociology* 9 (1983): 527–53.

Keck, Margaret E. *The Workers' Party and Democratization in Brazil.* New Haven: Yale University Press, 1992.

Keen, Sam. *Fire in the Belly: On Being a Man.* New York: Bantam Books, 1991.

Klandermans, Bert, and Sidney Tarrow. "Mobilization into Social Movements: Synthesizing European and American Approaches." In *From Structure to Action: Comparing Social Movements across Cultures,* edited by Bert Klandermans, Sidney Tarrow, and Hanspeter Kriesi, 1–38. Greenwich, Conn.: JAI Press, 1988.

Klosko, George, Edward N. Muller, and Karl-Dieter Opp. "Rebellious Collective Action Revisited." *American Political Science Review* 81 (June 1987): 557–66.

Koontz, Claudia. *Mothers in the Fatherland: Women, the Family, and Nazi Politics.* New York: St. Martin's Press, 1987.

Kornblith, Miriam. "Public Sector and Private Sector: New Rules of the Game." In *Venezuela under Stress,* edited by Jennifer McCoy, Andrés Serbin, William C. Smith, and Andrés Stambouli, 77–103. New Brunswick, N.J.: University of Miami North-South Center and Transaction Publishers, 1995.

Krejcí, Jaroslav. "Introduction: Concepts of Right and Left." In *Neo-Fascism in Europe*, edited by Luciano Cheles, Ronnie Ferguson, and Michalina Vaughan, 1–18. London: Longman, 1991.

Lanata, Jorge, and Joe Goldman. *Cortinas de humo: Una investigación independiente sobre los atentados contra la embajada de Israel y la AMIA.* Buenos Aires: Editorial Planeta, 1994.

Lancaster, Roger N. *Life Is Hard: Machismo, Danger, and the Intimacy of Power in Nicaragua.* Berkeley: University of California Press, 1992.

Le May, G. H. L. *The Afrikaners: An Historical Interpretation.* Cambridge, Mass.: Blackwell, 1955.

Leach, Graham. *The Afrikaners: Their Last Great Trek.* Johannesburg: Southern Book Publishers, 1989.

Levine, Daniel H., ed. *Constructing Culture and Power in Latin America.* Ann Arbor: University of Michigan Press, 1993.

Lijphart, Arend, and Carlos H. Waisman, eds. *Institutional Design in New Democracies: Eastern Europe and Latin America.* Boulder, Colo.: Westview Press, 1996.

Lindblom, Charles E. *Politics and Markets: The World's Political-Economic Systems.* New York: Basic Books, 1977.

Linz, Juan J. *Crisis, Breakdown, and Reequilibration.* Baltimore: Johns Hopkins University Press, 1978.

Linz, Juan J., and Arturo Valenzuela. *The Failure of Presidential Democracy.* Baltimore: Johns Hopkins University Press, 1978.

Lipset, Seymour Martin. "The Sources of the 'Radical Right.'" In *The Radical Right*, edited by Daniel Bell, 307–71. Garden City, N.Y.: Doubleday, 1964.

Madsen, Douglas, and Peter Snow. *The Charismatic Bond: Political Behavior in Time of Crisis.* Cambridge, Mass.: Harvard University Press, 1991.

Mainwaring, Scott, and Timothy R. Scully, eds. *Building Democratic Institutions: Party Systems in Latin America.* Stanford: Stanford University Press, 1995.

Mallaby, Sebastian. *After Apartheid: The Future of South Africa.* New York: Random House, 1992.

Mançano Fernandes, Bernardo. *MST: Movimento dos trabalhadores rurais sem-terra: Formação e territorialização em São Paulo.* São Paulo: Editora HUCITEC, 1997.

Marcus, George E., John L. Sullivan, Elizabeth Theiss-Morse, and Sandra L. Wood. *With Malice toward Some: How People Make Civil Liberties Judgements.* Cambridge: Cambridge University Press, 1995.

Martí i Puig, Salvador. *La Revolución enredada: Nicaragua, 1977–1996.* Madrid: Los Libros de la Catarata, 1997.

Martin, Meredith. *In the Name of Apartheid.* London: Hamilton, 1988.

Martins Rodrigues, Leôncio. *Quem é quem na Constituinte: Uma análise sócio-política dos partidos e deputados.* São Paulo: OESP-Maltese, 1987.

Maybury-Lewis, Biorn. *The Politics of the Possible: The Brazilian Rural Workers' Trade Union Movement, 1964–1985*. Philadelphia: Temple University Press, 1994.

McAdam, Doug. *Political Process and Development of Black Insurgency*. Chicago: University of Chicago Press, 1985.

McAdam, Doug, John D. McCarthy, and Mayer N. Zald, eds. *Comparative Perspectives on Social Movements: Political Opportunities, Mobilizing Structures, and Cultural Framings*. Cambridge: Cambridge University Press, 1996.

McCarthy, John D., and Mayer N. Zald. "Resource Mobilization and Social Movements: A Partial Theory." *American Journal of Sociology* 82, no. 6 (1977): 1212–41.

———. *The Trend of Social Movements in America*. Morristown, N.J.: General Learning Press, 1973.

McClosky, Herbert, and Dennis Chong. "Similarities and Differences between Left-Wing and Right-Wing Radicals." *British Journal of Political Science* 15 (July 1985): 329–63.

Mendes, Chico. *Fight for the Forest: Chico Mendes in His Own Words*. London: Latin American Bureau Research in Action, 1989.

Mignone, Emilio F. *Iglesia y dictadura: El papel de la Iglesia a la luz de sus relaciones con el régimen militar*. Buenos Aires: Ediciones del Pensamiento Nacional, 1986.

Milgram, Stanley. *Obedience to Authority: An Experimental View*. New York: Harper and Row, 1974.

Mosse, George L. *The Image of Man: The Creation of Modern Masculinity*. New York: Oxford University Press, 1996.

Muller, Edward N., and Karl-Dieter Opp. "Rational Choice and Rebellious Collective Action." *American Political Science Review* 80 (January 1986): 471–87.

Norden, Deborah L. *Military Rebellion in Argentina: Between Coups and Consolidation*. Lincoln: University of Nebraska Press, 1996.

———. "The Rise of Lieutenant Colonels: Rebellion in Argentina and Venezuela." *Latin American Perspectives* 90, no. 23 (1996): 74–86.

Norval, Aletta J. *Deconstructing Apartheid Discourse*. London: Verso, 1996.

Nunca Más: Report of the Argentine National Commission on the Disappeared. New York: Farrar Straus Giroux, 1986.

O'Donnell, Guillermo. *Modernization and Bureaucratic-Authoritarianism*. Berkeley: University of California Press, 1973.

O'Donnell, Guillermo, and Philippe Schmitter. *Transitions from Authoritarian Rule: Tentative Conclusions about Uncertain Democracies*. Baltimore: Johns Hopkins University Press, 1986.

Omi, Michael, and Howard Winant. *Racial Formation in the United States*. New York: Routledge, 1986.

Page, Joseph A. *The Revolution That Never Was: Northeast Brazil*. New York: Grossemen, 1972.

Paiero, Denise, and José Roberto Damatto Jr. *Foices e sabres: A história de uma ocupação dos sem-terra*. São Paulo: Annablume, 1996.

Payne, Leigh A. *Brazilian Industrialists and Democratic Change.* Baltimore: Johns Hopkins University Press, 1994.

Pereira, Anthony W. *The End of the Peasantry: The Rural Labor Movement in Northeast Brazil, 1961–1988.* Pittsburgh: University of Pittsburgh Press, 1996.

Przeworski, Adam. *Democracy and the Market: Political and Economic Reforms in Eastern Europe and Latin America.* Cambridge: Cambridge University Press, 1991.

———. "Some Problems in the Study of the Transition to Democracy." In *Transitions from Authoritarian Rule: Comparative Perspectives,* edited by Guillermo O'Donnell and Philippe C. Schmitter, 47–63. Baltimore: Johns Hopkins University Press, 1986.

Revkin, Andrew. *The Burning Season: The Murder of Chico Mendes and the Fight for the Amazon Rain Forest.* Boston: Houghton Mifflin, 1990.

Rogin, Michael Paul. *Ronald Reagan, the Movie, and Other Episodes in Political Demonology.* Berkeley: University of California Press, 1987.

Rosenberg, Tina. *Children of Cain: Violence and the Violent in Latin America.* New York: William Morrow, 1991.

Rustow, Dankwart A. "Transitions to Democracy: Toward a Dynamic Model." *Comparative Politics* 2 (April 1970): 337–64.

Sain, Marcelo Fabián. *Los levantamientos Carapintada, 1987–1991.* Volumes 1 and 2. Buenos Aires: Centro Editor de América Latina, 1994.

Sanford, Nevitt. "Authoritarian Personality in Contemporary Perspective." In *Handbook of Political Psychology,* edited by Jeanne N. Knutson, 139–70. London: Jossey-Bass, 1973.

Schedler, Andreas. "Anti-Political-Establishment Parties." *Party Politics* 2, no. 3 (1996): 291–312.

Schneider, Cathy. "Chile Shantytowns." In *The Making of Social Movements in Latin America: Identity, Strategy, and Democracy,* edited by Arturo Escobar and Sonia Alvarez, 260–75. Boulder, Colo.: Westview Press, 1992.

———. *Shantytown Protest in Pinochet's Chile.* Philadelphia: Temple University Press, 1995.

Shaw, Mark. "The Bloody Backdrop: Negociating Violence." *South African Review* 7 (1994): 182–203.

Shugart, Matthew Soberg, and John M. Carey, eds. *Presidents and Assemblies: Constitutional Design and Electoral Dynamics.* Cambridge: Cambridge University Press, 1992.

Shupe, Anson. "The Accommodation and Deradicalization of Innovative Religious Movements." In *Religion and Politics in Comparative Perspective: Revival of Religious Fundamentalism in East and West,* edited by Bronislaw Misztal and Anson Shupe, 28–42. Westport, Conn.: Praeger, 1992.

Slater, David, ed. *New Social Movements and the State in Latin America.* Amsterdam: CEDLA, 1985.

Smith-Rosenberg, Carroll. *Disorderly Conduct: Visions of Gender in Victorian America.* New York: Alfred A. Knopf, 1985.

Snow, David A., and Robert D. Benford. "Ideology, Frame Resonance, and Participant Mobilization." *International Social Movement Research* 1 (1988): 197–217.

Snow, David A., Burke E. Rochford, and Steven K. Worden. "Frame Alignment Process, Micromobilization, and Movement Participation." *American Sociological Review* 51 (1986): 464–81.

Sparks, Allister. *Tomorrow Is Another Country*. Chicago: University of Chicago Press,
1995.

Sprinzak, Ehud. *The Ascendance of Israel's Radical Right*. New York: Oxford University Press, 1991.

Stagenborg, Suzanne. "The Consequences of Professionalization and Formalization
in the Pro-Choice Movement." *American Sociological Review* 53, no. 4 (1988): 585–
605.

Stédile, João Pedro, ed. *A questão agrária hoje*. Porto Alegre: Editora da Universidade,
1994.

Stepan, Alfred, ed. *Democratizing Brazil: Problems of Transition and Consolidation*.
New York: Oxford University Press, 1989.

———. "The New Professionalism of Internal Warfare and Military Role Expan-
sion." In *Authoritarian Brazil: Origins, Policies, and Future*, edited by Alfred Stepan,
47–65. New Haven: Yale University Press, 1973.

———. "Paths toward Redemocratization: Theoretical and Comparative Consider-
ations." In *Transitions from Authoritarian Rule: Comparative Perspectives*, edited
by Guillermo O'Donnell, Philippe Schmitter, and Lawrence Whitehead, 64–84.
Baltimore: Johns Hopkins University Press, 1986.

———. *Rethinking Military Politics*. Princeton: Princeton University Press, 1988.

Stern, Kenneth S. *A Force upon the Plain: The American Militia Movement and the
Politics of Hate*. New York: Simon and Schuster, 1996.

Stokes, Susan Carol. *Cultures in Conflict: Social Movements and the State in Peru*.
Berkeley: University of California Press, 1995.

Sullivan, John L., Patricia G. Avery, Kristina Thalhammer, Sandra Wood, and Karen
Bird. "Education and Political Tolerance in the United States: The Mediating Role
of Cognitive Sophistication, Personality, and Democratic Norms." *Review of Education, Pedagogy, and Cultural Studies* 16 (1994): 315–24.

Sullivan, John L., James Pierson, and George E. Marcus. "An Alternative Conceptuali-
zation of Political Tolerance: Illusory Increases, 1950s–1970s." *American Political
Science Review* 73, no. 3 (1979): 781–810.

Tarrow, Sidney. *Struggling to Reform: Social Movements and Policy Change during
Cycles of Protest*. Ithaca, N.Y.: Cornell University, Center for International Studies,
1983.

Taylor, Diana. *Disappearing Acts: Spectacles of Gender and Nationalism in Argentina's
"Dirty Wars."* Durham, N.C.: Duke University Press, 1997.

Thalhammer, Kristina, Sandra Wood, Karen Bird, Patricia G. Avery, and John L.
Sullivan. "Adolescents and Political Tolerance: Lip-Syncing to the Tune of Democracy." *Review of Education, Pedagogy, and Cultural Studies* 16 (1994): 325–47.

Thompson, Keith, ed. *To Be a Man: In Search of the Deep Masculine*. Los Angeles: Jeremy P. Tarcher, 1991.

Tilly, Charles. *From Mobilization to Revolution*. Reading, Mass.: Addison-Wesley, 1978.

Timerman, Jacobo. *Preso sin nombre, celda sin número*. Buenos Aires: El Cid Editor, 1981. Translated by Toby Talbot as *Prisoner without a Name, Cell without a Number*. New York: Vintage Books, 1984.

Valenzuela, Luisa. *Cambio de armas*. Hanover, N.H.: Ediciones del Norte, 1982.

————. *Realidad nacional desde la cama*. Buenos Aires: Grupo Editor Latinoamericano, 1990.

Van Rooyen, Johann. *Hard Right: The New White Power in South Africa*. London: I. B. Tauris, 1994.

Verbitsky, Horacio. *El vuelo*. Buenos Aires: Planeta, 1995.

Wagner-Pacifici, Robin Erica. *The Moro Morality Play: Terrorism as Social Drama*. Chicago: University of Chicago Press, 1986.

Walker, Thomas W., ed. *Revolution and Counterrevolution in Nicaragua*. Boulder, Colo.: Westview Press, 1991.

Walton, John. "Debt, Protest, and the State in Latin America." In *Power and Popular Protest: Latin American Social Movements*, edited by Susan Eckstein, 299–327. Berkeley: University of California Press, 1988.

Weber, Max. *From Max Weber: Essays in Sociology*. Translated, edited, and with an introduction by H. H. Gerth and C. Wright Mills. New York: Oxford University Press, 1969.

Wood, Sandra, Kristina Thalhammer, John L. Sullivan, Karen Bird, Patricia G. Avery, and Kate Klein. "Tolerance for Diversity of Beliefs: Learning about Tolerance and Liking It, Too." *Review of Education, Pedagogy, and Cultural Studies* 16 (1994): 349–72.

Young, Crawford. "The Dialectics of Cultural Pluralism: Concept and Reality." In *The Rising Tide of Cultural Pluralism: The Nation-State at Bay?* edited by Crawford Young, 3–35. Madison: University of Wisconsin Press, 1993.

Zald, Mayer N., and Bert Useem. "Movement and Countermovement Interaction: Mobilization, Tactics, and State Involvement." In *Social Movements in an Organized Society: Collected Essays*, edited by Mayer N. Zald and John D. McCarthy, 247–72. New Brunswick, N.J.: Transaction Books, 1987.

INTERVIEWS

ARGENTINA

The author conducted all interviews in Spanish, in person, and in the Greater Buenos Aires environs, unless otherwise indicated. The political and occupational positions listed for each individual are the positions he or she held at the time of the interview. The author interviewed several individuals who will remain anonymous: a civilian MODIN leader (August 1994); a lower-ranking Carapintada soldier (July 1994); an army major and key Carapintada and MODIN leader, here called "Major Martínez" (August 1994); the lawyer for "Major Martínez" (August 1994); a MODIN youth leader (August 1994); Aldo Rico's "cultural adviser" (July 1994); and a top officer in the Argentine High Command (July 1994).

Daniel Adrogué, founder and leader, Federación Nacional Solidaridad, 28 July 1996

Geraldo Adrogué, political analyst, 1 July 1994

Griselda Aristí, press secretary, MODIN, 11 July and 8 August 1994

Alberto Asseff, president, Partido Nacionalista Constitucional, 5 July 1994

Heriberto Justo Auel, retired army major, 12 August 1994

Liliana Ayetz, MODIN congresswoman, 29 June and 4 July 1994

Hebe de Bonafini, founder, Madres de Plaza de Mayo, 26 July 1994

Atilio Borón, director, Centro de Investigaciones Europeo-Latinoamericanos (EURAL), 28 July 1994

Gustavo Breide Obeid, former army captain, Carapintada leader, 25 July 1994

Silvia Cristina Brogna, MODIN town council member, 29 June and 4 July 1994

Cristina Caiati, documentation director, CELS, 8 August 1994

Horacio Cambareri, president, Fuerza Republicana party, 5 July and 10 August 1994

Julio Carreto, MODIN provincial deputy for Buenos Aires, 8 July and 5 August 1994

Noemí Crocco de Rico, MODIN member, 11 July 1994

Carlos Doglioli, retired army lieutenant colonel, 26 July 1994

Roberto Alejandro Etchenique, MODIN constituent assemblyman, 27 June 1994

Félix Fernández, MODIN provincial deputy for Buenos Aires, 5 August 1994

Rosendo Fraga, executive director, Centro de Estudios Unión para la Nueva Mayoría, 15 June 1994

Orlando Juan Gallo, MODIN congressman, 28 June 1994

Carlos Gil, leader, Partido Nacionalista Constitutional, 2 August 1994

Guillermo Fernández Gill, MODIN congressman, 25 July 1994

Joe Goldman, journalist, United Press International, 27 July 1994

Mario Gurioli, leader, Federación Nacional Solidaridad, former MODIN leader, 29 July 1994

Anibal Laiño, brigadier general, secretary general of the army High Command, 8 July 1994

Angel Luis León, MODIN leader, former lieutenant colonel, Carapintada, 3 August 1994

Juan Carlos Maurossero, army captain, 30 July 1994

Martín Mendoza, congressman (Independent), 11 August 1994

Alejandro Montiel, MODIN town councilman, Federal Capital, 4 July 1994

Lilian Morelli, president, Women's Association of Patriotic Action, 10 August 1994

Emilio Morello, MODIN congressman, 29 June 1994

Luis Nicolás Polo, MODIN congressman, 28 June 1994
Luis Máximo Prémoli, retired army colonel, 9 August 1994
Aldo Rico, president, MODIN, Carapintada founder and leader, 24 June 1994
Juan Rico, president, La Matanza district of MODIN, MODIN town councilman
    for La Matanza, 7 July 1994
Enrique Rodriguez Day, MODIN vice president, 26 July 1994
Nicolás Saturnino Aparicio, manager of MODIN headquarters, 15 June 1994
Estella Maris Schiuma, MODIN congresswoman, 15 July 1994
Thomas Sheetz, researcher, EURAL, 28 July 1994
Juan Carlos Tudino, senator (Independent), 30 July 1994
Mario Luis Vivas, MODIN member in La Matanza, adviser to Schiuma and Ayetz,
    15 July 1994

BRAZIL

The author conducted the following interviews in Portuguese, and in person, unless otherwise noted. The interviews took place in various parts of Brazil between August and November 1995. The political and occupational positions listed for each individual are the positions he or she held at the time of the interview. The author interviewed several individuals who will remain anonymous: three rural labor leaders and two religious leaders (November 1995); and one large landowner who probably revealed more during his September 1995 interview than he intended to have published.

Kit Abdala, former UDR leader, telephone interview to Beltrão, Paraná,
    11 October 1995
Nagib Abude, former UDR president, telephone interview to Londrina, Paraná,
    9 October 1995
Jorge Agenor de Jesus Correa, settler, Sorocaba, São Paulo, 12 October 1995
Péricles Roberto Alves de Lima, landowner leader, telephone interview to
    Xinguara, Pará, 23 November 1995
Saulo Alves de Oliveira, former UDR leader, Ribeirão Prêto, São Paulo,
    27 September 1995
Deolinda Alves de Souza, Movimento Sem Terra leader, Pontal de Paranapenema,
    São Paulo, 15 and 16 October 1995
Francisco Assis Ferreira, inmate charged with rural murder, Americano, Pará,
    21 November 1995
Lourdes Azedo, social worker, Presidente Prudente, São Paulo, 15 and
    16 October 1995
Hugo Biehl, congressman (Partido Progressista Reformador–Santa Catarina),
    Brasília, 15 August 1995
João Bosco Umbelino dos Santos, president, Federation of Agriculture of Goiás
    and the Federal District, Goiânia, Goiás, 16 August 1995
João Branco, former UDR leader, São Paulo, 27 November 1995

Vicente Britto de Sousa, INCRA lawyer, Rio Branco, Acre, 29 November 1995

Lincoln Bueno, owner, Distribuidora Monte Rey, Belém, Pará, 20 November 1995

Antonio Cabrera, secretary of agriculture, State of São Paulo, São Paulo, 19 October 1995

Ronaldo Caiado, former president, UDR, Goiânia, Goiás, 17 August 1995

Pedro de Camargo Neto, director, Brazilian Rural Society, São Paulo, 1 August 1995

Pedro Ernesto Cardoso de Oliveira, UDR leader, Rio Preto, São Paulo, 8 October 1995

Gerson Carneiro Spindola Jr., former UDR-Youth leader, Brasília, 9 August 1995

James Cavallaro, director in Brazil of Human Rights Watch/Americas, Rio de Janeiro, 30 November 1995

José Oscar Cícero, former UDR leader, São José do Rio Preto, São Paulo, 8 October 1995

Valdir Colatto, congressman (PMDB–Santa Catarina), Brasília, 11 August 1995

Augusto Cunha, commander, military police, Presidente Prudente, São Paulo, 17 October 1995

Assuero Doca Veroñez, president, Federation of Agriculture of Acre State, Rio Branco, Acre, 17 November 1995

Henrique Duarte Prata, former UDR leader, Barretos, São Paulo, 29 September 1995

Edson Faccín, settler, Sorocaba, São Paulo, 12 October 1995

Salvador Farina, founder and former UDR leader, Goiânia, Goiás, 16 and 17 August 1995

Eliny Faulstich, director of public relations, INCRA, Brasília, 14 August 1995

Antonio Elói Ferriche Paz, *caminhonaço* organizer, Porto Alegre, Rio Grande do Sul, 12 November 1995

Ilzamar Gadelha Mendes, Chico Mendes's widow, Rio Branco, Acre, 19 November 1995

Irailton Gonçalves Souza, Movimento Sem Terra leader, Salvador, Bahia, 28 November 1995

Luis Carlos Heinze, mayor, São Borja, Rio Grande do Sul, 14 November 1995

Sigeyuki Ishii, president, Presidente Prudente Rural Sindicate, Presidente Prudente, São Paulo, 17 October 1995

Plínio Junqueira Jr., founder and former UDR leader, Presidente Prudente, São Paulo, 5 August 1995

Sylvio Lazzurini Neto, director, Sindicato Nacional dos Pecuaristas de Gado de Corte, telephone interview to São Paulo, November 1995

Américo Leal, lawyer, Belém, Pará, 22 November 1995

Antonio M. A. Licio, director of agricultural planning, Ministry of Agriculture, Brasília, 11 August 1995

Raimundo Araújo Lima, state superintendent, INCRA, Rio Branco, Acre, 29 November 1995

Edson López, former UDR leader in Ceará, telephone interview to Fortaleza, Ceará, 27 November 1995

Aparecido Lauinano López, squatter, Pontal de Paranapanema, São Paulo, 15 and 16 October 1995

Abelardo Lupión, congressman (Partido da Frente Liberal/Partido Trabalhista Brasileiro–Paraná), Brasília, 15 August 1995

João Carlos Machado Ferreira, former UDR leader, Porto Alegre, Rio Grande do Sul, 14 November 1995

Darci Machio, Movimento Sem Terra leader, Porto Alegre, Rio Grande do Sul, 12 November 1995

Madeleine Bedran Maklouf Carvalho, CPT leader, Belém, Pará, 22 November 1995

Bernardo Mançano Fernandes, professor, Faculdade de Ciências e Tecnologia, UNESP, Presidente Prudente, São Paulo, 7 August 1995

Joel Mascarenhas, vice president, Presidente Prudente Rural Syndicate, Presidente Prudente, São Paulo, 17 October 1995

Gilmar Mauro, member, National Coordinating Council of the Movimento Sem Terra, Pontal de Paranapanema, São Paulo, 15 and 16 October 1995

Flávio Pascoa Teles de Menezes, former SRB president, São Paulo, 28 July 1995

Alcides Modesto, congressman (PT-Bahia), president, Commission of Agriculture and Rural Policies, Brasília, 9 August 1995

Halim Mufarej, former UDR leader, Marabá, telephone interview to Marabá, Pará, 29 November 1995

Udelson Nunes Franco, former UDR leader, Ituiutaba, Minas Gerais, 30 September 1995

Gabriel Alfonso M. A. Oliveira, UDR leader, Ribeirão Prêto, São Paulo, 28 September 1995

Flavia Olivito Lancha Alves de Oliveira, former UDR-Woman leader, Franca, São Paulo, 28 September 1995

Meire Orlandino, lawyer, Presidente Prudente, São Paulo, 8 August 1995

Alysson Paulinelli, former minister of agriculture, Belo Horizonte, Minas Gerais, 5 October 1995

Paulo Paulista Leite Silva, UDR leader, Ribeirão Prêto, São Paulo, 27 September 1995

Aldo Pedreschi, former president, UDR of Alta Mogiana, Sertãozinho, São Paulo, 29 September 1995

Hamilton Pereira, president, Instituto de Formação e Assessoria Sindical, Goiânia, Goiás, 16 August 1995

Vilobaldo Peres, former UDR leader, Araçatuba, São Paulo, 7 October 1995

Geraldo Perri Morais, former UDR leader, Araçatuba, São Paulo, 7 October 1995

Luciano Piovesan Leme, former UDR-Youth leader, Ponte Nova, Minas Gerais, 4 October 1995

Adão Preto, congressman (PT–Rio Grande do Sul), member, Commission of Agricultural and Rural Policies, Brasília, 10 August 1995

Roque Quagliato, former UDR leader, telephone interview to Ourinhos, São Paulo, 24 November 1995

José Rainha Jr., director, Movimento Sem Terra in the Pontal de Paranapanema, 15 and 16 October 1995

José Rezende, congressman, former UDR member, Belo Horizonte, Minas Gerais, 2 October 1995

Luis Rezende, founder, UDR, Uberaba, Minas Gerais, 30 September 1995

Roberto Rodrigues, former president, Brazilian Rural Society, São Paulo, 1 and 3 August 1995

Roosevelt Roque dos Santos, president, UDR, Presidente Wenceslau and São Paulo, 18 August 1992, 31 July 1995, and 7 August 1995

Neuri Rosetto, national communications director, Movimento Sem Terra, São Paulo, 3 August 1995

Henri Roziers, leader, CPT–Rio Maria, telephone interview to Rio Maria, Pará, 27 November 1995

Tufi Rufael, former UDR leader, Marabá, Pará, 23 November 1995

Antonio de Salvo, director, ADS Assessoria de Comunicações Ltda, São Paulo, 19 October 1995

Regina Sandoval Gonçalves, former UDR-Youth leader, Presidente Prudente, São Paulo, 7 August 1995

Renata Sandoval Gonçalves Belfort, former UDR member, Presidente Prudente, São Paulo, 7 August 1995

Antonio Sandoval Netto, former UDR member, Presidente Prudente, São Paulo, 7 August 1995

Ana Maria Jorgens Sartori, former UDR leader, Porto Alegre, Rio Grande do Sul, 10 and 14 November 1995

Daniel Schwenk, lawyer, Presidente Wenceslau, São Paulo, 14 November 1995

Gilberto Mauro Scopel de Moraes, former UDR leader, Porto Alegre, Rio Grande do Sul, 14 November 1995

José Serafim Sales, inmate charged with rural murder, Belém, Pará, 21 November 1995

William Silva de Almeida, settler, Sorocaba, São Paulo, 12 October 1995

Francisca Maria Soares, settler, Sorocaba, São Paulo, 12 October 1995

Douglas Fanchin Taques Fonseca, former UDR leader, telephone interview to Ponta Grossa, Paraná, 11 October 1995

João Batista Tezza Filho, landlord and leader, Rio Branco, Acre, 15 November 1995

Nina Tonin, Movimento Sem Terra leader, Porto Alegre, Rio Grande do Sul, 12 November 1995

Creusa Maria Turato, squatter, Pontal de Paranapanema, São Paulo, 15 and 16 October 1995

Altair Veloso, founder and former UDR leader, Goiânia, Goiás, 17 August 1995

Lister Vianei Borges, Movimento Sem Terra leader, Imperatriz, Maranhão, 25 November 1995

Plínio Vidigal Xavier de Silveira, leader, Tradição, Família, e Patria (TFP),
    São Paulo, 4 August 1995
Peter von Medem, former UDR leader, Belo Horizonte, Minas Gerais,
    2 October 1995

NICARAGUA

With the exception of interviews with U.S. citizens, all of these interviews were conducted in Spanish. The interviews took place in person and in Managua unless otherwise indicated. The political and occupational positions listed for each individual
are the positions he or she held at the time of the interview. The author interviewed
several individuals who will remain anonymous: one member of the Organization
of American States peacekeeping mission (March 1995 and April 1996); two members of the Nicaraguan government—one Contra and one MRS—(April 1996); one
Contra-oriented representative to the Tripartite Commission on Verification (March
1995); one Contra leader of a social assistance agency (April 1996); and one Recontra
leader (April 1996).

Alfredo Cesar Aguirre, congressman (Partido Nacional Democrático), former
    Contra politician, 14 March 1995
David Alarid, second secretary, Economic/Commercial Section, U.S. embassy,
    9 April 1996
Elsa Alemán, member, Committee of Mothers of Heroes and Martyrs, Matagalpa,
    13 March 1995
Maria Auxiliadora Alemán, lawyer, Bufete Jurídico Rivera, Alemán y Asociados,
    11 April 1996
Rodolfo "El Invisible" Ampié, former Contra combatant, ex–National Guardsman,
    president, Centro de Acción y Apoyo al Desarrollo Rural (CENADE),
    9 March 1995
Roberto Arana Baez, president, Codex Tractor Parts, 11 April 1996
Miriam Argüello, congresswoman (Alianza Popular Conservadora), former
    Contra politician, 24 April 1996
José Argüello Cardenal, president, "Arges Sequeira Mangas" and Federation of
    Associations of Owners of Confiscated Property, 29 April 1996
Luis Ignacio Argüello Montiel, secretary, Council on the Nicaraguan War,
    11 April 1996
Adan Artola, former Contra combatant (Misurasata), Puerto Cabezas,
    25 April 1996
Fernando Avellán, former Contra combatant, ex–National Guardsman, director,
    PRN, 15 April 1996
Carmen Baltodano, assistant director, Nicaraguan Human Rights Center
    (CENIDH), 7 March 1995
Alejandro Bendaña, professor, Center for International Studies, 8 March 1995

Mario Noel Briones Loza, wounded war veteran, former Contra combatant,
14 April 1996

Kenneth Bushey Law, director, Yátama, former Contra combatant (Misurasata),
Puerto Cabezas, 26 April 1996

José Honores Caballo, PRN candidate for mayor in the municipality of La
Concepción, 19 April 1996

Walter "Toño" Calderón, former Contra combatant, ex–National Guardsman,
director, PRN, 14 April 1996

Adolfo Calero Portocarrero, former Contra politician, president, Partido Nacional
Conservador, 14 March 1995

Balberino Cano Cruz, member, Commission of Peace and Reconciliation,
Maleconcito, 12 April 1996

Humberto Castilla, congressman (PRN), 9 March 1995

Elmo Castillo, director, Jorge Salazar Cooperative, Matagalpa, 13 March 1996

Humberto Chavarría Salgado, member, Commission of Peace and Reconciliation,
Maleconcito, 12 April 1996

Osorno "Blas" Coleman, director, Yátama, former Contra combatant (Misurasata),
president, Association of Ex-Combatants, 15 April 1996

Valentina Cortedano, member, Center of Mothers and Widows of the Resistance,
Matagalpa, 13 March 1995

Manuel "Tigre-17" Cunningham, former Contra combatant (Misurasata), Puerto
Cabezas, 25 April 1996

Myrna Cunningham, congresswoman (MRS), rector, University of the
Autonomous Region of the Nicaraguan Caribbean Coast–Puerto Cabezas,
22 April 1996

R. Bruce Cuthbertson, president, Committee to Recover Confiscated American
Properties in Nicaragua, 10 April 1996

Miguel Echevarría, administrator, Managua Mayor's Office, 24 April 1996

Stedman Fagot Mueller, former Contra combatant (Misurasata), Puerto Cabezas,
26 April 1996

Azucena Ferre, congresswoman (Unión Demócrata Cristiana), former Contra
politician, 26 April 1996

Abner Figueroa, director, FSLN, Puerto Cabezas, 25 April 1996

Luis "Johnson" Fley, former Contra combatant (FDN), vice president, PRN,
10 and 12 March 1995 and 11 April 1996

Pablo Roberto Fley, former Contra combatant, farmer, Matagalpa, 14 March 1995

Fabio Gadea, president, PRN, owner of Radio Corporación, 10 March 1995 and
24 April 1996

Carlos "Chino" Garcia, former Contra combatant (FDN), president, Fundación de
Ex-combatientes, 16 April 1996

Freddy García, wounded war veteran, former Contra combatant (FDN), member,
PRN, 14 April 1996

Francisco Javier González, second secretary, U.S. embassy, 9 April 1996
Ramiro Granera, former Contra, medical doctor, 10 March 1995
Henry Herman, director, FSLN, Puerto Cabezas, 25 April 1996
Roger Herman, former Contra combatant (Misurasata), 14 March 1995 and
    15 April 1996
Lino Hernández, director, Permanent Commission on Human Rights (CPDH),
    8 March 1995
Marcos Hoppington Scott, governor, North Atlantic Autonomous Region, former
    Contra combatant (Misurasata), 25 April 1996
Jaquelín Hortegaray, departmental secretary, PRN, 14 April 1996
Enrique López, member, Jorge Salazar Cooperative, Matagalpa, 13 March 1995
Luis Angel "Leonel" López, former Contra combatant, Southern Command,
    ex-president, PRN, 6 March 1995
Ricardo Manchaverde, member, PRN, 14 April 1996
Bayardo Martínez, member, Jorge Salazar Cooperative, Matagalpa, 13 March 1995
Juan Carlos Martínez Urbina, secretary of international relations, PRN,
    10 April 1996
Eleuterio Mendoza Arancibia, wounded war veteran, former Contra combatant,
    14 April 1996
Felipe Mitchell, former Contra combatant (Misurasata), Puerto Cabezas,
    25 April 1996
Edgard "Richard" Molinari Blandón, former Contra combatant, Southern
    Command, Ministry of Social Action (MAS), 17 April 1996
Oscar Morales, Planning Department, National Institute of Agrarian Reform,
    26 April 1996
Daniel Nuñez Rodríguez, president, Unión Nacional de Agricultores y Ganaderos
    (UNAG), 8 March 1995
Rigoberto Nuñez, former Contra combatant (FDN), owner of La Plancha II,
    17 April 1996
Sergio Ojeda, departmental secretary, PRN, Department of Granada,
    14 April 1996
Eden "Comandante Cero" Pastora Gómez, former Contra combatant, Southern
    Command, president, Movimiento de Alianza Democrática (MAD),
    6 March 1995   •
Julia Patricia Peralta, secretary, Association of Mothers, Widows, and Orphans of
    the Resistance, 14 April 1996
Rosaneli Peralta López, administrator, War Veterans Foundation, 22 April 1996
Fanor Pérez Mejía, president, PRN, Jinotega, 11 April 1996
Timothy Phillips, co-chair, Project on Justice in Times of Transition, Boston,
    10 April 1996
Juan Reyes Acevedo, coordinator, Commission of Peace and Reconciliation,
    Maleconcito, 12 April 1996

Alejandro Reyes Casco, secretary, Commission of Peace and Reconciliation, Maleconcito, 12 April 1996

José Rivas, administrator, Managua Mayor's Office, 24 April 1996

Julío César Saborio, executive director, Nicaraguan Human Rights Association (ANPDH), 7 March 1995

Hector Sánchez Argüello, former Contra combatant (FDN), owner of Club Remanso, 19 April 1996

Adan Silva, director, FSLN, Puerto Cabezas, 25 April 1996

Rodolfo Smith, president, Autonomous Movement, Puerto Cabezas, 26 April 1996

Oscar Sobalvarro, Yátama mayor, Puerto Cabezas, 24 April 1996

Leonardo Somarriba, president, Almacenadora de Exportaciones S.A. (ALMEXSA), 11 April 1996

Sonia Soto, director, FSLN, Puerto Cabezas, 25 April 1996

Salvador "Esteban" Talavera, former Contra combatant (FDN), Recontra in FN 3-80, executive director, Center for Strategic Studies, 12 March 1995 and 15 April 1996

Doris Tijerino, congresswoman (FSLN), Madison, Wisconsin, 24 March 1995

Serapio Venerado Valles González, president, PRN, Maleconcito, 12 April 1996

Roberto Vassalli, president, ALPAC company, 19 April 1996

Monseñor Pablo Antonio Vega, former Contra priest, United Nations Project on Peace and Reconciliation, 29 April 1996

Guillermo Vega Herrero, municipal secretary, PRN, 14 April 1996

Alfonso Zamora López, former Contra combatant (FDN), member, PRN, 14 April 1996

Index

LIBRARY OF CONGRESS CATALOGING-IN-PUBLICATION DATA

Payne, Leigh A.
  Uncivil movements : the armed right wing and democracy in Latin America /
Leigh A. Payne.
      p.   cm.
  Includes bibliographical references and index.
  ISBN 0-8018-6242-6 (alk. paper)
  1. Latin America—Politics and government—1980– 2. Authoritarianism—Latin
America—Case studies. 3. Militia movements—Latin America—Case studies.
4. Paramilitary forces—Latin America—Case studies. 5. Carapintada Uprising,
Argentina, 1990. 6. União Democrática Ruralista (Brazil). 7. Fuerza Democrática
Nicaraguense. I. Title.
  F1414.2. P355 2000
  322.4'2'098 21—dc21   99-045860

February 2019
Unique Thrift
New Hope
$2 44